THE RELIGION OF THE MITHRAS CULT IN THE ROMAN EMPIRE

The Religion of the Mithras Cult in the Roman Empire

Mysteries of the Unconquered Sun

ROGER BECK

OXFORD

UNIVERSITY PRESS

OXFORD
UNIVERSITY PRESS

Great Clarendon Street, Oxford OX2 6DP

Oxford University Press is a department of the University of Oxford.
It furthers the University's objective of excellence in research, scholarship,
and education by publishing worldwide in

Oxford New York

Auckland Cape Town Dar es Salaam Hong Kong Karachi
Kuala Lumpur Madrid Melbourne Mexico City Nairobi
New Delhi Shanghai Taipei Toronto

With offices in

Argentina Austria Brazil Chile Czech Republic France Greece
Guatemala Hungary Italy Japan Poland Portugal Singapore
South Korea Switzerland Thailand Turkey Ukraine Vietnam

Oxford is a registered trade mark of Oxford University Press
in the UK and in certain other countries

Published in the United States
by Oxford University Press Inc., New York

British Library Cataloguing in Publication Data

Data available

Library of Congress Cataloging in Publication Data

Data available

Typeset by SPI Publisher Services, Pondicherry, India
Printed in Great Britain
on acid-free paper by
Biddles Ltd., King's Lynn, Norfolk

ISBN 978–0–19–814089–4 (Hbk.)   978–0–19–921613–0 (Pbk.)

1 3 5 7 9 10 8 6 4 2

To Richard Gordon, John Hinnells, and Luther Martin

Preface

This book has been many, many years in the making. So it is appropriate that I dedicate it to the three scholars who over the years have helped me most along the way with their friendship, encouragement, and wise counsel on the Mysteries of Mithras and how to address them. There are of course many others who have generously aided me, and I hope they will excuse me if I do not repeat here the acknowledgements recently made in the collection of my past articles and new essays, *Beck on Mithraism*.

I do however want to thank my editor Hilary O'Shea for her trust and forbearance over what must surely be one of the lengthiest projects to come to fruition and a record-holder in deadlines overrun. I also want to thank my research assistant Norman Valdez for his skilful production of the diagrams.

Since Chapter 1 is entirely programmatic, I shall refrain from introducing my subject and outlining my methods here. Let the Table of Contents which follows serve as a map of the road ahead.

Contents

List of Figures

Abbreviations

ANRW	*Aufstieg und Niedergang der römischen Welt*
BNP	Beard, North, and Price 1998
CCAG	*Catalogus Codicum Astrologorum Graecorum*
EM	*Études mithriaques* = Duchesne-Guillemin (ed.) 1978
EPRO	Études préliminaires aux religions orientales dans l'Empire romain
JMS	*Journal of Mithraic Studies*
JRS	*Journal of Roman Studies*
MM	*Mysteria Mithrae* = Bianchi (ed.) 1979
MS	*Mithraic Studies* = Hinnells (ed.) 1975
NEB	New English Bible
OLD	*Oxford Latin Dictionary*
SM	*Studies in Mithraism* = Hinnells (ed.) 1994
V	*Corpus Inscriptionum et Monumentorum Religionis Mithriacae* (= Vermaseren 1956–60)

1

Introduction to Interpreting the Mysteries: Old Ways, New Ways

1. AN AGENDA

A study of the 'religion' of an ancient cult may seem to entail an artificial, even perverse, distinction between the cult's religion and the cult itself, as if 'religion' were somehow the cream to be skimmed from the surface of the institutional milk. Such an undertaking would indeed be strange, especially these days when students of religion in the Roman empire are with good reason more interested in social formation than in *theologoumena*.

Please then be assured that in advancing a new interpretation of the 'mysteries' of Mithras I am not proposing to treat Mithraism as a self-contained and free-standing system separable in principle from actual Mithraists. We need not—indeed should not—think of the 'religion' of the Mithras cult as a sort of pre-existent package deal which a person bought into, as it were. Rather, we should see it as an *aspect* of a collaborative human enterprise of a particular time, place, and culture, constantly re-created and sustained by those initiated into it.

Its contemporaries spoke of 'the Mysteries of Mithras', not of 'Mithraism'. The latter, like all such '-isms', is but a modern label devised for comparison and taxonomy (cf. Stoicism, maenadism, and so on). Contemporaries of course made no distinction between the 'Mysteries' as an institution in the socio-cultural scene and the 'mysteries' as the peculiar sacred business or 'religion' of that institution. The conventions of modern English orthography (initial capital versus initial lower-case) allow me to draw this distinction. I stress that the distinction is for hermeneutic purposes only. The 'mysteries' (lower-case 'm') are inseparable from the 'Mysteries' (capital 'M'), and it is senseless to look for a point where the one starts and the other leaves off.

'What do you mean by "religion"?' is a fair question, to which I shall return three rather different answers. First, by 'religion' I mean what the theologian Gerd Theissen means by 'religion' in his book *The Religion of the Earliest Churches* (1999). Let me set this out formally:

> The Mithraic religion (i.e. the 'mysteries' of Mithras) : the institution of the
> Mithras cult (i.e. the 'Mysteries' of Mithras) (Beck) :: 'The religion of the
> earliest churches' : 'earliest churches' (Theissen).

This is a relational definition. I am also in sympathy with Theissen's own working definition of religion as 'a cultural sign language which promises a gain in life by corresponding to an ultimate reality', with the important proviso that the 'ultimate reality' is subjective: 'the statement... merely takes up the way in which the religions understand themselves; it does not expect anyone to adopt this understanding' (1999: 2).

My second answer is to say what I do *not* mean by 'religion'. As will become clear soon enough, I do *not* mean a 'faith' or a 'belief system'. That is the old 'package deal' approach. It never was appropriate to ancient paganisms, even to the mystery cults. Few now accept its applicability to very early forms of Christianity. As a model it is a retrojection from later times of creed and dogma.

For my third answer I turn to an ancient expert on religion, Plutarch of Chaeronea, writing at the turn of the first and second centuries CE. In his essay on Isis, her cult (mostly in Egypt), and her theological meaning, Plutarch describes the 'mysteries' of Isis as the gift of the goddess (*On Isis and Osiris* 27, trans. Gwyn Griffith):

Nor did she allow the contests and struggles which she had undertaken, and her many deeds of wisdom and bravery, to be engulfed in oblivion and silence, *but into the most sacred rites she infused images, suggestions and representations of her experiences at that time* (alla tais hagiōtatais anamixasa teletais eikonas kai hyponoias kai mimēmata tōn tote pathēmatōn), and so she consecrated at once a pattern (*didagma*) of piety and an encouragement (*paramythion*) to men and women overtaken by similar misfortunes. (Emphasis added)

Eikonas kai hyponoias kai mimēmata. I propose to treat the 'religion' or 'mysteries' of the Mithras cult as a system of (literally) 'likenesses and underthoughts and imitations' apprehended and realized by the initiate as the gift of Mithras. Just as 'likenesses' include but are not limited to material icons, so 'imitations' include but are not limited to mimetic rituals. As for the 'underthoughts', 'mental representations' best approximates the sense in which I take the term. My study of the 'religion' of the Mithras cult is thus a study in *cognition*, a study of how the initiate *gets to know* his mysteries in the context of the life and physical environment of the mithraeum, the 'cave' in which he and his cult brothers assembled.

The scholarly consensus is that the Mithraic mysteries were coterminous with the cult of Mithras; in other words, that wherever Mithraists met in a mithraeum, there too Mithraic mysteries were celebrated. To some this may seem self-evident, true only as part of a definition and hence trivial: Mithraism was a mystery cult; obviously, then, it had its mysteries and was nothing without them.

The ubiquity of its mysteries, however, is precisely what distinguishes Mithraism from the other 'mystery cults'. The mysteries of Isis were not coterminous with Isism, which was a much broader, more multiform phenomenon altogether. Initiation into a mystery, such as we read about in the eleventh book of the *Metamorphoses* of Apuleius, was but an option—and an option which we cannot assume was on offer in all or even most Isiac communities. The same is true of the other so-called 'mystery cults'.

Mithraism's distinctiveness in this regard is stated forcefully and without qualification by Giulia Sfameni Gasparro in an important study of the cult of Cybele and Attis, where it is all the more telling because the Mithraic mysteries are not there her primary concern (1985: p. xiv):[1] 'it [Roman Mithraism] constitutes an organic and autonomous religious context which had so entirely assumed a mystery "shape" that, of all the cults with an initiatory-esoteric structure in Antiquity, this alone deserves to be defined as a "mystery religion".'

I shall begin, in Chapter 2, with a critical look at twentieth-century approaches to the interpretation of the Mithraic mysteries. For the most part, these follow in, or react against, a tradition set by Franz Cumont in his magisterial two-volume study of the cult at the close of the nineteenth century (Cumont 1896, 1899). For all the gains in our understanding of the Mithraic mysteries effected in—or in opposition to—the Cumontian tradition, we sense that hermeneutics has now reached something of a dead end. This is as true of the relatively recent astronomical/astrological interpretations (Beck 2004c: 235–49) as of the more conservative approaches. As a consequence of this hermeneutic failure, a narrow positivism has in some quarters replaced interpretation. Hard facts about the cult, its membership, and its physical remains are valued above the interpretation of its mysteries, a venture which is deemed at best 'speculative' (Clauss 1990a, 2000) and at worst mere invention, the misattribution of high theology to unsophisticated folk manifestly incapable of sustaining it (Swerdlow 1991). In Chapters 2 to 4, then, we shall explore the shortcomings of the traditional hermeneutics, especially in its heuristic procedure and in the classic approach to deciphering doctrine by way of the cult myth and the iconography of the monuments which carry the myth.

In particular, I shall identify five problems with the traditional approach. In ascending order of seriousness these are: first, an undervaluing of the admittedly very small body of literary testimony to the mysteries in favour of an almost exclusive concentration on the monumental, that is, iconographic, testimony;

---

[1] Sfameni Gasparro's study of the Cybele/Attis cult has acquired additional significance in that it was used by J. Z. Smith (1990: 126–9) to establish, for purposes of comparison with early Christianities, a paradigm of the pagan mystery cults as uniformly 'locative' (this-worldly) rather than 'utopian' (other-worldly). In effect, by making an exception of Mithraism, Sfameni Gasparro disallows Smith's extension of her description of the Cybele/Attis cult as a paradigm for all ancient mysteries (see Beck 2000: 174, n. 135). For the full account of her views on Mithraism qua mystery cult, see Sfameni Gasparro 1979c.

secondly, an undervaluing of the design of the mithraeum, in comparison to the iconography of the 'figured monuments' (*monuments figurés*),[2] as a store and expression of ideological meaning; thirdly, an assumption—albeit a waning one—that doctrine is the primary object of the heuristic quest; fourthly, as a complement to the third problem, the positivist assumption that, absent doctrine, the mysteries cannot have been a serious and sophisticated cognitive enterprise; fifthly, the total disregard of semantics and semiotics, a failure to ask not merely *what* the iconography means but also *how* it means.[3] And not just the iconography; the design of the mithraeum too, and of the rituals enacted there.

In fairness, one cannot fault an interpretation for failing to take into account methods which lay beyond its time horizon. So rather than speak of a sixth deficiency, I shall list as 'an opportunity' the availability of new methods pioneered by cognitive science, especially in anthropology and psychology, during the last decade or so. More on this later.

From Chapter 5 onwards I shall propose a new hermeneutics based on a new heuristic procedure. In place of the hermeneutics of doctrine, I shall offer an interpretation of the mysteries as *a system of symbols*, both complex and orderly, apprehended by the initiates in cult life and especially in ritual. Indeed, to experience the mysteries, I shall argue, was precisely to apprehend the symbols. At least, that is the most fruitful way I now see of describing the mysteries.

As a banner text for this enterprise we might take a phrase from a passage of Origen, *Contra Celsum* 1.12. Origen claims that a distinction which he drew within Egyptian religion between the approaches of the wise (*sophōn*) and the vulgar (*idiōtōn*) is valid also for the 'Persians' (by whom he means the Mithraists). The 'mysteries' (*teletai*) of the Persians, he says, 'are cultivated rationally by the erudite but *realized symbolically* by common, rather superficial persons (*par' hois eisi teletai, presbeuomenai men logikōs hypo tōn par' autois logiōn*, symbolikōs de ginomenai *hypo tōn par' autois pollōn kai epipolaioterōn*)' (trans. Chadwick). My aim is not to show that the rank and file got it right while their betters got it wrong—for that would be to accept the distinction between the two types of initiate at face value—but rather that mysteries 'come into being via their symbols' and are apprehended in that form by their initiates, both high and low.

Interpreting the mysteries of Mithras as a system of symbols inevitably places me in a particular anthropological camp, the symbolist camp,[4] and from my perspective the most important proponent of the interpretation of cultures and their religions as systems of symbols is Clifford Geertz (1973). My new hermeneutics will be unashamedly Geertzian—which reveals that it is 'new' only

---

[2] For want of a better, I use a literal translation of Cumont's term for the sculptures and frescos which carry the iconography.

[3] If the author were to be brought to trial on these charges, he would plead guilty to the third. Of a fault more usually imputed to him, the extravagance of his astronomical interpretations, he remains entirely unrepentant.

[4] Catherine Bell (1997: 61–92) has a good survey of the symbolists.

in its application to Classics.[5] To an anthropologist it will be very old news indeed.

Before attempting to apply the new hermeneutics to the mysteries in any detail, I shall postulate some fundamental principles of the Mithraic mysteries to direct and control our analysis of the symbol system. Obviously, I shall not backtrack and propose these principles as Mithraic 'doctrines'. Rather, they are what the anthropologist Roy Rappaport, in an important study which was the culmination of his life's work (1999), called the 'ultimate sacred postulates' of a religion, and Gerd Theissen, in his work of the same year (1999),[6] called a religion's 'axioms'. Since 'axiom' is the simpler term, I shall use it, remarking that in this context it loses, at least for the secular scholar, its implications of 'logical deduction from'.

Although they are known to their religion's members and are usually explicit, axioms are not generally understood by them as a limited set. As such, they are strictly a scholar's hermeneutic device. 'Axioms' are the overarching truths of a religion which ultimately sanctify, and so sanction, the thoughts, the words, the deeds, of its members thinking, speaking, and acting within the context of that religion. They are obvious, simple, and often tautologous or merely definitional. Generally, they are neither verifiable nor falsifiable, and they are invalidated not by argument but only by the death of the religion in question. In this sense, all Mithraic axioms are now invalid because there are no Mithraists left to live by them. An example, often cited by Rappaport,[7] of a religious axiom is the Jewish *Shema* ('Hear, O Israel, the Lord our God, the Lord is One'), words which are ideally the first a child learns and the last the dying hope to utter. Theissen (1999: 271–307, esp. 273) finds just two axioms for the early Christian churches, covenantal monotheism (inherited of course from Judaism) and acceptance of Jesus as the effective redeemer, the latter encapsulated in the saying 'Christ is Lord'.

For the Mithraic mysteries I shall propose, likewise, just two *axioms* (ultimate sacred postulates):

1. DEUS SOL INVICTUS MITHRAS. As every ancient Mithraist once knew (presumably it was explained to the illiterate), and as every modern student of Mithraism now knows, this is the god's cult title and the normal formula for dedications; it establishes that the religion's effective power is a GOD, is the SUN, is UNCONQUERED, is MITHRAS.

---

[5] 'No work has appeared so far which applies the theory of Geertz to any Greco-Roman religion' (Segal 1989: 155). An exception, in spirit if not in explicit alignment, might be Gordon 1980*b*.

[6] Theissen, as the subtitle of his book ('creating a symbolic world') makes explicit, also aligns himself with the symbolist tradition. Mithraism, however, was demonstrably the more literal 'symbol system'; for while early Christianity may by metaphor be called 'a marvellous cathedral of signs' (Theissen 1999: 306), the mithraeum was designed and constructed, literally and physically, as a symbol-equipped 'image of the universe' (Porphyry, *De antro nympharum* 6).

[7] 1999: see index s. 'Judaism, *Shema*'.

2. 'HARMONY OF TENSION IN OPPOSITION'. This axiom is presented here as it appears in Porphyry *De antro nympharum* 29, at the conclusion of a list of fundamental oppositions (e.g. night and day): *palintonos hē harmoniē kai toxeuei dia tōn enantiōn*. It was originally a saying of Heraclitus (Fr. 51 DK). Elsewhere (Beck 2000: 167–71) I have argued that it was the Mithraists who adapted it and integrated it with the list of opposed pairs.[8] However, the principal expression of this axiom of 'harmony of tension in opposition' in the Mithraic mysteries is the pair of images of the torchbearing divinities: Cautes with his raised torch and Cautopates with his lowered torch.[9]

These two axioms find expression in an indeterminate number of *motifs* (the term, the concept, and the relation of 'motifs' to 'axioms' are Theissen's—1999: 271–82, 290–1). Examples of an important motif in the Mithraic mysteries would be descent and ascent.

I further propose that axioms and motifs operate in various *domains*. Four domains are particularly germane to the Mithraic mysteries: (1) the sacred story, the deeds of Mithras; (2) the cosmos; (3) the sublunary world; (4) the destiny of human souls, and in particular the souls of the initiates of Mithras.

These four domains are not mutually exclusive. Obviously, the sublunary world is a part of the cosmos. Thus domain 2 contains domain 3; and, in accordance with ancient cosmology, domain 3 is at rest at the centre of domain 2, which moves in a complex dance around it.

Furthermore, 'domain' is not intended solely in the literal sense of an area—or, since we are dealing with a three-dimensional universe, a volume of space in which activities take place and power is exercised. The cosmos and the sublunary world (domains 2 and 3) are clearly domains of that sort, but the Mithras story and the destiny of human souls (domains 1 and 4) are clearly not. Rather, the latter are, as it were, envelopes for divine and human actions, actions which take place in cosmic or earthly space. They have a temporal dimension, but not one that is reducible to dating on any earthly continuum of linear time. As to the relating of domains, much of the narrative of the first and fourth domains has to do with bridging the second and third domains, the terrestrial with the celestial or cosmic.

---

[8] I also argued that the image of Mithras as bowman is an expression of this axiom, as is the image on the Mainz ritual vessel of the cult Father miming the archery of Mithras in an act of initiation (Beck 2000: 149–54, 167–71).

[9] It may be objected that with the second axiom I am crudely mistaking the medium for the message. Many would argue (Lévi-Straussian structuralists, for example) that eliciting and reconciling oppositions is simply the way in which religions and other socio-cultural systems work. True enough, but my point will be that in the Mithraic mysteries, untypically, the oppositions are displayed on the surface—literally so in the iconography—and are so omnipresent and explicitly structured that 'harmony of tension in opposition' may reasonably be claimed as an axiom.

The symbol system conveying the axioms and motifs of Mithraism in their several domains are manifested concretely in three distinctive *structures*: (1) the physical structure of the icon of the tauroctony (with its occasional reverse, the banquet scene, and other peripheral scenes); (2) the physical structure of the mithraeum; (3) the organizational structure of the seven grades. I shall pay particular attention to the first and second of these structures because, unlike the third, they are attested ubiquitously in the Mysteries.

What you will not find in these chapters is a comprehensive reconstruction of Mithraic theology and other beliefs; or of the myth cycle in all its episodes. Those goals, which dominated much of twentieth-century Mithraic scholarship, I no longer consider either achievable or, for that matter, worth pursuing.

I shall distinguish four *modes* in which, singly or concurrently, the symbol system of the Mithraic mysteries could be apprehended by its initiates: (1) ritual action; (2) the perception of meaningful iconography; (3) the giving and receiving of words (logia, explications, teaching, esoteric epigraphic phrases, etc.); (4) ethical behaviour consonant with the mysteries (e.g. Mithraic Lions behave in an esoterically appropriate leonine way). The first three modes are esoteric; they characterize types of internal behaviour within the cult and (literally) inside the mithraeum. The last is more public; presumably, one is expected to behave in an ethically appropriate fashion not just to one's cult brethren but also in one's wider social relations.

Further, I shall argue throughout, but specifically in Chapters 8 and 9, that the Mithraic mysteries, across their axioms, motifs, domains, structures, and modes, communicated symbolically in a peculiar *idiom*. This idiom is a form or jargon of one of Graeco-Roman culture's most pervasive languages, the language of astronomy and astrology. Partly to avoid the clumsy repetition of those two constituents, and partly because a new or at any rate radically different concept requires a new term, I shall call this idiom 'star-talk'.

By 'star-talk' I do not intend merely talk in words or symbols *about* the stars. I intend also, following the ancients' own conception of the stars as language signs and the heavens as text, the talk *of* the stars. From the ancient point of view, this is the primary celestial language of which the discourses of astronomy, astrology, and astral symbolism such as we find in the Mithraic mysteries are earthly replications. Primary star-talk is thus a highly peculiar language, in that the celestial bodies which are its signs and signifiers are themselves also its speakers, holding discourse in and by their rotations and revolutions. And if not they, then the power or powers who move them.

From the modern scientific perspective, of course, primary star-talk does not exist: the stars are without mind or meaning, and so do not and cannot communicate. Here, however, what science tells us can and cannot transpire in the physical heavens is of less relevance than the construction placed upon the physical heavens by the human mind in the particular cultural context of

Graeco-Roman antiquity. The ancients' supposition that the stars communicate is of far more interest to us than the scientific fact that they don't.

However, even if for analytical purposes we entertain the ancients' conception of an astral language, a more cogent objection remains. 'Star-talk', in my definition of the ancients' conception of it, is a language of symbols; and a language of symbols, it has been argued by the anthropologist Dan Sperber (1975), is an oxymoron: symbols are not language signs. Consequently, before I can deploy 'star-talk' in my description of the Mithraic mysteries, I have to clear what one might call 'Sperber's bar'. I must show not only that star-talk was deemed a language by the ancients, but also that as a (to us) imaginary language it does indeed function as a language on criteria that Sperber set as the necessary conditions for language status. Specifically, I must show that astral symbols, as deployed in the Mithraic mysteries, can and do function as language signs.

From my past interest in interpreting certain aspects of the mysteries by reference to Graeco-Roman astronomy and astrology, a sceptical reader might suspect that I am ushering back in through the back door as astral 'language' the same disreputable creature whom I have expelled through the front door as astral 'doctrine'. In a sense, that is indeed what I am doing. Nevertheless, I plead that the creature has undergone a reformation. No longer is it the 'astral truths of the mysteries'; rather, it is the 'truths of the mysteries astrally expressed'. It is now medium, not message.

Of the five problems of traditional Mithraic hermeneutics, I identified as the most serious 'the total disregard of semantics and semiotics, a failure to ask not merely *what* the iconography means but also *how* it means. And not just the iconography; the design of the mithraeum too, and of the rituals enacted there.' The concept of star-talk as a language and as the proper idiom of the Mithraic mysteries is intended to remedy that deficiency. It will enable us to translate traditional substantive ('what') questions into modal ('how') questions of communication, of the giving and apprehending of signs and symbols, and ultimately of cognition itself. In posing and answering the old questions in this novel way, we shall actually be traversing much the same traditional terrain of cult theology, cosmology, and salvation.

2. A WORD ON ONTOLOGY

Some of our categories are obviously anchored in the actual world: their matter or, rather, propositions about their matter are susceptible, at least in principle, to empirical verification. This is mainly so of matter which falls within the categories of 'structure' and 'mode'. The categories themselves are no more than heuristic and hermeneutic organizing principles. Accordingly, my statement that the mysteries were conveyed and given expression in three structures and four modes is actually just a claim (non-factual, hence neither verifiable nor falsifiable) that the mysteries can be re-described most effectively in terms of those categories so delimited. However, what you find brigaded under the banners of the three structures and four modes are facts; or at least the propositions which assert them can be empirically verified or falsified. It is a fact, verifiable from the extant exemplars, that there were Mithraic icons and mithraea designed so and not otherwise. It is a fact that there was a (probably non-ubiquitous) hierarchy of grades ordered so and not otherwise. It is a fact that the initiates performed certain actions, and not others, of a sort which we call 'ritual'.

In the preceding sentence I have deliberately problematized 'ritual'. It would have been all too easy to say simply, 'it is a fact that the initiates performed certain rituals rather than others'. That, however, would beg an enormous ontological question. What makes a particular action a ritual? Or more precisely, how does one verify/ falsify *empirically* the proposition that such-and-such a piece of business is a 'ritual', for example a 'sacrifice' rather than routine butchery? Of course we all 'know the difference'—or think we do—but how can we confirm it empirically on real-world criteria and without appeal either to our own modern scholarly taxonomies (as above) or, more dangerously, to a meta-realm of 'the sacred'?

The problem is well posed by Dan Sperber (1996: 24), whose solution we shall follow. It is the *representations* of sacrifice in the minds of those who perform and witness the deed, not the sacrifice qua sacrifice, that belong in our common world where empirically verifiable/falsifiable propositions can be made about them. Whether or not one wants to reduce these representations to states or changes in the neural circuitry of the brain,[10] the fact remains that for every representation there must necessarily be a corresponding neural event. These events, whether mental or neural or both, occur in the course of nature in the empirically accessible world.

Ontologically, according to Sperber (1996), cultural phenomena, of which religions constitute a set, are clusters of representations of two types, 'mental' and 'public'. Mental representations are obviously those discussed in the preceding paragraph. Public representations are the expression of mental representations in the common world: the observable ritual, the visible icon, the legible text. Of all these representations, mental as well as public, one can state that they are/were so and not otherwise. Those propositions, in principle if not in practice, are subject to empirical verification/falsification.[11]

---

[10] Sperber's explicit materialism points him that way (pp. 9–31), but there is no need to follow. His theory of representations, as I employ it here, is compatible with a dualist position, provided one accepts that every mental representation is physically anchored in a corresponding neural state or event and is hence part of an individual's physical history; hence an event in the material history of the world; hence accessible in principle to verification/falsification: either it did happen or it did not happen.

[11] 'Of course, we have records of only a few of the public versions and none of the mental ones, but complementing observations with hypotheses about unobserved—and even unobservable— entities is plain normal science' (Sperber 1996: 27).

Consequently, under 'modes' I speak not of Mithraic 'ritual' and so on *per se*, but of the 'apprehension' of the Mithraic 'symbol system' in and by 'ritual action', in and by 'the perception of meaningful iconography', in and by 'the giving and receiving of words', in and by esoterically appropriate 'ethical behaviour'. What I seek to describe and to analyse is the interplay of those mental and public representations the sum of which constituted the mysteries.

Like 'structures' and 'modes', my categories of 'axioms', 'motifs', and 'domains' are in and of themselves just scholars' heuristic and hermeneutic devices for ordering representations. But they too are grounded in the actual world. Our postulated 'axiom' DEUS SOL INVICTUS MITHRAS is also a dedicatory formula, hence a public representation in Sperber's sense, existing openly in the actual world. Moreover, it was a public representation only because it was a (complex) mental representation in the minds/brains of the initiates. Precisely because we suppose it a definitive representation of Mithras we identify it as an 'axiom'.

In sum, we may say that *ontologically* all axioms, motifs, domains, structures, and modes, are, or are reducible to, *mental* and/or *public representations* or clusters of representations (as defined by Sperber 1996).

3. TEMPLATE FOR A RE-DESCRIPTION OF THE MITHRAIC MYSTERIES

In this section I lay out in summary form the re-description of the Mithraic mysteries developed over the preceding sections.

The description comprises six propositions, A–F. Each proposition except the last (F) has alternative openings (A1 and A2, B1 and B2, etc.). This is to reflect different perspectives: the first line represents the mysteries as an autonomous system acting on the initiate; the second line represents the mysteries from the initiate's point of view as something apprehended and accepted. Obviously, my preference is for the latter, for it captures the interplay of mental and public representations of which the mysteries, as a matter of fact, consisted.

Elsewhere (Beck 2004*c*: 45–9) I have presented a third alternative which better reflects the ancient way of looking at things: it represents the mysteries from the divine perspective as the gift of the god, mediated in part by a 'prophet' or 'law-giver' ('Zoroaster' for the Mithraists) and received by the initiate.[12] Unsurpassed as a paradigm for this third way is Plutarch's account of the transmission of her mysteries by Isis in the form of 'likenesses and underthoughts and imitations' (*On Isis and Osiris* 27), a passage we examined at the beginning of this chapter.[13]

---

[12] An imaginary first-person 'Mithraic aretalogy' on the Isiac model is interleaved with the summary description presented in the second, initiate-centred form only.

[13] Compare the Homeric *Hymn to Demeter* 270–4, 470–82, on Demeter's institution of her mysteries and her mandate to the Eleusinian princes.

A description of the Mithraic mysteries

A1. The mysteries give *symbolic* expression to . . .
A2. In the mysteries, the initiate apprehends *symbolically* . . .
two *axioms* or *ultimate sacred postulates*:
  1. DEUS SOL INVICTUS MITHRAS
  2. 'Harmony of tension in opposition.'

B1. These axioms are conveyed . . .
B2. The initiate experiences these axioms . . .
in an indeterminate number of *motifs*:
  e.g. the motif of descent and ascent.

C1. Axioms and themes operate . . .
C2. The initiate apprehends the axioms and themes . . .
in one or more of four *domains*:
  1. the sacred story, the deeds of Mithras
  2. the cosmos
  3. the sublunary world
  4. the destiny of human (especially initiates') souls.

D1. The complexes of symbols conveying the axioms and motifs of the mysteries in their various domains are manifested concretely . . .
D2. The initiate apprehends the symbol complexes conveying the axioms and motifs of the mysteries in their various domains . . .
on *structured sites*; in the mysteries there are three principal and distinctive *structures*:
  1. the physical structure of the icon of the tauroctony (with its reverse = the banquet scene, plus peripheral scenes)
  2. the physical structure of the mithraeum
  3. the organizational structure of the seven grades
(*note*: only the first two structures are attested ubiquitously).

E1. The symbols are activated . . .
E2. The initiate apprehends the symbols . . .
in one or more of four *modes*:
  1. ritual action
  2. the perception of meaningful iconography
  3. the giving and receiving of words (logia, explications, teaching, esoteric epigraphic formulae)
  4. ethical behaviour consonant with the mysteries (e.g. Mithraic Lions behave in an esoterically appropriate leonine way).

F. The mysteries' common *symbolic idiom* across axioms, motifs, domains, structures, and modes is the language of astronomy/astrology or *star-talk*.

4. ON COMPARISONS

I am confident that this new heuristic/hermeneutic approach and template for a re-description of the Mithraic mysteries, developed as they are from recent initiatives in anthropology (Rappaport, Sperber) and Christian origins (Theissen), will allow us to make more interesting, deeper, and better-nuanced *comparisons* than heretofore. The making of interesting comparisons, I agree with the distinguished scholar of ancient religions, Jonathan Z. Smith (1990), is at the heart of the enterprise of the study of religion. The importance of Smith's comparative project has been endorsed and its centrality emphasized in the recent work of a senior New Testament and Christian origins scholar, Burton Mack (2001: 59–80).[14]

Accordingly, you will encounter here comparisons not only with the systems of Christianity in its early forms,[15] but also with those of cultures closer to us in time and as distant as the indigenous Chamula of southern Mexico (Gossen 1979); also with those of certain contemporary Western 'cults' (in the modern sense), in particular the celestially oriented cults of the Solar Temple and Heaven's Gate, groups which achieved notoriety in the 1990s for the bizarre murder-suicides of their initiates.[16]

Wide comparisons over space, time, and levels of economic and scientific sophistication help us both to familiarize the exotic and—no less important—to exoticize the familiar. We aim to create, as it were, a level playing-field for all mysteries, in particular one on which those of Mithras are not set at a disadvantage with those of Christ. Though no longer in the spirit of Christian triumphalism, we classicists still tend to overprivilege the latter, especially on the intellectual plane. We may (or may not) concede some intellectual value to the ancient philosophical allegorizations of the pagan mysteries. But by and large we treat the real-life initiates as an intellectually scruffy lot, reserving our respect, if not our liking, for the minds of their Christian rivals. 'Jerusalem' might have wanted little to do with 'Athens', but we extend it honorary Athenian citizenship nonetheless. Not so the pagan mysteries.

---

[14] Mack's Christian origins project aims at an explanation of Christian myth-making which disengages the extant texts and their predecessors (e.g. 'Q') from the 'historical Jesus'. As a result, his reconstructed early Christianities approximate more closely to the pagan mysteries than did previous paradigms of Christianity at its genesis. Welcome to our pagan field, where the historical Mithras never was a problem!

[15] For some novel comparisons, made possible by the discovery and identification of previously unknown Mithraic rituals on the Mainz cult vessel, see Beck 2000 (171–8).

[16] Beck 1998*b*: 343. Cf. J. Z. Smith's well-known comparison of the Jonestown cult with Dionysiac maenadism (1982).

5. ON COGNITION

As one of the shortcomings of the traditional interpretations of the Mithraic and other ancient mysteries, we have identified the lack of adequate semiotics and semantics, specifically of a paradigm of how symbols in the mysteries convey meaning. To that semantic deficiency we added the absence of any *cognitive theory*, that is, a paradigm of how the initiates *apprehended* the symbol systems of their mysteries. Classical scholarship here tends to take a commonsensical approach (as it does all too often), supposing it sufficient that the initiates believed their beliefs, that they thought their thoughts (if the mystery is allowed intelligent and intelligible content),[17] and that the rest was affect or more-or-less edifying emotion.

Since we postulate that Mithraism was a serious cognitive enterprise, it is incumbent on us to have at least a working paradigm of cognition in the context of religion. Fortunately, the new *cognitive science of religion* (CSR) provides just such a paradigm. As an approach to a particular subset of mental and cultural phenomena, CSR is part of a more general cognitivist methodology which I shall describe at the start of Chapter 6 when I begin to employ it in my hermeneutics. Suffice it to say here that Dan Sperber's theory of representations, which I adopted above, exemplifies this method.[18]

A precursor of the cognitivist approach is a theory known (not very informatively) as *biogenetic structuralism*.[19] Biogenetic structuralism proposes a model of the operation of the human brain and the autonomous nervous system functioning as an integrated whole, especially in certain non-everyday situations, notably meditation, ecstasy, and participation in ritual. It is, of course, the theory's focus on religious states of mind and their corresponding physiological states that

[17] Particularly unfortunate is the assumption that belief starts where rational thought leaves off (e.g. Hopkins 1999: 323, asterisked note), as if the mental state of the initiate could be signalled by little coloured lights switching on and off, green for rational thought, yellow for belief, and red for emotion. It is, perhaps, the last gasp of Platonist psychology.

[18] Jensine Andresen (2001*a*, 2001*b*) gives a good overview of the new cognitive approach in the study of religion. See also the articles in Pyysiäinen and Anttonen 2002. Apart from Dan Sperber's works already cited (1975, 1996), the most important studies germane to our hermeneutics are by E. Thomas Lawson and Robert N. McCauley (1990), Harvey Whitehouse (2000), Pascal Boyer (2001), and the authors/editors of the recently inaugurated 'Cognitive Science of Religion Series' (Altamira Press): Whitehouse 2004; Pyysiäinen 2004; Barrett 2004; Whitehouse and Laidlaw 2004; Whitehouse and Martin 2004. For the neural processes of the conscious brain/mind, I rely (as a rank layman) on Gerald M. Edelman and Giulio Tononi (2000); for the evolutionary history of the same, on Steven Mithen (1996). I here acknowledge my deep indebtedness to Luther Martin for integrating me, quite recently, into the CSR enterprise (Beck 2004*b*).

[19] See Laughlin 1997; Newberg and d'Aquili 1998. Of central importance is d'Aquili *et al.* 1979 on ritual.

attracted my attention. This approach too I shall describe in more detail when I come to make use of it towards the end of Chapter 7.[20]

6. SYNCHRONIC VERSUS DIACHRONIC; STRUCTURE AND MEANING VERSUS HISTORIC CAUSE AND EFFECT; INTERPRETATION VERSUS EXPLANATION

If one were to ask why, for example, the tauroctony is composed of a certain set of symbols in a certain arrangement, one of two different sorts of answer may be returned: first a synchronic answer, that the tauroctony is so and not otherwise because it gives expression, via an apparent narrative episode, to the axioms and certain key motifs of the Mithraic religion; secondly a diachronic answer, that the tauroctony is so and not otherwise because it is the end product of a historical evolution, whether of an underlying set of ideas or of the iconography itself (or both). These two broad types of answer are not of course mutually exclusive, but they should be kept distinct, at least conceptually. One should differentiate clearly between an explication in terms of meaning and an explication in terms of antecedents.

My study takes a synchronic approach. I shall attempt to explicate the mysteries as a symbolic system in terms of the system's meaning(s) and structure. To some extent, this is inevitable. There is simply not enough evidence to reconstruct the development of the tauroctony (to retain that example) in the way in which historians of Christian origins can reconstruct, through the methods of source-, redaction-, and form-criticism, not only the development of early Christianity's pre-canonical texts but also the earliest forms, social and ideological, of the religion itself. In part, however, my choice of approach is deliberate. In these chapters I am more concerned with *interpreting* the mysteries than with *explaining* them historically in terms of cause and effect.[21]

There are of course diachronic stories to be told, not only about the social formation of the Roman Mysteries of Mithras but also about the development of the cult's mysteries. Indeed, the whole Cumontian narrative of the transmission of Mithra-worship from Persia to Mesopotamia to Anatolia to Rome was as

---

[20] Here again I wish to acknowledge a debt: to Colleen Shantz (2001) for alerting me to biogenetic structuralism and its explanatory potential. Latterly, biogenetic structuralism has evolved into so-called 'neurotheology', a development which poses problems for the secular academic. We shall have to face this problem when we come to it in Ch. 7, sect. 13.

[21] 'Interpretation' and 'explanation' are technical terms in the anthropology of religion. Although they are not mutually exclusive, scholars tend to take one route or the other. Explanations translate or reduce a religious system into other terms; interpretations explicate the system largely in (but not on!) its own terms. See Lawson and McCauley 1990: 12–18. Explanation is these days generally preferred to interpretation, being deemed the more 'scientific' of the two.

much (if not more) about the creation and modification of a set of beliefs as about the institution and transformations of a social group.

Paradoxically, to validate my synchronic account, I found that towards the end of this study, specifically from section 11 of Chapter 9 and in Chapter 10, I had to tell an elaborate diachronic story. This, you will find, is not even about the mysteries of Mithras, or at least not primarily so. Rather, it is the reconstructed history of a set of astronomical and astrological—that is, 'star-talk'—concepts and representations in which, I claim, the prehistory and origins of the mysteries of Mithras are embedded.[22] Large though that claim is, there is fortunately no need to say more about it here at the outset.

7. CONCLUSION

Such, then, is our hermeneutic agenda. In the next chapter we shall look at the traditional interpretations of twentieth-century Mithraic scholarship and their *fons et origo* in the great two-volume work of Franz Cumont, which appeared in the closing years of the century before. Concurrently, we shall start to lay the foundations of our new approach.

[22] The role of the great astrologer-politician Ti. Claudius Balbillus in the story is treated in an essay in Beck 2004c: 323–9. See also Beck 1998a, 1999, 2001, both on Balbillus and on the earlier role of the kingdom of Commagene as the matrix of Mithraic astrology.

2

Old Ways: The Reconstruction of Mithraic Doctrine from Iconography

1. A GATEWAY TO AN INTERPRETATION OF THE MYSTERIES: PORPHYRY, *DE ANTRO NYMPHARUM* 6, ON THE FORM AND FUNCTION OF THE MITHRAEUM

An exploration such as ours should have a specific point of departure, gateway data, as it were, to use as a concrete example as one starts to address the theoretical issues. For our gateway into the Mithraic mysteries I have chosen a passage from Porphyry, *De antro nympharum* 6, on the form and function of the mithraeum:

Similarly, the Persians call the place a cave where they introduce an initiate to the mysteries, revealing to him the path by which souls descend and go back again. For Eubulus tells us that Zoroaster was the first to dedicate a natural cave in honour of Mithras, the creator and father of all. This cave bore for him the image of the cosmos which Mithras had created, and the things which the cave contained, by their proportionate arrangement, provided him with symbols of the elements and climates of the cosmos. (trans. Arethusa edition)

Porphyry, a Neoplatonist of the third century CE, here tells us two things of great importance. In the context of a foundation legend about an archetypal mithraeum,[1] he specifies first the esoteric *significance* or *meaning* of Mithraism's sacred space and secondly the *function* of that space within its mysteries. (1) The mithraeum is designed as, and called, a 'cave' because it is meant to represent the

---

[1] Porphyry derives his information from a predecessor, Eubulus. Eubulus, and probably the Mithraists too, ascribed the institution of Mithraism to the Persian sage Zoroaster. This sort of attribution to a remote and alien sage was common in antiquity (Momigliano 1975). It is ahistorical, although Zoroaster himself, as the prophet of Iranian Mazda-worship ('Zoroastrianism'), is of course real enough. By 'Persians' Eubulus means the Mithraists, not real-life Persians. Our passage also contains the information that the original mithraeum 'was located in the mountains near Persia and had flowers and springs'. The reference to water is significant but does not immediately concern us here.

universe. (2) It is an 'image of the universe' in order to realize a mystery of the descent and return of souls.

De antro 6 is actually the sole explicit testimony from antiquity as to the intent of Mithraism's mysteries and the means by which that intent was realized. Porphyry, moreover, was an intelligent and well-placed theoretician of contemporary religion, with access to predecessors' studies, now lost.[2] So his remarks, you might think, would be an obvious entry point to an interpretation of the mysteries.

In fact, however, *De antro* 6 has never been Mithraic scholarship's point of departure. So before we set out thence, I should review the traditional route and justify my divergence.

First, though, notice two interesting features of the passage which will recur in our discussions: (1) The intent of the mithraeum's design is to enable initiation into a mystery. Ritual is signalled as well as (rather than?) belief. In due course, we shall need to look carefully at Porphyry's language and its modern explications in order to assess the balance. (2) More obvious is the emphasis on symbols and on symbolism as the driving mechanism for what the Mithraists accomplish in their mithraeum: the mithraeum is an 'image' (*eikona*) of the universe; it is made so by a certain disposition of 'symbols' (*symbolois*) within it.

2. THE TRADITIONAL ROUTE: FROM THE ICONOGRAPHY OF THE MONUMENTS TO THE MYTH OF MITHRAS TO THE BELIEFS OF MITHRAISTS

The heuristic royal road, opened more than a century ago by Franz Cumont (1896, 1899), starts from the iconography of the monuments. From the monuments, and especially from the icon of the bull-killing Mithras, the so-called 'tauroctony',[3] first (1) the cult myth, centred on the story of Mithras, is reconstructed, and then (2) from that myth the cult's doctrines and beliefs are deduced.[4]

---

[2] e.g. Eubulus, as in the present passage.   [3] The term is modern.

[4] Cumont did not invent this heuristic procedure entirely *de novo*. As we shall see, it has its roots in antiquity; and long before Cumont early modern scholars and antiquarians had explicated the mysteries piecemeal by interpreting the iconography of the monuments, especially the tauroctony: see e.g. the early interpretations of the Ottaviano Zeno monument, V335, discussed in Vermaseren 1978: 8–17, pls. XI, XII). Cumont's accomplishment was (1) to collect the data of the 'monuments figurés', thus rendering the iconography amenable to systematic interpretation, and (2) to reconstruct from the scenes on the monuments the first credible Mithras myth, postulated as the object of the Mithraists' beliefs and the expression of their doctrines. For simplicity's sake, I concentrate here on the story of Mithras himself. For Cumont this was but a part, albeit the central part, of a grander story, likewise told in scenes on the monuments, involving divine powers other than Mithras. Cumont's ultimate goal, as Richard Gordon pointed out (1975: 216), was the full theology embodied in the totality of scenes and symbols.

This heuristic procedure involves two stages. Logically, it must indeed be so, for one cannot deduce doctrine and belief from myth without first deciphering the story told by the scenes on the monuments (by no means a straightforward task, as we shall see). Nevertheless, in practice, the two parts of the programme are usually run in tandem: meanings are deduced while the narrative is explicated. Furthermore, not all of the symbolism on the monuments contributes to the narrative, at least not in any obvious way. When that is so, the symbols are translated directly into doctrines and beliefs with little or no reference to the story. An example would be the explicit astrological symbolism with which the monuments are so richly embellished.

The architecture of Cumont's fundamental study, *Textes et monuments figurés relatifs aux mystères de Mithra*, makes this heuristic procedure—iconography to story to doctrine and belief—abundantly clear. Note first, however, the emphasis in the title: it is the 'monuments figurés', those monuments which carry interpretable iconography, which are privileged. The silent deficit in that title, the mithraea, the epigraphy, and the small finds, could not be addressed as adequately as the iconography until they were catalogued in a more appropriate format half-a-century later in M. J. Vermaseren's *Corpus Inscriptionum et Monumentorum Religionis Mithriacae* (1956–60).[5]

Although Cumont's interpretive first volume (1899)[6] starts with the literary texts, it disposes of them in forty-four pages (pp. 3–46), only twenty-six (pp. 21–46) of which concern the Greek and Latin texts directly relevant to the Graeco-Roman Mysteries. The monuments, in contrast, occupy 168 (pp. 53–220) out of the remaining 174 pages (pp. 37–220) of the first part ('Critique des documents') of this volume.[7] Even if we deduct the first seventeen pages (on the mithraea and small finds) and the last eight ('intérêt artistique') of these 168, that still leaves 143 pages devoted to the iconography of the 'monuments figurés', the story they tell, and the meanings they convey. Manifestly, this is the engine of Cumont's project, a perception confirmed when we find the very same data deployed again as 'La doctrine des mystères', the title of the fourth chapter in the volume's second part ('Conclusions'). As 'The Doctrine of the Mithraic Mysteries' it occupies the same position in the popular, still current English translation of those 'Conclusions' published as a separate book (Cumont 1903).

Among the leading twentieth-century interpreters of Mithraism, Robert Turcan exemplifies most transparently the continuation of Cumont's heuristic procedure. The fourth chapter of his short, general study of the cult is entitled 'L'Imagerie mithriaque', and it opens thus (Turcan 2000: 47; emphasis mine):

---

[5] A high point in the display of the full range of the archaeological evidence is undoubtedly Manfred Clauss's survey of the cult (1990, trans. 2000). 'Small finds' are now receiving proper attention: see Martens and De Boe 2004, the proceedings of a conference devoted to the subject in 2001.

[6] Vol. 1 was published *after* Vol. 2 (1896). Vol. 2 is the actual collection of texts and monuments.

[7] The balance, a scant six pages, is assigned to the inscriptions.

Le mithriacisme nous est accessible surtout et directement par l'*iconographie*. C'est dire l'importance des *monuments figurés* qui doivent servir de base à toute discussion sur les origines, la formation et la *signification* du culte gréco-romain de Mithra.

Mithraism is directly accessible to us above all through the iconography, which speaks to the importance of the figured monuments which ought to serve as the basis of all discussion on the origins, the formation, and the meaning of the Graeco-Roman cult of Mithras.

There could be no clearer programmatic statement. In the ground it covers (though not of course in its findings, which mark a real advance over those of Cumont),[8] Turcan's chapter on 'imagerie' runs more or less parallel to Cumont's chapter on 'doctrine'. The difference is that while Cumont's title signals the latter part of the course and its goal, Turcan's signals the earlier part and the starting line. In a nice symmetry, the equivalent chapter in the other of the two most recent general surveys (Clauss 1990; English translation 2000) signals the middle of the course, the cult myth: 'Mithras-Legende', 'The sacred narrative'.

In an article explicating an iconographically unusual detail in the banquet scene on the reverse of the Fiano Romano tauroctony (V641),[9] Turcan spells out this heuristic procedure more fully, but with equal clarity and with his customary eloquence (1986: 221). I quote the passage *in extenso*, for we shall need to return to it to take up various threads in its argument. Bear in mind that the strangeness ('bizarrerie') of the particular detail which he is addressing is the prompt for a more generalized reflection on where the iconography of the monuments leads us and how it conducts us there. Note especially the emphasis on *doctrine* as the end product of the imagery of the monuments, and on the *inculcation of doctrine*, in a liturgical or ritual context, as the goal of initiation into the mysteries. Note too how iconography functions as or like a *language of instruction* in the transmission of doctrine.

La bizarrerie de la représentation doit tenir pour une grande part au fait qu'elle s'efforce de transcrire par une image quelque chose d'un enseignement philosophico-religieux. D'une part, en effet, nous savons que le mithriacisme a intégré, adapté certaines théories grecques, voire certains mythes grecs . . . Et d'autre part, une caractéristique essentielle de ce culte est qu'il se répand par l'image, moyennant une initiation et une liturgie qui comportent l'explication rituelle des images. L'iconographie n'y a, comme on sait, aucune fin esthétique. Elle se veut porteuse d'une doctrine. D'une extrémité à l'autre du monde romain, avec certaines variantes autour de figures fondamentales, elle véhicule un même enseignement. C'est un langage à déchiffrer, et l'on ne peut guère hasarder de déchiffrement qu'en

---

[8] Mainly in the shedding of the baggage of Mazdaism, of which Cumont supposed Mithraism to be the Roman form or expression, in favour of a more Graeco-Roman ideology; also in a heightened attention to the cult's principal icon, the tauroctony, and to the scene of the banquet which both follows the bull-killing in the myth cycle and serves as the charter for the cult meal.

[9] For present purposes, the specific detail does not matter: in fact, it is the flames which spring up at the base of an altar where one of the torchbearers points the head of a caduceus.

se fondant sur la sémantique courante des motifs ou des attributs, en fonction de certaines idées communes au monde gréco-romain.

[The strangeness of the representation has to do in large measure with the fact that it is trying to transcribe by an image some piece of philosophical or religious teaching. On the one hand we know that Mithraism integrated and adapted certain Greek theories, certain Greek myths . . . On the other hand an essential characteristic of this cult is that it spread by means of the image, through an initiation and a liturgy which carried the ritual explication of the images. The iconography, as we know, has no aesthetic purpose. It is meant to be the carrier of a doctrine. From one end of the Roman world to the other, with certain variants on fundamental figures, it conveys the same teaching. It is a language to be deciphered, and one can only try deciphering it by relying on the then current semantics of the motifs or attributes, in terms of certain ideas common to the Graeco-Roman world.]

3. THE MERITS AND ACHIEVEMENTS OF THE TRADITIONAL HEURISTIC PROCEDURE

Of course there is good warrant for the traditional Cumontian procedure—were there not, scholars would hardly have followed it for the duration of the twentieth century. The most obvious and compelling reason is the sheer quantity of the iconographic evidence. Notoriously, there are no extant sacred texts, other than a few short symbola, from within the Mysteries of Mithras; and even from the external but contemporary ancient sources which discussed or touched on the Mysteries there are only some brief and fragmented testimonies. By contrast, an amazing plethora of monuments with narrative scenes and other groupings of symbols survives, mostly in the form of relief sculpture, but also in fresco and in sculpture in the round.[10] Mithraism typically expressed itself in and through the medium of the visual arts, just as early Christianity typically expressed itself in and through the medium of the spoken and, before long, the written word. Accordingly, it was as proper and as inevitable that Mithraic scholarship, or at least that part of it concerned with interpreting the mysteries, should start with the monuments and their iconography as that the scholarship of early Christianity should start with New Testament criticism.[11] One begins, rightly, where the data is thickest, most voluminous, and most complex.

[10] The abundance of the archaeological evidence, in stark contrast to the paucity of the literary remains, is stressed by Clauss (2000: pp. xxi, 15).

[11] More precisely, with the criticism of early canonical and extra-canonical literature and its postulated antecedents (e.g. the 'Q' gospel) in both narrative and non-narrative forms. The aim is twofold: (1) to identify and differentiate the earliest forms of Christianity (ideological as well as social), and (2) (for those who maintain that the goal is achievable) to isolate and characterize 'the historical Jesus'. The second of those two quests has no counterpart in Mithraic scholarship, although a search for Mithraism's actual human founder(s) is a legitimate historiographical endeavour (Beck 1998). It is worth noting that these days the scholarship of Christian origins does not work exclusively with and from the written record. Archaeology too plays a substantial role: see e.g. the use of recent archaeological evidence from the Lower Galilee in Crossan 1998: 209–35.

Secondly, focusing first on the iconography of the monuments, and in particular on the icon of the bull-killing Mithras, places the emphasis where, one
senses intuitively, it belongs. The tauroctony is one of Mithraism's few defining
essentials. Every Mithraic group, as far as one can tell, displayed one in a
prominent location, usually in a special niche at the end of their mithraeum.
Indeed, it was the icon's presence there that privileged that part of their sacred
space. Often, the mithraeum was embellished elsewhere with secondary exemplars of the tauroctony,[12] and there seem also to have been small portable
versions, perhaps for private devotion.[13] Since it was manifestly the focus of
the Mithraists' attention, surely it ought to be the primary focus of the scholar's
attention too; and if the primary focus, why not the heuristic point of departure?

The argument for the centrality of the tauroctony is sound, and in fact there
are no nay-sayers. Again, an analogy with the interpretation of Christianity
(though not in its most antique forms) is germane. The siting of the image of
the crucified Jesus in the sanctuary above the altar persists as a norm in Western
church design from the Middle Ages onwards. From it one could infer, even in
default of all other evidence, the centrality of the crucifixion in the Christian
system. So it is with the image of the bull-killing Mithras and the event which it
both represents and proclaims. Although, for good reason, I select a different
entry point into the mysteries, we must and shall pay no less attention to the icon
of the tauroctony.

Thirdly, the iconography conducts us, both directly and via the myth, to
Mithraic praxis. The tauroctony in relief form sometimes carries on its reverse a
second scene, in which Mithras and the Sun god feast together.[14] The two gods
recline on the hide of the slaughtered bull. Their banquet, then, is manifestly the
next episode in the myth. It follows immediately on the bull-killing. But is it just
an event of myth, a culmination in a story told of the gods? Again, it is the
iconography, not the texts, that tells us otherwise. The banquet of the gods, so the
monuments make clear, was replicated in the cult meal which the initiates
celebrated together on the ubiquitous side-benches which are the mithraeum's
defining feature. In other words, the story of the banquet of Mithras and Sol is
the charter myth of the initiates' cult meal.

In an analogous fashion, the story of Jesus's 'last supper' is or, more precisely,
became the charter myth for the Christian cult meal and the liturgy of the
eucharist which developed from it. The difference is that while we discern the
relation of myth to ritual in certain forms of early Christianity from the literary

[12] Vermaseren lists over fifty as certainly or most probably from the same mithraeum at
Sarmizegetusa (Dacia), V2027–2140.

[13] e.g. the roundel, only 7.5 cm in diameter, found in the Caesarea mithraeum but likely of
Danubian provenance (Bull 1978: 79–83; pl. II, fig. 4). On small and miniature icons, see Gordon
(2004).

[14] e.g. V1083 (Heddernheim I). The scene also occurs on separate reliefs; also as a side-scene on
complex tauroctonies. See Beck 1984: 2010 f., 2083 f.

sources (i.e., the gospels, their antecedents, and the Pauline epistles),[15] for Mithraism we discern it from the iconography, notably from those representations of the banquet which elide the celestial and mythic event into the terrestrial and actual. This they do by intimating in one way or another that the participants and attendants are not only deities (Mithras, Sol, Cautes, Cautopates) but also initiates of various grades in the hierarchy. The banquet transpires at both levels or in both worlds simultaneously: it is the heavenly feast of Sol and Mithras, but it is also the feast of their earthly surrogates, the Father and the Sun-Runner, with Mithraic Lions and Ravens in attendance.[16] From the iconography, then, we may reasonably deduce that the Mithraic cult feast was not simply a meal shared and enjoyed by the initiates—though it was certainly that too and never less than that[17]—but also a sacrament, if by 'sacrament' we may understand a ceremony whose participants understand it to reach, through symbols, into a world beyond that in which it was performed.

Starting, then, from the iconography, one can establish first the link between two crucial events in the Mithras myth, the bull-killing and the banquet, and then the link, which is a charter relationship, between the events of myth and Mithraism's normative ritual.[18] These are huge pieces of the mysteries. If the iconography can guide us so far, why backtrack to a different point of departure?

Finally, the iconography, unlike the texts, never imparts erroneous information. In its own bailiwick it is incontrovertible. Its data are self-evidently authentic. One cannot argue, for example, with the fact that the tauroctony regularly includes a dog, a snake, a scorpion, and a raven. That, manifestly, is how the Mithraists decided to compose their icon. It is simply so and not otherwise. What better base, then, from which to launch one's hermeneutics?

4. THE SHORTCOMINGS OF THE TRADITIONAL HEURISTIC PROCEDURE

Unfortunately, iconography's bailiwick does not extend very far. As soon as we start to interpret the iconography, to say what it 'means', we enter the domain of error, or at least of potential error. There is of course a considerable zone of

[15] Mark 14: 22–5, Matt. 26: 26–9, Luke 22: 17–19, 1 Cor. 11: 23–5. I subscribe to the widely held modern view that this 'charter' was imposed, in the light of the crucifixion/resurrection, on a pre-existing common meal in the Jesus movement (Crossan 1998: 423–44; Theissen 1999: 121–60).

[16] For the relevant monuments see Clauss 2000: 108–13; also Beck 1984: 2010 f., 2028, 2083 f. In the Konjic banquet scene (V1896) only a Lion and a Raven can be identified with certainty from among the four attendant figures as grade-holders (Turcan 1999: 225–7).

[17] According to J. D. Crossan (1998: 427, on 1 Cor. 11: 17–22), Paul upbraids his Corinthian followers on precisely this point: that the well-off Christians had perverted the common meal by admitting their poorer members only to token communion, not to shared food. Certain it is that the eucharist did eventually develop into a purely symbolic meal, a mistake—if it is a mistake—which the Mithraists apparently avoided.

[18] 'La liturgie ordinaire', as Turcan rightly calls it (2000: 78).

agreement in the interpretation of the monuments (for example, on the intent of the banquet scene, as discussed above), and little likelihood that the consensus of scholars there is completely mistaken. However, this clear zone of agreement soon gives place to thickets where the intent of the iconography is by no means self-evident and the inferences which are hazarded can at best be no more than plausible.[19]

Here an ancient text such as Porphyry's *De antro* has a clear advantage. The intent of the mithraeum's symbolism may or may not be what Porphyry says it is, but at least we are listening to a contemporary of the Mysteries making the inference, and there is a good chance that he is drawing (albeit at second hand) on sources within the Mysteries. This likelihood I shall discuss in due course. In contrast, no ancient authority tells us *why*, for example, the tauroctony regularly includes a dog, a snake, a scorpion, and a raven. We are on our own—though not resourceless. The iconography, garrulous enough on its own turf, is mute on meaning.

A defect of Clauss's survey in particular (1990, 2000) is the casual assumption that, because the archaeological data (i.e. excavated mithraea and their furnishings, 'figured monuments',[20] epigraphy, small finds) are hard data and in themselves incontrovertible, their esoteric intent will to some extent be self-evident, at least to the trained eye of the classicist. Contingently, no doubt, most of Clauss's inferences are correct. But the method, because it is entirely *ad hoc*, is actually more speculative than the speculation of the systematic interpreters whom he faults (1990: 8; 2000: p. xx).[21]

Let us allow that the Cumontian method has successfully reconstructed the story of Mithras—which in broad terms it has;[22] also, that some of the story's most important non-narrative implications are thereby revealed, for example the charter implications of the mythic banquet of Mithras and Sol for the cult meal of the initiates in the here and now. What then? Have we exhausted the recoverable 'meaning' of the monuments and of the mysteries thereby? We have not—and the five faults in twentieth-century hermeneutics and heuristic procedure, which we identified in the preceding chapter (sect. 1), still remain to be addressed.

---

[19] Which is not a reason for not making them: in this field warrantable or grounded speculation is not a vice but a necessity.

[20] I shall use this literal translation of Cumont's *monuments figurés* (in future without quotation marks) because English has no suitable corresponding phrase.

[21] A good example of Clauss's randomness of interpretation is his treatment of the torchbearers (2000: 95–8).

[22] All of the comprehensive surveys of the Mysteries retell the basic story, though with somewhat different 'spins': Cumont 1903: 130–40; Vermaseren 1960: 63–88 (56–8 on the bull-killing); Turcan 2000: 95–8; Clauss 2000: 62–101 (108–13 on the banquet). Merkelbach 1984 is the most idiosyncratic: the episodes in the story are correlated each with one of the grades (pp. 86–133), except for the bull-killing itself which is first correlated with all seven of the grades (pp. 80–2) and then explicated at greater length as a cosmogony (pp. 193–208). On some remaining methodological problems for the explication of the Mithras myth, see the appendix to this chapter.

Of those five faults, we are already on the road to rectifying the first two. These were (1) undervaluing the literary evidence as against the monumental, and (2) undervaluing the mithraeum as against the figured monuments.[23]

The choice of Porphyry, *De antro* 6 as our gateway to the mysteries redresses the balance on both counts. It is text, and it privileges the mithraeum. It confronts us with the fact—or the possibility, if one harbours reservations about the reliability of the testimony—that the mithraeum, symbolizing the universe and enabling a mystery of the descent and return of souls, was itself a store of esoteric meaning no less than the figured monuments which it contained.[24]

The three more serious faults remain. These we identified as: (3) the presumption—admittedly, less pervasive now than formerly—that a Mithraic 'doctrine' or 'faith' is the ultimate object of the heuristic quest and the category into which narrative and non-narrative iconography are to be translated; (4) the contrary—and now more prevalent—positivist assumption that, in default of *self-evident* doctrine on the figured monuments, the iconography conveys little of significance above and beyond the story told—hence that the mysteries cannot have been a serious and sophisticated cognitive enterprise; and (5) the disregard of semantics and semiotics, a failure to ask not merely *what* the iconography means but also *how* it means. This last fault is by far the gravest, for it empowers the other two with an illusory confidence that common sense and the standard tools of classical scholarship suffice.

In addressing these three fundamental heuristic flaws, I shall also lay the groundwork for an alternative and, in my opinion, better approach. This new method, as well as making greater use of the literary texts, especially Porphyry's *De antro*, will return us to the iconography of the figured monuments and the design of the mithraeum viewed as the two principal complexes of symbols in an integrated system of symbols. In effect, we shall pull back from that second stage in the traditional explication of the iconography, the translation of the myth conveyed by the figured monuments into doctrine. This retreat from

---

[23] The figured monuments, it is clear, are valued because they tell a story, while the mithraeum does not. Consequently the former, especially the tauroctony, are seen as the conveyors of esoteric meaning, the latter primarily as *venue* for the mysteries and above all for the cult meal.

[24] Devaluing or ignoring *De antro* 6 has led to bizarre consequences. Thus Clauss, in his earlier background chapters on 'Religious perspectives in the Roman empire' and 'Mystery religions' (2000: chs. 2 and 3), admirably describes the very cosmology and theory of the destiny of souls which undergirds Porphyry's testimony in *De antro* 6. Yet, in his chapter on the mithraeum (2000: ch. 7), in the meticulous description of its material remains, you will find not a word about the mithraeum's *function* as a highly intelligent contemporary source reports it! Although Clauss does indeed cite *De antro* 6 and mention the mithraeum's cosmic symbolism, it is clear from the wording of the original German edition (1990: 60) that he does not see the symbolism as functional: 'Der Kultraum wird somit ein Abbild der Welt, durch die der Mensch schreitet, hin zu Gott, der im Hintergrund sichtbar wird.' Note, too, how Michael White, in an otherwise admirable descriptive section on the mithraeum in a book on the topic of 'building god's house in the Roman world' (1989: 47–59 and title), is entirely silent about this aspect of the mithraeum's intent.

hypothetical doctrine back to actual symbols will eventually help us confront on firmer ground that basic semiotic question which classical scholarship, with its commonsensical methods, has failed to pose—let alone answer—concerning Mithraic iconography: do symbols *mean*? If so, *what* do they mean and *how*? First, however, to the chimaera of doctrine, which we shall approach via the question of *referents*: to what outside itself and the narrated myth does the rich and complex iconography of the monuments *refer*? Reference and referents will be the topic of the next chapter.

APPENDIX: SOME REMAINING METHODOLOGICAL PROBLEMS FOR THE EXPLICATION OF THE MITHRAS MYTH AS REPRESENTED ON THE FIGURED MONUMENTS

1. Some of the episodes remain obscure, because details in the scenes that represent them are difficult to discern on account of weathering and smallness of scale. For example, what is the object which Mithras brandishes over Sol's head in the 'commissioning' scene (Gordon 1980*a*: 216, scene 'S'; Hinnells and Gordon 1977–8: 213–23; Beck 1987: 310–13): a haunch or forequarter of an ox, a Phrygian cap, both of the above (on different monuments of course), something else altogether (e.g. a military sack)?

2. The sequence of the episodes in the myth is not guaranteed by the composition or, rather, by the disposition of the scenes on the complex monuments. There are broad regional norms, not strictly observed, for the sequence of the subsidiary scenes around the bull-killing, but there is certainly no canon. (On the regional sequences, from which earlier scholars tried to deduce a history of the cult's spread—unsuccessfully, in my view—see Saxl 1931; Will 1955; Beck 1984: 2074–8; Gordon 1980*a*; Turcan 2000: 53–60.) The absence of a canonical sequence of scenes suggests that the myth as an ordered narrative was not of primary importance to the Mithraists (cf. the pre-passion gospel narratives in early Christianity). Scholars are therefore surely justified in searching the scenes, individually or in limited sets, for intent beyond the mere narration of a story.

3. The bizarre, unnaturalistic quality of the representation of the principal event, the bull-killing itself (contrast, in this respect, the all too shocking realism of the crucifixion in the Christian passion narratives). The problem with 'reading' the tauroctony as an incident in a story is not so much the miraculous—for example the transformation of the bull's tail into ears of wheat—as the clutter of detail: that Mithras should slay a bull—that is, the core of the event—is credible at the level of episode in a narrative; that he should do so in the company of a dog, a snake, a scorpion, a raven, and two clones of himself, one with an elevated torch, the other with a lowered torch, is not. Manifestly, we have to do with an aggregation of symbols, and we need to ask, to what end? An important distinction between the tauroctony as 'theophany' and the framing side-scenes as biographic narrative is drawn by Zwirn (1989). To the non-narrative intent of the tauroctony's clutter of detail we shall return, more than once, in the chapters which follow.

3

The Problem of Referents: Interpretation with Reference to What?

1. ICONOGRAPHY AND THE PROBLEM OF REFERENTS

If we are to interpret the iconography, or the myth which we have reconstructed from the iconography, we have to decide what we will interpret it *with reference to*. This is not a given in the iconography in the way that it is a given in some of the written testimonies. For example, in *De antro* 6 Porphyry interprets the mithraeum as an image of the cosmos complete with 'symbols of the elements and climes of the cosmos', and he attributes that interpretation to the Mithraists themselves (via Eubulus). Consequently, if we think Porphyry's interpretation worth exploring, we know exactly where to look—to cosmology. And when, later in his essay, he talks about the signs of the zodiac, about planetary houses, about solstices and equinoxes, we know that we must focus particularly on astronomy and astrology in their Graeco-Roman manifestations.

The iconography, with the one major exception of the explicit astronomical symbols, gives us no such leads. We are on our own and must choose which way to look. Clauss's solution, as we have seen in the preceding chapter, is to ignore the problem and to treat the referents of the iconography as somehow self-evident. If there is incoherence or apparent contradiction, this merely proves that Mithraism was not 'a unified religion' (2000: 16). In fact, it does no such thing: it shows only that the researcher has begged the question and so absolved himself from a serious search for systematic referents and meaning.

2. REFERENTS IN THE SURROUNDING CULTURE?

Turcan's approach to the question of referents is altogether more reflective and sophisticated. In the passage I have already quoted (1986: 221), he addresses the problem as one of deciphering a language, and he bids us use as a reference text the 'common ideas of the Graeco-Roman world': 'C'est un langage à déchiffrer, et l'on ne peut guère hasarder de déchiffrement qu'en se fondant sur la séman-tique courante des motifs ou des attributs, en fonction de certaines idées com-munes au monde gréco-romain.' In other words, look to the relevant ideas in the Mysteries' surrounding culture and in particular to the customary meanings of the iconographic symbols we want to decipher. This is sensible advice, and it has led in practice to substantial findings concerning many aspects of the Mysteries, not least by Turcan himself.[1]

Iconographic symbols, however, are notoriously slippery signifiers, whose 'meanings' are difficult to decipher precisely because of their multivalence, the multiplicity of their referents. How, then, do we decide to what part of antiquity's common culture we should refer, in order to decipher what any given symbol 'means' within the mysteries? Again, Turcan has helpful answers, which we may summarize in three principles: (1) select the most usual connotations; (2) do not force the data into an a priori scheme; (3) consider the whole context in which the symbol is deployed.

(1). In the article from which I have quoted, the symbol at issue is the caduceus, the rod entwined by a pair of snakes in a figure-of-eight. In the banquet scene on the reverse of the Fiano Romano relief (V461), one of the torchbearers extends a caduceus towards the base of an altar, and at that exact place flames appear to leap up from the ground. Turcan (1986: 221–6) argues that since the caduceus is the customary attribute of Mercury, and since Mercury is the conductor of souls (*psychopompos*), the caduceus will maintain this connotation of the conduct of souls in the novel context of the Mithraic banquet scene. So the eliciting of flames by the caduceus refers to the dispatch of human souls,[2] and the scene expresses, among other things, Mithraic doctrine on this matter. I have no quarrel with Turcan's conclusion. Indeed, I find it entirely plausible. Neverthe-less, the principle on which it rests, that the symbol carries its most usual connotation, is a working assumption, not a self-evidently true premise. It is not inconceivable—indeed it is quite likely—that the Mithraists sometimes employed their symbols in unusual ways and with unusual connotations.

(2). Turcan (1986: 218–21) rightly pointed out that preconceived schemes had led his predecessors into untenable identifications of the symbols in this exemplar of the banquet scene. Cumont (1946), in applying a doctrine of the

---

[1] e.g. Turcan 1981 on the idea and practice of sacrifice within and beyond the Mysteries. The best example of this approach, in my view, is Gordon 1980b on the grades, where reference is made to the stock of Graeco-Roman animal lore in order to understand better what it meant to be a Mithraic Lion or Raven. This method also helps one draw distinctions between Mithraic ideas and the ideological mainstream of pagan antiquity. As Gordon has commented (pp. 22–3), new cults, especially in their ideologies, must walk a fine line between innovation and conservatism. They must remain comprehensible and familiar and yet must offer something appealing in its cognitive distinctiveness—a new and different way of understanding the world, yet recognizably still the old ways renovated.

[2] Whether into or out of the world (or both) must still be determined (Turcan 1986: 223).

four elements, had identified the flames as water; Leroy Campbell (1968: 189), in line with his blended Neoplatonic and Iranian interpretation, had identified the altar as an urn for water. Neither identification is at all plausible. Nevertheless, the interpreter must have some point of reference in the ideas current in the culture, if only as a working hypothesis: one cannot interpret out into a void. In fact, Turcan in his study of this banquet scene oriented his explication towards Stoic ideas of the nature of the soul. Turcan's interpretation is superior to Cumont's and to Campbell's not because he avoids a preconceived referent among current ideas, but because the symbols fit his referent without forced and implausible identifications.

(3).   Turcan's interpretation of the Fiano Romano banquet scene carries added persuasiveness because he integrated it with the scene of the tauroctony on the obverse of the relief in a single explication. The blood of the sacrificed bull, he explained, has soaked the ground at the base of the altar, and it is from the blood so shed that souls are elicited in fiery form by the torchbearer's caduceus (1986: 224 f.). The context is enlarged and the interpretation is enriched in relation to its postulated referent, the Stoic conception of the soul. It is hard to quarrel with this criterion of comprehensiveness. As a working principle it is indeed admirable. One notes only that it affords no guarantee of certainty in interpretation. A cluster of visual symbols has much greater elasticity than a sequence of words. How can we tell if we have divined *the* correct, or even *a* correct, 'meaning'?

3. IRANIAN REFERENTS?

In following Turcan's principles of interpretation, I have accepted his assumption that the culture to whose 'common ideas' we should refer is that of the 'Graeco-Roman world'. Historically, however, Mithraic scholarship has always looked as well to the Iranian world, and particularly to the ancient religion of that world, Zoroastrianism or Mazdaism. Of this Turcan is, of course, well aware; he would not deny, any more than I would, an Iranian component in, or in the background to, these self-confessed 'Persian' Mysteries. It is a matter, finally, of emphasis: how much weight one gives to things Graeco-Roman and how much to things Persian; also whether one construes the 'Persian' component as genuinely Iranian or as reinvented *Perserie*.

This is not the place to confront this question directly, let alone try to answer it.[3] My present concern is merely with its implications for heuristic procedure. Here we need only note the fact that, historically, Mithraic studies evolved around the question.[4] Cumont himself started with the working assumption that the mysteries of Mithras were the Roman expression of Mazdaism, and that

---

[3] Tentative answers: Gordon 1975, 1978, 2001; Beck 1998a.
[4] For a survey, see Beck 1984: 2063–71; updated in Beck 2004c: 27–9.

was the conclusion which he thought the data finally warranted. Although the last three decades of the twentieth century saw a swing towards interpreting the mysteries much more by reference to their Graeco-Roman context, scholars continue to put forward Iranizing interpretations, either in whole or in part.[5]

It is not merely uncertainty about the culture of the referents of Mithraic iconography that complicates our heuristic procedure. The iconography is seldom so straightforward that one can assign different components of a standard composition to unambiguous referents in one culture or the other, labelling, for example, this item in the tauroctony 'Graeco-Roman' and that 'Iranian'. Even to suggest such a distribution is to expose its absurdity. If both cultures are indeed represented in the mysteries, their presence is necessarily blended in the iconography of the monuments. We face, once again, the multivocality of the symbols: they can 'speak' different cultures simultaneously.

In point of fact, certain components of the iconography are indeed unilingual; or rather, they speak about referents in one culture only. These are the explicit astronomical symbols, and what they refer to are things in the heavens as constructed in Graeco-Roman culture, for example the zodiac and its signs. To my knowledge, there is no equivalent feature in the iconography that refers solely to a referent in Iranian culture or in Mazdaism. The classic case is the bull-killing Mithras himself. Iranian Mithra is not a bull-killer: why, then, do the occidental icons represent him as such?[6] If straightforward Iranian referents are hard to come by for the persons represented on the monuments, how much more difficult it is to decipher there a pure Iranian/Mazdean ideology.

It is not my intention to decry the search for Iranian/Mazdean antecedents to, or elements in, the referents of Mithraic iconography. That search has undoubtedly been a fruitful one.[7] My point is only that, in the absence of referents which are themselves manifestly and exclusively Iranian or Mazdean, the conclusions can only be more or less credible, more or less plausible, but never certain.[8]

The question of Iranian or Mazdean antecedents poses the further issue of historical depth. Even those who favour a scenario of radical reinvention of the

[5] For a select bibliography, see Gordon in Clauss 2000: 185 f. The acme of Iranizing interpretations, both in scope and complexity, was undoubtedly Campbell 1968. See also Widengren 1966, 1980. The modern surveys, though they also do justice to eastern Mit(h)ra, on the whole treat the Western mysteries as an autonomous creation: Turcan 2000, Merkelbach 1984, Clauss 1990/2000. The last of these marks the most radical break with an Iranian past. Nevertheless, strong voices still rightly insist on substantial continuities from East to West: Boyce and Grenet 1991: 468–90; Kreyenbroek 1994; Russell 1994; most recently, Bivar 1999; Weiss 1994, 1996, 1998, 2000.

[6] The other intensely problematic figure is the Mithraic lion-headed god. An indication of the frailty of the Iranizing case is that its proponents offer two mutually exclusive identities, Zurvan and Ahriman; for a summary, Beck 1984: 2087–8.

[7] To choose one example out of many, see Hinnells 1975 on Iranian ideas of sacrifice in the Mithraic bull-killing.

[8] Strangely, Iranizing interpretations are often regarded as more secure than 'speculative' astronomical interpretations (e.g. Swerdlow 1991). With the latter we can at least be sure that we are always in the right cultural ballpark.

mysteries in the West do not propose that the tauroctony, the side-scenes, and the entire ideology to which they give expression were drafted in a single comprehensive exercise. Antecedents are of course of even greater concern to those who favour continuity from Mazdaism and Iran. The Cumontian story, for example, is quite complex. Here is his well-known summary, expressed in an elaborate geological metaphor of stratification (1903: 30–1):

The basal layer of this religion, its lower and primordial stratum, is the faith of ancient Iran, from which it took its origin. Above this Mazdean substratum was deposited in Babylon a thick sediment of Semitic doctrines, and afterwards the local beliefs of Asia Minor added to it their alluvial deposits. Finally, a luxuriant vegetation of Hellenic ideas burst forth from this fertile soil and partly concealed from view its true original nature.

Again, the veracity of this and other such scenarios is not at issue here. Displaying it does, however, raise again the important distinction, introduced above (Ch. 1, sect. 6), between the two types of account that one can give of the iconography of the monuments: the synchronic, which provides an explanation in terms of structure and meaning; and the diachronic, which explains in terms of antecedents. It is essential to be transparent about which type of account one is offering at every stage.

4. CELESTIAL (ASTRONOMICAL/ASTROLOGICAL) REFERENTS?

I have alluded already to another class of referents invoked by Mithraic scholarship, especially in the final quarter of the last century: the astronomical and/or astrological. The warrant for looking in that direction is obvious and incontrovertible: Mithraic iconography is awash with explicit astronomical symbols, notably zodiacs;[9] the Sun god and the Moon goddess are present in the principal cult icon, the tauroctony; the Sun god is a major player in the episodes of the Mithras myth; and Mithras is himself the (Unconquered) Sun.[10] In cult life, moreover, each of the seven grades was under the protection of, and exemplified, one of the seven planets. Lastly, as Cumont himself observed (1899: 198), most of our very few ancient literary explications of the monuments point in the same direction, to the visible heavens as constructed in Graeco-Roman astronomy and astrology. We have already taken a first look at the principal such testimony, Porphyry's *De antro* 6, on the mithraeum as 'image of the universe' equipped with 'symbols of the elements and climes of the universe'.

---

[9] In H. G. Gundel's catalogue of ancient zodiacs (1992), eleven of twenty-eight arciform zodiacs (type I.5) are Mithraic, as are seven of thirty-six ring zodiacs in stone (type I.4a). Mithraea, as well as 'figured monuments', are embellished with astronomical symbols, e.g. the 'Seven Spheres' mithraeum in Ostia, which I shall discuss in a later chapter.

[10] I bypass, for the moment, the paradox of one solar person and two solar gods.

Now, whatever else the explicit astronomical symbols intimate, their primary referents are unambiguous. A zodiac cut in stone refers to the zodiac in the heavens: a notional band of twelve 'signs' modelled on twelve constellations through which—more precisely, along the central line of which, that is, the ecliptic—the Sun appears to pass in the course of his annual journey around the earth.

Not only is there a wealth of explicit astronomical symbolism on the monuments, but there is also good reason to suppose that in the tauroctony, in particular, reference is made to the visible heavens by deploying astronomical symbols in a less obvious, less conventional form as elements in what appears superficially to be an episode in a story.[11] Mithras slays a bull, and around these two are grouped a dog, a snake, a scorpion, a raven, a pair of twins, and not infrequently (particularly in Germany and to a lesser extent on the Danube) a cup and a lion too; the bull's tail is metamorphosed into an ear (or ears) of wheat. In the heavens (see star-chart, Fig. 1) we find, within a band extending along and below the zodiac from Taurus to Scorpius, constellations imagined in ancient uranography as a bull (Taurus), two dogs (Canis Major and Minor), a snake (Hydra),[12] a scorpion (Scorpius), a raven (Corvus), a pair of twins (Gemini), a cup (Crater), a lion (Leo), and finally a star called the 'wheat ear' (Spica = Alpha Virginis).[13]

It is improbable in the extreme that this set of correspondences between elements of the tauroctony and constellations in the heavens is an accidental, unintended coincidence.[14] That said, it must be admitted that most Mithraic scholars have in fact either ignored the correspondences altogether or treated them as too trivial and marginal to the tauroctony's meaning to warrant serious consideration.[15] In Clauss's survey (1990/2000), you will find not a word about them, just as you will find not a word about the specifics of the astronomical symbolism that makes the mithraeum an 'image of the universe'. Yet, paradoxically, his introductory chapter (ch. 2) on the background of religious thought ('Religious perspectives in the Roman Empire') concentrates precisely on the ancient view of the heavens and the stars as the goal of the soul's escape from the confines of terrestrial mortality. This strange state of affairs in Mithraic scholarship requires some explanation.

That scholars shy away from the mysteries' astronomical/astrological symbolism is explicable partly in terms of modern attitudes and reactions to the subject

---

[11] On the strangeness of the scene as narrative episode, see above, Ch. 2, app., sect. 3.

[12] One of three serpentine constellations; the other two, Serpens and Draco, are in different parts of the celestial sphere from the zone defined above.

[13] The first scholar to draw attention to the correspondences between elements of the tauroctony and constellations was K. B. Stark (1869).

[14] In a new essay in Beck 2004c (251–65) I demonstrate that the probability of unintended coincidence is statistically negligible.

[15] Turcan (2000: 106) does allow them 'secondary' importance.

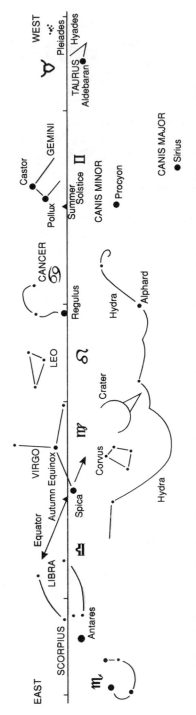

Fig. 1. The ecliptic and zodiac from Taurus to Scorpius, with southern paranatellonta of the summer quadrant, epoch of 100 CE

matter. First, we are not as routinely and experientially familiar with the visible heavens and the motions of the celestial bodies as were the ancients. Consequently, we do not recognize the referents of the symbols and their interrelations as readily as did they. We are diffident because we do not effortlessly comprehend what it is that the astronomical/astrological signifiers in this or that context might be signalling. Put bluntly, we don't understand 'how it all works', either in the apparent world or in the syntax and semantics of the astronomical/astrological sign systems.

Secondly, astronomy and astrology have long since parted company. The former is a respected science, the latter a derided superstition, all the more suspect because not yet eradicated. By and large, the best historians of ancient astronomy focus on the scientific—in the strictly modern sense—accomplishments of their predecessors in antiquity. They pan for astronomical gold in a stream of astrological grit and gravel. With some exceptions, they are uninterested in, and dismissive of, the predictive and theological goals which motivated ancient astronomy on the Babylonian side and the equally theological but also philosophical motivation of the Greeks.[16] The very people, then, who do understand 'how it all works', both in the world of appearances and in astronomical/astrological sign systems, are those least disposed to find sophisticated and systematic reference to the heavens in the religious context of Mithraic iconography.[17] Mithraism has next to nothing of strictly astronomical interest to teach a positivist historian of astronomy.[18] By contrast, it has a great deal to teach those concerned with the religious deployment of astronomy in antiquity's cultural constructs.

There are two further reasons, specific to the study of Mithraism as it has developed historically, why the astronomical/astrological referents in both the

---

[16] For the narrow aim of reconstructing the 'mathematical' astronomy of the ancients, the exclusion of all astrological (in the modern sense), theological, and philosophical (again, in the modern sense) considerations is unquestionably necessary. We would do well to remember, however, that the scientific astronomy thus reconstructed is *our* construct not the ancients'. It is salutary to recall the preface to Ptolemy's *Almagest*, in which the greatest of the ancient astronomers locates his subject midway between theology and physics, as a philosophical discipline concerned with immortal and unchanging, yet visible, entities, the contemplation of which is both an aesthetic and an ethical activity. This of course is the same Ptolemy who wrote the *Tetrabiblos*, a treatise on astrology (in our sense).

[17] I indicate a bias rather than an incapacity. Of course historians of ancient astronomy can and do produce excellent studies of the social and religious contexts in which astronomy and astrology flourished (e.g. Jones 1994, on 'the place of astronomy in Roman Egypt').

[18] Hence, I suspect, the animus of N. M. Swerdlow's (1991) attack on the astronomical interpretations of the mysteries. Swerdlow is a distinguished historian of astronomy, and his particular target, David Ulansey (1989), had the temerity to propose that the tauroctony encoded one of ancient astronomy's most important and highly technical discoveries, the 'precession of the equinoxes'. On the limited question of precession I agree with Swerdlow against Ulansey. Nevertheless, it is revealing that in rescuing high science from the domain of religion Swerdlow could not resist belittling the Mysteries of Mithras, although he explicitly acknowledged (1991: 58)—and amply demonstrated—his lack of scholarly competence in the study of religion.

iconography and the texts of the mysteries have been minimized. First, in the Cumontian story of the evolution of Mithraism the astronomical/astrological components are late and superficial, 'les propos d'antichambre dont on entretenait les prosélytes de la porte avant de les admettre à la connaissance de la doctrine ésotérique et de leur révéler les traditions iraniennes sur l'origine et la fin de l'homme et du monde' (1899: 202). Cumont never demonstrated that this was so: it was merely asserted as part of his scenario of the reception and realization of essentially Iranian mysteries in the West. Nevertheless, it was accepted as historically true by those following in Cumont's footsteps. Cumont's status as a historian also of ancient astrology gave it additional weight.[19] If an authority in both fields said it was so, why should one suppose differently?

The second reason for trivializing astronomical/astrological reference in the mysteries has to do with the quality and thrust of the celestial interpretations themselves. These, for the most part, have concentrated on decoding the constellation symbolism of the tauroctony, while overlooking the more explicit symbolism of the mithraeum as 'cosmic image'. An astronomical interpretation of the mithraeum has a greater and more immediate plausibility than an astronomical interpretation of the tauroctony, not only because the key symbols are 'in clear' (for example, the signs of the zodiac on the benches of the Sette Sfere mithraeum), but also because, as we saw in Chapter 4 (sect. 1), an intelligent and well-informed contemporary source tells us—and tells us how and why—the mithraeum was constructed on a principle of correspondence with the celestial macrocosm. For that reason, I have chosen to make Porphyry, *De antro nympharum* 6 and the ideal mithraeum the gateway for our explorations of the mysteries. Other astronomical interpretations, I sense, have made weaker cases by plunging more or less precipitately into a decoding of the tauroctony. Consequently, they have lacked persuasiveness. Like Adonis gardens, they flourish briefly and wither, because they are ungrounded in proper contextual soil.

The astronomical interpretations are also suspect because they pose, or seem to pose, a stark either/or choice: either the tauroctony has an exclusively astral meaning or it has no astral meaning at all (or only a marginal one). The choice, however, is illusory, and in fact the astronomical interpreters do not pose it; at worst, their interpretations are mute as to non-astrological significance. In fighting shy of the astronomical interpretations, scholars may well be confusing medium and message. As we shall explore later, the constellation correspondences do not imply, in and of themselves, that the tauroctony conveys an astral meaning. The position I shall eventually take, simply put, is that the celestial symbols convey a cluster of messages which are primarily about Mithras, not about the heavens. More precisely, the symbols mirror their counterparts in the

---

[19] See Cumont's popular *Astrology and Religion among the Greeks and Romans* (1912) and his *L'Égypte des astrologues* (1937). Cumont was also one of the most active founders, promoters, and editors of the important multi-volume *Catalogus Codicum Astrologorum Graecorum* (1898–1953).

heavens, the actual constellations, and it is these latter which convey messages about Mithras. 'The heavens declare...', and what they declare is not self-referential, or at least not primarily so.

For the most part, the astronomical interpretations have concentrated on narrow questions of identity, in particular the celestial identity of Mithras.[20] If the elements of the tauroctony correspond to the various constellations listed above, then what constellation is indicated by Mithras in the centre of the composition? The plausibility of the approach is greatly undercut by the multiplicity of the answers returned and the fact that they appear to be mutually exclusive.[21] Michael Speidel (1980) proposed Orion, David Ulansey (1989) Perseus, K.-G. Sandelin (1988) Auriga. It does not help that none of these three constellations is at the centre of the constellation group signified by the other elements in the composition of the tauroctony (see star-chart, Fig. 1).[22]

Reactions to these and other celestial identifications are polarized. Some find them totally persuasive, others totally unconvincing. Their attractiveness lies in their power to inject a meaning into the tauroctony which is precise, objective (if you buy into the logic of the argument), and precisely describable. They explain by deciphering, by translating one set of signs into another. They thus give a sense of accomplishment and discovery. The new sign set, moreover, is more readily comprehensible, more straightforwardly articulated, and thus much more congenial to the reductionist mentality than the strange, loosely co-ordinated, unconfined symbolism of the violent and threateningly numinous scene on the tauroctony's surface.

Negative reaction takes one of two forms. Positivists sceptical of the logic of the argument consider the theory a misappropriation of scientific astronomy and the reduction spurious.[23] Those more profoundly and sympathetically committed to interpreting the mysteries instinctively object to the reduction precisely because it both demystifies the mystery and trivializes the tauroctony. In other words, the astronomical translation of the strange, unconfined symbolism of the numinous scene is taken pejoratively. Is the tauroctony really no more than a star-chart posing a riddle of identity? What larger purpose could possibly be served by making the tauroctonous Mithras this or that constellation? Scepticism along these lines is certainly salutary, and I sympathize—though I do not agree—with

[20] I critique this approach in more detail in a new essay ('The rise and fall of the astral identifications of the tauroctonous Mithras') in Beck 2004c: 235–49.

[21] Actually, given the multivalence of symbols—the usual law of non-contradiction does not apply, in that one symbol can simultaneously signify several referents—a case could be made for identifying the tauroctonous Mithras with as many constellations as seem apposite. In fact, however, none of the scholars mentioned makes such a case.

[22] Orion is in the lower right corner (south-west), Perseus and Auriga in the upper right (north-west). (NB: In a star-chart the directions of east and west are inverted from those in a terrestrial map.)

[23] Swerdlow 1991 (review article of Ulansey 1989) is the best example.

Turcan's counter-arguments (2000: 105–8), based as they are on an admission of the *secondary* significance of the constellation correspondences.[24]

Before passing on from the astronomical/astrological referents postulated for the tauroctony, we should briefly survey the remaining claimants.

First, the constellation of Perseus is not the only celestial identity proposed by David Ulansey (1989) for the tauroctonous Mithras. Ulansey postulates a more profound identity for Mithras as the power responsible for an arcane but fundamental cosmic phenomenon, discovered in antiquity (by Hipparchus in the second century BCE), known as the 'precession of the equinoxes'. Precession, we now know, is caused by a wobble in the earth's axis of rotation. It manifests itself in an apparent, very slow shift of the position of the celestial poles and of the equinoxes (the points at which the ecliptic and the celestial equator intersect). According to Ulansey, the Mithraists believed that their god had effected this shift of the world axis. The tauroctony is thus an allegorized display of the power of Mithras in accomplishing this cosmic feat. This is not the point at which to engage with Ulansey's theory.[25] In due course I shall demonstrate that there are more plausible ways to account for those features of the tauroctony on which Ulansey bases his case for Mithras as the agent of precession. Currently, Ulansey's theory is the best-known—or most notorious, depending on one's point of view—of the late twentieth-century celestial identifications. It is certainly the most sensational, since it claims that astronomical knowledge previously thought to be the preserve of a few highly sophisticated astronomers was not only known to the Mithraists but also appropriated by them into the arcana of their mysteries.

Secondly, there are two interpretations which involve reference to the constellation of Leo (see star-chart, Fig. 1) but do not assert the outright equation of the tauroctonous Mithras with that constellation. The first of these is Alessandro Bausani's theory (1979) that the ultimate archetype of the tauroctony is the Near Eastern motif of the bull-killing lion, which in turn can be interpreted (following Hartner 1965) as a very old expression of the seasonal cycle in which the lion of summer (Leo) overcomes the bull of spring (Taurus). Constellation lore thus lies in the 'prehistory' of the tauroctony's composition. The second interpretation centrally involving Leo was advanced by me (Beck 1994*b*), starting with the

---

[24] One is less sympathetic to Clauss's total disregard of the evidence, on the unargued assertion that astronomical interpretations are 'unconvincing speculation' (2000: p. xx). See also his review of the German translation of Ulansey's book (Clauss 2001).

[25] For critiques see Swerdlow 1991, Beck 1994*b*: 36–40. Clauss's review (see preceding note) is as polemical and contemptuous as Swerdlow's, but it attacks not Ulansey's use of ancient astronomy *per se*, but rather his historical methods in constructing a narrative link connecting Hipparchus to the Mithraists. Here Clauss's criticisms, like Swerdlow's, hit the mark. Where both critics are wrong and Ulansey is right is in the evidence for astronomy's massive and sophisticated presence in the symbolism of Mithraic monuments. This requires a causal explanation; if not Ulansey's, then some other. But the necessity of an explanation is something neither Swerdlow nor Clauss will concede even in principle, the former because the very idea of learned astral symbolism affronts his standards for serious astronomy in the ancient world, the latter because it requires understanding of a kind not in the repertoire of the exemplary ancient historian.

postulate—the very obvious can sometimes be overlooked—that the tauroctonous Mithras is precisely what the monuments call him, the Unconquered Sun.
Leo lies in the middle of the band of constellations intimated by most of the
other elements in the tauroctony. Therefore the tauroctonous Mithras is the Sun
in Leo. The proper question to ask of the tauroctony is not '*who* is Mithras?' but
'*where* is Mithras?' or, since the position of the Sun in the signs/constellations of
the zodiac indicates seasonal time, '*when* is Mithras?'—or in other words, at what
time of year does he do what he does?

I drew on an interpretation of the tauroctony by A. J. Rutgers (1970), equating
Mithras with the Sun and the bull with the Moon. (There is as good warrant for
the latter identification as for the former, as we shall see later.) Now, the most
dramatic astronomical phenomenon observable as the Sun and the Moon pursue
each other around the heavens is the eclipse, when the light of one or other of
these bodies is quite suddenly and unexpectedly dimmed. In these terms, then,
the victory of Mithras (Sun) over the bull (Moon) can be interpreted as a lunar
eclipse. Less dramatic, but equally explicable as the victory of the Sun over the
Moon, is the monthly disappearance of the old crescent Moon into the Sun's
brilliance, followed by her reappearance a couple of days later as the 'New Moon'.
Lastly there are those rare occasions when the conjunction of Sun and Moon is so
close that the latter actually passes in front of the former, causing a solar eclipse.
Any account of the mysteries which takes the solar persona of Mithras seriously
must accommodate this setback in the career of the 'Unconquered Sun'.

To return to the bull as Taurus, the most recent interpretation, that of Bruno
Jacobs (1999), relates the bull-killing to the heliacal setting (i.e. last evening
visibility) of Taurus the constellation at the time of the spring equinox. The
tauroctony thus represents the overcoming of winter and proclaims Sol Mithras
the paragon of seasonal renewal, youth, and invincibility.

Thirdly, there is a recent interpretation which, in a seeming paradox, un-
couples Mithras from the Sun and identifies him with the vault of heaven itself,
particularly the night sky, in which the doings of the celestial gods are made
manifest. In this interpretation, by Maria Weiss (1994, 1996, 1998, 2000), the
classic formula DEUS SOL INVICTUS MITHRAS is explained paratactically: the
Sun god (and) Unconquered Mithras.

Fourth are astronomical interpretations which refer the tauroctony primarily
to *time*. Time and calendrics have always been the concern of astronomy and
much of its *raison d'être*, since the apparent motions of the celestial bodies are the
very measures of time. Time, moreover, especially seasonal time, is deeply
implicated with the sacred. It is no mere matter of measured duration. Thus, it
is plausible to descry in the tauroctony references to time as well as to bodies in
celestial space, temporal relationships as well as spatial relationships. Of the two
interpretations which look to time, that of Stanley Insler (1978) is to be
commended for adducing the important fact that the positioning of the elements
of the tauroctony, right to left, matches approximately the sequence of the

corresponding constellations from west to east, and hence the sequence in which they rise and set heliacally during the course of the year.[26] Right = west = earlier; left = east = later. I shall have more to say later about this pair of fundamental structural equations.

The second temporal interpretation is that of the historian of science John D. North (1990). As one might expect, North's interpretation is technically the most accomplished in astronomical terms. He interprets the tauroctony more as a clock than a calendar, correlating thirteen features in the tauroctony with constellations or parts of constellations which set successively at intervals of one hour, more or less.[27] One wonders, however, why observing the passing of the hours should have been of such fundamental importance to the Mithraists that they encoded it in their principal icon. The striking of the hours on the parish clock is not at the heart of the Christian mystery: why should we suppose it so in the Mithraic mystery? Although he introduces much detailed star lore, North does not tell us. Strangely, North also misses the one piece of archaeological evidence which securely relates ancient time-telling to ancient star maps, albeit in a secular context (as far as anything in antiquity can be called truly secular). This is the device of the anaphoric clock, whose 'dial' or clock-face was a star map rotating once every twenty-four hours (Vitruvius 9.8; Drachmann 1954).

Fifthly and finally, there is the interpretation of Reinhold Merkelbach (1984: 81). The reference to the heavens which Merkelbach sees in the tauroctony is indirect and follows from his identification of various elements of the tauroctony with each of the seven grades. Since the grades are correlated with the planets, each element in the basic tauroctony, the bull excepted, alludes secondarily to a planet. Thus, the four subsidiary animals in the tauroctony (raven, snake, scorpion, dog) correspond to the first four grades (Raven, Nymphus, Miles, Leo), and hence intimate, respectively, the planets Mercury, Venus, Mars, and Jupiter. Merkelbach's planetary correspondences follow a priori from the primary correlations. Hence they stand or fall with the latter, since the direct links between animals and planets are not overwhelmingly compelling.[28]

The more ways in which the tauroctony and its features are referred to the heavens, the less convincing the entire enterprise becomes. One can only plead the multivalence of symbols so far; after a point, which has probably now been reached for all but enthusiasts, the law of diminishing returns sets in. One sympathizes with those who turn away, in weariness or scepticism, to simpler

---

[26] Insler proposed that the heliacal setting of Taurus in April was the time of year signalled by the tauroctony.

[27] 'Set' is used here in the everyday sense in which we speak, e.g., of a sunset, as opposed to the once-a-year 'heliacal' setting of a star.

[28] With the exception, perhaps, of the equation raven = Mercury. The problem is that while individually each trail from animal to planet is viable, all the correspondences are effected by different routes, so that the set of correspondences as a whole is ultimately unconvincing.

interpretations—or to no interpretation at all, just a reading of the tauroctony at face value without translation. Yet the basic constellation correspondences of the tauroctony cannot be denied, nor can the basic correspondence of the mithraeum to the universe via its 'cosmic symbolism'.

If we are to reach a more convincing interpretation via astronomy and astrology, we should listen again to some words of Robert Turcan quoted already in this and the preceding chapters: 'C'est un langage à déchiffrer.' If the iconography is a language and if many of its signs are astral, one cannot assume that its messages too are necessarily astral. Some of them no doubt are; perhaps many of them are. I propose, however, in future chapters to focus on astral symbolism more as medium than as message, less on questions of 'what'—what, celestially, do the elements of the tauroctony refer to?—and more on questions of 'how' and 'why'—how and why does the tauroctony refer to the heavens, how and why does the mithraeum function as an 'image of the universe'? 'Star-talk', in my model, is the *idiom* of the Mithraic mysteries, not its substance.

5. CONCLUSION

Scholarly interpretation of the Mithraic mysteries, which started so promisingly with Cumont's great two-volume work at the turn of the nineteenth and twentieth centuries, appears to have reached something of a dead end at the turn of the twentieth and twenty-first. All avenues of reference—whether to the Graeco-Roman cultural milieu, or to Iranian religion, or to ancient astronomy and astrology—have been explored, and the intuitively obvious inferences have been drawn. The veins appear to be exhausted, the mines worked out. In any case, omnibus interpretations are now out of fashion, and likewise grand causal explanations which privilege Iranian antecedents or astronomical constructs. Indeed, there is a tendency now to disperse and pluralize the mysteries into regional variations over limited time spans.[29] The local and the particular predominate, and perhaps that is as it should be—it is certainly safer. Grand narratives are perhaps just grand illusions.

It might therefore seem that in deconstructing 'doctrine', as I intend to do in the next chapter, one is demolishing a straw man—no very arduous feat. There is, nevertheless, good reason to proceed, not because there is still a widespread belief in a fixed Mithraic doctrine now lost but in principle recoverable, but because demolition to date has been, paradoxically, both less radical and more radical than it should be. It has been insufficiently radical, in that while scholars now seldom postulate a lost *corpus* of Mithraic doctrine, the Cumontian assumption

---

[29] Turcan 1999 is a good example. Turcan there suggests that the correlation of grades to planets attested at the Felicissimus mithraeum in Ostia (V299) and the Sta Prisca mithraeum in Rome (V476) was a local third-century phenomenon.

that Mithraism was first and foremost a 'faith' with 'beliefs', and hence with 'doctrine' in a more diffuse sense, still flourishes. Not that 'doctrine' as a category has to be entirely extirpated: no one doubts that teaching and exegesis took place in the mithraeum; and what is taught and explicated can properly be called 'doctrine'. Rather, what needs to be modified is the presupposition that the inculcation of *beliefs* was the primary function of the mysteries. When made explicit, that assumption loses much of its credibility; but left implicit, as it usually is, it is dangerous. As I shall show in the next chapter, it has seriously compromised the understanding of at least one important piece of evidence, our 'gateway' text of Porphyry on the mithraeum (*De antro* 6).

Much more serious are the ill effects of an out-and-out dismissal of doctrine. For the vacuum which it leaves seems to legitimate a prejudice, both elitist and naive, to which classicists are still all too liable: the assumption that doctrine is an index of a thoughtful religion. Absence of doctrine, so runs this logic, is thus precisely what one would expect in a plain man's religion such as Mithraism. Why look for doctrine where one's model of reason predicts that it cannot be found? And why look for anything in doctrine's place? To the new positivism these are simply non-issues.

In the next chapter I shall demonstrate how deeply rooted is this attitude. Indeed, it is one of our less fortunate legacies from antiquity itself. Exposing it, and the naive theory of mind on which it depends, will be part of our continuing task.

4

Doctrine Redefined

1. BACK TO PORPHYRY, *DE ANTRO* 6

For our discussion of 'doctrine' we return to our gateway text, Porphyry's *De antro* 6, on the form and function of the mithraeum:

Similarly, the Persians call the place a cave where they introduce an initiate to the mysteries, revealing to him the path by which souls descend and go back again. For Eubulus tells us that Zoroaster was the first to dedicate a natural cave in honour of Mithras, the creator and father of all.... This cave bore for him the image of the cosmos which Mithras had created, and the things which the cave contained, by their proportionate arrangement, provided him with symbols of the elements and climates of the cosmos. (trans. Arethusa edition)

Porphyry, as we have already noted (Ch. 2, sect. 1), tells us here two things of great importance: (1) that the mithraeum was intended to be, and was designed and furnished as, 'a model of the universe', a microcosm in the literal sense of a self-contained miniature replica of the cosmos; and (2) that in this setting the initiates of Mithras were inducted into a mystery of the soul's descent and return.

We also observed (3) that Porphyry appears to be talking about *ritual*, specifically a ritual of initiation, rather than instruction; and (4) that whatever is effected for the initiates in the mithraeum works by *symbolism*.

2. 'INDUCTION INTO A MYSTERY': THE DOCTRINAL MISCONSTRUCTION OF *DE ANTRO* 6

Now it might seem over-cautious to say that Porphyry in *De antro* 6 'appears' to be talking about ritual rather than instruction. Surely ritual *is* what Porphyry is talking about, and 'appearances' can be dispensed with. That, however, is precisely the point at issue. Scholars have mostly assumed—mostly, too, without argument—that what is transmitted to the initiate at his initiation is *teaching* about the descent and ascent of souls. One can see this in the translations of the first sentence. Here is the Greek:

houtō kai Persai tèn eis katō kathodon tōn psychōn kai palin exodon mystagōgountes *telousi ton mystēn, eponomasantes spēlaion ton topon.*

The Arethusa edition, as we have seen, translates (my italics):

Similarly, the Persians call the place a cave where they introduce an initiate to the mysteries, *revealing* to him the path by which souls descend and go back again.

The more recent English translation (Lamberton 1983, my italics) runs:

Likewise the Persian mystagogues initiate their candidate by *explaining* to him the downward journey of souls and their subsequent return, and they call the place where this occurs a 'cave'.

The key word is the participle *mystagōgountes*, which means literally 'inducting into a mystery'. Grammatically, the *kathodos* ('road down') and *exodos* ('road out') of souls are the participle's direct objects: they are what the Mithraists both make a mystery *of* and induct the initiate *into*. In so doing they make him 'perfect' in the mystery (*telousi*). Accordingly, I would render the sentence thus:

Thus too the Persians perfect their initiate by *inducting* him *into a mystery* of the descent of souls and their exit back out again, calling the place a 'cave'.

Neither the Arethusa rendering nor Lamberton's is a *mis*translation; but both are tendentious in that they explain the mystagogy by suggesting modes of delivery unwarranted by the text. In place of the literal 'induction' ('leading', *-agōgē*) into the mystery, we are offered (1) a revelation and (2) instruction. Of the two, 'revealing' adds less to the literal sense, for in certain mysteries, notably the Eleusinian, we know that 'showing' (hierophany) and 'viewing' (*epopteia*) were of the essence. With 'explaining', however, we—and the initiates—are sent down a different route altogether: 'explaining' implies instruction; the initiate, in a word, is *taught* about the descent and exit of souls.[1] Thus the mystery is transformed into a *doctrine*, and the mithraeum into a classroom and/or a visual aid to *learning* about one's entry into and exit from this mortal world.

3. TEACHING VERSUS ENACTING THE 'DESCENT AND DEPARTURE OF SOULS': THE COMMONSENSICAL ANSWER

In a subsequent chapter we shall pursue the literal intent of *De antro* 6. Here, however, the role of doctrine in the Mithraic mysteries is the issue, and the question we need to ask next is why the plain sense of *De antro* 6 has been so misunderstood.

---

[1] Simonini's translation (1986: 45) commendably avoids the error: '... i Persiani danno il nome di antro al luogo in qui durante i riti introducono l'iniziato al mistero della discesa delle anime sulla terra e della loro risalita da qui.'

Common sense is the first culprit. If I am inducted into a mystery of the 'descent and departure of souls', surely it must be something I am taught, not something I enact, because my soul has already descended at or prior to my birth and will not depart until my death. What can possibly be done in a mithraeum to re-enact and pre-enact these processes? So it follows, doesn't it, that what I undergo in a mithraeum must be instruction about the two processes, the transmission of esoteric information about what happened to me before my birth and what will happen to me after my death? Nicodemus' point is well taken (John 3: 4): 'Can [a man] enter his mother's womb a second time and be born?'

In an earlier study (Beck 1988: 77–9) I have combated the casual assumption that the 'journey back out again' can only refer to the *posthumous* ascent of the soul and therefore that initiation into the mystery must necessarily have taken the form of instruction. Nicodemus received one answer concerning rebirth; the Mithraists would give another concerning both a second birth and an anticipation of death: yes, in our ritual you can indeed experience what you were before you were born and what you will be after you die. Or rather, in the 'time out of time' of the mithraeum-universe you can experience your arrival, sojourn, and departure from earth as stages in an ampler continuum of being.[2]

Ritual, then, predominates; but we need not doubt that the 'descent and departure of souls' was *also* explained verbally to the initiates. In this weak sense of *ad hoc* teaching, it is likely that there was indeed a 'doctrine' of the descent and departure of souls in the Mithraic mysteries. That, however, is an independent probability; it is not an entailment of Porphyry's text, and there is certainly no warrant here for discerning 'doctrine' in the strong sense of fixed, uniform, written teaching. (In fairness to contemporary scholarship, I should add that an extreme doctrinal view, postulating a definite corpus of written text no longer extant, is a theoretical limiting case, not one, as far as I know, which is seriously entertained today.)

4. AN EXPECTATION OF APPROPRIATE BEHAVIOUR

That the Mithraists were taught about their posthumous destiny in and as a rite of initiation is not just the commonsensical interpretation of *De antro* 6; it is also the most conformable to our expectations of how people behave. It is easy for us to imagine the initiates receiving instruction about the celestial journey their souls would undertake after death (and the reverse journey down from the heavens which they had already undertaken prior to birth); easy, too, to imagine the Father or other senior member giving that instruction from his stock of authoritative learning and using his mithraeum, with its store of cosmic symbolism 'appropriately arranged', as teaching aid.

---

[2] On 'time out of time' in ritual, see Rappaport 1999: 216–25.

Far less easy is it to imagine our 'average' Mithraist—the veteran in Dacia, say, or the petty official of the customs bureaucracy at Poetovio, or the successful Ostian freedman—actually undergoing in the here and now an experience of celestial soul travel, an intimation of what he was before he was and of what he would be after he was. Intuitively we confine such experiences to the shaman, to the solitary adept of arcana such as the Graeco-Egyptian magician and other-worldly voyager who put together the so-called 'Mithras Liturgy'.[3]

My point at this stage is not that the Mithraists actually did have experiences of celestial soul travel but that scholars instinctively and automatically discount the possibility. Evidence about a ritual performed is accordingly transformed into evidence of instruction given, hence of a doctrine about the soul's posthumous (and prenatal) destiny. This transformation is effected below the threshold of the scholar's conscious consideration of the interpretive options available. We simply cannot envisage the Dacian veteran, the petty bureaucrat at Poetovio, the Ostian freedman *experiencing* celestial soul travel, albeit in ritual. Ergo he must be *learning* about it—for future reference.

It is our imaginations, not the imaginations of the Mithraists, which are deficient. Scholarship has unthinkingly assumed, against the plain intent of Porphyry's testimony, that the Mithraists, being the people they were, were incapable of the sort of experience attributed to them. What explains this attitude, apart from commonsensical but misleading expectations about the behaviour of 'ordinary' people? It is a long and not very creditable story, and it has its origin in the attitudes of our scholarly predecessors back in antiquity. Let us start with the ancients, moving at the same time from the particular testimony of *De antro* 6 to the more general question of 'doctrine' in the Mithraic mysteries and in the wider religious world beyond.

5. 'REASON FOR THE WISE, SYMBOLS FOR THE VULGAR'

Information about the Mithraic mysteries has been passed on to us by the Neoplatonists, primarily by Porphyry in his *De antro*, not because they were interested in Mithraism *per se*—let alone in the rank-and-file membership—but as grist to the mill of their own philosophical and theological speculations. On this all modern scholars agree. Opinion diverges, however, on the next question: did the ancients report their data from the Mithraic mysteries *accurately*? Here we must immediately concede two points: first that modern research standards of objectivity and accuracy would be irrelevant to Porphyry and his colleagues; secondly that they would regard massaging the data (as we would see it) not

---

[3] I cite the Mithras Liturgy (text and translation Betz 2003) not because of its (tenuous) connection to the actual Mysteries of Mithras but because it is the best example of the magical ascent.

only as justifiable but also, if the data did not already fit, as methodologically necessary in order to access a higher truth on the philosophical/theological plane. There is, then, no presumption of accurate reportage such as one would expect of a modern ethnographer or a sociologist describing a sub-culture.

Elsewhere I have argued that the testimony of Porphyry and his sources in *De antro* is substantially accurate.[4] They did not misrepresent the data because they did not need to; the Mithraic evidence already said what they needed it to say. However, the contrary opinion is also widely held: that while there is a core of accurate information (e.g. mithraea really were called 'caves', some of them were actually sited in natural caves, and many others were made to look like caves), the Mithraic mysteries as they are presented to us in the *De antro* and similar works are essentially the construct of Neoplatonist (and Neopythagorean) philosophers. The champion of this view is Robert Turcan, the title and subtitle of whose influential *Mithras Platonicus: recherches sur l'hellénisation philosophique de Mithra* (1975) say it all.

The issue of my disagreement with Turcan—who is right and who is wrong— is not our immediate concern, which is rather with the heuristic implications of the divergent views. Turcan's view implies that the Neoplatonic testimonies, since they are unreliable witnesses for the actual Mithraic mysteries, are of little value to the modern project of interpreting the mysteries. My view of course implies the opposite: that the testimonies, since they are for the most part factually accurate, are hermeneutically valuable.

However, my confidence in the accuracy of most of the Mithraic data conveyed by Porphyry and his colleagues and predecessors does not extend to their *interpretations*, either of religion in general or of the Mithraic mysteries in particular. Factually sound data can always be perverted—'enhanced', the Neoplatonist could say with a clear conscience—to mistaken ends. I shall maintain that this has indeed happened and that, despite the accuracy of their data, the Neoplatonists' *construction* of the mysteries is indeed, from the modern perspective, a misrepresentation.

Here I am in agreement with Turcan. We agree both on the character and on the intent of the Neoplatonic construction of the mysteries and on its distancing from the actual mysteries. We disagree solely on whether or not the Neoplatonic construction is a conduit for reliable information on the latter; perhaps also on quite how far distant were the constructed mysteries from the actual: I would give Porphyry and company rather more credit than would Turcan for respecting the empirical facts in constructing their model.

The Neoplatonic model of religion, apart from its own intrinsic interest, is important because it shows us how the contemporary intelligentsia constructed the mysteries. Moreover, their model did not vanish with the ending of antiquity and its philosophical culture. Rather, it propagated itself into modern represen-

---

[4] Beck 1984: 2055–6; 1988: 42, n. 93 (cf. pp. 92–4), 80–2; 1994a: 106–7; 2000: 158–9, 177–9.

tations of what a mystery religion should and should not be. In other words, the ancient philosophical template for 'mysteries' is still applied. When coupled with similar preconceptions transferred from the Christian mysteries, the ancient philosophical model has seriously distorted modern representations of the mysteries—and nowhere more seriously than with regard to 'doctrine'. We therefore need to look at the Neoplatonic construction of the mysteries with some care.

In the *De antro*, as elsewhere, Porphyry assumes that religion, or rather *what matters* in religion, is (1) the product of the sages of the past and (2) comprehensible and fully meaningful in the present only to the wise. Mysteries, then, represent an intellectual elite calling to an intellectual elite across the gulf of time. The meanings transmitted by the wise and deciphered by the wise are primarily allegorical: what certain symbols 'really' mean at a higher, that is, philosophical, metaphysical, theological, level. These meanings may or may not be comprehended by the cult initiate who employs them. It scarcely matters, for the meanings are entirely independent of the initiate who handles, speaks, or otherwise apprehends them. One can access them just as well, perhaps better, from the text of Homer, which is precisely what Porphyry does in the work whose full title is *On the Cave of the Nymphs in the Odyssey*. Homer has his honoured, indeed pre-eminent, place among the ancients (*palaioi*) and theologians (*theologoi*) on whom Porphyry so often draws for the truth behind material symbols and symbolic practices.[5]

The co-option of the mysteries into an autonomous intellectual tradition had two unfortunate consequences (unfortunate, that is, from the modern perspective of the accurate reconstruction of ancient religion). First, ownership of the mysteries passed from the actual workaday initiates to an imagined quasi-philosophical elite. Secondly, the core of the mysteries was metamorphosed into doctrine, arcane wisdom transmitted from the wise to the wise. Ideal intellectual filiations were extended into remote times and places, where their sources and the founts of their wisdom could be traced to antique sages, usually of the Orient or Egypt.[6] Thus Zoroaster, 'prophet' of the Persian mysteries, was reconstructed on the pattern of a Greek philosopher, indeed as the putative teacher of Greek philosophers.[7] In this way the Mysteries/mysteries of Mithras, as a real-life human enterprise, were misrepresented both socially and cognitively. Modern scholarship still lives with the consequences of this distortion.

---

[5] On 'Homer the theologian' see Lamberton's book of that title (1986). On the ancient philosophical construction of an Ur-religion see Boys-Stones 2001.

[6] On this 'alien wisdom' see Momigliano 1975.

[7] The classic study of the ancient reconstruction of Zoroaster is Bidez and Cumont 1938 (note the title: *Les Mages hellénisés: Zoroastre, Ostanès et Hystaspe d'après la tradition grecque*); see also Beck 1991: 521–39, esp. 525; Kingsley 1990, 1995 (both on earlier, i.e., pre-Neoplatonic, Greek constructions). That the real-life Mithraists also looked to Zoroaster as their founder we may legitimately infer from Porphyry, *De antro* 6; that they further encumbered him with much, or indeed any, of the baggage of the extant Zoroastrian pseudepigrapha, I very much doubt.

The ancient construction of exotic religion is nicely caught in the first book of Origen's *Contra Celsum* (1.9 ff.). Origen is there defending Christianity against the familiar charge that it exalts blind faith over reason. While stoutly championing the necessity for, and the virtue of, faith among the humble and intellectually challenged (and shrewdly counter-charging that adhesion to a philosophical school often involves a leap of faith and passionate rather than reasoned conviction), Origen concedes all of his opponent's principal points about what religion should be and ideally is: a rational, cognitive enterprise, of which the philosophical school is the paradigm and which is traceable to a philosophical founder. As well as protesting that Christianity too has its intellectuals, Origen criticizes Celsus for excluding Judaism (of which Christianity for Origen is the proper continuation) from the honour roll, despite the high standing of its founder Moses and the Mosaic law. The criticism is warranted, for Moses and the law do indeed fit the ancient paradigm of proper and reasonable religion, a fact, says Origen, which the Neopythagorean Numenius is to be complimented on for appreciating (1.15).[8] In excluding Judaism, and therefore Christianity, Celsus must have some other—and unpleasant—axe to grind. Origen is probably right.[9]

Our main concern, however, is with the substantial agreement of Origen, Celsus, and Numenius that religions, in particular the exotic, non-civic cults and mysteries, are constituted on the one hand of a rational elite and, on the other, of a vulgar membership incapable of intellectual endeavour beyond the most rudimentary. Social status, it is understood, generally correlates with intellectual status. In the first of two references to Mithraism in this part of the *Contra Celsum* (1.9), Origen says that Celsus classed the Mithraists entirely with the latter group, the vulgar 'believers'. But in the second reference (1.12), to which I drew attention in Chapter 1 (sect. 1), both classes 'among the Persians' are engaged in the *teletai*.[10] These mysteries of initiation are 'cultivated rationally' (*logikōs presbeuomenai*) by the erudite, but expressed symbolically (*symbolikōs ginomenai*) by the 'common, rather shallow people'. The differentiation is actually more complex than a mere contrast between more and less sophisticated interpretations of the mysteries, but the primary distinction is clear: the erudite 'cultivate' the mysteries 'rationally'; common, shallow people do not. Whatever it is that the latter do—and we shall return to it later—it is not an activity of reason. The distinction is perhaps clearer in Egyptian religion as Origen explicates it before turning to the 'Persian' *teletai*: 'Egyptian wise men who have studied their traditional writings give profound philosophical interpretations of what they

[8] Numenius was an extreme xenophile, going so far as to call Plato an 'Atticizing Moses' (Fr. 8 Des Places, cf. 1a).

[9] As Boys-Stones's study (2001) amply demonstrates, there was a nasty strain of what we would now call anti-Semitism running through the ancient philosophical construction of the Ur-religion.

[10] Though he likely thought he was speaking of actual Persians, Celsus is referring to Roman Mithraism, the most accessible form of 'Persian' religion to a Greek or Roman writer.

regard as divine, while the common people hear certain myths of which they are proud, although they do not understand the meaning' (ibid., trans. Chadwick).

Now modern scholarship has of course long since deconstructed the ancient stereotype of Zoroaster and his ilk as the source of philosophical or quasi-philosophical traditions. Whatever they were, we now know that they were not Greek thinkers in disguise. We are also both more interested in, and less contemptuous of, the 'common people'. Nevertheless, the old paradigm of an intellectual elite transmitting doctrine over the heads of an unenlightened rank-and-file still haunts us. But since the facts, as modern research has revealed them, no longer appear to support the paradigm, its two elements have been uncoupled and inquiries into them are pursued independently or in uneasy juxtaposition: into Mithraic doctrine on the one hand, and into the social profile and cult activities of the membership—the relatively humble membership—on the other. On balance, the latter approach has probably been the more fruitful, although it has not been the dominant one historically and its successes are more recent.

One solution, as we have already noticed, is to divorce much of the doctrine from the Mysteries and to return it to the philosophers. Robert Turcan (1975) takes this route, at the end of which we find not Mithras but *Mithras Platonicus*, and not Mithraism but the 'hellénisation philosophique de Mithra'.[11]

Another solution is to find systematic and coherent doctrine in the Mysteries but to treat it as somehow generically Mithraic, skirting the difficult question of whether real-life Mithraists or groups of Mithraists could possibly have held it— and if so, which groups and what sorts of individuals. As we saw in the preceding chapter, an indubitable residuum of things Persian in the Mysteries and a better knowledge of what constituted actual Mazdaism have allowed modern scholars to postulate for Roman Mithraism a continuing Iranian theology. This indeed is the main line of Mithraic scholarship, the Cumontian model which subsequent scholars accept, modify, or reject.[12] For the transmission of Iranian doctrine from East to West, Cumont postulated a plausible, if hypothetical, intermediary: the Magusaeans of the Iranian diaspora in Anatolia.[13] More problematic, and never properly addressed by Cumont or his successors, is how real-life Roman Mithraists subsequently maintained a quite complex and sophisticated Iranian theology behind an occidental façade. Other than the images at Dura of the two 'magi' with scrolls,[14] there is no direct and explicit evidence for the carriers of such doctrines. The argument, then, is essentially a priori: establish the doctrine

---

[11] This, of course, is not Turcan's sole mode of treating 'doctrine' in the Mysteries. For the fuller picture see Turcan 2000: 93–114 (cf. Beck 1984: 2078 f.).

[12] Cumont 1899, 1903/1913, elaborated in Bidez and Cumont 1938. Though with numerous modifications and nuances, M. J. Vermaseren (1960/1963) and R. Turcan (2000) have remained essentially within this tradition. For a brief overview see Beck 1984: 2003–8, 2056–79.

[13] Cumont 1903: 11–32; cf. Beck 1991: 492 f., 539–50.

[14] V22a, 22b. The figures, in any case, are probably images of ideal rather than real conveyors of *hieroi logoi*.

(from a reading of the monuments and their iconography), and infer doctrine-holders therefrom. The more abstruse the doctrine, the more sophisticated the doctrine-holders implied.[15] So the shades of the magi return to the Mysteries, not as Greek philosophers but as Mazdaists metamorphosed into the leaders of the Roman cult.

The other pattern for a doctrinal elite is the astronomical or astrological. Here again the starting point is the iconography of the monuments which, as we also saw in the preceding chapter (sect. 4), do indeed exhibit a remarkable array of overt and covert astronomical symbols. Systematic astronomical/astrological doctrine is then deduced, which in turn implies learned doctrine-holders. With David Ulansey's hypothesis (1989/1991) that Mithraism descends from those who made a religion out of the phenomenon now known as the precession of the equinoxes, the point has been reached at which the underlying astronomy is so arcane that both doctrine and doctrine-holders have become quite implausible.[16]

Meanwhile, solid and less controversial work has been pursued on the social construction of the Mysteries,[17] and a bias towards this line of research has been reinforced by the perception that the quest for doctrine has been rather too speculative and its results unsound. The studies of Manfred Clauss typify this reaction (1990/2000, 1992).[18]

Most revealing is the response of N. M. Swerdlow (1991) to the astronomical/astrological interpretations of the Mysteries. Swerdlow in effect redeploys the ancient paradigm of doctrine in a mystery religion, not in the old Numenian way as an imagined ideal, but rather as an implicit intellectual and social standard against which Mithraism may be judged—and found wanting. The ancient paradigm, as we have seen, made two assumptions: first, that a proper mystery, as a quasi-philosophy, has at its core a rational, coherent, intellectually comprehended system; second, that the system is the preserve of a learned elite.[19] Only on criteria such as these can Swerdlow move directly from his dismissal of Mithraism's astronomy and astrology as a superficial and unsystematic farrago

---

[15] The extreme case for Mithraic doctrine as a thoroughgoing translation of Iranian thought is made by L. A. Campbell (1968). A. D. H. Bivar (1999) dispenses with the translation by postulating a single form of 'esoteric Mithraism' spanning East and West.

[16] Ulansey 1989; on the implausibility see Beck 1994*b*: 36–40. I have to acknowledge that my own earlier studies of the cult's astronomy/astrology were to some extent guilty of the fault of which I now complain: insufficient attention paid to the doctrine-holders implied by the postulated doctrines—and indeed to the whole question of what one can realistically intend by 'doctrine' in the Mithras cult.

[17] See esp. Gordon 1972, Liebeschuetz 1994.

[18] See esp. the explicit criticisms in the foreword to the former (2000: p. xx) and the all-out assault on Ulansey's historiographic methods in Clauss 2001.

[19] Not surprisingly, the criteria are those which ancient mathematical astronomy, of which Swerdlow is a distinguished historian, happens to meet. Astronomy, qua science, is nothing if not a rational, coherent, intellectually comprehended system, and in antiquity its more recherché reaches (such as the theory of precession, the matter primarily at issue between Swerdlow and Ulansey) were indeed the preserve of a tiny specialized elite.

to his astonishing conclusions: first, that the cult was not a real religion ('... nothing much, and perhaps not a serious religion after all'); and second, that its members, now stripped of doctrinal pretensions, were manifestly the ignorant and the base ('a rude fraternal cult of soldiers on the frontier, many of them adolescents, and perhaps of ancient veterans back in Rome and Ostia').[20] Here the Mithraists' social profile—or a travesty of it—is used against them. We are back in the mentality of a Celsus: the proletariat is incapable of sustained rational thought and so may not aspire to religious 'seriousness'.[21] The disdain is palpable, the anthropology jejune.[22] Of course no actual mystery did or could measure up to the intellectual rigour and systematic coherence of mathematical astronomy. More tellingly, it would have had no interest in doing so. The doctrines of the Mithraic Mysteries were neither translated science nor science *manquée*.[23] That does not mean that they were not, among other things, serious cognitive enterprises, capable of drawing eclectically and intelligently on the science of their times.

6. MITHRAIC DOCTRINE AND ITS STAKEHOLDERS: VARIOUS VIEWS

The positions of Ulansey and Swerdlow exemplify two extreme views of Mithraism and its adherents: on the one side, a doctrinal system based on the most rarified astronomy; on the other, the mindless good cheer of the soldiery in their

---

[20] Swerdlow 1991: 62. Though with a certain reluctance (for he finds it better argued), Swerdlow also bids farewell to 'Cumont's Iranian interpretation' (ibid.). If Mithraism is no more than 'a rude fraternal cult of soldiers', it cannot harbour a crypto-Mazdean elite either.

[21] Somewhat illogically, the possibility of a 'great popular religion' is allowed (Swerdlow 1991: 62). It is clear from context that Christianity is intended. 'Great' and 'popular' ought to be mutually exclusive; but, presumably, weight of numbers, success, and a highly literate leadership eventually confer respectability on the humbler followers. The Christian perspective is important to Swerdlow, for it is from the near silence of the church fathers concerning Mithraism that he deduces the latter's negligibility (ibid.): Mithraism was not a 'serious' religion because contemporary Christian authors did not treat it seriously. One may fairly argue that Christian silence implies that the Christians did not perceive Mithraism as a serious competitor; alternatively, that Mithraism was barely noticed because it maintained a low profile (which is certainly true); but that Mithraism was intrinsically non-serious only follows with the aid of a further concealed premise: that the Christian fathers are privileged as objective judges of 'seriousness'. The comparative study of religion has long since moved on from such casual *parti pris*.

[22] Even as characterized in Swerdlow's dismissive final paragraph (1991: 62 f.), an unbiased cultural anthropologist or comparative religionist would surely recognize in the Mysteries a system of considerable depth and complexity.

[23] In this Swerdlow (1991) was entirely right. Contra Ulansey, Mithraism harboured no astronomical arcana, such as precession, at its core. Perceptively, Swerdlow traces facile astronomical reductionism of this sort back two centuries to the *Origine de tous les cultes, ou religion universelle* of Charles François Dupuis (ibid. 54–6). Would that Swerdlow himself had not swung so heedlessly to the opposite extreme! There is a middle ground between astronomical arcana and 'mumbo-jumbo'.

'mock grottos'.[24] Between these improbable poles there are of course paradigms which accord Mithraism a more realistic measure of doctrinal knowledge. Up to a point, Cumont's Iranian paradigm, especially in Turcan's modified form,[25] is certainly plausible. Three other approaches also merit attention.

First, Reinhold Merkelbach (1965; 1984: 193–244) has delineated a cosmology for the cult which is basically in the Platonic tradition and thus occidental. It does not imply an unrealistically high level of learning. The surviving Iranian elements are accommodated by postulating a founding individual from the borders of the empire, working specifically in Rome but steeped in the religious traditions of Iran.[26] Following Merkelbach (and Cumont, in that I too look to Anatolia and Anatolians), I have proposed a tentative profile of the cult's founding group as centred on the retainers, military and civilian, of the Commagenian royal family at the time of its participation in the Judaean and Civil Wars and subsequent exile in Rome (Beck 1998a). These, then, would be the hypothetical doctrine-holders of the first generation of Mithraists, combining the 'farrago'— the term need not be pejorative—of Graeco-Roman and Persian learning detectable in the Mysteries and their monuments. The scenario has additional plausibility in that the Commagenian dynasty had acquired as a kinsman by marriage the foremost astrologer-politician of the times, Ti. Claudius Balbillus. Balbillus may be viewed as the source of Mithraism's astrology (Beck 1998a: 126 f.; 2001: 67–71; 2004c: 324–9). Alternatively, taking an analogical rather than a genealogical approach, Balbillus' astrology and that of his probable father, Ti. Claudius Thrasyllus, may be viewed as exemplary of the astrology available in the culture of the times to a new religion interested in such matters.

Secondly, a substantial comparative assessment of Mithraic doctrine in relation to the other mystery cults and the philosophies of the times was undertaken by Ugo Bianchi (1979a) and Giulia Sfameni Gasparro (1979a, b, c) in the context of the International Seminar on the Religio-Historical Character of Roman Mithraism.[27] In addition to the apparatus, doctrinal and otherwise, of a mystery cult (its 'mysteric' aspects), Bianchi and Sfameni Gasparro detected a relatively sophisticated, pervasive, and systematic 'mysteriosophy'. This mysteriosophy, they found, was focused on 'ascent', both in a general way as movement from lower to higher levels in the cosmos and in the particular sense of the initiate's ascent through the esoteric grades and through the spheres of heaven.[28] What

[24] Swerdlow 1991: 62.
[25] See above, n. 11.
[26] Merkelbach 1984: 77, 160 f. Merkelbach acknowledges his debt to Nilsson (1967/1974: 675 f.) for the idea of a founding 'genius'.
[27] Held in Rome in 1978; the seminar was the third in a series of international conferences on Mithraism.
[28] See esp. Sfameni Gasparro's concluding paragraph (1979c: 407 f.); also the seminar's 'final statement' (Bianchi 1979: pp. xiv–xviii).

concerns us here is not so much the specifics of the mysteriosophy as the fact that the Mithraists were deemed sufficiently intelligent to have had one.[29]

At the time of the International Seminar (1979) the working assumption was that there was doctrine in the Mysteries, that it was probably fairly coherent and probably widespread throughout the cult. Nowadays one would not start with that assumption—which brings us to the third approach, the one currently predominant. This approach questions whether one can properly speak of Mithraic doctrine in a general sense and without qualification. To be sure, few would deny the existence of a loose 'cluster of ideas'[30] which must be deemed generically Mithraic because they are vouched for empire-wide by the cult's material remains. The universality of the standard cult icon, for example, implies some minimum of universally held ideas, coherent or incoherent, on the whys and wherefores of Mithras' bull-killing. But beyond that minimum, why assume a coherent, systematic, universal Mithraic doctrine? Why, indeed, use the term 'doctrine' at all, with its implications of an integrated system deliberately transmitted?

These are reasonable questions, and they seem all the more so in the postmodern critical age. Nowadays we tend to discount the very idea of 'doctrine' as a religious category, something which, in principle at least, can be objectively determined for a given religion. We are interested in it (if at all) as proxy discourse in the negotiation of power relations, not as what it superficially claims to be, an autonomous system of beliefs and claims to knowledge.

The new sceptical approach to Mithraic doctrine tends to explain the appearance of ideological concerns on the monuments, beyond the standard and the commonplace, as the speculative initiatives of local leaderships: doctrinal flotsam, rather than the peaks of some great submerged ideological continent. A recent study by Turcan of the Mithraic grade structure and astrology (1999), limiting the correlation of the seven grades and the seven planets and even the sevenfold hierarchy itself to Rome and Ostia during the restricted time span of their documentation there, exemplifies the approach. In the much wider context of their *Religions of Rome* (1998), Mary Beard, John North, and Simon Price set out a very reasonable paradigm of this approach, posed as a question of cult 'homogeneity', doctrinal and otherwise:[31]

By and large, however, in discussing the religions of the empire we have tried to avoid thinking in terms of uniformity, or in terms of a central core 'orthodox' tradition with its

---

[29] It is worth bearing in mind that A. D. Nock, in his influential article 'The genius of Mithraism', gave as one of the cult's six definitive features the possession of 'its own cosmogony and eschatology' (1937: 111). 'Further, other mystery-religions could be interpreted by the use of Greek philosophic concepts; but in Mithraism, as in Judaism and Christianity, there was what seemed a core or philosophy.' In doctrine, it seems, Nock was of the opinion that Mithraism should be brigaded with Judaism and Christianity rather than with its pagan peers among the mystery cults.

[30] For the term, BNP 1: 249.

[31] BNP 1: 248 f., 278, 301–12 (quotation at p. 249).

peripheral 'variants'; we have preferred to think rather in terms of different religions as clusters of ideas, people and rituals, sharing some common identity across time and place, but at the same time inevitably invested with different meanings in their different contexts.

My own position is not that far removed: that the Mysteries were loosely disseminated and maintained by largely autonomous leaders best described as ideological *colporteurs*.[32]

That said, there were, I maintain, if not 'orthodoxies', then demonstrable *norms*.[33] These norms were more widespread, more systematic, and more sophisticated intellectually than the now predominant type of inquiry supposes. The new approach has rendered a great service in that it has discredited the old and lazy assumption of free-floating, generic 'Mithraic doctrine'. But it has perhaps gone too far to the other extreme in restricting ideas, other than the very basic and standard, to the narrow circles of Mithraists immediately associated with the monuments from which the ideas are inferred. There is often, I argue, good reason to postulate some more generalized teaching, even when the particular monument from which one starts, such as the Mainz ritual vessel or the Seven Spheres mithraeum in Ostia, is untypical.

7. DOCTRINE AND BELIEF: THE CHRISTIAN 'FAITH' PARADIGM

In Chapter 2 (sect. 2) we noticed how *doctrine* is the ultimate goal of Cumontian heuristics, which we may characterize as follows: From the *monuments*, reconstruct not only (1) a sacred *narrative*, which is the *myth* of Mithras, but also (2) a *doctrine*, which is what the monuments *intend* over and above their *literal referents*. The doctrine so deciphered is the *faith* of the Mithraists, their *religion*.

That Mithraism and even its antecedent forms were 'faiths' with 'doctrines' in which its initiates 'believed' was axiomatic to Cumont. In this 'faith model', as we might term it, Mithraism and the other mystery cults (Christianity included), in contrast to the public cults of paganism, evolved as religious systems of 'belief'. Their initiates not only gave their confidence and devotion to the respective gods of the cults ('belief *in*') but also subscribed intellectually to notions, of greater or less sophistication, expressed or expressible in propositional form, concerning those gods and their roles in the cosmos and in relation to mankind ('belief *that*'). Accordingly, the interpreter's task, which Cumont saw as part of the 'scientific' study of religion, is to reconstruct and elucidate those beliefs, presenting them as the 'doctrines' of the cults. 'Doctrine' is belief objectified, existing independently

---

[32] The term is Richard Gordon's (1994: 463).   [33] Beck 2000: 170 f.

of the individual believer; it is the matter of esoteric instruction, what the believer is taught to believe.

How the dynamics of 'faith', 'belief', and 'doctrine' animated Cumont's model can be vividly illustrated by a passage from his *Mysteries of Mithra* (1903/1956: 30–1) which I have already quoted (above, Ch. 3, sect. 3). I repeat the quotation as Luther Martin (1994: 217) presented it in an article whose explicit aim was to escape the preconceptions about doctrine and beliefs in Cumontian and post-Cumontian interpretation:

The basal layer of this religion... is the *faith* (*foi*) of ancient Iran... [upon which] was deposited in Babylon a thick sediment of Semitic *doctrines* (*doctrines*), and afterwards the local *beliefs* (*croyances*) of Asia Minor... Finally, a luxuriant vegetation of Hellenic *ideas* (*idées*) burst forth from this fertile soil... (Martin's italics, French terms from Cumont 1913: 27 in parentheses)

Noteworthy here is the layering of beliefs: not only was Mithraism a faith, but it also evolved by accretion of earlier faiths, a process strikingly captured in the geological/botanical metaphor.

Clearly, Christianity was the paradigm. The Cumontian model was cloned from the then dominant model of early Christianity, not deliberately but simply because that was the way the late nineteenth-century Western mind confronted religion. If you could make the case that a religion was doctrine-centred, then it was self-evidently a faith in which its initiates believed, and so could be brigaded with Christianity over against the sacrifice-centred pieties of the ancient public cults. It helped of course that Mithraism in its Roman form was an almost exact contemporary of Christianity. Both originated in the first century CE (Mithraism a decade or so later than its peer), and both grew and flourished within the same cultural milieu.

As Cumont's Christian contemporaries immediately recognized, his paradigm of Mithraism was not only very similar to theirs of Christianity, but also, when coupled with a narrative of Mithraism's evolution from Iranian Mazdaism, downright threatening. For if Mithraism could be explained as the product of historical evolution, what was to prevent the application of the same sort of evolutionary template to early Christianity as a sufficient explanation of its origins and development?[34]

Times change, but old models linger on, especially when there is no sensed need for a new explanatory paradigm. The tide of secularism carried Cumont's faith model into less controversial waters, where it stayed afloat long after it had ceased to be the sole model entertained for early Christianity, the paradigm case. Most notably and most influentially, Robert Turcan has not only continued to

[34] The threat posed by Cumont's model was serious enough to block his appointment to the instructorship in Roman history at Gand/Ghent to which the scholarly world thought him entitled. The matter was even debated in the Belgian Senate. The full story and its implications are related by Corinne Bonnet (2000).

use the language of 'faith', 'doctrine', and 'belief' in treating of the Mithraic mysteries but has also perpetuated thereby the assumptions concerning the mysteries' content and mode of transmission which those terms imply.[35] I quote again a passage which we discussed briefly in an earlier chapter (Ch. 2, sect. 2):

La bizarrerie de la représentation [of a detail in the relief under discussion] doit tenir pour une grande part au fait qu'elle s'efforce de transcrire par une image quelque chose d'un enseignement philosophico-religieux. D'une part, en effet, nous savons que le mithriacisme a intégré, adapté certaines théories grecques, voire certains mythes grecs... Et d'autre part, une caractéristique essentielle de ce culte est qu'il se répand par l'image, moyennant une initiation et une liturgie qui comportent l'explication rituelle des images. *L'iconographie n'y a, comme on sait, aucune fin esthétique. Elle se veut porteuse d'une doctrine. D'une extrémité à l'autre du monde romain, avec certaines variantes autour de figures fondamentales, elle véhicule un même enseignement.* C'est un langage à déchiffrer, et l'on ne peut guère hasarder de déchiffrement qu'en se fondant sur la sémantique courante des motifs ou des attributs, en fonction de certaines idées communes au monde grécoromain. (Turcan 1986: 221; emphasis mine)

Again I draw attention to the emphasis on *doctrine* as the end product of the imagery of the monuments and on *teaching* ('*enseignement*') via the imagery, even in a liturgical or ritual context, as the route of initiation into the mysteries. We are back to the mithraeum as classroom.

Turcan speaks of the imagery as a 'language' of instruction. We shall return to this perceptive analogy in a later chapter, for it poses some highly germane questions (is it more than a metaphor, do iconographic symbols really communicate in the same way as natural language signs?). However, some implications of this idea should be raised here. They concern the teacher and the taught in this 'language of instruction':

Les images sont un langage dont les éléments sont faits pour être compris en fonction d'un vocabulaire commun au sculpteur et au spectateur de son oeuvre, en l'occurrence au responsable et aux fidèles de la communauté mithriaque. (1986: 220)

[The images are a language whose elements are made to be understood by means of a vocabulary common to the sculptor and viewer of his work, in context to the person responsible and to the faithful.]

Who, then, are the language users of the language of Mithraic iconography? For Turcan the answer is obvious and straightforward. Those who speak and

---

[35] Turcan is somewhat ambivalent about doctrine. In his 1986 article he seems to envisage the mysteries primarily as a doctrinal belief system taught to initiates. Elsewhere, as we have seen in the preceding sections of this chapter, he (1) transfers doctrine attributed to the Mithraists by the Neoplatonists back to the same Neoplatonists, and (2) restricts what he regards as learned elaborations to local Mithraic elites. Perhaps it is a matter of level: a general, intellectually undemanding set of doctrines for ordinary initiates; more sophisticated doctrines as the optional speculations of the learned—when not Neoplatonic inventions.

listen to the iconographic language of the mysteries are the sculptors and viewers of the monuments; alternatively, the mithraeum's leadership (including, presumably, those who commissioned and dedicated the monuments) and the 'faithful' (note the characterization!). Of the two pairs, we should concentrate on the latter. Since the 'figured monuments' were commissioned for internal use within the mithraeum, never for public display, the 'viewers' and the 'faithful' were one and the same. The sculptors (and the fresco painters), moreover, were not primary 'speakers', for they merely executed the design of 'those responsible' (*responsable*).

Turcan's distinction between 'those in charge' who spoke the language of Mithraic iconography and 'the faithful' who listened to it certainly helps us to understand the initiates as a community of quasi-language users and their mysteries as something communicated by a quasi-language. Nevertheless, the distinction imports some dangerous baggage of its own, in addition to the questionable presentation of the mysteries as a faith with a belief system and initiation as a type of instruction. Most insidiously, the paradigm of unidirectional discourse flowing from teacher to learner implies that what is encoded and decoded via the iconography is a determinate body of information, that is, Mithraic doctrine. Output matches input. If the language is efficient and the teachers and learners fully competent, then the 'faithful' get from the iconography what 'those in charge' put into the iconography, ideally without remainder. If we read the clues aright, we too can recover that input/output. But can we? Our explorations so far lead us to doubt whether such a goal is achievable in practice or in principle.

8. MITHRAIC DOCTRINE: THREE MAIN ISSUES

The problem of deciphering Mithraic doctrine may be broken down into three main issues. The first is solely a practical matter and assumes that there is 'doctrine' of whatever sort out there on the monuments awaiting decipherment. The second and third are more theoretical and beg no questions, at least about the nature and presence of doctrine on the monuments.

First is the issue of generalizability. What is the evidential base in the monuments necessary for postulating some element of Mithraic doctrine? Is it ever reasonable to infer some more widely held doctrinal norm from features on relatively few monuments—or even on a single monument? If so, in what circumstances?

The second issue is the nature of 'doctrine' itself. So far in this chapter the term remains undefined. Yet it is not an obvious category. It is not self-evidently something which a religion either has, in large or small measure, or doesn't have. Nor does it stand out sharply from other aspects of a religion such as myth and ritual. What, then, are we to understand by 'Mithraic doctrine' when and if we postulate it for the mysteries?

The third question returns us to unfinished business from the preceding sections: can we do better than the old dichotomous paradigm of a learned elite (of questionable reality) and an unthinking commons? This third question is inseparable from the second, for what we make of doctrine depends on how we construe the doctrine-holders—and vice versa.

9. (i) GENERALIZING ABOUT MITHRAIC DOCTRINE FROM UNUSUAL MONUMENTS

Our entry point into the question of Mithraic doctrine was from a literary source, Porphyry's *De antro* with its testimony on the form and function of the mithraeum. This of course is unusual. Since the 'monuments' of Mithraism far outweigh the 'texts', Mithraic doctrine, as we saw in Chapter 2, is reconstructed mostly from the monuments, especially from the rich and complex iconography of the reliefs, frescos, and statuary. So implicated is Mithraic doctrine in the design of the monuments that the transmission of doctrine is properly considered a matter of the transmission of norms of design: the design of the mithraeum, the design of the bull-killing icon, and so on.[36] In this respect, an account of *colporteurs* and *colportage* is but another version of the traditional scholarly narrative of the spread of Mithraism, doctrine and all. What the *colporteur* transports and unpacks, the wares he puts on offer, is a bundle of designs (perhaps literally so) for cult room and cult artefact, and a blueprint (metaphorically so) for cult life led within and in relation to the sacred structures implicit in those designs. So expressed, what I intend by 'Mithraic doctrine' is precisely the Mithraic pedlar's rationale of his portfolio of designs, literal and metaphoric. Quite properly, then, the reconstruction of doctrine, beyond what can be elicited from the very few external literary testimonies, is largely the explication of the contents and compositions of the monuments.

One cannot formulate in advance a hard-and-fast quantitative rule on the volume of monumental evidence necessary to support a doctrinal principle. Obviously, at one end of the spectrum there are features so commonplace that one may reasonably suppose empire-wide norms. For example, the principal elements in the tauroctony and their disposition in the scene are so standard, so universally exemplified, that one cannot but suppose some basic underlying teaching: for example, why Mithras is accompanied by a dog, a snake, a scorpion, and a raven, and why these creatures are placed where they are in the composition. What that teaching actually was is of course another question, but that explications, whether rudimentary or sophisticated, were brought by the *colporteurs* and passed down through the membership of the groups seems unarguable. The persistence of the iconographic norms implies the persistence of the underlying

[36] Beck 1984: 2074–8.

doctrine, though doubtless with some fraying at the edges. No enforcement of the norms need be presumed, merely sufficient *ad hoc* liaison between groups to maintain their continuity and overall coherence. At the other extreme there are unique or extremely rare features which are obvious transgressions. For example, in the Moesian tauroctony (V2327) the scorpion is positioned not at the bull's genitals but at those of Mithras: clearly the artist or the *colporteur* or the local Mithraic group collectively has 'got it wrong'. Flagrantly incorrect iconography implies misapprehension or plain forgetfulness of story and customary explication.

Between these two extremes lies a debatable field where certain features or sets of features are attested in a minority of monuments. They cannot be construed, self-evidently, as empire-wide norms, but neither are they obvious aberrations. What do we infer about their underlying rationale (assuming there was one and that the feature in question was not just a stylistic flourish—a possibility we should always bear in mind)? Do we infer some local or regional elaboration of Mithraic doctrine or instead a more general element of doctrine about which, for whatever reason, the generality of monuments is silent? The question cannot be answered on a priori grounds, for that would simply beg it. Whether Mithraism was a religion with a broadly coherent ideology or a religion of local options is precisely the point at issue. The inquiry, then, must be case by case, and most answers will be tentative. Beyond the number of occurrences and their spread, the criteria are necessarily qualitative and *ad hoc*. There is no nice calculus to deliver an answer one way or the other. With few exceptions, we shall achieve likelihoods, not certainties.

The foremost test is coherence: do the hypothetical rationales cohere in broad doctrinal themes? Can these themes, even in default of written documentation (which is usually the case), be inferred from structures and features universally current in the monuments? If so, in any given instance is it a case of theme or of variation? When is an instance better explained as an integral element of widespread doctrine, and when as a piece of local/regional speculation enshrined in local/regional iconography, and so on? The process is inductive and cumulative. The more we discern coherence, the greater the overall likelihood of a corpus of doctrine, a larger rather than a smaller *colporteur*'s pack, a submerged continent rather than ideological flotsam. We shall find that even highly unusual monuments, such as the Seven Spheres mithraeum and the Mainz ritual vessel, more often than not exemplify general Mithraic doctrine rather than local elaboration. Or, more subtly, they exemplify local elaboration of broad doctrinal themes. Because they also tend to be unusually informative, the unusual monuments are those which, carefully explicated, disclose both theme and variation.[37]

---

[37] For just this reason, several of my previous studies have focused on the explication of unusual monuments: Beck 1976 and 1978 on the Ponza zodiac; Beck 1988 on the Ottaviano Zeno monument (pp. 42–72) and the Barberini tauroctony (pp. 91–100); Beck 2000 on the Mainz vessel.

10. (ii) WHAT DO WE MEAN BY 'DOCTRINE' IN THE CONTEXT OF THE MITHRAIC MYSTERIES? AN ARRAY OF ANSWERS

To address our second question, we should not think of doctrine as something determinate, a body of propositions recoverable, in principle at least, in its entirety. 'Doctrine' is at best a somewhat nebulous category. It is scarcely relevant to much ancient religion (the public cults, for example), and in Mithraism, where it is arguably germane, it finds expression, as we noted above, in the medium of room design and iconography rather than creed and sacred text. We have already characterized Mithraic doctrine as the various rationales for the designs of mithraeum and icon imported, literally and metaphorically, by the Mithraic *colporteur*. To the structures of cult room and cult icon, we need only add the structures of cult life and authority. We might think, then, of Mithraic doctrine as an indeterminate set of explanations which senior Mithraists would impart to their juniors or explore among themselves: why our 'cave' is designed as it is (and why it's a 'cave'); why this icon of our bull-killing hero is composed as it is; why we initiate and celebrate as we do; what it means that I am a Father, he is a Lion, and you are a Raven.[38]

There are some useful lessons to be drawn from this functional paradigm of Mithraic doctrine as explication in context. It helps to break down the old preconception of doctrine as an autonomous category, as something self-contained and pre-existent, which is then inserted into the monuments, like statements of belief into a creed. Although one may argue, as I do, for broad doctrinal themes in the mysteries, there is no reason to suppose a comprehensive doctrine, articulated in all its parts.

Moreover, not every point of doctrine will have been expressed verbally in written or spoken form. Mithraic doctrine, I argue, is largely implicit in structures of design in the monuments. It is not necessary to suppose that, at one time or another and in one place or another, each and every component was explicated by a Mithraic Father. Paradoxical though it might seem, one might well posit Mithraic doctrine which was never given verbal expression. Doctrine in such cases exists as a *potentiality* within the monuments. It is the explication that a Mithraic Father would give, were he asked, the explication demanded by the structural logic of his mithraeum and its icons. Recovering Mithraic doctrine is largely a matter of tracing that internal logic.

In tracing the themes of Mithraic doctrine across the monuments, we should not expect to uncover meanings radically different from what lies on the surface. There is no Big Secret to be decoded, no privileged hermeneutic route to

---

[38] The papyrus catechism P.Berol. 21196 (Brashear 1992) is just such a dialogue in the form of questions asked of and answered by an initiate.

doctrines more profound. Confronting the Mithraists' monuments, not a single item of which was intended for external display, we are already within their esoteric world, literally and physically so. We view what they viewed, we locate ourselves, where no ancient outsider did, in their sacred space. Why, then, search for more profound arcana? That Mithras is the Unconquered Sun, that he slew the bull, these are the truths of the religion, patently displayed—but only within the 'cave'—in icon and inscription. Our task in reconstructing doctrine is to discover how these truths were apprehended and related, glossing them in propositional language; it is not to translate them into something wholly other. With Mithraism, as the saying goes, 'what you see is what you get'.

The pursuit of arcana is yet another of antiquity's dubious legacies to our comprehension of the mystery cults. The assumption that every mystery has its *logos* known to the wise, and thus decipherable by the wise of a later generation, was fundamental to the ancient authorities, as we have seen. Something of the same assumption, in modern guise, underlies the scholarly 'translations' of Mithraism, whether into full-blown Mazdaism or into rarified astronomy. The attraction of this sort of approach is that it 'gets results'—or appears to. Whether by the antique philosopher's intuition or by the methods of modern research, new facts about cult doctrine are established, and because these facts are more than restatements of the obvious truths displayed on the monuments (Mithras slew a bull, etc.), our comprehension is advanced—or seems to be. There are other gains, just as illusory. The postulated doctrine is deep doctrine, so its discovery seems to have great explicative power: it tells us what the mystery 'really' was. The modern reformulations of doctrine thus contain and control the mystery. As the product of historical research, we seem to know what even the most learned ancient insider could but dimly comprehend: that is the exact theological equations which convert Iranian *yazatas* into the divinities of Roman Mithraism; or, if one prefers, the precise astronomical phenomena of which Mithras' bull-killing is the expression. Finally, there is the lure of simplicity. David Ulansey's astronomical reconstruction (1989/1991), for example, flows (with great elegance, it must be allowed) from two primary doctrinal 'facts': that Mithras is the constellation Perseus and that the bull-killing encodes his cosmic victory as the power who shifts the world's axis by means of what astronomers term the 'precession of the equinoxes'. To know these facts, so it seems, is to know *in nuce* the entire meaning of the tauroctony.

The present study has no such implicit goal. Except on the form and function of the mithraeum, where a modicum of Mithraic doctrine in propositional form is recoverable from Porphyry's *De antro*, our explorations will necessarily be tentative and our findings inconclusive and lacking coherence in the same measure that Mithraic doctrine was itself inchoate and not fully coherent. This is a fault neither in the mysteries nor in their explication. It resides in the nature of the thing studied and the appropriate way of studying it. Accordingly, I cannot leave the reader with a satisfying sense of easy comprehension ('Ah, so that is what it was really all about!'). No mystery can be translated into a neat set of propositions about something else. Plutarch, commenting on the seasonal and agricultural explanations of Isis and Osiris, long ago exposed reductionism of that sort as a strategy for reassurance which gives the illusion of intellectual mastery by substitution of the familiar for the unfamiliar (*On Isis and Osiris* 64–7). Consequently, the coming chapters, while they engage with and explore what may legitimately be called Mithraic 'doctrine', do not pretend to decipher it in a definitive and comprehensive way. If that is the expectation, these chapters will inevitably disappoint.

Mithraic doctrine is not an autonomous and self-contained ideological domain. Quite the contrary, its territory lies squarely in the thought world of the times. Consequently, much of it is recoverable by reference to common intellectual systems which have left their signatures on the records of the cult. One such system is astrology. Astrology is a system whose articulation and significations we know from extant treatises, some of them (e.g. Ptolemy's *Tetrabiblos* and the *Anthologies* of Vettius Valens) contemporaneous with the heyday of the Mysteries. Consequently, traces of technical astrology on the monuments, for example of the system of 'houses' correlating planets and signs, are especially informative, for they illuminate what is esoteric and unknown by means of what is exoteric and known.[39] The more precise the astrology implicated, the greater its explicative power. On the same premise, that the Mysteries cannot have constituted an entirely closed doctrinal system, I make frequent appeal to the 'encyclopaedia', antiquity's store of accumulated knowledge, the body of facts about the world which 'everyone knows', best exemplified in compendia such as Pliny's *Natural History* or Aelian's *On the Nature of Animals*. These were not of course real facts, as we understand them scientifically; rather, they were agreed constructions, the consensus, for example, on 'lions' or 'ravens' or 'hyenas'. For that very reason they are indispensable if we are to comprehend Mithraic Lions and Ravens as the Mithraists comprehended them or to understand why 'they called women "hyenas"' (Porphyry, *De abstinentia* 4.16).[40] The mind world of the Mithraists was peopled with such constructs. In that respect it will have differed little from the mind world of their enveloping culture. Necessarily, even their most esoteric doctrine will have been but reformulations, new 'takes' on old truths expressed largely in the common idiom. This is not to deny the Mithraists originality, but merely to acknowledge the constraints within which doctrinal creativity operates. It is the common idiom that affords us the possibility of access. Had Mithraic doctrine been strictly and solely esoteric, it would indeed be literally incomprehensible.

[39] On the use of ancient astrology and astronomy to interpret the monuments and thus to elucidate doctrine, see particularly Beck 1976*a*, 1977, 1978, 1979, 1988, 1994*a*, 1994*b*, 2000.

[40] The concept of the 'encyclopaedia', together with the examples cited was introduced by Richard Gordon (1980*b*, see esp. n. 8) drawing on Sperber 1975: 91–110.

Finally, we should bear in mind that 'doctrine', formulated as a set of propositions, is sometimes just a proxy—a necessary scholar's proxy—for describing what is apprehended by the initiates not as information imparted in propositional form, but in other modes altogether. Truly to comprehend the 'meaning' of the Mysteries was to experience them by sight, hearing, and action in the context of the mithraeum and its ritual. Only thus would that extraordinary array of visual symbols 'make sense'. We may think of this as a form of cognition, but not as the assimilation of propositional knowledge, or at least not primarily so. To know your 'cave' as cosmos was not to take lessons about it. Lessons there may have been, but that is not what our gateway text, Porphyry's *De antro* (6), tells us: the Mithraists 'perfect the initiate' (*telousi ton mystēn*) not by teaching but 'by *inducting him in a mystery* (*mystagōgountes*) into the 'descent and departure of souls'. In 'reconstructing doctrine' we are not really aiming to recover a lost system of propositional knowledge, but rather to recapture and express in scholars' language—thus necessarily in propositional language—something of the *mystagōgia* of the Mithraic 'cave'.

My contextual definition of 'doctrine' will perhaps seem frustratingly vague. This is unfortunate—but unavoidable. A crisper definition would merely return us to the old preconception of doctrine as an explicit body of knowledge which, at least in principle, can be reassembled in its original form, just as a material object—a pot for example—can be reconstructed, given enough sherds and the restorer's expertise. But doctrine in that concrete, self-contained form never existed in the Mithras cult, and it would be misleading to imply by definition that it can be recaptured as such. Nevertheless, if something more succinct is looked for, it may be extrapolated, appropriately enough, from an ancient account of the institution of a mystery cult. In his *On Isis and Osiris* (27), as we saw in Chapter 1, Plutarch relates how the goddess herself founded her mysteries by 'mixing into the holiest rituals images, thoughts, and imitations of her former experiences' (*tais hagiōtatais anamixasa teletais eikonas kai hyponoias kai mimēmata tōn tote pathēmatōn*). Doctrine, we might say, is that central term *hyponoia*, the 'under-thought' which is the realization of the mysteries in the mode of cognition, just as their visual realization is the icon and their performative realization the ritual.[41] We, of course, must treat the mysteries as a human rather than divine institution, but Plutarch's pious attribution of them to the goddess, for all its apparent naivety, accommodates a truth which we would do well to remember: that 'doctrine' is an expression of the mysteries, not vice versa; it is elicited from them (largely from their constituent 'images' and 'imitations'), not built into them, by their human expounders.

---

[41] A strict differentiation between visual 'images' and performed 'imitations' was probably not intended by Plutarch. It is, though, a reasonable refinement of his meaning.

11. (iii) DOCTRINE AND THE ORDINARY INITIATE

The looser conception of doctrine proposed above may help us break out of the old stereotypes of leaders with intellect and followers without. As long as doctrine is considered to be a systematic and formulated body of knowledge, one has to presuppose a learned elite whose possession it was. Consequently, a gulf is opened up between the leaders and the led, the guardians of doctrine and those nurtured on less-intellectual fare. This false dichotomy can be avoided by abandoning the search for a lost body of comprehensive knowledge, but without going to the other extreme of dismissing the Mysteries as intellectually trivial. Instead, doctrine can be discerned in the Mysteries and its ownership located with the generality of members if we construe it not as a monolithic, logically articulated system, but as a diffuse network of ideas, many of them implicit in the structure of the monuments, many of them mere potentialities for thought, which each initiate would apprehend in a manner appropriate to status, context, and occasion.

It is easy enough to envisage doctrine as explanations given or rationales explored by the Fathers of Mithraic groups. Less straightforward is the apprehension of doctrine by the ordinary cult member in situations other than the formal giving and receiving of instruction as in a catechism.[42] If we keep *context* in mind, however, our question 'what is doctrine?' might fruitfully be rephrased as follows: how, intellectually, did the ordinary Mithraist apprehend (1) the sacred environment of his 'cave' qua 'image of the universe', (2) its sacred furniture ('proportionately arranged') and especially the dominant icon of the bull-killing, (3) the ritual actions which he and his cult brothers performed therein, and (4) the esoteric relationships with cult brothers and with the deity into which he had entered as an initiate and which were played out in the ongoing life of the mithraeum? These are the familiar 'doctrinal' questions of cosmology, theology, soteriology, and hierarchy reformulated with reference to their principal stakeholder in his proper environment, the ordinary Mithraist in the Mithraic 'cave'.

12. CONCLUSION

In the preceding sections we have, as it were, *unpacked or unbundled* doctrine.[43] In place of doctrine as a definite body of explicit teaching, we have re-characterized it as a loose web of interpretation, both actual and potential, located in the symbol system of the mysteries. A piece of doctrine, in this sense, is legitimated (1) by its

---

[42] P.Berol. 21196 (Brashear 1992) appears to confirm such occasions in the life of the Mysteries.
[43] Had the term not become suspect, we might say that we had *deconstructed* it.

coherence with other pieces on the web, and (2) by being what the local Father approved, or would approve if asked, with an assumption that most of his peers, if asked, would likewise approve. That the minds of Mithraic Fathers are now inaccessible does not matter, for we seek only to *define* doctrine, not to rule on whether a particular idea was or was not a point of doctrine. Indeed, the latter is precisely the trap we want to avoid. Nor does it matter that we define as pieces of 'doctrine' certain elements which may never have undergone explicit verbal formulation and actual consent in real time. That merely shows that Mithraism managed to retain its norms without recourse to expensive and contentious synods. In this regard the Mithraic solution seems to me superior to the Christian solution in that it reached consensus without coercion. No blood was spilled, as far as we know, in reconciling the singularity of the Sun with the distinct personae of Sol and Mithras.

Transition: from old ways to new ways

In these last four chapters we have completed the necessary preparations for the hermeneutic road ahead. In the first stage of this journey (Chapter 5) we shall begin to explore the symbol system in which Mithraic doctrine, in our redefined sense, was located. Our method will be based on symbolist anthropology and in particular the approach of Clifford Geertz. We shall see how the symbol system of the Mithraic mysteries functions as an expression of the ethos and world view of the Mithraists' culture, itself a subset of the surrounding Graeco-Roman culture of the imperial age. Since this approach thrives on comparison, I shall make extensive use of a comparison culture. I have selected for our comparator the culture of the Chamulas, an indigenous Mexican people whose ethos and world view stem from a fusion of missionary Christianity with local Mayan sun worship.

Since symbols function in their apprehension—strictly speaking, there is no such thing as a symbol without someone to apprehend it as such—we next explore in a general way what apprehending a symbol system entails (Chapter 6). Here I introduce the methods of the new 'cognitive science of religion', in particular the approaches of Pascal Boyer and Dan Sperber and the latter's theory of culture as an 'epidemic' of representations.

At this stage we will be ready to explore (Chapter 7) the complex of symbols which is the mithraeum. We shall examine its blueprint as an 'image of the universe' and see how it functions as the instrument for 'inducting the initiates into a mystery of the descent of souls and their exit back out again' (Porphyry *De antro* 6).

In the chapter following (8) we turn to 'star-talk' as the postulated idiom of the mysteries (Proposition F in our 'template for the re-description of the mysteries' in Chapter 1). I shall show how in an unusual, perhaps unique, way the astral symbols of the mysteries function together as quasi-language signs. That is a very risky claim, because on the whole I agree with Dan Sperber's argument (1975) that symbols do not 'mean', at least not in the sense that words and strings of words do. However, I shall maintain that the claim is warranted by the ease with which reading the symbols of the mysteries as ordered language signs led in the previous chapter (7) to an understanding of the precise form and function of the mithraeum. In other words, the mithraeum *communicates meaning* through the medium of its complex of symbols. As supporting evidence I shall also show that although the concept of 'star-talk' might seem bizarre to us today, to the ancients the idea of talking stars and a celestial text was far from strange. If the mithraeum was a true image of the universe, its ancient initiates would expect it to replicate among other properties the *rationality* of its grand original.

The penultimate chapter (9) brings us to the symbol complex which is the tauroctony, the image of the bull-killing Mithras and the cult's principal icon. My explication of the tauroctony will be informed by all the methods and approaches introduced in the preceding chapters. But let there be no false expectations. The tauroctony conveys no message of the sort which can be simply stated in a sentence or paragraph. Or rather, its message is what we and the initiates have known all along: DEUS SOL INVICTUS MITHRAS. The task is to discern not *what* the tauroctony says but *how* it says it.

In the course of these chapters I shall also reintroduce, albeit in a somewhat piecemeal fashion, the categories of our descriptive template for the Mithraic mysteries summarized in Chapter 1: axioms or ultimate sacred postulates (the first of which is the formula displayed above, the second the principle of 'harmony of tension in opposition'), motifs, domains, structures, modes, and the idiom of 'star-talk'. To 'star-talk', as already explained, I devote a full chapter (8), as also to two of the three definitive 'structures', the mithraeum (7) and the tauroctony (9). (The third, non-ubiquitous structure, the grade hierarchy, I touch on in Chapter 9.) Finally, in the 'Conclusions' we revisit the descriptive template briefly but more systematically.

5

The Mithraic Mysteries as Symbol System: I. Introduction and Comparisons

It is a cluster of sacred symbols, woven into some sort of ordered whole, which makes up a religious system.

(Geertz 1973: 129)

1. RELIGION AS A SYSTEM OF SYMBOLS: AN ANTHROPOLOGICAL APPROACH

In his justly celebrated essay, 'Religion as a cultural system', the anthropologist Clifford Geertz (1973: ch. 4) defined 'a religion' as 'a system of symbols'.[1] As indicated at the outset (Ch. 1, sect. 1), I shall apply Geertz's definition and the interpretations which stem from it to the Mithraic mysteries.[2]

Fortunately there is no need—yet—to worry about the further definitional question: what is a symbol? What Geertz meant and what I mean by a symbol will be obvious enough as we examine particular instances. Geertz spent little time on definition and none on lists or examples of symbols in isolation. Symbols manifest themselves in particular contexts and these contexts are specific to particular cultures. For Geertz, the exemplary context is not the icon or the sacred space so much as the performance or ritual in which 'symbolic forms' are constructed, apprehended, utilized (1973: 91).

Geertz's approach can only be captured by quotation *in extenso*. This is because the symbol or complex of symbols is inseparable from, and incomprehensible

---

[1] The full definition reads: 'a religion is (1) a system of symbols which acts to (2) establish powerful, pervasive, and long-lasting moods and motivations in men by (3) formulating conceptions of a general order of existence and (4) clothing these conceptions with such an aura of factuality that (5) the moods and motivations seem uniquely realistic' (1973: 90). Geertz's approach of 'interpretation' (as opposed to 'explanation') and 'thick description', it must be admitted, is now somewhat out of favour. Nevertheless, the essay is a classic, and 'out of favour' is not the same as 'out of date'.

[2] There are naturally other eminent symbolist anthropologists whom we could profitably have followed, notably Victor Turner, Mary Douglas, and Edmund Leach. On the symbolists see Bell 1997: 61–92.

apart from, the activity which it informs; and the activity, so informed, is an expression of the culture—its world view and its ethos[3]—which the symbol system constructs and holds in place. 'They [the concrete symbols involved] both express the world's climate and shape it' (1973: 95).

Let us take as our example Geertz's description of the Navaho 'sing' and the symbol of the 'sand painting' which is an integral component of this rite (1973: 104–5):

A sing—the Navaho have about sixty different ones for different purposes, but virtually all of them are dedicated to removing some sort of physical or mental illness—is a kind of religious psychodrama in which there are three main actors: the 'singer' or curer, the patient, and, as a kind of antiphonal chorus, the patient's family and friends. The structure of all the sings, the drama's plot, is quite similar. There are three main acts: a purification of the patient and audience; a statement, by means of repetitive chants and ritual manipulations, of the wish to restore well-being ('harmony') in the patient; an identification of the patient with the Holy People and his consequent 'cure'. The purification rites involve forced sweating, induced vomiting, and so on, to expel the sickness from the patient physically. The chants, which are numberless, consist mainly of simple optative phrases ('may the patient be well', 'I am getting better all over', etc.). And, finally, the identification of the patient with the Holy People, and thus with cosmic order generally, is accomplished through the agency of a sand painting depicting the Holy People in one or another appropriate mythic setting. The singer places the patient on the painting, touching the feet, hands, knees, shoulders, breast, back, and head of the divine figures and then the corresponding parts of the patient, performing thus what is essentially a bodily identification of the human and divine. This is the climax of the sing: the whole curing process may be likened, Reichard says,[4] to a spiritual osmosis in which the illness in man and the power of the deity penetrate the ceremonial membrane in both directions, the former being neutralized by the latter. Sickness seeps out in the sweat, vomit, and other purification rites; health seeps in as the Navaho patient touches, through the medium of the singer, the sacred sand painting.

Note that Geertz is content to leave the specific form and content of the sand painting quite imprecise. Of course at that early stage in the essay detailed analysis would be inappropriate. Later, Geertz does indeed go into considerable detail, especially when discussing the 'cultural performances' of Bali (1973: 114–18) and of Java (ibid. 132–40, 'the shadow-puppet play or *wajang*'). But his aim is always to capture through sympathetic yet meticulous description the symbolic intent of the whole, not the individual meanings of its constituent elements. In so far as he ever states what it is that symbols symbolize (what they are signs *of*), he specifies only very broad categories: 'They ["the Cross", etc.] are all symbols, or at least symbolic elements, because they are tangible formulations

---

[3] See the next essay in Geertz's collection (ch. 5: 'Ethos, world view, and the analysis of sacred symbols').

[4] G. Reichard, *Navaho Religion*, 2 vols. (New York, 1950), no page number(s) cited.

of notions, abstractions from experience fixed in perceptible forms, concrete embodiments of ideas, attitudes, judgements, longings, or beliefs' (ibid. 91).

The intent of a complex of symbols, especially when energized in a performative context (of which the religious ritual is the archetype), is to construct, to express, and to legitimate the *ethos* and the *world view* of the culture concerned.

... sacred symbols function to synthesize a people's ethos—the tone, character, and quality of their life, its moral and aesthetic style and mood—and their world view—the picture they have of the way things in sheer actuality are, their most comprehensive ideas of order. In religious belief and practice a group's ethos is rendered intellectually reasonable by being shown to represent a way of life ideally adapted to the actual state of affairs the world view describes, while the world view is rendered emotionally convincing by being presented as an image of the actual state of affairs peculiarly well arranged to accommodate such a way of life. (Ibid. 89–90)

Whatever else religion may be, it is in part an attempt... to conserve the fund of general meanings in terms of which each individual interprets his experience and organizes his conduct.

But meanings can only be 'stored' in symbols: a cross, a crescent, or a feathered serpent. Such religious symbols, dramatized in rituals or related in myths, are felt somehow to sum up, for those for whom they are resonant, what is known about the way the world is, the quality of the emotional life it supports, and the way one ought to behave while in it. (Ibid. 127)

A symbol system, in Geertz's well-known formulation (ibid. 93–4) is thus both a 'model *of*' the world and a 'model *for*' living in it. Observation of Navaho ritual and description of the symbol system in action find accordingly 'an ethic prizing calm deliberateness, untiring persistence, and dignified caution complement[ing] an image of nature as tremendously powerful, mechanically regular, and highly dangerous' (ibid. 130).

2. ARE GEERTZIAN DESCRIPTION AND INTERPRETATION APPLICABLE TO THE SYMBOL SYSTEM OF THE MITHRAIC MYSTERIES?

Initially, it might seem that Geertz's method of carefully describing cultural symbol systems in action cannot be applied to Mithraism because the cult's performances are inaccessible to us. Field work, cultural anthropology's prime method, is of course impossible, and the archaeological record of the Mithraic mysteries is neither sufficient nor of the sort amenable to 'thick description'.[5]

In answer, it is worth observing first that Geertz himself uses the written record of the past as effectively as field work, his own or others', in the present.

---

[5] On 'thick description' see ch. 1 of Geertz's *Interpretation of Cultures* (1973).

For example, in chapter 6 of *Local Knowledge* (1983) he brilliantly captures, from factual descriptions and imaginative literature, the ethos and world views symbolically instantiated in the Royal Progresses of 'Elizabeth's England' (sixteenth century), 'Hayam Wuruk's Java' (fourteenth century), and 'Hasan's Morocco' (late nineteenth century). The past, in itself, raises no insuperable barrier.

Certainly, then, it is possible to take a Geertzian approach to rituals and other formalized activities in antiquity which are well documented in extant literature, such as the Roman triumph and the games. On the latter, K. M. Coleman's landmark article, 'Fatal charades: Roman executions staged as mythological enactments' (1990), can legitimately be read as a Geertzian 'thick description' which elicits through the interpretation of energized symbol complexes the mutually reinforcing ethos and world view of imperial Rome.

But how is 'thick description' possible for Mithraism when it is precisely the extant *literary* record which is so sparse? Would not a symbolist interpretation of the tauroctony be as fruitless as, say, an interpretation of a Navaho sand painting without record or observation of the 'sing' which activates its intent and meaning?

3. YES, GEERTZIAN DESCRIPTION AND INTERPRETATION ARE POSSIBLE, PROVIDED WE BEGIN *NOT* WITH THE TAUROCTONY BUT WITH THE MITHRAEUM AND THE GRADE STRUCTURE

If we focus on the tauroctony as, superficially at least, Mithraism's most obvious symbol complex, then a Geertzian interpretation would indeed be a hopeless endeavour. That is because, despite its manifest richness and evocativeness as a complex of symbols, it has (for us) no immediate ritual context. Perhaps when the mysteries were a living religion it did have such a context, perhaps not. It does of course have an indirect link to ritual in that the bull-killing was the necessary precursor of the feast of Mithras and Sol, and the feast of Mithras and Sol was the divine archetype of the sacramental feast of the initiates in the mithraeum.[6] It may well be that this was sufficient. But the fact remains that the tauroctony, although amenable to symbolic interpretation, cannot now be interpreted—if it ever could have been—as a complex of energized symbols or symbols-in-action analogous to the Navaho sand painting. For all its centrality in the mysteries, the tauroctony is an accessory to ritual action, not an instrument of action.

The tauroctony is one of the three distinctive symbolic constructs of the Mysteries of Mithras. The other two are the mithraeum and the hierarchy of the seven grades. This important fact I incorporated into my descriptive template of the mysteries (Ch. 1, sect. 3) as follows:

---

[6] This holds whether or not the serious eating and drinking was done outside, as at the recently discovered Tienen mithraeum (Martens and De Boe 2004).

D1. The complexes of symbols conveying the axioms and motifs of the mysteries in their various domains are manifested concretely...
D2. The initiate apprehends the symbol complexes conveying the axioms and motifs of the mysteries in their various domains...

on *structured sites*; in the mysteries there are three principal and distinctive *structures*:

1. the physical structure of the icon of the tauroctony (with its reverse = the banquet scene, plus peripheral scenes)
2. the physical structure of the mithraeum
3. the organizational structure of the seven grades.

Unlike the tauroctony, the mithraeum and the grade hierarchy are structures which can be *entered*, though of course in very different senses. One can 'get into' them—literally: 'into' the mithraeum because it is a *room*, a three-dimensional space designed to be entered physically; 'into' the grade hierarchy because it is a *career*, extended in the dimension of time and designed to be entered by initiation at a particular moment. In contrast, the tauroctony is an *impenetrable* three- or two-dimensional object, a mass or a surface to be apprehended from the outside only. No one, except in the imagination, ever entered the tauroctony to relate to its symbols from within. In a phenomenological sense one 'intends' the symbolic structures of mithraeum and grade hierarchy from inside, of the tauroctony from outside.

Because they could be entered and in a manner of speaking *lived*, the symbolic structures of mithraeum and grade hierarchy are in principle amenable to Geertzian description and interpretation. And if properly described and interpreted they can tell us much about both the ethos and the world view of Mithraism.

There is of course a necessary condition for an adequate description, and that is sufficient information. Do we know enough not just about the structure and elements of the two symbol complexes but about their functions in performance, about how the initiates actually engaged with them? To repeat, it is no use knowing everything about the iconography of the 'sand painting' if you know nothing about the 'sing'; better a modicum of information about both.

4. A CULTURE WITHIN A CULTURE: MITHRAISM AS A SUBSYSTEM WITHIN THE CULTURAL SYSTEM OF GRAECO-ROMAN PAGANISM. THE HERMENEUTIC IMPLICATIONS

Mithraism was not an autonomous and autarkic culture. Few cultures are, although the 'pre-contact', 'primitive', 'tribal' culture used to be anthropology's ideal case precisely because it is uncontaminated by the alien. But Mithraism was comfortably embedded in the society of the Roman empire. If there is one trait which scholars unanimously ascribe to the Mithraists, it is social conformism. Whatever their esoteric values, we may be sure that the initiates shared and echoed the values of the surrounding culture and subscribed, reflectively or unreflectively, to its world view.

Consequently, in our descriptions and interpretations we may properly deploy much information about the symbolism and symbol complexes current in Graeco-Roman culture, not just in Mithraism where the available data on the significance of symbols (as opposed to just the symbols themselves) are so limited. In point of fact, drawing selectively on the ethos and world view of the wider culture is what Mithraic scholarship has been doing hermeneutically for the past century. This was the topic I addressed specifically in Chapter 3 as the problem of 'referents', although in that context I addressed it from the traditional standpoint of the iconography of the monuments. Scholarship, we saw, has found three fields of reference: first (Ch. 3, sect. 2), the lore and learning (the 'encyclopaedia') of the surrounding Graeco-Roman culture; secondly (sect. 3), Iranian religion, with the proviso that we can never be entirely sure what in the assimilated religion was or had been 'real existing' Mazdaism and what mere *Perserie* constructed (in all sincerity) by the founders of the Mysteries or by others in the late Hellenistic world; thirdly (sect. 4), astronomy and astrology, or more precisely the heavens as systematically constructed in Graeco-Roman culture.

5. THE SYMBOL COMPLEX OF THE GRADE HIERARCHY

Of the mysteries' three major complexes of symbols, the 'structures' (D) in our description, two are ubiquitous: the mithraeum and the tauroctony. The distinctive space and the distinctive icon, it appears, were functional necessities. One cannot conceive of the Mysteries of Mithras without them. The third symbol complex, the grade structure, appears to have been optional. Few would now argue that the hierarchy was established in all Mithraic communities, whether or not it is attested in the archaeological record. Currently, a minimalist position is in vogue. Manfred Clauss (most recently, 2000: 131–3) claims that only those whose rank in the hierarchy is explicitly attested were grade-holders in the Mysteries, a group amounting to about 15 per cent of the thousand or so known initiates. Likewise, Robert Turcan (1999) asserts that the well-known correlation of the seven grades with the seven planets was restricted to the area (Rome and Ostia) and the time span (end of the second century to second half of the third) of actual archaeological record.

I do not think that the minimalists are right; but even if they are, it is beside the point. The important question from our perspective is whether the symbol complex of the grade structure as attested may legitimately be read as an expression of the ethos and world view of the initiates. No one, as far as I know, has ever suggested otherwise. Indeed it is manifestly absurd to imagine that the grade structure reflects an ethos and world view contrary to those in communities where the hierarchy happens not to be attested in the archaeological record.

In 1980 Richard Gordon published a comprehensive study of the grade structure entitled 'Reality, evocation and boundary in the Mysteries of Mithras'. In effect, as in intent, this study interpreted the symbolism of the grades, both individually and together as a structured whole, in relation to the Graeco-Roman 'encyclopaedia', that immense fund of facts and factoids, lore and learning, scattered across the literature of classical antiquity but lodged particularly in certain works of the second and third tier such as Pliny the Elder's *Natural History* and Aelian's *Nature of Animals* (Gordon 1980*b*: n. 8). The 'encyclopaedia' is the key—at least *a* key and arguably the best key—to the culture's basic ethos and world view. I intend 'basic' in a non-trivial sense, for the 'encyclopaedia' instantiates, albeit in an uncodified, unsystematic, and discontinuous form, the culture's fundamental attitudes and beliefs: that which 'everyone knows' about the world, about how to behave in it, and about what to expect of the behaviour of others, whether kin or friend or foe.

By exploring the symbolism of the grades with reference to the 'encyclopaedia' Gordon was able to see what aspects of the ethos and world view of Graeco-Roman society the Mithraists had selected, for the most part unconsciously, and amplified. For example, the 'encyclopaedia's' facts and factoids about real-life ravens and lions enabled him to clarify what it meant to be make-believe Mithraic Ravens and Lions (in ascending order initiates of the first and fourth grades respectively). Consequently we can now better interpret and set in context data such as (1) Porphyry's testimony (*De antro* 15) that Mithraic Lions wash their hands with honey as a fiery liquid inimical to water, and (2) the Sta Prisca painted text that the Lions are incense-burners 'through whom we offer incense, through whom we ourselves are consumed' (V485).

Much of the small extant stock of Mithraism's symbols-in-action relates to the grades, as demonstrated by the two examples above, honey and incense. Because they are symbols realized in performance—in doing, not knowing—they reveal in particular the *ethos* of the mysteries, 'how we as Lions behave, what values we stand for'. Consequently, it is through the symbolism of the grade structure that we can recapture and describe with a modicum of depth something of the fourth 'mode' of experiencing Mithraism (E4 in our descriptive template), 'ethical behaviour consonant with the mysteries'.

There is no need here to continue with how Mithraic Lions exemplify through their performative symbols the virtues of austerity, dryness, and purity, or how and why 'dryness' is an esoteric virtue in the Mithraic mysteries. For that I can do no better than to recommend Gordon's article to the reader. Like Geertzian 'thick description', such presentations are best read unabridged.[7] Their impact is in the richness of their detail, and summary only drains them of their power to represent the evocations of the original. Besides, my intent in this book is not to present new findings or new hypotheses about the grades or any other component of the Mithraic Mysteries, but by devising proper hermeneutic methods to render a more adequate account of what scholarship has long known by intuition and *ad hoc* empiricism.

6. A MODERN COMPARATOR: THE SYMBOL SYSTEM OF THE CHAMULAS

The two examples of symbols-in-action cited above, the honey ablutions of Mithraic Lions and their incense-burning, prompts a comparison with the symbol system of another culture in which comparable symbols both evoke and express comparable values in ethos and world view.

The culture is that of the Chamulas, a people of southern Mexico (central Chiapas highlands), described by Gary Gossen. The religion of the Chamulas is a blend of Christianity and Mayan sun cult, and their culture and thought are structured on a grid of 'discriminations' in which the Sun is 'the first principle of order' (Gossen 1979: 118). Hence, of course, the relevance of the Chamula symbol system to the Mithraic: both are fundamentally solar. Both are also syncretic. Just as Chamula religion blends Christianity and Mayan sun cult, so Mithraism in its day blended Persian—or what it believed to be Persian—religion with Graeco-Roman paganism, most obviously in its pantheon.

Chamula culture is different from Mithraic culture in two major respects: it is a self-contained regional and ethnic culture, and it is a contemporary, living culture. Interestingly, while Chamula religion drew on the alien system of Christianity (via Dominican missionaries), their own developed system as a whole has long enabled the Chamulas to insulate themselves mentally and physically from the surrounding Christian and Ladino culture. The Mithraic mysteries, in contrast, were supremely integrative; or at least from the membership profile in the epigraphic record we can safely say that they attracted those well integrated into the society of the Roman empire. But these dissimilarities between Mithraic and Chamula cultures, far from invalidating comparisons, enhance their value.

To understand the structure of their 'symbolic discrimination' (Gossen 1979: 121), one must recognize that 'Chamula cosmological symbolism has as its

---

[7] 'Geertzian' would be an appropriate label for Gordon's description and analysis of the Mithraic grades. Geertz was a major influence on Gordon's work at that time (see Gordon 1979: 17, n. 53), although, as the term 'evocation' in the title indicates, Gordon was most influenced by Dan Sperber, who was then challenging the symbolists' assumption that symbols have meanings (see Sperber 1975).

primary orientation the point of view of the Sun as he emerges on the eastern horizon each day, facing his universe, north on his right hand, south on his left hand' (ibid. 119). The risen Sun, in Chamula imagination, then travels round to the north, thus proceeding counterclockwise and to his right, until he sets in the west. His subterranean nocturnal journey back to the east is accordingly a journey round to the south. It is also represented as a winter journey, just as the northern sector of the journey is represented as a summer journey.

The logic of the solar stance and the solar journey structures the system of Chamula oppositions ('symbolic discriminations' in Gossen's terms)—see table.

Superior ('senior')	Inferior ('junior')[8]
Sun	Moon
on/to the right	on/to the left
counterclockwise	clockwise
east and north	west and south
up/high	down/low
hot/fiery	cold/earthy
male	female

The 'fundamental orientation' (i.e. Sun rising in the east, 'facing his universe, north on his right hand, south on his left'), says Gossen,

may also contribute to an understanding of Chamula ritual treatment of space. It is first of all necessary to understand that religious cargo-holders [office-holders] themselves have an aspect of deity in that they share with the sun and the saints (the sun's kinsmen) the responsibility and the burden of maintaining the social order. While imparting a sacred aspect to themselves through exemplary behavior and constant use of sacred symbols and objects such as strong rum liquor, incense, candles, fireworks and cigarettes, most of which have actual or metaphoric qualities of heat, they metaphorically follow the sun's pattern of motion by moving to their own right through any ritual space which lies before them. (Gossen 1979: 119)

Before we turn to the 'ritual treatment of space', which will of course lead us to a comparison with the mithraeum in the Mithraic mysteries, we should first take a look at the 'sacred symbols and objects' of Chamula culture mentioned above and compare them to the two 'symbols-in-action' of the Mithraic mysteries already introduced, incense and honey. To the Mithraic pair in the following table I add (in parentheses) another three to balance the Chamula pentad.

The first and most obvious point of comparison is that both sets of symbols/objects are physically and/or 'metaphorically' *hot*. Secondly, certain of the symbols/objects in each set are incandescent: they emit *light* as well as heat. Thirdly,

---

[8] 'Senior/junior' are Gossen's terms. A better/worse discrimination seems to be implicit, though definitely not a Manichaean good/bad discrimination.

Chamula symbols/objects	Mithraic symbols/objects
incense	incense
rum	honey
candles	(plethora of lamps)
fireworks	(light effects)
cigarettes	(*pyrōpon asthma*—'fiery breath')

and more importantly, both sets of symbols/objects serve to define, to validate, and to sanctify the lives and actions of *males in a hierarchy*, the Chamula cargo-holders[9] on the one hand and the Mithraic grade-holders on the other. Lastly, and most importantly, in handling the symbols/objects of their respective systems Chamula men and the all-male initiates of Mithras engage in a *mimesis of the Sun*.

It is worth noting that the 'ritual height' and hence the solarity of Chamula cargo-holders

is expressed by special pole and branch towers, fifteen feet high, which are constructed at their homes at the time when they leave office. A representative of the Alférez [religious cargo-holder] sits in the tower and thus symbolizes the new heights of the desirable which the outgoing official has achieved in his year in office. In so doing, he has helped the sun to maintain order and thus partakes of the sun's good, rising aspect. (Gossen 1979: 121)

Comparable in the Mithraic system is the rank of Sun-Runner (Heliodromus), the second highest in the grade hierarchy, whose tutelary planet is the Sun himself.[10] He is the Sun's special representative in the cult economy, and at the sacred meal he sits in for the Sun, just as the Father sits in for Mithras. Furthermore, as I have argued in my interpretation of the second of the two newly discovered rituals represented on the Mainz vessel (Beck 2000: 154–67), the Sun-Runner has his own ritual procession in mimesis of his celestial patron. It is a misrepresentation to suppose the Sun-Runner a mere courier who 'runs' the Sun's errands (that function would belong to the most junior grade, the Raven, under Mercury's protection). No, in mimesis he runs the Sun's own course; for technically, in astronomical parlance, a *dromos* is an arc of the planet's own orbit.

Some line-by-line comparisons are now in order, although we should bear in mind that these cannot be made except by reference to the intent of the two sets of symbols/objects as integrated wholes in each culture. The first pair (incense) appears in identical form in both lists and so needs no comment. The second pair instantiates a paradox: rum and honey are liquids which are 'fiery', not watery as intuitive physics (folk physics) would suggest. To match 'candles' on the

[9] Chamula women cannot be cargo-holders. Significantly, the Chamula word for 'mother' is prefixed to a husband's cargo title to designate his wife.

[10] We can now also appreciate why the tutelary planet of the Father, the highest grade of all, is Saturn. In Greek astronomical parlance, Saturn is literally the 'highest' of the planets because it is the furthest from earth and the nearest to the ultimate sphere of the fixed stars.

Chamula side I have proposed for Mithraism a 'plethora of lamps' such as was found massed around the altar in the Caesarea mithraeum (Blakely *et al.* 1987: 150). In a Chamula 'household curing ceremony' the candles are arranged by 'seniority' so that the 'largest, most expensive and longest-burning candles remain closest to "conceptual East"' (Gossen 1979: 128, Fig. 6C). As analogues to modern fireworks I suggest 'light effects', notably the piercing of monuments so that the solar rays or the lunar crescent could be illuminated from behind (e.g. V847; Schwertheim 1974: 35, no. 36). Finally, as an analogue to cigarettes, a text from the Dura mithraeum evokes a comparable mixture of fire and air, the 'fiery breath which for the magi too is the lustration (*niptron*) of holy men' (V68).[11]

7. THE CONSTRUCTION OF SPACE IN MITHRAIC AND CHAMULA CULTURES

To understand a culture's 'ritual treatment of space' one must first understand how that culture constructs and represents space itself, from the level of its cosmos down to its actual environment.[12]

For the Mithraists this is easy and straightforward. Mithraic space and the Mithraic cosmos merely replicate the standard Graeco-Roman conceptions of space and the cosmos. There is nothing at all esoteric about it. It is the same public text—'in bold' as one might say, since the Mysteries, as the plethora of cosmic symbols attests, placed a greater emphasis on the celestial cosmos (*to periechon*, that which 'surrounds' the earth) than did the culture at large.

In the Hellenized culture of the Roman empire the universe was represented as a nest of rotating spheres centred on a spherical but immobile earth. There are eight of these spheres, seven inner and one outer. The outer sphere carries the 'fixed' stars rotating westwards (from left to right for a south-facing, northern-hemisphere observer) in the period of a twenty-four-hour day. The inner seven, while also participating in 'universal' motion, rotate in the opposite direction (eastwards, right to left), each in a different period. The function of these spheres is to carry the seven planets, that is, the Sun, the Moon, and the five planets visible to the naked eye, in their individual orbits. The Moon's sphere rotates in the period of a month,[13] the Sun's in the period of a year, and the other five in the periods appropriate to each. On the common-sense assumption that the slower the planet, the farther away it must be, the ancients ordered the seven planetary spheres as shown in the table (from the earth outwards to the sphere of the

[11] See Gordon 1980*b*: 36–7. Note that this blend of fire and air is a medium for ablution too. So it is even more paradoxical than honey, which is at least a liquid.

[12] For this and subsequent sections J. Z. Smith's *To Take Place: Toward Theory in Ritual* (1987) is essential reading.

[13] A sidereal month (27.32 days), not the longer synodic month of 'new moon' to 'new moon' (29.53 days).

Planet	Period of rotation of sphere
Moon	one month
Mercury	one year
Venus	one year
Sun	one year
Mars	two years
Jupiter	twelve years
Saturn	thirty years[14]

fixed stars). Since the 'inferior' planets Mercury and Venus have the same average geocentric sidereal period as the Sun, this trio could be and was in fact arranged in different orders. That shown in the table was eventually preferred, largely because it places the Sun in the centre of the sequence to orchestrate and to illuminate the dance of the celestial bodies.

Not only do the spheres of the planets turn in the opposite direction to the sphere of the fixed stars, but they also rotate around different poles. Consequently their equators are oblique to the equator of the sphere of the fixed stars. The equator of the latter we call the celestial equator;[15] the common equator of the former, which is actually the Sun's orbit, we call the ecliptic.[16] The ecliptic is oblique to the celestial equator by approximately 23½°.

The points at which the ecliptic intersects the equator are the spring and autumn equinoxes. At the spring equinox the Sun crosses the equator from south to north; at the autumn equinox from north to south. Midway between the spring equinox and the autumn equinox is the summer solstice. This is the northernmost point on the ecliptic, the point at which the Sun changes direction (hence the term 'tropic')[17] and starts to move back southwards. Opposite the summer solstice is the winter solstice, the southernmost point on the ecliptic, from which the Sun starts to move back northwards again. As should be clear from this explanation, the equinoxes and the solstices are equally points in celestial space and moments in annual time.

The ecliptic is defined not only by these four tropic points but also by the twelve 'signs' (*zōidia*) into which it is divided. Strictly speaking, the zodiac is a band encircling the heavens, 12° in width, of which the ecliptic is the median

[14] Figures rounded off to the nearest year for the three 'superior' planets.

[15] The celestial equator is a projection of our terrestrial equator outwards onto the sphere of the fixed stars. In speaking of 'the equator' unqualified, we moderns usually intend the terrestrial equator; the ancients intended the celestial equator.

[16] Rather than dealing with seven different planetary equators, astronomers ancient and modern use the ecliptic as the common planetary equator and treat the actual orbits of the Moon and the other five planets as deviations from it. Consequently, the lunar and planetary orbits are to the ecliptic as the ecliptic is to the equator.

[17] In ancient parlance the equinoxes can also be called 'tropics'.

line. Each sign is 30° in length (12 × 30° = 360°) and the sequence custom-
arily begins with Aries at the spring equinox. The signs are named after the actual
constellations with which in antiquity they roughly coincided.[18]

All this is elementary stuff. The model (excluding the divisions of the zodiac) is
essentially that established by Plato in the *Timaeus*.[19] His authorship does not
imply that it is astronomically 'learned'; it is not: the work's sophistication lies
entirely in its metaphysics. The very simplicity of its *physical* cosmology, backed
by Plato's almost divine authority, guaranteed its persistence as antiquity's default
model long after the advances of Hellenistic mathematical astronomy had made
it scientifically obsolete. It even has its standard iconographic representation: the
world globe with the crossed bands of equator and ecliptic/zodiac.[20]

Two features of the cosmology of the *Timaeus* should be noted here. First, as
we saw with respect to the celestial tropics, the heavens are where Time and Space
are related. The celestial bodies are created specifically to instantiate Time in the
cosmos: 'as a result of this plan and purpose of god for the birth of time, the sun
and moon and the five planets... came into being to define and preserve the
measures of time' (*Timaeus* 38c2–6, trans. Lee).

Secondly, the macrocosm is linked to the microcosm of the rational human
soul as original to copy in a very literal way. The human soul is rational because
and only because it replicates the two celestial orbits described above, the
revolutions of the Same (universal motion) and of the Different (planetary
motion), and maintains them undistorted (41–7). Speaking of the human eye,
Plato says (47b5–c4, trans. Lee):

Let us rather say that the cause and purpose of god's invention and gift to us of sight was that
we should see the revolutions of intelligence in the heavens and use their untroubled course
to guide the troubled revolutions in our own understanding, which are akin to them, and so,
by learning what they are and how to calculate them accurately according to their nature,
correct the disorder of own revolutions by the standard of the invariability of those of god.

Ideal Space is thus internalized. The rational human soul contains, in Geertzian
terms, both a *model of* and *model for* the universe.[21]

This is not just an ontological matter (what sort of thing is the soul and where
does it fit in the general scheme of things?). More important in the present
context are its spatial implications. The *Timaeus* (with the *Phaedrus*) stands at the
head of a long and rich tradition of soul journeys, frequently on the pattern of a
descent from the sphere of the fixed stars down into mortal genesis on earth and

---

[18] As a result of the phenomenon known as 'the precession of the equinoxes', the signs of the
zodiac and their eponymous constellations have long since parted company.

[19] Astronomically, the signs of the zodiac were adopted in order to measure longitude (i.e.
distance along the ecliptic from the vernal equinox). Their primary intent is of course astrological.

[20] To take a Mithraic example, in V543 the lion-headed god is posed on just such a globe.

[21] It would be truer to the language of the *Timaeus* to say that the rational human soul physically
instantiates the revolutions of heaven within the human head, which was made spherical for
precisely that purpose.

an ascent back up again at death. Later we shall look at the Mithraic version of this travelogue which boldly enacted the celestial journey in ritual. The point here is that in this widely held model constructed extraterrestrial space is not untrodden space. People go there.

And what of terrestrial space? In the Mysteries this was of little concern in and of itself, although as the arena for the processes of birth and death, growth and decay, seed-time and harvest, cold and heat, moisture and aridity, Earth clearly mattered.[22] Presumably the Mithraists' geographic sense was much the same as that of other denizens of the Roman empire, though perhaps sharper and more informed among those with military or bureaucratic experience. Mithraists of that sort might well have a greater sense of the extent of the empire and thus of the *oikoumenē*. What would be peculiar to the imaginative initiate would be the awareness that his mysteries came from 'elsewhere', specifically from 'the mountains near Persia' where 'Zoroaster first hallowed a natural cave in Mithras' honour' (Porphyry, *De antro* 6).

The celestial and terrestrial reach of the Mithraists' construction of space stands in sharp contrast to the very bounded construction of the Chamulas. Laterally the Chamula world ends or fades into the unknown and irrelevant not far from their own highland region. The lowlands to their south (reached from the western end of their territory) have significance because they are the source of 'hot' ritual products and ingredients: 'tobacco, rum, incense, candles, and fireworks' (Gossen 1979: 123):

Resin for incense, beef tallow and wax for candles, the ingredients for gunpowder, sugarcane for rum, and tobacco for cigarettes do in fact come from, or at least through, the lowlands. This tropical origin is interesting because it illustrates a paradox in Chamula thinking about the world. Although the highlands are closer than the lowlands to the sun in a vertical sense, the climate of the highlands is actually much colder than that of the lowlands. It may be that the ambiguous quality of the lowlands (physically hot yet socially distant) makes them a logical source for some sacred symbols and substances.

We shall meet paradoxes of this sort in Mithraic cosmology too. They are what distinguish sacred geography from mere economic geography.

To the north and east there is no dramatic change of terrain. Moreover, the Chamulas have no economic incentive to travel there, as they do to the lowlands to the south via the west. However, on the principle that 'higher is better' because closer to the Sun, the north and the east are viewed positively. This is especially so of the east, the direction of sunrise. 'Significantly, Tzontevitz Mountain, the highest in the Central Chiapas Highlands and the most sacred of all mountains,

---

[22] Leroy Campbell's (1968) valiant attempt to correlate different patterns of composition and iconography with different geographical climates is now more or less forgotten. The general significance for the Mithraists of Earth as the source of fertility is made clear by Line 1 at Sta Prisca: *Fecunda Tellus cuncta qua generat Pales* (Vermaseren 1960: 144; 1963: 187–92; Betz 1968: 64–6).

lies both to the east of Chamula ceremonial center and within Barrio San Juan, which is the highest ranking of the three barrios' (ibid. 118).

Obviously the same principle 'higher is better' informs the vertical construction of the Chamula world. Underground in caves dwell the 'earthlords' who 'provide all forms of precipitation, including accompanying clouds, lightning, and thunder', snakes 'which are the familiars and alternate forms of the earthlords', and 'demons': 'all are associated with dampness, darkness, and lowness' (ibid. 118)

As well as this underground world there is an antipodal world where dwell the dead:

The dead eat charred food and flies in place of normal food. The dead must also refrain from sexual intercourse. With these exceptions, life in the underworld is much like life on earth. People do not suffer there. Those who have murdered or committed suicide are exceptions. These are burned by the sun as he travels his circuit there during the night on earth. (Ibid. 118)

Interestingly, the extreme of lowness seems to be correlated not with an extreme of cold but with a malefic extreme of heat: charred food, sunburnt sinners.

The Chamula heavens are described by Gossen (ibid. 118) as follows:

Three layers, which informants draw as concentric domes, make up the sky. The first and smallest of these domes is the only level of the sky which is visible to most human beings. This level, however, is only a reflection of what is happening at the upper two levels. The moon (who is conceptually equivalent to the Virgin Mary, *hmʔetik* or 'Our Mother') and minor constellations travel in the second level. The sun (who is conceptually equivalent to Christ, *htotik* or 'Our Father'), Saint Jerome, the guardian of animal souls, and major (bright) constellations reside and travel in the third level. The heat and brilliance of the sun's head are so great that they penetrate the two inferior levels of the sky. Thus, it is only the reflection of the sun's face and head which we perceive on earth.

Perhaps the most interesting feature of this cosmology is the doubling of the Sun. The visible Sun of our everyday experience is but a pale image of the real Sun, exalted and dazzling, two spheres above. Whatever the reason for this strikingly Platonic conception, there is a salutary lesson to be learnt. As emphasized throughout this study, one should never underestimate the capacity of 'simple folk' to create and sustain sophisticated systems of representation.

8. MITHRAISM'S SECOND AXIOM: 'HARMONY OF TENSION IN OPPOSITION'[23]

To the extent that Mithraic cosmology is more sophisticated than Chamula cosmology it is because it is derived from the learned, philosophical model of its Graeco-Roman cultural matrix. We can see this in the distinction between the

[23] Despite its different time frame G. E. R. Lloyd's *Polarity and Analogy: Two Types of Argumentation in Early Greek Thought* (1966) is germane to our inquiry in a fundamental way.

two cosmic motions, universal daily motion and planetary motion, described above. The Mithraic mysteries, as we shall see, incorporated this fundamental opposition; Chamula cosmology does not. In particular, Chamula cosmology conflates the two solar journeys, the daily and the annual/seasonal. This makes intuitive sense but is scientifically less fruitful. It is also less generative of paradox and opposition of the sort that the Mithraists eagerly exploited.

These considerations bring us to Mithraism's second 'axiom' or 'ultimate sacred postulate', as I termed the mysteries' two fundamental principles in our descriptive template in Chapter 1:

A1. The mysteries give *symbolic* expression to...
A2. In the mysteries, the initiate apprehends *symbolically*...
two *axioms* or *ultimate sacred postulates*:
 1. DEUS SOL INVICTUS MITHRAS
 2. 'Harmony of tension in opposition.'

Binary opposition is not only inevitable in a solar religion, it is also inevitably *explicit*. This point is of fundamental importance. Mere binary opposition or polarity can be said to characterize the world view and ethos of virtually any religion, indeed of virtually any culture. It is not a contingent property of such systems. Rather, it is an ineluctable consequence of the way we as a species organize our cognized world, of the way we think. Our postulated second axiom must therefore do more than reinvent the wheel of Lévi-Straussian structuralism.

Hermeneutically, I intend with the second axiom the claim that in contrast to the deeply buried, intuitively unobvious oppositions of most structuralist analysis,[24] the oppositions in the Mithraic system are on the surface, explicit, and as readily accessible to the membership then as to scholars now. This accessibility is a function of the solar focus of the cult. It needs/needed no Lévi-Strauss to tell a modern scholar or a Mithraist or a Chamula that day (Sun present) is opposed to night (Sun absent) and that summer (Sun highest) is opposed to winter (Sun lowest). Binary pairs and polarities come with the turf.

The second axiom is expressed in the form of a quotation from Porphyry's *De antro nympharum* (29), where it concludes and encapsulates a list of binary oppositions:

> Since nature arose out of diversity,
> the ancients everywhere made that which has a twofold entrance her symbol.
> For the progression is either through the sensible or the intelligible;
> and when it is through the sensible,
> it is either through the sphere of the fixed stars or through the sphere of the planets;
> and again it is made either by an immortal or a mortal road.

---

[24] To take an example from classical antiquity, see Lévi-Strauss's own well-known analysis of the Theban myth (1955).

> There is a cardinal point above the earth and another below it,
> one to the east and one to the west.
> There are regions to the left and right,
> there is night and day.
> And so there is a tension of harmony in opposition,
> and it shoots from the bowstring through opposites.[25]

The saying itself, displayed here as the final two lines, is an adaptation of a fragment of Heraclitus (51 DK). Elsewhere (Beck 2000: 167–71) I have argued that it was the Mithraists who adapted it. The commonplace image of Mithras as a bowman is thus the visual counterpart of the verbal *symbolon* which expresses the mysteries' second axiom. The recovery of an actual Mithraic ritual (depicted on a cult vessel from Mainz) in which the Father mimes Mithras-as-archer by drawing a bow at an initiand has dramatically confirmed my interpretation of the adapted Heraclitus fragment in *De antro* 29 (Beck 2000: 149–54, 167–71).[26]

The original Mithraic *symbolon* has been disguised by its redeployment in *De antro* 29. There is however another extant *symbolon* of the Mithraic mysteries which is explicitly identified as such. In *Contra Celsum* 6.22 the Christian apologist Origen states:

These things [i.e. the celestial ascent of souls] the *logos* of the Persians and the *teletē* of Mithras intimate.... for there is therein a certain *symbolon* of the two celestial revolutions (*periodōn*), that of the fixed stars and that assigned to the planets, and of the route of the soul through and out (*diexodou*) of them. Such is the *symbolon*: a seven-gated ladder and an eighth [sc. gate] on top (*klimax heptapylos, epi de autēi ogdoē*).

This hugely important testimony tells us (1) that the Mithraic *symbolon* was a material object (i.e. a ladder of a certain construction) rather than a verbal formula; (2) that it signified the two celestial revolutions, universal and planetary, discussed in the preceding section of this chapter; (3) that it also signified the journey of souls 'through and out'.

The symbol's first significance, the two celestial revolutions, returns us to the primary cosmological opposition of Plato's *Timaeus*, the opposition between universal motion which instantiates Sameness and Uniformity and planetary motion which instantiates Difference and Multiplicity. It thus locates the mysteries' second axiom and thereby the mysteries themselves firmly within the Platonic tradition.

The second significance, the 'through-and-out journey' of souls, does not—it is essential to note—elevate the symbol's intent to a metaphysically higher plane. To assume so would be a modern misapprehension triggered by the reference to 'souls' (*psychōn*). The route of souls lies through the actual heavens which we can

---

[25] Trans. Arethusa edn., modified to restore 'mortal' and 'immortal' to their correct order.

[26] In discussing the adaptation of the Heraclitus fragment, I argued that the original *Mithraic* subject of the second clause (*kai toxeuei dia tōn enantiōn*) was Mithras himself: '*he* shoots through opposites.'

descry in the here and now with our mortal eyes. It is not just a metaphor for a 'spiritual journey' in the modern sense.

However, the 'route through and out' is not *merely* an itinerary through extraterrestrial space, although it is fully that too. It is also a 'way out' in the sense of an escape, a release from mortality back into immortality, a return whence we came, a recovery of our ontologically superior selves. These larger claims are not of course literally intended by the *symbolon* in and of itself. Rather, they are the Platonic entailments of the *symbolon* in the context of the mysteries. In this sense it is not improper to say that the symbol of the ladder becomes a symbol of salvation, as a Mithraist—and a Platonist—would understand the term.[27]

From the way 'through and out' of Origen, *Contra Celsum* 6.22, we return to the 'downward path of souls and their route back out again' (*tèn eis katō kathodon tōn psychōn kai palin exodon*) of Porphyry, *De antro* 6, the passage we selected as our 'gateway text' to the Mithraic mysteries (Ch. 2, sect. 1; Ch. 4, sects. 1–3). Note that the soul journey is here explicitly dichotomized, whereas in the former passage it was left implicit: presumably, there is a 'way in' to balance the 'way through and out'. Note also that Porphyry does not here link the entry/descent and the exit/ascent of souls to the two celestial motions. That occurs later, in ch. 29, where the two celestial motions are added to the list of binary pairs. Finally, note the important correlations:

$$\text{downward} = \text{way in}$$
$$\text{upward} = \text{way out}$$

Now in the context both of the mysteries and of our two literary sources, the way down and in is the way of genesis into mortality and the way up and out is the way of apogenesis into immortality. Accordingly, we may formulate the correlations:

$$\text{descent from heaven to earth} = \text{genesis into mortality}$$
$$\text{ascent from earth to heaven} = \text{apogenesis into immortality}$$

or as oppositions:

| descent from heaven to earth | vs. | ascent from earth to heaven |
| genesis into mortality | vs. | apogenesis into immortality |

In *Contra Celsum* 6.22 the route of souls passes through both 'revolutions', that is, through the planetary spheres and the sphere of the fixed stars, and the same double route is implied in *De antro* 29, though as alternatives ('either through...or through'). Elsewhere in *De antro* (chs. 21–4) we discover that the entrance and exit lie at opposite points on the sphere of the fixed stars, namely the summer solstice and the winter solstice respectively. It would be a mistake,

---

[27] For more on Origen, *Contra Celsum* 6.22, see Beck 1988: 73–85.

however, to try to integrate the data into a single coherent set. That way 'doctrine' lies, the chimaera we exorcised in the preceding chapter. Better to leave the data unreconciled as equally valid cosmological, anthropological, and soteriological riffs on the grand theme of 'harmony of tension in opposition'.

APPENDIX: ON PORPHYRY'S *DE ANTRO NYMPHARUM* AS A RELIABLE SOURCE OF DATA ON THE MITHRAIC MYSTERIES

Here we must meet the following potentially serious objection: does Porphyry's testimony appear to corroborate our thesis about a Mithraic principle of 'harmony of tension in opposition' not because there really was such a principle but because it suited Porphyry's allegorical purpose to pretend there was?

This objection should be set in the broader context of scepticism about the accuracy of Porphyry's testimony on the Mithraic mysteries. The testimony is unreliable, so the argument runs, because it is more Porphyry's own philosophical construction and/or the construction of his philosophical sources than evidence for actually existing Mithraism. I will not counter this larger charge here. It is essentially that made by Robert Turcan in his *Mithras Platonicus* (1975), the title and subtitle (*Recherches sur l'hellénisation philosophique de Mithra*) of which encapsulate his case. I have argued against it elsewhere,[28] in some detail (Beck 2000: 158–9, 177–9). The main counter-argument consists in demonstrating that nothing in the archaeological data conflicts with the evidence of the *De antro* and that much in fact confirms it. The sceptical case is further weakened when we no longer have to assume that the Mithraic data challenged by the sceptics and accepted by their opponents must have constituted a formal doctrine of the faith. As we established in the preceding chapter, there is now no need to make this assumption. We may treat Porphyry's Mithraic data at face value as bits and pieces of Mithraic practice and theory, the latter tentative explications rather than fixed teaching. We do not have to reconcile the data into a formally coherent doctrinal whole.

Let us then turn to the narrower objection that it is Porphyry's allegorical intent in the *De antro* rather than any inherent Mithraic principle that has moulded the Mithraic data into the appearance of a system of structured polarities. Now it is certainly true that the *De antro* is far from being a disinterested discussion of the mysteries of Mithras. In fact, Mithraism is quite incidental to its primary purpose, which is to explore certain philosophical and cosmological themes through an allegorical explication of the cave described by Homer in *Odyssey* 13.102–12, the cave near which the sleeping hero is set on his return to his native land.[29] So peculiar is Homer's description, Porphyry argues (*De antro* 2–4), that we cannot believe such a cave ever existed or could exist in the actual world. Obviously, then, since it is neither a real cave to be found on Ithaca nor yet a realistic fiction, Homer must intend something different. That something can only be allegory. Homer's description is indeed bizarre from a naturalistic point of view, so one has every sympathy with Porphyry's premise, if not with his solution.

---

[28] Beck 1984: 2055–6; 1988: 42, n. 93, 80–2; 1994*a*: 106–7.
[29] On the Neoplatonic allegorization of Homer see Lamberton 1986 (66–76, 119–33, 318–24 on this particular passage of the *Odyssey*).

Caves, Porphyry shows (*De antro* 5–9), are traditional symbols of the cosmos. That, then, must be the intent of the Homeric cave, and for the balance of his essay and with considerable ingenuity Porphyry argues that the cave's peculiar features bear this meaning out.

Among these features are the cave's two 'doors' (*thyrai*), of which Homer says (*Od.* 13.110–12): 'the northern is for men to descend by, the southern is more for gods (*theōterai*); men do not enter by the latter, for it is the route of immortals (*athanatōn*).' For Porphyry this is perhaps the clearest indication of Homer's allegorical intent: for while natural caves do not normally exhibit such features, the universe, as construed by 'theologians' (*De antro* 22), does. According to this cosmology, the universe possesses a pair of gates set opposite each other. Not only do these gates lie to the north and the south, but they are also transit points respectively for mortals and immortals. Through the northern gate souls descend to earthly mortality, through the southern gate they ascend again to celestial immortality. These of course are the soul gates already introduced in the preceding section of this chapter.

As well as the unnamed 'theologians', Porphyry gives as his sources for the theory of cosmic soul gates the second-century Neopythagorean 'Numenius and his associate (*hetairos*) Cronius' (*De antro* 21, cf. 22). It was the same Cronius whom he had cited initially as his authority for allegorizing the Homeric cave because of the lack of realism in its description (2, 3).[30] Porphyry, in other words, received much of his argument ready made. We have to construe the information contained in ch. 6, that the Mithraists celebrated in their microcosmic 'caves' a mystery of the soul's descent and return, as part and parcel of the same argument, even though the authority cited there is not Cronius or Numenius but a certain Eubulus.[31]

In the ampler passage on the soul gates (20–9) the Mithraists are not initially mentioned, but their cosmology—or their imputed cosmology—makes an explicit appearance in ch. 24 with a detail concerning the celestial location of Mithras 'on the equator... at the equinoxes' which is then related to the location of the soul gates at the solstices. The passage is of immense importance, and I shall accord it proper consideration in due course. For the moment my concern is simply with its context—and because of its context, with its reliability.

In sum, the Mithraic data of *De antro* 6 and 24 are so well dovetailed with the body of evidence which Porphyry adduces to prove his point about the necessarily allegorical intent of Homer's cave in general, and of its 'doors' in particular, that one cannot but wonder if the data were not crafted or adapted to that end by Porphyry and/or his sources. Are they really facts about Mithraism or 'facts' spun out of Mithraism by the requirements of Neoplatonic explication?

That Porphyry and/or his philosophical sources might have cooked their data on the mysteries is not in itself unlikely. Ancient authorities cannot be held to modern canons of objectivity. If what they attribute to the mysteries is not what the Mithraism actually practised or preached, then it is not a question of lies or fabrication, but rather, as it would seem to them, the expression of an underlying intent or truth which a philosopher, qua

---

[30] On Cronius and Numenius in relation to the *De antro*, see Turcan 1975: 62–5; Lamberton 1986: 318–24; on Numenius, Des Places 1973; Lamberton 1986: 54–77.

[31] On Eubulus see Turcan 1975: 23–43.

ideal initiate, was surely better qualified to elucidate than the cult's actual membership of the moment.

Nevertheless, the fact that Porphyry and/or his sources would have had no scruples about adapting or even inventing Mithraic data to suit their arguments does not necessarily mean that they actually did so. It is far more likely that Mithraic doctrine (in the weak sense of the term!) really was what the philosophers said it was. In that case there would have been no need for invention or adaptation. The Mithraists would be saying independently what the philosophers too were saying. Indeed it is likely, given the chronological precedence of the Mysteries over the philosophical sources, that the philosophers actually acquired from the Mysteries the cosmological details which they attributed to them: in other words, a process of adoption, not adaptation. We should not assume, surely, that inventiveness necessarily lies within the philosophical tradition rather than the working religion.

As mentioned above, I have already demonstrated elsewhere that there are no insuper-able discrepancies between Mithraic practice and theory as attested in Porphyry and Mithraic practice and theory as archaeology has allowed us to recover them. Even if there were major discrepancies, they would matter only in the context of the old model of an internally consistent and monolithic Mithraic doctrine. In the end, I think, only the outdated preconceptions about the 'wise' and the 'vulgar' and the formers' monopoly on intelligence, which we exposed in the preceding chapter, prevent one from construing the *De antro*'s Mithraic data at face value. Mithraic concepts in the *De antro* are polarized into binary pairs because that was the way they were formulated in the Mithraic mysteries, not because Porphyry and his philosophical sources twisted them into that shape for allegorical ends.

6

Cognition and Representation

1. THE COGNITIVE APPROACH: ONTOGENETIC/ PHYLOGENETIC VERSUS CULTURAL

It is sometimes difficult to date the arrival of a new method or approach in scholarship, but at least since the 1990s a new method focused on *cognition* has been available to scholars of religion—including, since it is not restricted as to date or culture, scholars of the religions of Graeco-Roman antiquity. The method originated in the cognitive sciences, in particular evolutionary psychology, and in anthropology. It is known as 'the cognitive science of religion' (Andresen 2001*a*, *b*). I shall speak of it here simply as the 'cognitive method/approach' and of scholars and scholarship that take it as 'cognitivist'.

The cognitive method is a powerful *explanatory* tool. It is not, and does not claim to be, *interpretive*. We will not understand Mithraism *qua Mithraism* any the better for using it, but we may understand better how the Mithraic mysteries functioned *qua religion*.

Cognitivist scholarship tends towards radical reductionism: to explain is to explain away.[1] I see no heuristic benefit in making that larger negative claim. Whether the representation-forming minds of Mithraists—or, for that matter, of Christians or Muslims—touched on some otherworldly reality seems to me, in a secular academic context, as idle to deny as to affirm. The cognitive method need not be forced to answer ontological questions at a metaphysical level; sufficient that it addresses, and addresses well, the modal question of *how* the human mind forms and organizes 'religious' ideas in the here and now.

The human mind forms—and, as far back as the record shows, always has formed—representations of supernatural beings. This is not a necessary activity of the mind, for one can get through life without it, but it is certainly a very common activity.

Not all representations of supernatural beings are 'religious', in the sense of belonging to that domain of life which we label 'religion'. Nor do all religious representations necessarily involve supernatural beings. Nevertheless, there is a

---

[1] Notably S. E. Guthrie (1993, 1997).

high degree of coincidence: more often than not, the mental representation of supernatural beings is a vital part of practising a religion. Certainly, that was so for the religions current in classical antiquity. Paganism was literally unthinkable without the mental representation of the Olympian and other gods; likewise Judaism without representation of Jahweh, or Christianity without the additional representation of Jesus as the Christ. And so Mithraism: to be a Mithraist, one must have (or feign having) Mithras 'in mind'.

While there is little religious thought that does not in a primary or secondary way involve supernatural beings, the human mind does construct and entertain representations of innumerable supernatural and paranatural beings entirely outside the religious domain. Folk tale and fantasy literature abound with inventions of this sort, whose connection with 'religion' is tenuous or nonexistent. And that is precisely the point. Except in the degree of ontological commitment, there is no essential difference between an ancient Athenian's representation of Pallas Athena or an ancient Roman's of Jupiter Optimus Maximus and a twenty-first-century person's representations of wizards, elves, orcs, and dementors *à la* J. R. R. Tolkien or J. K. Rowling.

The first achievement of the cognitive approach is thus to strip away the special status of 'religious' representations of supernatural beings, and consequently to de-mystify and de-problematize them. The ability to form mental representations of supernatural and paranatural beings is simply part of the evolved mental endowment of the species *Homo sapiens*. As a further consequence, the cognitive approach radically redefines the 'why' questions: why religion, why the gods? Granted our *natural* propensity to entertain representations of the non-natural, it is not the presence of the gods in our minds that requires explanation so much as their expulsion in relatively recent times; not 'why religion?' but rather 'why religion no longer?' As the cognitivists emphasize, religion is 'natural', science is not (McCauley 2000).

The second achievement of the cognitive approach is to divert part of the inquiry into religion from the socio-cultural level both upwards to the phylo-genetic and downwards to the ontogenetic. We form representations of supernatural beings not by virtue of membership in societies and cultures but by virtue of membership in the species *Homo sapiens*. Our particular societies and cultures shape and standardize our representations, conforming them to the various explicit traditions current and licensed in our various times and places. But it is we who construct the gods, not 'society', not 'culture'; and 'we' means the human mind functioning in the human brain. Hence the reorientation of the inquiry from society or culture to the individual and the species.[2]

At first glance this reorientation might seem to doom any project directed towards an ancient, dead religion. How can we possibly access the representations of minds long dead and gone? It is precisely here, however, that evolutionary

---

[2] For an overview of this new approach, see Tooby and Cosmides 1992.

theory comes to the rescue. Societies may come and go, cultures may change with
great rapidity, but the adaptive changes which significantly modify a species are
measured at the least in tens of millennia, not mere centuries. Evolutionary
science postulates no change in the human brain and mind which would have
rendered them markedly different now from what they were and how they
functioned in classical antiquity. Quite the contrary, we may safely assume that
we form our representations of supernatural beings, to all intents and purposes,
just as the ancients did. Any adaptive changes, so cognitive theory argues, took
place in earlier and far longer epochs as our remote ancestors passed through
the hunter-gatherer phase, and they took place in response to the exigencies of the
hunter-gatherers' environment. They occurred because they gave those hunter-
gatherers with these adaptations a competitive and reproductive edge over those
without. This is not to say that the capacity (and neural circuitry) for imagining
supernatural beings itself conferred a competitive edge, merely that it cannot
be a recent acquisition, something which radically differentiates us from our
conspecifics a score of centuries ago.

Same brain, same mind. Consequently, one may argue with some confidence
from the way we form 'religious' representations now to the way the ancients
formed them then. Given the comparatively rapid and radical shifts of culture,
we are actually on much firmer ground with the phylogenetic and the ontogenetic than with the socio-cultural.

While a comprehensive solution to the mind–body problem still eludes both
scientists and philosophers (is it even in principle attainable?), much is now
known about the neural processes in the brain which accompany various mental
states and events. This now opens up, for the first time, the possibility of
correlating what happens in the brain with what happens subjectively in the
mind of someone undergoing a religious experience. We shall touch on some of
this research later, but since it mostly involves unusual states of consciousness
(e.g. meditation, ecstasy), we shall pass it by for now and return to the more
pedestrian topic of the mind's representation of supernatural beings. Here one
may surely assume that just as there is nothing distinctively 'religious' about the
mental event of forming representations of beings not normally encountered in
the natural world, so the concomitant neural events do not differ, or do not
necessarily differ, according to whether or not the representations belong to the
subject's religious world. Different neuronal groups do not fire in different ways
whenever the mind is, as it were, 'doing religion'. The human brain has no
dedicated circuits for religion or 'the sacred'.

The topic of cognition in the religious domain is caught up in a much wider
debate taking place in the social sciences and in those disciplines, particularly
psychology and anthropology, which straddle the boundary between the life
sciences and the social sciences. The debate is about the acquisition and location
of 'culture'. Are cultural systems, of which religions constitute a particular form,
downloaded in a process of teaching and learning as content into an originally

content-free human mind/brain? Or is the human mind/brain already endowed with systems—software running on 'wetware', as the saying goes—selected in and by the evolutionary process, which form representations *modified, not created*, by interaction with conspecifics in a particular society and culture?

I incline to the latter scenario. Fortunately, a concise summary of its underlying model already exists in the introductory essay to a volume of studies by some of its leading proponents (Tooby and Cosmides, in Barkow *et al.* 1992: 24). These cognitivists call it the 'Integrated Causal Model' (ICM). I quote their summary:

a. the human mind consists of a set of evolved information-processing mechanisms instantiated in the human nervous system;[3]

b. these mechanisms, and the developmental programs that produce them, are adaptations produced by natural selection over evolutionary time in ancestral environments;

c. many of these mechanisms are functionally specialized to produce behavior that solves particular adaptive problems, such as mate selection, language acquisition, family relations, and cooperation;

d. to be functionally specialized, many of these mechanisms must be richly structured in a content-specific way;

e. content-specific information-processing mechanisms generate some of the peculiar content of human culture, including certain behaviors, artifacts, and linguistically transmitted representations;

f. the cultural content generated by these and other mechanisms is then present to be adopted or modified by psychological mechanisms situated in other members of the population;

g. this sets up epidemiological and historical population-level processes; and

h. these processes are located in particular ecological, economic, demographic, and intergroup social contexts or environments.

To understand what is new and different about the ICM, we should also look at the traditional model which the ICM challenges and aims to supplant. This 'Standard Social Science Model' (SSSM—again the term is that of the cognitivists), is likewise conveniently summarized by Tooby and Cosmides (1992: 31 f.). Though they are of course opposed to this model, their summary of it is fair and untendentious. I quote the first seven propositions (abbreviating where feasible without loss of substance).[4] They convey the implicit assumptions which usually underlie inquiries, such as ours, into cultural phenomena. These are cards which ought to be on the table, but seldom are:

1. Particular human groups are properly characterized typologically as having 'a' culture, which consists of widely distributed . . . behavioral practices, beliefs, ideation

---

[3] In this sort of context, 'nervous system' includes, but is not limited to, the brain (my footnote).
[4] The remaining four propositions (8–11) in effect elaborate the first seven. Though useful, they can be omitted here without prejudice to the SSSM or to its alternative, the ICM.

systems, systems of significant symbols, or informational substance of some kind. Cultures are more or less bounded entities, although cultural elements may diffuse across boundaries.

2. These common elements are maintained and transmitted 'by the group', an entity that has cross-generational continuity.

3. The existence of separate streams of . . . culture . . . is the explanation for human within-group similarities and between-group differences. In fact, all between-group differences . . . are referred to as cultural differences and all within-group similarities are regarded as the expressions of a particular culture. . . .

4. Unless other factors intervene, the culture . . . is accurately replicated from generation to generation.

5. This process is maintained through learning, a well-understood and unitary process.

6. This process of learning can be seen . . . as a group-organized process called social-ization, imposed by the group on the child.

7. The individual is the more or less passive recipient of her culture and is the product of that culture.

What difference does it make in practice that we adopt the 'integrated causal model' (ICM) rather than the 'standard social science model' (SSSM) for our inquiry into the Mithraic mysteries? We are already committed, by placing ourselves in the Geertzian symbolist tradition,[5] to treating the Mithraic mysteries as a cultural system, which would seem to position us more comfortably in the SSSM camp. Of course, the ICM does not preclude treating religion as a cultural system (propositions 'f' through 'h'); so our question is rather, what advantage does the ICM confer over the SSSM?

At one level the answer is, none at all. When, for descriptive purposes, we uncouple the mysteries from their actual initiates, it makes sense to treat them as an autonomous cultural system, or more precisely as a subsystem of the wider culture of Graeco-Roman paganism. This we did in our 'template for the re-description of the mysteries' presented in Chapter 1 (sect. 3), where the propositions were stated in alternative forms: 'the first line [in each proposition] repre-sents the mysteries as an autonomous system acting on the initiate; the second . . . from the initiate's point of view as something apprehended and accepted.'

Clearly the first of the alternative forms coheres better with the 'standard social scientific model' and the second with the 'integrated causal model'. Since, as I have already stated, our ultimate quarry is the initiates' *apprehension* of their mysteries (qua symbol system) rather than the mysteries *per se*, the ICM will be my preferred model both over the longer haul and especially in the present chapter in which I focus on cognition.

---

[5] Above, Ch. 1, sects. 1–2.

2. GODS IN MIND: COGNITION AND THE REPRESENTATION OF SUPERNATURAL BEINGS

Perhaps the best application to date of the cognitivist approach to religion, and certainly one of the most accessible, is Pascal Boyer's *Religion Explained* (2001). We shall accordingly hew quite closely to his model of religion in tracing the mental representations of an initiate of the Mithraic mysteries. Remember, as we do so, that the sole and sufficient warrant for this seemingly audacious project is the general evolutionist postulate that the lapsed time between Mithraists and moderns is simply too short for the brains and minds of our species to have undergone adaptations significant enough to render invalid extrapolations from 'mind doing religion now' to 'mind doing religion then'. Because of this we are at no insurmountable disadvantage to Boyer and other cognitivists who treat of contemporary religion and have access to contemporary minds by way of psychological, sociological, and ethnographic research.

To the diachronic postulate of the sameness of the brain/mind now and two millennia ago must be added a synchronic postulate: that there is no essential difference in the way in which believers and non-believers construct mental representations of supernatural beings. The *content and associations* of a Persian's, a Roman's, and a Christian's representations of Mithras no doubt differed, and all these certainly differed from a modern historian of religion's representations of Mithras, but the mental and underlying neural *processes* of representation did not and do not differ.

The cognitive approach, we have already seen, locates a religion in the representation-forming minds of those who adhere to it, whether actively or passively. As humans we all form representations of beings which do not exist in the natural world, at least in a normal, empirically testable way. Such representations are for the most part evanescent. Some representations, however, because they are conformable to the representations of others in the same socio-cultural group, are preserved, fostered, and modified by the interaction of mind with mind; also of mind with the projections of mind in the actual world: text, creed, artistic representations, mimetic ritual, and so on. Very occasionally, a new religion is born, or an old religion substantially modified, when the novel representations of a single mind, then of the minds of a small founding group, successfully commend themselves over wider and wider circles, and the apparatus of the religion, in whatever form is deemed necessary or appropriate, is constructed in the common objective world.[6] A religion dies when no one remains to energize its outward forms and, more fundamentally, to make its subjective representations within the context of those outward forms. Because they exist

---

[6] Boyer 2001: 46–7. Dan Sperber (1996) treats cultures, and a fortiori religions, as epidemics of mental representations. He intends 'epidemics' literally, not metaphorically.

in the external, objective, common world, the forms linger on in the fossilized record of text and artefact. From the record we seek to recapture, as far as an external inquirer can, something of the mental representations that were the living religion.

To avoid over-privileging religion or 'religious' representations, we should recall that the very same mental processes create and perpetuate representations of make-believe beings, whether natural or supernatural, in the domain of art, both visual and verbal. Sir John Falstaff, inanimate in Shakespeare's text, lives on in the representation-forming minds of audiences and readers, as do the aforementioned wizards, elves, orcs, and dementors of Tolkien and Rowling. Thus too have the Olympian immortals fled mortality by migrating to the aesthetic domain—where of course they were always at home: a consideration which merely returns us to our postulate that the process of forming representations of the gods did not—and does not—vary; regardless of whether those forming the representations were witnessing a sacrifice in some ancient community, a tragedy in fifth-century BCE Athens, or a pantomime in first-century CE Rome.

Religion, then, exists in, and consists of, a ferment of representations in the minds of its living adherents. From the general to the particular, it follows that the Mithraic mysteries were the mental representations of successive generations of initiates in their far-flung 'caves' and autonomous brotherhoods throughout the Roman empire.

3. NEGOTIATING REPRESENTATIONS

Adopting a cognitive approach and locating 'religion' in the minds of its adherents pays two rich and immediate dividends. First, the cognitive model accommodates well the rather fluid concept of doctrine which I proposed towards the end of Chapter 4: 'In place of doctrine as a definite body of explicit teaching, we have re-characterized it as a loose web of interpretation, both actual and potential, located in the symbol system of the mysteries' (sect. 12); alternatively, as 'an indeterminate set of explanations which senior Mithraists would impart to their juniors or explore among themselves' (sect. 10). From a cognitive perspective, then, doctrine is *that which within the given religious group is negotiated (or negotiable) concerning legitimate representations.* As we said above (preceding section) of humanity's propensity for forming mental representations of supernatural beings, 'some representations . . . because they are conformable to the representations of others in the same socio-cultural group, are preserved, fostered, and modified by the interaction of mind with mind; also of mind with the projections of mind in the actual world: text, creed, artistic representations, mimetic ritual, and so on.'

Legitimate representations can—but need not necessarily—be negotiated explicitly and by formal process. They are thereby reified—and sanctified—in creeds, catechisms, canons of scripture, and the like. This was the road taken by Christianity. Mithraism followed another and less divisive road: from the overall conformity of its mithraea and figured monuments to certain norms, one may infer that it managed to maintain a coherence of mental representation without resort to explicit doctrinal formulations. Creeds and the like, once formulated, objectify and sanctify doctrine, and so make it something to defend and police, a criterion for inclusion and exclusion. It may be (though I doubt it) for want of extant evidence, but it seems improbable that there were Mithraic heretics. 'Heresy' and the odium which attaches to it only become possible when there is an 'orthodoxy' to measure it against.

It is hermeneutically liberating to shake off the task of reconstructing an explicit but no longer extant Mithraic doctrine; likewise the task of rebutting the opposite but more insidious charge that Mithraism, lacking formulated doctrine, was for that reason a second-class or inferior religion. If anything, its coherent yet unprescribed way of normalizing the mental representations of its initiates seems, if not more sophisticated, at least more admirable. It is certainly more irenic.

The cognitive approach compels us to interpret and explain the mysteries always in terms of *actual* on-the-ground Mithraism. We focus not on an abstracted system (although for descriptive purposes one must sometimes treat it as such), but on those interactive processes of mental representation by which successive cohorts of initiates in their autonomous 'caves' apprehended and communicated their mysteries. These surely are the *hyponoiai*, the 'under-thoughts' which, as we saw in Chapter 4 (sect. 10), Plutarch so perceptively listed together with the 'images' (*eikones*) and 'imitations' (*mimēmata*) as the gifts of another mystery-cult deity to her initiates.

As a benign consequence, much that was in dispute can now be deproblema-tized. For instance, the issue of 'generalizing about Mithraic doctrine from unusual monuments' which we addressed in Chapter 4 (sect. 9) becomes less urgent. We still want to explore whether or not an unusual monumental feature points to a more widespread element in Mithraic thought, but whether it is orthodox or heterodox is not at issue. First and foremost, it is the product of negotiation, explicit or tacit, between the representation-forming minds of those particular initiates in that particular group. It is what *they* thought consonant with their mysteries then and there. We return to our point that Mithraic doctrine is whatever accords with what a Mithraic Father thinks is Mithraic doctrine. Since there was no overarching objectified code to which appeal could be made, merely norms perpetuated for the most part in iconography and the design of sacred space, there was little constraint on innovation. The surprise is not the occasional variant, but the unpoliced integrity, amounting almost to unanimity, of the mysteries over such an expanse of time and territory.

The cognitive approach also lets us deproblematize what appear to be doctrinal contradictions. For example, I have referred to the paradox that Mithras both is and is not the Sun: is, because the Unconquered Sun is his cult title; is not, because Sol is a separate person in certain episodes (notably, the banquet following the bull-killing) in which the two deities participate. Cognitive theory predicts, and can demonstrate experimentally, the generation of such contradictions in the formation and transmission of religious concepts (Boyer 2001: 78–89).[7] Although their contents may defy logic, their genesis in the mental representation of supernatural beings is a normal enough process psychologically. Consequently, while they may be described and explored, there is nothing to explain or resolve—unless the religious group itself chooses to problematize the paradox, as Christianity notoriously has done with, for example, the dual nature of Christ.

4. REINTEGRATING THE WISE AND THE VULGAR

Now to the second dividend paid by the cognitive approach. Here I shall risk a value-judgement. To some extent I have already done so, in that I have suggested that Mithraism, in eschewing explicit doctrine and yet successfully transmitting doctrinal norms by instantiation in the symbol complexes of its monuments, was in this regard superior to Christianity. That judgement entailed of course a more general judgement about the baleful effect of formulated doctrine as a cause of discord—and worse. If you consider explicit doctrine benign or at least harmless, my claim for Mithraism's superiority will not have been persuasive.

Now, however, I make a larger claim, not for the mysteries of Mithras but for the paradigm of religion which the cognitive approach implies. In locating 'religion' in the representation-forming minds of its adherents, the cognitive approach emphasizes its creative and egalitarian strain.

That assertion might surprise both the cognitivists and their opponents. The cognitive approach is necessarily associated with evolutionary psychology. We form our representations as we do because the minds/brains of our hunter-gatherer ancestors evolved as they did. So we are prisoners of the mental/neural adaptations they underwent, doomed to repeat their thinking and behaviour until our post-Neolithic age has clocked sufficient tens of millennia to generate and select for further mind/brain adaptations more suited to an environment which will then itself be slipping inexorably into the irrelevance of the past.

---

[7] Note the experiment (p. 88) in which a group of subjects was asked first to read stories about an omnipotent and omnipresent god who (e.g.) saves a man's life and *simultaneously* helps a woman find her lost purse, and then to retell the stories. Without giving up the divine attributes of omnipotence and omnipresence, 'many subjects said that God had helped one person out *and then* [italics in original] turned his attention to the other's plight'. The observed effect was the same with believers and non-believers and in India and the USA. (Not without interest is the gender stereotyping both of God and of his imagined beneficiaries, so easy is it to represent a male god and a female human losing her purse.)

This gloomy scenario may be countered in one of two ways. Opponents of evolutionary psychology reply that because we have reached a level at which we can communicate and store information transgenerationally, societal evolution has more or less replaced biological evolution and so emancipated our species from the snail's pace of the latter. A better response, so it seems to me at least, is to retain evolutionary psychology's model, since it is supported by a growing body of hard neurological evidence, but to set aside the entailment of determinism with which it is invested. That our brain/mind adaptations were selected for in our hunter-gatherer ancestors manifestly does not condemn our inference systems, thus evolved, to think only hunter-gatherer thoughts and to solve only hunter-gatherer problems until at long last natural selection rolls out a phenotype better adapted to its environment.

Let us then postulate a measure of individual human autonomy within the broad scenario modelled by evolutionary psychology. There is no contradiction, unless one is committed a priori to determinism as a universal principle.

Evolutionary psychology's theory of mind frees us from another and more insidious tyranny, *societal* determinism. This you may readily appreciate by reviewing the two models, 'Integrated Causal' and 'Standard Social Science', presented earlier in this chapter. It is of course true that we are largely conditioned by and into our social systems—what else, after all, is education? But that we are entirely the product of these systems, that our minds are virtually empty slates on which our cultures inscribe themselves, this we need not—indeed should not—accept; for psychological research shows otherwise.

A religion, then, while it lives, is a dialogue of minds: admittedly, a lopsided dialogue in which the voice of authority preponderates, whether the actual voices of leaders and exegetes or the recorded and materialized voices of sacred text, creed, liturgy, artefact, and so on; but a dialogue nonetheless, because the representation-forming minds of the led are as necessary to it as the representation-forming minds of the leaders.

Our cognitive approach focuses, in an egalitarian way, on individual minds calibrating their representations in negotiation, mostly below the level of conscious intent, with other minds in the culture and environment of Mithraism—which itself is the product or instantiation of those negotiated representations. In so doing, we return some measure of agency to the rank and file, breaking the mortmain on the mysteries assigned to the 'wise' in antiquity and in modern times to the system itself as socio-cultural construct. We return ownership, not of course to the led alone, but to the members, the 'hand-claspers' (*syndexioi*), each in his proper status, gathered in their 'caves'.

I take this position not just to indulge a sentimental egalitarianism, but to correct a 'folk theory of mind'[8] which lurks unexamined among the learned,

---

[8] I use the term in its technical sense of a non-specialist commonsensical set of working assumptions about the way other minds—and by inference one's own—operate.

though fortunately less so now than in earlier generations. This folk theory of mind assumes that the less learned are substantially less sophisticated, less discriminating in their mental representations, than the more learned. As a purely aesthetic judgement about informed and uninformed taste, this is perhaps so; likewise as an intellectual judgement about understanding an argument and failing to understand an argument. But as a cognitive judgement about processes of representation and inference it is nonsense—and pernicious nonsense at that. In religion and in the study of religion, as we saw in Chapter 4, it licenses the spurious separation of the 'wise' and the 'vulgar' on which the ancients harped and a no less spurious *class* dichotomy which modern scholars of antiquity occasionally still apply.

In contrast, the cognitive approach adopted here treats religion in general, and of course 'mysteries' in particular, as works continuously in progress, re-created across the generations as their members, leaders and led alike, fashion their mental representations by interaction both with each other and with the religion's external memory archived in text, ritual, symbolic iconography, and so on. In this way the cognitive approach, as I claimed above, emphasizes that which in religion is creative and egalitarian.

As it happens, Mithraism towards the end of its historic lifespan furnishes an excellent example of a religion in which ownership, through an implicit claim to monopolize the agenda of representation, gravitated to the leadership. The lost set of inscriptions V400–5 from the S. Silvestro in Capite mithraeum in Rome records a series of grade initiations undertaken by two members of the pagan senatorial aristocracy, Nonius Victor Olympius and Aurelius Victor Augentius, between the years 357 and 376. The former was the latter's (biological) father; in the mysteries he held the rank of 'Father of Fathers' (*pater patrum*) and his son that of Father. By 376 Aurelius Victor Augentius had ascended to his father's rank, probably on the latter's death, since in the inscription of that year (V403) his father is not mentioned. What is so interesting about these inscriptions is what they do *not* say. There is no mention of Mithras, and there is no mention of those inducted into the various grades—with one exception: in 376 (V403) Aurelius Victor Augentius initiates *his 13-year-old son* Aemilianus Corfinius Olympius into the initial grade of Raven. Clearly, what the mysteries were largely 'about' for this noble family was the noble family itself, not Mithras, not the cult brothers, but themselves. What it was 'about' for the rank and file of this cult group, presumably composed largely of the family's clients and household, we can never know. But one may reasonably conjecture that appropriate representations of the patronal hierarchy were encouraged. This is not to say that the mysteries practised under this noble family's aegis were less genuine, less alive, than those of earlier times and other places. Rather, it is to infer from the evidence of surface symptoms a change in how the initiates represented the mysteries to themselves and each other.

APPENDIX: COMPREHENDING THE PANTOMIME: LUCIAN, *ON THE DANCE*

The capacity to form representations of non- or supernatural beings, we have accepted, is a constant of the human mind, and it does not operate exclusively in some special religious domain. As an example from antiquity I gave the audience's representation of supernatural beings at the pantomime in first-century CE Rome. The example of Roman pantomime was not chosen at random, for it also helps to give the lie to the assumption challenged in the preceding section: namely that cognition in the learned differs radically from, and is superior to, cognition in the unlearned. (To avoid confusion latent in the term 'representation', note that I am not of course talking about the artist's public and performative 'representation' of the supernatural being, but of the audience's inner mental representations prompted by the artist's representation in performance.)

The pantomime, as an art form in ancient Rome, was both hugely popular and very demanding on the audience because of the extreme artificiality of its conventions. To comprehend the pantomime, to 'get it', the audience had to run, simultaneously and subconsciously, an array of mental programs (to use the computing metaphor) to co-ordinate and translate into a unified and meaningful experience an audio-visual input quite remote from the input that they would receive if viewing/hearing the corresponding events in real time and real life. To the artificialities of other forms of ancient drama (principally tragedy and comedy) the pantomime added the convention of divorcing the spoken or sung word from the physical action, with the primary focus on the latter. The pantomime—the term properly belongs to the actor rather than the genre—conveyed the action by dance and gesture alone, accompanied by music. Words sung by a choir or spoken by a narrator were optional and strictly unnecessary in that to rely on them for communication of meaning would be considered an artistic failure. The pantomime was of course masked, and so could convey nothing by facial expression. Moreover, the acme of his art was the ability to carry *all* the roles sequentially, even of characters who in real time would be interacting concurrently.

The pantomime is irretrievably lost, since, unlike tragedy and comedy, such fragments of texts as have survived are obviously of slight importance to the art. We do, however, possess some testimony to the pantomime of much greater value to our present purpose: a comprehensive and intelligent critique of the pantomime as an art form, written while it was still performed. This work, composed as a dialogue, is entitled *On the dance* (*De saltatione*); it was written by Lucian, a satirical essayist of the second century CE. The work is particularly relevant to our present topic, for like much ancient criticism of drama it is more concerned with how the audience comprehends and responds to the performance than with a formal definition and description of the art.

Lucian makes it clear that the mass audience of the pantomime did indeed 'get it': that is, they reacted in a way that, to a cognitivist, shows that the inference and data-processing systems of their minds, operating for the most part below the conscious level, took the pantomime's highly complicated and unnaturalistic conventions in their stride. They translated effortlessly the stylized movements and gestures of a single silent performer into a sequence of meaningfully related interactions and verbal exchanges between a multi-plicity of persons. Lucian tells the story of an unnamed pantomime who in Nero's reign undertook to refute the charge that his art owed its success solely to the accessories ('the silk vestments, the beautiful mask, the flute and its quavers, and the sweet voices of the singers') by performing without music and chorus:

Enjoining silence upon the stampers and flute-players and upon the chorus itself, quite unsupported, he danced the amours of Aphrodite and Ares, Helius tattling, Hephaestus laying his plot and trapping both of them with his entangling bonds, the gods who came in on them, portrayed individually, Aphrodite ashamed, Ares seeking cover and begging for mercy... (*De salt.* 63, Loeb trans.)

The challenger, a Cynic philosopher named Demetrius, withdrew the charge, shouting to the pantomime still on stage: 'I *hear* the story that you are acting, man, I do not just see it; you seem to me to be talking with your hands!' The point, for us, is that Demetrius now 'gets' and verbalizes what the groundlings have 'got' or apprehended all along.

Lucian has much to say about the way in which ordinary people respond to the pantomime, particularly about their emotional responses, of which he—or perhaps we should say, the speaker whom he privileges in the dialogue—generally approves, thus accepting the moral and educative value of the performance (*De salt.* 72, 79, 81). People weep when they rightly should, and they feel and express indignation when they rightly should. This, of course, they can only do if they have comprehended the intent of the highly abstracted and artificial show which their eyes and ears have taken in. Successful cognition is the necessary precondition for appropriate affective response.

Another indication of successful cognition among the groundlings can be seen in their banter with the performers. Again, Lucian (or his dialogue persona) treats this not censoriously but positively as a form of popular quality control by which 'entire peoples' (*holoi dēmoi*)—he is speaking here specifically of the Antiochenes—'regulate (*rhythmizein*) its [i.e. the dance's] good and bad points'. The examples he gives seem quite trivial:

When a diminutive dancer made his entrance and began to play Hector, they all cried out in a single voice, 'Ho there, Astyanax! where's Hector?' On another occasion, when a man who was extremely tall undertook to dance Capaneus and assault the walls of Thebes, 'Step over the wall', they said, 'you have no need of a ladder!' (*De salt.* 76, Loeb trans.)

However, for all their simplicity, these and other examples indicate a high level of cognitive sophistication. Together, the anecdotes demonstrate the audience's ability not only to comprehend the performance but also to discriminate consciously between that which is represented in performance and the performative representation. They heckle because they can detect, and consciously represent to themselves, an amusing dissonance between character and actor. Metatheatricality, it seems, was well understood by the dregs of the Orontes, and presumably of the Tiber too. To reach that level of conscious appreciation, the mind—of the learned and unlearned alike—must first have developed a massive capacity for complicated feats of cognition below the threshold of reflective consciousness.

I offer one final example of audience response, because Lucian uses it to contrast the reaction of the vulgar with the reaction of the refined. It is the story of a pantomime who got carried away by his own performance of the mad Ajax:

He tore the clothes off one of the men who beat time with the iron shoe, and snatching a flute from one of the accompanists, with a vigorous blow he cracked the crown of Odysseus, who was standing near exulting in his victory. . . . [9] Coming down among the public, he seated himself among the senators, between two ex-consuls, who were very much afraid that he would seize one of them and drub him, taking him for a wether. (*De salt.* 83, Loeb trans.)

The crowd, as the saying goes, went wild, 'leaping, and shouting and flinging up their garments'. Lucian (or his dialogue persona) treats it as a case of triple madness: the actor, miming the madness of Ajax, goes mad himself, and the 'riff-raff and absolutely unenlightened (*surphetōdeis kai . . . idiōtai*) went mad along with him (*synememēnei*)'. However, Lucian has already said far too much to make this diagnosis credible, for all that it is rhetorically effective and conforms to class stereotypes. More likely, the groundlings comprehended the actor's transgression of performative boundaries just as well as did the 'politer sort' (*asteioteroi*) who Lucian says 'understood and were ashamed', covering their embarrassment with lukewarm applause rather than stony silence. The vulgar, I suggest, understood the transgression perfectly well; they thoroughly enjoyed it and entered into its spirit. If 'Ajax' could break convention and export his madness into the real world, then the audience could reciprocate from the real world by 'madly' entering the performance. The audience didn't *go* mad with Ajax, they *played* mad with 'Ajax'.

[9] This performance clearly involved more than a single dancer.

7

The Mithraic Mysteries as Symbol System:
II. The Mithraeum

1. THE SYMBOL COMPLEX OF THE MITHRAEUM AS 'IMAGE OF THE UNIVERSE'

As we saw in Chapter 5, the Graeco-Roman model of the universe instantiates, in the broadly Platonic tradition to which the Mithraic mysteries belonged, a hierarchy of binary oppositions such as we find in *De antro* 29. The Mithraists replicated this model of the universe by designing their meeting places as authentic microcosms, models in the literal, physical sense of the word. We know this of course from our 'gateway text', Porphyry's *De antro* 6:[1]

Similarly, the Persians call the place a cave where they introduce an initiate to the mysteries, revealing to him the path by which souls descend and go back again. For Eubulus tells us that Zoroaster was the first to dedicate a natural cave in honour of Mithras, the creator and father of all; it was located in the mountains near Persia and had flowers and springs. This cave bore for him the image of the Cosmos (*eikona kosmou*) which Mithras had created, and the things which the cave contained, by their proportionate arrangement, provided him with symbols of the elements and climates of the Cosmos (*tōn d' entos kata symmetrous apostaseis symbola pherontōn tōn kosmikōn stoicheiōn kai klimatōn*). After Zoroaster others adopted the custom of performing their rites of initiation in caves and grottoes which were either natural or artificial. (trans. Arethusa edn.)

There are surely few religions for which we are told so succinctly the esoteric name, the form, the design principle, the function, and the postulated origin of their sacred space. More to the present purpose, we are also told that the effectiveness of the Mithraists' 'cave' as an instrument for getting the initiates from heaven to earth and back again depends on *symbolic* authenticity. It is because its complex of symbols is 'proportionately arranged' that the mithraeum is an accurate 'likeness of the cosmos' and so can realize its ritual intent.

---

[1] See the opening sections of Chs. 2 and 4, above.

2. THE BLUEPRINT FOR THE MITHRAEUM

In this chapter I shall sketch out the design of the Mithraic 'cave' as 'cosmic model'. There is no need to do this at any great length, for I have described the blueprint in earlier studies (Beck 1994*a*; 2000: 158–63).[2] The 'blueprint', both as diagram (see Figs. 2 and 3) and as description, is a reconstruction of an ideal mithraeum based on data from Porphyry's *De antro* and actual mithraea, notably the Ostian Mithraeum of the Seven Spheres ('Sette Sfere', V239–49). By 'ideal mithraeum' I mean just that; I do not mean the mithraeum that all mithraea should have been but, with the exception of Sette Sfere, failed to be.

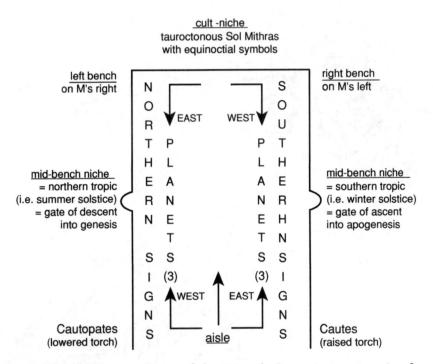

Fig. 2. The mithraeum as 'image of the universe'. Composite reconstruction from Porphyry, *De antro nympharum* (esp. 6 and 24) and excavated sites, principally the Mithraeum of the Seven Spheres, Ostia

---

[2] See also Gordon 1976*a*; 1988: 50–60. There is thus no need to redeploy the supporting argumentation or once again to justify my reliance on Porphyry's input.

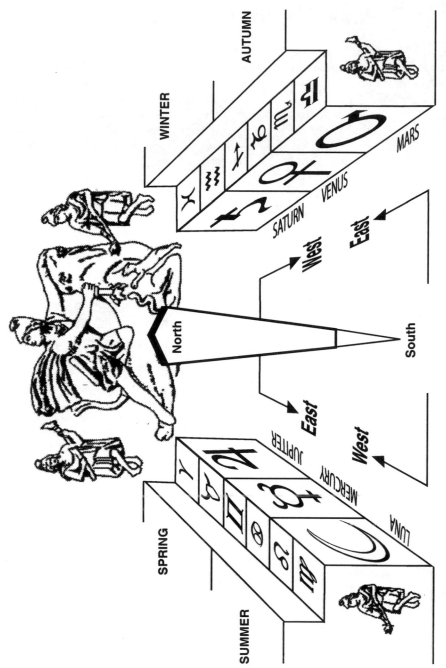

Fig. 3. The Mithraeum of the Seven Spheres (Sette Sfere), Ostia, with symbols substituted for the images of the planets and signs of the zodiac

The mithraeum is 'structure D2' in our 'template for the redescription of the mysteries' (Chapter 1):

D1. The complexes of symbols conveying the axioms and motifs of the mysteries in their various domains are manifested concretely...

D2. The initiate apprehends the symbol complexes conveying the axioms and motifs of the mysteries in their various domains...

on structured sites; in the mysteries there are three principal and distinctive structures:

1. the physical structure of the icon of the tauroctony
2. *the physical structure of the mithraeum*
3. the organizational structure of the seven grades

1. The mithraeum, as also the tauroctony, is a *necessary* structure. No mithraeum, no Mysteries of Mithras.

2. As Porphyry correctly reports, all mithraea are 'caves', both in nomenclature and intent. Where feasible they were sited in natural caves. They are 'caves' in conformity with the ancient trope 'cave = universe'.

3. As to shape, the most faithful model of the universe would be a dome replicating the celestial sphere (as most obviously in a modern planetarium). Domed structures however are relatively expensive. Consequently, cosmic models of this sort tend to be large public structures such as the Pantheon, which Dio (53.27.2) thought was 'domed so as to resemble the heavens' (*tholoeides on tōi ouranōi proseoiken*). The Mithraists of course were not in that league. They had to be content with rectangular rooms, as often as not recycled from some other function. Fortunately, barrel vaulting in the lower levels of multipurpose buildings provided a cave-like curvature in cross-section which would intimate the vault of heaven. Important 'caves' of this type include the Caesarea mithraeum (Bull 1978), the mithraeum at S. Maria Capua Vetere (V180, Vermaseren 1971), the Marino mithraeum (Vermaseren 1982); in Rome the San Clemente (V338), Barberini (V389), Thermae Antoninianae (V 457), and Sta Prisca (V476) mithraea; and in Ostia the Terme del Mitra (V 229) and 'di Fructosus' (V 226) mithraea. Apart from affordability, a rectangular room has the great advantage that it allows the designer to display cosmic polarities by means of the room's opposite sides and ends.

4. An appropriate shape and 'proportionate arrangement' within generate for the mithraeum the vital quality of *epitēdeiotēs* = 'fitness', 'suitability', 'functionality'. *Epitēdeiotēs* is defined in this illuminating passage from Sallustius (*De diis et mundo* 15, trans. Nock): 'The providence of the gods stretches everywhere and needs only *fitness* for its enjoyment (*hypodochēn*). Now all fitness is produced by imitation and likeness (*mimēsei kai homoiotēti*). That is why temples are a copy of (*mimountai*) heaven, altars of earth, images of life...' Interestingly, our 'gateway text' from *De antro* 6 continues in much the same vein: 'Just as they consecrated to the Olympian gods temples, shrines and altars, to terrestrial deities and heroes sacrificial hearths, and to the gods of the underworld ritual pits or trenches, so

they dedicated caves and grottoes to the Cosmos.' 'Imitation and likeness' are clearly the key to 'fitness'. But fitness for what? To function, surely. And the function of the Mithraic 'cave' = cosmos is to get the initiates in and out, down and up again along the route of souls.

5. The Mithraic 'cave' is indefinitely replicable.[3] No mithraeum, as far as we know, is any more special or authentic than any other mithraeum, except of course the mithraeum that never was, Zoroaster's cave 'in the mountains near Persia'. Put another way, there is no unique or proper place on earth to worship Mithras and to perform his mysteries. How could there be, when the entire universe is his creation and the 'cave' where he is worshipped *is* the universe?

6. A cave is an appropriate image of the universe because, like the universe, it is an inside without an outside. That is why, ideologically at least, the exterior of a mithraeum, in dramatic contrast to the exteriors of standard Greek and Roman temples, does not matter. Literally, it does not signify. Economic considerations no doubt played their part, but in an urban context an anonymous room or suite of rooms makes good symbolic sense.

6.1. To point up the paradox of containing a symbol of the universe within something that is necessarily less than the universe, the Mithraists designed—though not as a conscious exercise—what one might call 'the Marino experience'. Marino is a small town in the Alban Hills. The mithraeum there is a cave bored deep into the hillside below.[4] As you move down the entrance ramp and into the unusually long (29.2 m) and narrow (3.1 m) cult room, your focus of attention is of course the tauroctony, here painted, as in the Capua and Barberini mithraea, on the end wall. The bull-killing, as is normal in the media of fresco and relief sculpture, takes place within a cave. At Marino the cave is represented carefully and naturalistically. So at the heart of the actual cavern which is also an esoteric 'cave' qua image of the universe you confront another cave in two-dimensional representation. By the inexorable logic of the symbolism which here holds sway this cave too must be a universe—a universe inside a universe. But that is not the end of it, for as your eye is drawn inwards into the scene within this painted cosmic cave you see yet another universe; and this final inmost universe is not a cave, not a symbol, but the real thing—or as close to the real thing as a two-dimensional painted representation can get. As is usual, Mithras' cloak is shown billowing out behind him as if in a strong wind,[5] revealing the cloak's lining. But

---

[3] On replicability see Smith 1987: 74–95 (the chapter of *To Take Place* nicely entitled 'To replace').

[4] The Marino mithraeum is the subject of a monograph by M. J. Vermaseren (1982). See in particular plate I, a view back up the aisle towards the entrance ramp, and the fold-out diagram at the end, showing (fig. 5) the floor plan and longitudinal and latitudinal cross-sections with an analogous diagram (fig. 6) for the Barberini mithraeum (V389).

[5] Vermaseren 1982: pls. III and IV. The intent of this convention is not, I think, to suggest that there happened to be a strong wind blowing on the day of the bull-killing, but to convey the impression of cosmic motion. Appearances to the contrary, DEUS SOL INVICTUS MITHRAS rushes through space and so creates both Space and Time.

that lining is no piece of fabric. In fact it is no thing at all; rather it is an emptiness, a transparency, a window on a field of stars. Six out of the array of stars are distinguished by their size and brilliance. Clearly the planets are intended, the missing seventh, the Sun, being Sol Mithras who wears the cloak. The stars spill out over Mithras' tunic, giving the god a peculiar transparency, as if he belongs both in the universe of the painted cave and in the universe of stars and planets framed by the cloak—which of course he does because the universe at all levels is his. In sum, a painted universe of stars and planets, its sphericity emphasized by lightly brushed arcs of blue and gold, is nested within a painted image of the universe, the cave which frames the scene of the bull-killing, which in turn is nested in a three-dimensional image of the universe, the symbolic Mithraic 'cave' which in this instance is a real physical cave deep within the earth. The moral? The inside is ampler than the outside; the contained contains the container; *totum pro toto.*

7. The key to the design of the mithraeum's interior is Porphyry *De antro* 24:

[A.] To Mithras, as his proper seat, they assigned the equinoxes.

[B.] Thus he carries the knife of Aries, the sign of Mars, and is borne on the bull of Venus; Libra is also the sign of Venus, like Taurus.

[C.] As creator and master of genesis, Mithras is set on the equator with the northern signs on his right and the southern signs to his left.

[D.] They set Cautes to the south because of its heat and Cautopates to the north because of the coldness of its wind.

7.1. Proposition 'B' gives two iconographic 'facts' about the composition of the tauroctony which validate Proposition 'A' concerning Mithras' cosmic setting. The logic is that of astrological 'star-talk' and has to do with the system of planetary 'houses'.[6] Proposition 'C' expands on 'A', again by star-talk logic: to the placement of Mithras is added his orientation there. Proposition 'D', adding the setting of the auxiliary torch-bearing deities Cautes and Cautopates, is validated not by star-talk logic but by the logic of terrestrial geography.[7]

8. In the macrocosm Mithras commands the celestial equator, the great circle which separates the northern celestial hemisphere from the southern, and the equinoxes, the points at which the equator intersects the ecliptic, the path of the Sun's annual journey. If you wish to envisage Mithras enthroned on his 'proper seat' (*oikeian kathedran*), imagine him at the spring equinox facing inwards across the universe to the autumn equinox diametrically opposite. The ecliptic with the northern signs (Aries, Taurus, etc.) curves upwards to his right; the southern signs (in reverse order: Pisces, Aquarius, etc.) curve downwards to his left.

---

[6] For an explication and the necessary emendation to make sense of the text, see Beck 1976*b*; 1994*a*: 106–15; 2000: 160–2, with n. 68.

[7] The brilliant emendation of the Arethusa edition which restores the torchbearers to the text is generally accepted.

9. This macrocosmic setting is replicated in the microcosm of the mithraeum (Figs. 2 and 3) by siting the image of the tauroctonous Mithras in sculpture in the cult-niche or in fresco on the end wall. From there Mithras commands the aisle extending before him towards the entrance. The cult-niche is thus the spring equinox, the entrance the autumn equinox, and the aisle is the diameter of the universe between those two points. Now imagine this aisle/diameter opened up vertically into a hoop. Its top above the ceiling is the north celestial pole, its bottom below the floor is the south celestial pole; the hoop itself is the equinoctial colure, the great circle of the celestial sphere which passes through both poles and both equinoxes. The longitudinal section of the mithraeum is thus the plane of the equinoctial colure.

10. At Sette Sfere, the most cosmologically garrulous of all extant mithraea, the mosaic images of the signs of the zodiac set on the side-benches make this setting of Mithras explicit. Along the bench to the right of Mithras run the northern signs from Aries (nearest to Mithras) to Virgo (farthest from Mithras); along the bench to his left run the southern signs from Libra next to the entrance and opposite Virgo back to Pisces opposite Aries and next to the Mithras in the cult-niche. Thus the cult-niche 'is' the vernal equinox because it lies on the Pisces–Aries cusp which is the vernal equinox by definition; and the mithraeum's entrance 'is' the autumn equinox because it lies on the Virgo–Libra cusp which is the autumn equinox by definition.

11. The side-benches represent and so 'are' the ecliptic/zodiac. But they also represent and so 'are' the celestial equator. This is the sort of paradox which the imagining mind takes in its stride, the logician despairs of, and the historian of religion is left to explicate. Fortunately, the cognitive approach, introduced in the preceding chapter, can be of assistance.

11.1. Let us take the equatorial 'meaning' first. If the longitudinal section of the mithraeum is the plane of the equinoctial colure (see above, para. 9), then the plan of the mithraeum ('plan' in the usual sense of 'floor plan') must be the plane of the celestial equator, for that is the horizontal plane which is at right angles to the plane of the equinoctial colure. It follows that the side-benches, construed as two semicircles joined together at the cult-niche and the entrance, must represent—and 'be'—the celestial equator. And so they are.

11.2. How then can they also represent, as they must, the ecliptic/zodiac? By *imagination* and by a different train of inference. Initiates on the bench to the right of Mithras know that their bench, qua the ecliptic/zodiac from the spring equinox to the autumn equinox, is 'higher' and more 'northerly' than the opposite bench to the left of Mithras which represents the other half of the ecliptic/zodiac from the autumn equinox back again to the spring equinox. This 'knowing' is not propositional knowledge, and it requires no great feat of intellectual discernment. Rather, it is apprehended subliminally, perhaps after some initial instruction, as an entailment of the equations 'universe = cave = mithraeum' and 'celestial north = up/above/higher, celestial south = down/below/lower'. Intending it so makes it so. The attuned initiate on the 'northern' bench is aware that he is 'higher'—but only in terms of cosmic location—than his colleague on the 'southern' bench. This awareness could be brought to conscious knowledge and formulated on star-talk logic as the true proposition: 'I am now to the north of/ higher than my colleague opposite.'

11.3. The apparent contradiction, that the benches are both the equator and the ecliptic, is easily resolved. A symbol, even a complex symbol such as the side-benches of the mithraeum, can signify two (or more) different things concurrently, although at the conscious level the perceiving mind must discriminate between the two. Thus for the initiate the side-benches can 'mean' both equator and ecliptic/zodiac at once. That is simply how symbols work: they are multivalent.

11.4. This ambiguity is nicely captured in the design of the stucco ceiling of the Ponza mithraeum (Vermaseren 1974; Beck 1976a, 1978). The ceiling represents the northern celestial hemisphere, for within the ring of the twelve signs of the zodiac are shown two bears, a mother and her cub, which obviously signify the two polar constellations Ursa Major and Minor (Vermaseren 1974: 17–26; Beck 1978: 116–35).[8] The pole itself is marked with an indentation on the body of Ursa Major. Since this spot is at the centre of the zodiac ring, it ought in strict logic to signify the pole of the ecliptic. But the pole signified by the Bears in the popular imagination is not the pole of the ecliptic but the north celestial pole around which the universe appears to revolve. So in two very different ways the marked centre concurrently signifies *both* of the poles. We do not have to choose between them—nor did the original users of the mithraeum. We do not even have to suppose that the designer was conscious of the two options or that any of the initiates there ever thought about them or discussed them explicitly. One cannot even appeal to precise astronomical placement, for the designer has put his central marker *neither* at the pole of the ecliptic *nor* at the north celestial pole of that era (see Beck 1976a: 8, fig. 2; cf. 2, fig. 1).

12. We have spoken of north and south, and have deduced that one side of the mithraeum is more 'northerly' than the other. What can we now say about east and west in the context of the mithraeum?

12.1. Now the universe, of which the mithraeum is an image, has a northern hemisphere and a southern hemisphere, a north pole and a south pole. The line connecting the two poles is of course the axis on which the universe turns (or appears to turn, from the modern point of view). This axis is represented in the mithraeum by a notional vertical line intersecting the floor plan at the longitudinal and latitudinal midpoint of the central aisle (see Fig. 3).[9] Where this line

---

[8] The ring which separates the Bears from the zodiac is occupied, for a full semicircle, by a large writhing snake. Though its primary intent is other (Beck 1976a: 9–13; 1978), it also signifies both of the serpentine constellations in the northern hemisphere, Draco and Serpens (ibid. 7–9).

[9] This orientation (north up, south down) supersedes that in my previous study (Beck 2000: 158–63). See below, sect. 5.

pierces the ceiling lies the north celestial pole. Equidistant downwards from the floor of the mithraeum lies the invisible south celestial pole.

12.3. This point at the centre of the mithraeum represents, and so 'is', the earth. Stand at this point and you will have aligned yourself with the axis of the universe. Now spin in a counterclockwise direction to your left and you will be replicating the rotation of the earth. But the earth for the ancients (except the Aristarchan minority) did not rotate; it was stationary and the entire universe revolved around it. So instead you must imagine the entire mithraeum revolving around you in a clockwise direction. That this is the proper direction you may verify by reference to the actual universe: step outside and you will see the Sun (or the Moon or the planets or the stars) moving clockwise from your left to your right—*westward*.

12.4. So there you have it. From the centre of the mithraeum motion clockwise or to the right is motion to the west, motion counterclockwise or to the left is motion to the east (see Figs. 2 and 3). Now go to the mithraeum's entrance, where you are no longer on earth but at a specific point in the heavens, the autumn equinox, and move (or sweep your gaze) around the mithraeum. If you first turn to your left and move clockwise up the 'northern' aisle, across, and back down the 'southern' aisle, you are moving westwards; if you first turn to your right and move counterclockwise up the 'southern' aisle, across, and back down the 'northern' aisle, you are moving eastwards.

12.5. In the microcosm of the mithraeum east and west are *directions*, not destinations or points of departure or places. To nowhere in the mithraeum can you point and say, 'that's the east' or 'that's the west'. This is not a paradox: it is merely the necessary entailment in star-talk of a rotating sphere: two poles and a direction of rotation, not four cardinal points.

13. It follows that trying to correlate the cosmic orientation of the mithraeum, whether the ideal mithraeum or its actual exemplars, with terrestrial north, south, east, and west is a pointless endeavour—pointless because the universe and a place on the earth's surface are incommensurable. The terms 'north/northern' and 'south/southern' applied to the benches or sides of mithraea refer here solely to the unvarying *symbolic* north and south, not to the actual terrestrial orientation of particular mithraea.

14. While one cannot indicate an eastern or western 'part' of the mithraeum, it should be clear from the preceding paragraphs that one can indicate a 'north' and a 'south'. The mithraeum itself, envisaged as a hemispherical volume of space, represents the northern celestial hemisphere, everything, that is, above (= to the north of) the plane of the celestial equator represented by the mithraeum's side-benches. Alternatively, when the benches are construed as the ecliptic the mithraeum is the hemisphere to the north of the plane of the ecliptic (and its zenith is the north pole of the ecliptic).

14.1. Corresponding to the northern hemisphere (in either sense) is a southern hemisphere. In the microcosm this southern hemisphere is purely notional: it is the hemispherical volume of terrestrial space beneath the floor/benches of the mithraeum, complementary to the upper hemisphere.

15. The side-benches in 'virtually all excavated mithraea' (Gordon 1976*a*: 132) are pierced at the midpoint by a pair of niches facing each other. These niches represent, and so are, the solstices. On the 'northern' bench to Mithras' right (= the zodiac/ecliptic from Aries to Virgo) the niche represents and so is the summer solstice in or at the start of Cancer. On the 'southern' bench to Mithras' left (= the zodiac/ecliptic from Libra to Pisces) the niche represents and so is the winter solstice in or at the start of Capricorn. The summer solstice is of course the most northerly point in the ecliptic, the winter solstice the most southerly. Through the northern/summer solstice souls descend into mortality, through the southern/winter solstice they ascend back into immortality. From an earthly perspective the summer solstice is the way in, the winter solstice the way out. These cosmological 'facts' are explored by Porphyry at some length in *De antro* 20–31.

15.1. The identities of the mid-bench niches are most explicit at Sette Sfere, where the mosaic image of Cancer is close to the 'northern' niche and the image of Capricorn to the 'southern' niche. At the Vulci mithraeum too (Sgubini Moretti 1979) the solstitial identities of the niches are clear. The benches are carried on arches, three each side of the niches, which are themselves shallower indentations in the central supports (i.e. between the third and fourth arch on each side). The three arches on either side of the niches are the three signs of the zodiac on either side of the solstices. At the Dura mithraeum (phase 3, 240–56 CE) one of the columns along the front of the 'northern' bench is obligingly labelled *eisodos/exodos* (V66, graffito 'in minute letters'). One would be ill-advised to attempt literal entry or egress since there is no physical doorway there—and never was. Clearly this is a soul-gate, and its function is ritual or psychagogic. On the wall on the same side in the Capua mithraeum, approximately above the mid-bench niche representing the gate of entry of souls, is affixed a relief of Cupid and Psyche (V186). Whether the relief was actually commissioned for the mithraeum or opportunistically recycled there, it is an unusual instance of an exoteric composition in this esoteric setting. In context it speaks of the Soul conducted into the world by Love.

15.2. Just as the longitudinal section of the mithraeum bisects the universe at the equinoctial colure, so the cross (latitudinal) section bisects the universe at the solstitial colure, the great circle which joins the solstices to the poles. The latitudinal diameter linking the niches is the route of souls, the longitudinal diameter linking the tauroctonous Mithras in the cult-niche to the mithraeum's entrance is the line of balance, control, equilibrium, of Mithras *mesitēs*, the god 'in the middle'.[10]

---

[10] This epithet for Mithras is taken from Plutarch, *On Isis and Osiris* 46, where 'in the middle' is intended in the very different sense of intermediate between the good Horomazes and the evil Areimanios.

16. The star-talk logic of *De antro* 24 requires that Cautopates, the Mithraic torchbearer with the lowered torch, be associated in the mithraeum with the northern bench, the summer solstice, and genesis; and that Cautes, the torchbearer with the raised torch, be associated with the southern bench, the winter solstice, and apogenesis. This pair of associations is confirmed by the actual siting of images of the torchbearers in mithraea where they are represented at or on the bench ends nearest the entrance, as they are at Sette Sfere. Invariably Cautopates is to the left as you enter (to the right of the tauroctonous Mithras), which links him to the celestial north, to the summer solstice, and to genesis; Cautes is to the right as you enter (to the left of the tauroctonous Mithras), which links him to the celestial south, to the winter solstice, and to apogenesis (Gordon 1976*a*: 127).

(17. For hermeneutic reasons I postpone this paragraph on the place of the planets in the 'blueprint' until section 4 of this chapter.)

3. TO *REPRESENT* IS TO *BE*

This then is the blueprint for the mithraeum as an image of the universe. A structure designed to these specifications, if properly used by the proper people, can realize the mystery of the soul's descent and entry into mortality and its exit and ascent back up again to immortality.

In his important study of sacred space—or 'place' as he preferred—Jonathan Z. Smith (1987: 96–103) drew attention to the watershed in Reformation thought which divorced in the ritual of the eucharist the symbol from the thing symbolized, the bread from the Body, the wine from the Blood. Deliberately selecting a scholar from outside the Western tradition, Smith quotes J. P. Singh Uberoi on the genesis of this 'crucial distinction' so necessary to the genesis of the modern 'western world view' (Smith 1987: 99; Uberoi 1978: 25):

Zwingli insisted that in the utterance 'This is my body' (*Hoc est corpus meum*) the existential word 'is' (*est*) was to be understood, not in a real, literal and corporeal sense, but only in a symbolical, historical or social sense (*significat, symbolum est* or *figura est*). . . . Zwingli had discovered or invented the modern concept of time in which every event was either spiritual and mental or corporeal and material but no event was or could be both at once. . . . Spirit, word and sign had finally parted company for man at Marburg in 1529; and myth or ritual . . . was no longer literally *and* symbolically true. (Emphasis in original)

Smith himself speaks of 'a major revolution in thought' (1987: 100): 'ritual is not "real"; rather, it is a matter of "signification" for Zwingli, or of "metonomy" for Theodore Beza. A wedge was decisively driven between symbol and reality; there was no necessary connection between them.'

The Mithraic 'cave' pre-dates this revolution by a millennium-and-a-half. Actually, it was developed both as structure and as concept at the same time as that Christian group which came to prevail historically was developing the cult meal into a sacramental ritual within the same Graeco-Roman cultural milieu.[11] If we are to understand the mithraeum or, more to the point, to understand the initiate's apprehension of his mithraeum, we have to withdraw that 'wedge . . . between symbol and reality' and reseal the gap. We have to co-imagine with the initiate that in *representing* the universe the mithraeum *is* the universe; the authorized microcosm *is* the macrocosm.

We are now in a position once and for all to dispose of that misconstruction of Porphyry, *De antro* 6 which explicates the mystery of the soul's descent and return as doctrine taught in the mithraeum functioning as teaching aid (above, Ch. 4, sects. 1–3). No, the descent and return of souls actually 'takes place' (in J. Z. Smith's sense) there because 'there' is the universe by virtue of being a valid representation of the universe.

4. THE BLUEPRINT CONTINUED: THE PLANETS

Let us join the initiates on their benches. We are in heaven, from where we come and to which we return, on the periphery in the circle of signs. Above us is the north of the universe, below us is the south. Those of us to the right of Mithras are in the northern signs; we are 'above' or 'higher' than our colleagues in the southern signs to Mithras' left.

Now look inwards to the point where the equinoctial line down the centre of the aisle intersects the solstitial line linking the mid-bench niches. Vertically through that point, from the roof of the 'cave' to the floor and deep into the ground below, runs the axis of the universe. We can, if we wish, imagine ourselves turning with that axis, but of course we detect no change of spatial relationship between ourselves and our colleagues on either side of us and opposite, for none has in fact occurred.

The world of change, our earth, where simultaneously we still are, is the merest point. Our view of earth is that of Scipio in the 'Dream' which bears his name (*Somnium Scipionis*) at the close of Cicero's *De republica*: 'From here the earth appeared so small that I was ashamed of our empire which is, so to speak, but a point on its surface' (3.7, trans. Stahl). Or, expressed mathematically, as Ptolemy demonstrated (*Almagest* 1.6), 'the earth has the ratio of a point to the heavens'.[12]

(The next paragraphs belong with and complete the 'blueprint' of the mithraeum in section 2, above. For hermeneutic reasons we postponed them until this point in the chapter.)

---

[11] On the parallel development of the sacramental mentality see Beck 2000: 176–8.

[12] The infinitesimally small size of the earth's globe was an astronomical commonplace. See Macrobius, *Comm. in Somn.* 1.16.8–13 with Stahl 1952: 154, n. 6.

17. The space between the peripheral benches and the dimensionless centre, between the ultimate heaven and the earth, is occupied by the seven planetary spheres. This is made explicit at the Sette Sfere mithraeum, as the name indicates, where the planetary spheres are represented by outlines of seven arches set in mosaic up the aisle, one above another, from the entrance towards the cult-niche. The arciform representation of the seven spheres is in all likelihood determined by the perception of the planetary spheres as gates through which the soul must pass, both descending from heaven to earth and ascending again from earth to heaven. As we saw in the preceding chapter (sect. 8), passage through the planetary gates was intimated in the Mithraic mysteries by the 'symbol' of the *klimax heptapylos*, the 'seven-gated ladder' (Origen, *Contra Celsum* 6.22). It is generally accepted that the floor mosaic of the seven-arched arcade at another Ostian mithraeum, V287–93, has the same significance; hence its modern name, 'the Mithraeum of the Seven *Gates*' (Sette Porte). The series of mosaic panels up the aisle of the Felicissimus mithraeum (V299, also in Ostia) would likewise intimate the succession of planetary gates, for each panel contains the symbol of a planet. However, as the other symbols in the panels indicate, the primary significance is passage through the grades of initiation from Raven up to Father, for the sequence is that of the grade hierarchy and the planetary symbols follow that order rather than the classic planetary order of relative distance from earth.[13]

17.1. At Sette Sfere individual mosaic images of six of the planetary gods are also set, three each side, on the front of the side-benches. (The seventh is of course the Sun represented by Sol Mithras in the cult-niche.) Whatever the precise significance of their arrangement at Sette Sfere (Jupiter, Mercury, Luna on the 'northern' bench to the right of Mithras; Saturn, Venus, Mars on the 'southern' bench to the left of Mithras), setting their images at certain points on the benches necessarily indicates that each is at a particular location or at least in one semicircle of the zodiac rather than the other (Beck 1979). Now the motions of the planets define time. Without them there is no time. In particular the Sun defines the day and the year, the Moon the month. But as the *Timaeus* declares (39c5–d7), the other five also have their proper periods, and the seven together define what was to become known as the Great Year by their simultaneous return to their points of departure. Thus what Sette Sfere 'says' at the most general level is that 'Time' and temporal difference exist and with them a past and a future defined by a moving 'now'. These are features not only of our sublunary world but also of the world of the seven planets.

17.1.1. The design of the mithraeum at Vulci (Sgubini Moretti 1979) offers a more elegant and versatile way of representing Time and Change by planetary position. As we saw above (sect. 2, para. 15.1), the benches are carried on low arches, six each side, with a mid-bench 'solstitial' niche dividing each set of six into two triads. The triads, I propose, represent the four quadrants of the zodiac:

---

[13] On all these matters see Beck 1988, *passim*.

starting on the right of Mithras in the cult-niche and proceeding counterclock-wise:

(1) from spring equinox—Aries, Taurus, Gemini
(2) from summer solstice—Cancer, Leo, Virgo
(3) from autumn equinox—Libra, Scorpius, Sagittarius
(4) from winter solstice—Capricorn, Aquarius, Pisces

Into these 'signiferous' arches could be set images of the seven planets in the form of statuettes of their deities. The mithraeum could thus demonstrate any time, past, present, or future, including the changing 'now', by moving the markers from sign to sign as appropriate.

17.2. Among the planets the Sun, whether as Sol Mithras or as Sol the companion of Mithras, is privileged in these solar mysteries. In addition to the sign he occupies in any particular month, his contingent place in the world of change, he possesses also his 'proper seat at the equinoxes' represented by his image in the cult-niche (above, sect 2., para. 8). The cult-niche represents the spring equinox on the cusp of Pisces and Aries. This then is his place in the Platonic higher world, the world of invariance which is and does not become, the world of Eternity. Wherever else he is, he is always there.

5. AN IMPROVED RECONSTRUCTION

Readers familiar with my previous descriptions of the mithraeum may have noticed a difference in the description presented here. Before I explain the alteration, please bear in mind that what I call the 'blueprint' of the mithraeum is not an actual plan existing in the external world about which one can be right or wrong empirically. I am not, then, correcting a mistake. Rather, I am modifying my reconstruction of how the initiates represented to themselves and so validated the esoteric 'fact': 'our "cave" is an image of the universe for the descent and ascent of souls.'

Certainly reconstructions can be *wrong* if they are false to the data from actual excavated mithraea on what Porphyry (*De antro* 6) calls the 'proportionate arrangement of the symbols'. But representations which conform to the data are another matter, and likewise one's reconstructions of those representations. What I now offer is a better—not truer—reconstruction: better because simpler, more in tune with ancient imagining, and with a greater regard for symbolic multivalence.

The mithraeum as I have just described it represents the universe as a sphere rotating on an axis whose poles 'are' (are represented by) the zenith of the ceiling and the subterranean nadir (para. 12.1). In earlier studies (Beck 1994*a*; 2000: 160–3), starting from the (true) premise that the side-bench to Mithras' right is 'northern' and the side-bench to his left 'southern', I had represented the cosmic axis as the transverse line from one side of the mithraeum to the other. In that representation the equatorial cross-section of the cosmos turns in daily revolution like a Ferris wheel in the vertical plane. In my newly postulated representation the same cross-section turns in the horizontal plane like a merry-go-round.

Why is the new reconstruction an improvement on the old? The answer is that the newly postulated representation conforms better to representations of the universe which were actually made in classical antiquity and which picture the equatorial and/or ecliptic cross-sections as discs rotating in the horizontal plane. First, in the 'Myth of Er' at the close of the *Republic* Plato uses the metaphor of a whorl on a drop spindle; and Nigidius Figulus is reported by Augustine (*City of God* 5.3) to have used a potter's wheel to demonstrate the speed with which points on the sphere of the fixed stars, specifically on the zodiac, revolve. Secondly, star-talk logic which correlates celestial north with 'up/above' and south with 'down/below' implies that any circle rotating eastward or westward does so in the horizontal plane. Thirdly, there is an exact precedent, in Plato's whorl on the 'Spindle of Necessity', for the representation of universal and planetary motion in the same plane. The Mithraists, I proposed (sect. 2, para. 11), represented their side-benches both as equator and as ecliptic/zodiac. Symbolic multivalence allowed them in effect to suppress the obliquity of the ecliptic, to return to the model of the spindle's whorl from Plato's later and more astronomically sophisticated model (*Timaeus* 36b6–d7) of the two strips of cosmic soul-stuff joined front and back in a *chi*-cross.

6. SYMBOLS, REPRESENTATIONS, AND STAR-TALK

In my description of the mithraeum's 'blueprint' I have spoken both of 'symbols' and of 'representations'. That is to say, I have treated the mithraeum as a complex of symbols within the larger symbol system that carried, and in a sense *was*, the Mithraic mysteries; and I have also treated the mithraeum as the public representation generated from and in turn generating the initiates' mental representations of the universe as 'cave'. The symbolic approach I laid out in Chapter 5, the cognitive/representational in Chapter 6.

You will also have noticed my appeal to 'star-talk' as the logic which holds together the symbol complex of the mithraeum as an integrated whole and likewise relates the mental and public representations of the parts of the mithraeum to the representation of the whole. In starting to apply 'star-talk' arguments before explaining the concept at a more theoretical and general level I am reversing the order of presentation. Star-talk as a heuristic and hermeneutic device is my invention, so I cannot explain it in advance as a ready-made and known method. Let this brief section serve then as an interim definition, on which I shall expand in the chapter which follows.

Perhaps the most important point to make at this stage is that because the mental representations of the mithraeum and their physical instantiations in actual mithraea follow the logic of 'star-talk', we can fine-tune our reconstruction of those representations to an extent that would be impossible if the ideal mithraeum and the actual mithraeum were mere congeries of representations and symbols. There is nothing esoteric about 'star-talk'; it is a public language which a modern scholar—or layperson for that matter—can 'hear' and apprehend quite as well as could an ancient initiate.

7. THE VIEW FROM THE BENCHES: ANALOGIES OF WORLD VIEW AND ETHOS TO 'SCIPIO'S DREAM'

I have mentioned already (above, sect. 4) that the initiate's view of the world from his bench corresponds to that of Scipio in the 'Dream' at the close of Cicero's *De republica*. Put less cautiously but more precisely, the initiates' view of the universe *is* Scipio's view, for the two occupy the same vantage point, the same celestial belvedere. What differs is how each of them got there. 'Scipio' (that is, Cicero's construction of Scipio) got there in a 'dream', a dream which is actually Cicero's literary fantasy. The Mithraic initiate got there by apprehending his mithraeum as an image of the universe and his position on the bench as a particular place on the zodiacal circumference.

Please notice what I am *not* postulating. I am not postulating a direct genealogical link. I do not claim that Mithraism's founder(s) had read 'Scipio's dream' and encoded it in the mithraeum's blueprint. Yes, there is a common ancestor, but that ancestor is a certain mental representation of the universe, a complex representation constructed of simpler representations according to strict star-talk logic. In Sperberian terms (1996), 'Scipio's dream' and the mithraeum belong to the same 'epidemic' of cosmological representations.

Notice too how irrelevant has become that old objection based on the dichotomy between antiquity's educated elite (the 'wise') and the rude masses (the 'vulgar'). By proper apprehension of his 'cave' the rank-and-file Mithraist was as capable of 'getting it' as the most cultured reader of 'Scipio's dream'.

And so, with confidence that it reflects the view of the cosmos that was to become Mithraism's too, I reproduce the relevant portions of 'Scipio's dream' (trans. Stahl 1952). Interestingly, the text reflects not only Mithraism's 'world view' (how things really are) but also its 'ethos' (how one should comport oneself in the context of how things really are). This earth, Scipio is told, is not our final home: it is an arena where we must serve honourably, faithfully, and piously in the station to which each of us is called. To say that a Mithraic Father could not have put it better is neither to evoke a fortunate coincidence nor to hint at the contents of a Mithraist's library. Rather it is to confirm a prediction that within the same larger epidemic of representations world view and ethos will tend to run in tandem.[14]

(3.4)[15] 'Men were created with the understanding that they were to look after that sphere called Earth, which you see in the middle of the temple. Minds were given to them out of the eternal fires you call fixed stars and planets, those spherical solids which, quickened with divine minds, journey through their circuits and orbits with amazing speed. (5) Wherefore, Scipio, you and all other dutiful (*piis*) men must keep your souls in the custody of your bodies and must not leave this life of men except at the command of that One who gave it to you, that you may not appear to have deserted the office (*munus*) assigned to you. . . . But cherish justice and your obligations to duty (*pietatem*) . . . (6) This sort of life is your passport (*via*) into the sky, to a union with those who have finished their lives on earth and who, upon being released from their bodies, inhabit that place at which you are now looking' (it was a circle of surpassing brilliance gleaming out amid the blazing stars), 'which takes its name, the Milky Way, from the Greek word'.

(7) As I looked out from this spot, everything appeared splendid and wonderful. Some stars were visible which we never see from this region, and all were of a magnitude far greater than we had imagined. Of these the smallest was the one farthest from the sky and nearest the earth, which shone forth with borrowed light [i.e. the Moon]. And, indeed, the starry spheres easily surpassed the earth in size. From here the earth appeared so small that I was ashamed of our empire which is, so to speak, but a point on its surface.

(4.1) As I gazed rather intently at the earth my grandfather said: 'How long will your thoughts continue to dwell upon the earth? Do you not behold the regions (*templa*) to which you have come? The whole universe is comprised of nine circles, or rather spheres. The outermost of these is the celestial sphere, embracing all the rest, itself the supreme god (*summus deus*), confining and containing all the other spheres. In it are fixed the eternally revolving movements of the stars. (2) Beneath it are the seven underlying spheres, which revolve in an opposite direction to that of the celestial sphere. One of these spheres belongs to that planet which on earth we call Saturn. Below it is that brilliant orb, propitious and helpful to the human race, called Jupiter. Next comes the ruddy one, which you call Mars, dreaded on earth. Next and occupying the middle region, comes the sun, leader, chief, and regulator of the other lights (*dux et princeps et moderator luminum reliquorum*), mind and moderator of the universe (*mens mundi et temperatio*), of such magnitude that it fills all with its radiance. The sun's companions, so to speak, each in its own sphere, follow—the one Venus, the other Mercury—and in the lowest sphere the moon, kindled by the rays of the sun, revolves. (3) Below the moon all is mortal and transitory (*nil est nisi mortale et caducum*), with the exception of the souls bestowed upon the human race by the benevolence of the gods. Above the moon all things are eternal. Now in the center, the ninth of the spheres, is the earth, never moving and at the bottom. Towards it all bodies gravitate by their own inclination.

---

[14] If there is a divergence it is that Mithraism, perhaps as a legacy from Mazdaism, retains a more positive view of Earth and life on Earth. There is no hint in Mithraism that the earthly creation is intrinsically anything but good, while in 'Scipio's dream' Earth, although not in itself evil, is no more than an arena for fighting the good fight.

[15] The speaker at this point in the dream is Scipio's adoptive grandfather, P. Cornelius Scipio Africanus the Elder. The dreamer and narrator is P. Cornelius Scipio Africanus the Younger.

8. THE CHAMULA CHURCH

It is time to return to our cultural and religious comparator, the Chamulas of the Chiapas highlands in Mexico. In Chapter 5 we saw how the world view and ethos of the Chamulas are expressed in a string of opposed pairs, one term of which is privileged over the other (see table).

Superior	Inferior
Sun	Moon
on/to the right	on/to the left
counterclockwise	clockwise
east and north	west and south
up/high	down/low
hot/fiery	cold/earthy
male	female

How are these cosmological principles and priorities instantiated in the Chamula church, in their 'Place' *par excellence*?

First, as we did for the mithraeum, we must establish the privileged stance, relative to which things are 'on/to the right' or 'on/to the left'. Gary Gossen (1979: 125) provides the answer: things are on/to the right or left 'from the point of view of the patron saint San Juan, who stands above the altar in the center of the east end of the church'.

As we pursue the obvious analogies with the 'blueprint' of the mithraeum, in which the tauroctonous Mithras in the cult-niche has north to his right and south to his left, we must bear in mind that the logic of orientation in the Chamula church is terrestrial, not celestial (as in the mithraeum). The terms 'north', 'south', 'east', and 'west' do not refer to the poles and directions of motion on a rotating sphere. Instead they revert to their usual terrestrial senses of the four cardinal points. Thus the Chamula church has an east end and a west end, a north side and a south side. Following the traditional Christian norm, the sanctuary with the image of S. Juan is in the east end and the entrance in the west end.

Thus, (1) S. Juan in the Chamula church is in the geographical east, having geographical north to his right and geographical south to his left, while (2) in the mithraeum the tauroctonous Mithras at the spring equinox has the northern signs and the northern (summer) solstice to his right and the southern signs and the southern (winter) solstice to his left.

S. Juan in the east end of the Chamula church is the microcosmic equivalent of the Sun rising in the east in the Chamula macrocosm, a 'universe' which we saw is limited to Chamula territory, its immediate surroundings, the sky above, and the earth beneath. In contrast the Mithraic universe is so vast that the globe of earth is a mere point at its centre. This immensity is captured in the microcosm of the mithraeum which, by definition, cannot be a place on earth having an east and a west, a north and a south. What we have been calling the 'privileged stance' is accordingly one and the same in the macrocosm and in the microcosm of the mithraeum: the 'proper seat' of Mithras at the (spring) equinox. In the macrocosm he is 'really' there; in the microcosm he is there as the tauroctonous god in the cult-niche.

In what way is the privileging of the north/right side of the Chamula church over the south/left side manifested? Primarily by the association of the north side with the male and the south side with the female. We can do no better than quote Gossen (1979: 125 and fig. 4):

The female saints reside on the left side (south) of the church from the point of view of the patron saint San Juan, who stands above the altar in the center of the east end of the church. While there are no female saints on the 'male (north) side', there are a few unimportant male saints on the 'female (south) side'. I believe that it is also significant that an oil painting of Hell (a very dark one which has never been cleaned), the cross of the dead Christ, and the baptistery are all found in the 'most negative', 'female' part of the church, the southwestern corner. These objects are negative within the symbolic scheme. The opposite (northeastern) corner of the church is the 'most positive', 'most masculine' part of the church. This point lies to the patron saint's immediate right. It is here that the major male saints and images of Christ (the sun) line the north and east walls.

The same point is made by motion as by location (ibid. 125 and fig. 5):

When processions take place at the climax of some major fiestas in honor of male saints, the male saints march out of the church and around the atrium to the right (counterclockwise). Female saints, on the other hand, march out to the left (clockwise) around the atrium, meet at the half-way point (the west entrance to the atrium) and bow to each of the male saints in sequence. The female saints then reverse their direction of motion and line up behind the last male saint. They march around the last 180 degrees of the circuit behind the male saints, but this time in counterclockwise direction, which is associated with the male principle. The female saints thus 'capitulate' symbolically to the male principle and follow the male saints as the moon follows the sun and Chamula women follow their husbands.

9. OTHER 'IMAGES OF THE UNIVERSE' IN ANTIQUITY: (I) THE PANTHEON, NERO'S DOMUS AUREA, VARRO'S AVIARY, THE CIRCUS

The Mithraists' invention of an 'image of the universe' was far from unique in the ancient world. We have already noticed (sect. 2, above) how Cassius Dio (53.27.2) thought that the Pantheon was domed 'so as to resemble (*proseoiken*) the heavens'. Similarly, a dining-room in Nero's Domus Aurea, so Suetonius says (*Nero* 31.2), was designed 'to revolve continuously day and night as a proxy for the universe (*vice mundo*)'. Presumably it was the dome of the ceiling that revolved, and it did so once every twenty-four hours, bringing the images of the stars and constellations on to the meridian in synchronization with their macrocosmic referents (Beck 2000: 167, n. 96). The orientation is essentially that of the mithraeum: 'north' is up, 'south' is down, 'westward' is the clockwise direction of the dome's rotation (to the interior observer's right), and 'eastward' is the opposite direction of motion. This proxy universe was an engineering triumph, requiring the emperor's resources to realize. However, the mithraeum, whose exemplars started coming into being a few decades later, is conceptually the more elegant and sophisticated, and it was achievable at a fraction of the cost. It had to be. For while Nero's dining-room was about Nero as a cosmocrat on earth,[16] the mithraeum had the more demanding though less vainglorious function of ferrying ordinary initiates in a mystery from heaven to earth and back again.

The shift of the vantage point, the belvedere, from earth (the emperor and his guests at the centre) to heaven (the initiates on their *side*-benches on the periphery) validates the affordable, no-moving-parts Mithraic model. To those on the periphery in the changeless heavens twenty-four-hour rotation with its alternation of day and night is unnoticed, for nothing up there changes in relation to anything else. Paradoxically, only for us mortals is so-called 'universal motion' relevant.[17] In a mithraeum a revolving dome, even if achievable, would not have been an improvement. It would have been a mistake.

The mithraeum is of course also a dining-room, both in the literal sense of a place designed for actual feasting and good-fellowship and in the sacramental sense of a place designed for the replication of the feast of Mithras and Sol following the former's sacrifice of the bull. To the mithraeum and Nero's dining-room we may add a third combination of cosmic model cum feasting-place from the preceding century, Varro's ingenious aviary near Casinum, which he describes in his *De re rustica* (3.8–17).[18] The aviary was designed in a set of concentric rings with the dining-room at the centre in the form of an open, columned rotunda. The rings collectively intimate the concentric celestial spheres, although individually they relate rather to the terrestrial elements (earth, water, air), not to particular celestial bodies. The dining-room/rotunda was set on a circular island surrounded by a circular pond, well stocked with waterfowl and fish, with access across a single bridge. Around the pond was a circular portico. At the outer ring of columns, in place of a wall, was a net made of gut, and similarly a fowling net

---

[16] On the Domus Aurea as the epitome of this project, see L'Orange 1942; Stierlin 1986: 40–7.

[17] In the next chapter, on 'star-talk', we shall look at Plotinus' treatment of this point-of-view problem. In classical antiquity it was a serious philosophical question, given the construction of the celestial bodies as rational self-conscious beings capable of communication.

[18] On Varro's aviary as an exemplar of the self-promoting cosmic model see Stierlin 1986: 141–7.

was suspended around the inner ring, thus forming a secure aviary in which the birds could be viewed against the natural background of the tree trunks and countryside beyond.

This cosmic model, like Nero's, had its moving parts. First, the table was what we would call a 'dumb waiter': it took the form of a rotatable spoked wheel carrying on its circumference a circular wooden trough two-and-a-half feet wide and a palm in depth. Secondly, 'inside under the dome, the morning star by day and the evening star by night move around the base of the hemisphere in such a way as to indicate the hour' (3.8.17). This effect could be achieved by rotating (by means of a water-clock drive, if done automatically) a diametrical rod. At each end of the rod images of the morning star (Lucifer) and the evening star (Vesperus) would function as pointers, and one would select the appropriate pointer to 'tell the time' (Lucifer in the day, Vesperus in the night). The twelve hours of the day and the twelve hours of the night would be painted in a circle on the inside of the dome, much as the twenty-four 'hours' of 'right ascension' are shown on a modern star map.[19] The clock would be accurate only at the equinoxes. At other seasons it would continue to 'tell the time' in equinoctial hours.[20] However, precision is probably beside the point. The intent of the clock was not really to 'tell the time' in our sense but to demonstrate Time itself in the universal order. Thirdly and lastly, 'in the centre of the hemisphere, surrounding a protruding spindle, is painted the circle of the eight winds, as in the *horologium* at Athens which the Kyrrhestian constructed, and a radial pointer projecting from the spindle to the wind-rose so moves that it touches the wind which happens to be blowing with the result that you can know it inside' (3.8.17). In other words, the oscillations of the weather-vane above are transmitted to a pointer below, indicating to the diners the direction of the wind.[21] Again, the point is not really to transmit information—the diners would be well aware which way the wind was blowing since the dining-room was purposefully open to the breezes—but to show how the actual wind relates to the scheme of the eight cardinal and intra-cardinal points and so to the idea of Direction itself in the cosmos. Varro compares his weather-vane to that in the still-standing Tower of the Winds at Athens, designed not long before by Andronikos of Kyrrhos.[22]

[19] In a map of the circumpolar regions the hour lines radiate from the pole, just as do the longitude lines on a map of the terrestrial polar regions.

[20] i.e. equal twenty-fourths of a 24-hour day measured from the equinoctial sunrise and sunset, i.e. 6 a.m. and 6 p.m. in modern time.

[21] The three devices rotate around a common vertical axis which represents the axis of universal revolution. In the material model, the spindle for the wind device is driven from above and the support of the table from below. It follows that one or other of these axles (probably the latter) must be hollow in order to accommodate the axle for the hour indicator.

[22] The Tower of the Winds and the anaphoric clock which it is now thought to have contained may also be considered an elaborate 'model of the universe': Noble and Price 1968.

One last feature of Varro's aviary is worth a look. From front to back the aviary 'was constructed in steps like a little bird-theatre with many perches on all the columns to serve as seating for the birds (*gradatim substructum ut theatridion avium, mutuli crebri in omnibus columnis inpositi, sedilia avium*, 3.5.13)'. So who are the spectators in this *theatridion avium* and who are the performers? Varro's description is unambiguous: birds view men, not men birds. Varro's dinner guests might think themselves bird-watchers, but the reality is otherwise. However, those who had read their Plato would quickly get the point: the heavens on the periphery belong to winged souls; the wingless inhabit earth at the centre. Think now of the Mithraists on their peripheral benches and of the dreaming Scipio gazing inwards to an insignificant earth.

Among structures with multiple exemplars the circus, that immensely popular arena for chariot-racing, was explicitly likened to the universe, and although the extant sources for this are mostly late,[23] there is good reason to suppose that the simile and its constituent comparisons go back at least to the first century CE (Wuilleumier 1927).[24] Naturally, the race-course itself is the great cosmic periphery, 'carrying round' the stars and planets. In particular it represents the solar year, and the seven laps allude to the seven days of the week and to the seven eponymous planetary gods, while the twelve starting-gates allude to the twelve months and the twelve signs of the zodiac through which the Sun passes. So we may properly compare the Mithraists facing each other on the side-benches of their mithraeum to the spectators at the circus (Mithraists no doubt among them) facing each other across the long central *spina* separating the two halves of the track.

10. OTHER 'IMAGES OF THE UNIVERSE' IN ANTIQUITY: (II) ORRERIES AND THE ANTIKYTHERA MECHANISM, THE SUNDIAL

Next we should take a brief look at those 'images of the universe' which were purpose-built to replicate in miniature the universe's motions and 'periods'. These are actually 'scale models' of the universe, but it is not space which is 'to scale', but time. The most like in appearance is the orrery, a type of *sphaera* so-called, in which a small earth-globe is suspended in the centre of a much larger transparent globe representing the sphere of the fixed stars. Between earth and heaven revolve seven other small globes representing the Moon, the Sun, and the remaining five planets. The most famous exemplar in antiquity—there cannot have been many—was that made by Archimedes in the third century BCE and taken to Rome in the spoils from the sack of Syracuse. It was described by Cicero

---

[23] With the exception of Tertullian (late 2nd cent.), the earliest is Cassiodorus (6th cent.).

[24] See also Stierlin 1986: 163–70 (cf. 140–1); Lyle 1984.

(*De republica* 1.21–2), who also tells of another *sphaera* of this type which 'our friend Posidonius recently made' (*De natura deorum* 2.88).[25]

How did it work? By clockwork, is the short answer. The proof of this is the Antikythera Mechanism, a luni-solar 'calendar computer' (Price 1975: subtitle) constructed in about 80 BCE, recovered from an ancient shipwreck excavated by sponge-divers in 1900–1, and reconstructed, as far as the extensive corrosion allowed, by Derek De Solla Price (1975) and A. G. Bromley (1986). The mechanism consists of a complex train of meshing bronze gear-wheels. Its function was to transmute an initial impetus, probably the turning of a crank (the mechanism's *primum mobile* as it were), via the gear train, into a replication of the time-defining motions of the Sun and Moon. On a dial on the front of the mechanism were displayed the progress of the Sun and Moon around the ecliptic/zodiac and of the Sun through the 365-day Egyptian year,[26] and on dials in the back the Moon's progress through the synodic month and the Sun's progress through the twelve lunations of the lunar year.

Archimedes' and Posidonius' orreries were driven by similar gear trains (Price 1975: 55–60), probably less complicated for the Sun and Moon,[27] and for the other five planets incorporating only mean motion in longitude (for example, the thirty-year sidereal period of Saturn).[28] Superficially the orreries resembled antiquity's imagined universe more closely than did the Antikythera Mechanism. They 'looked like' the universe. But to the Platonic way of thinking, antiquity's default mode, the Antikythera Mechanism is surely the purer image, for it dispenses with mere appearance and confines its output to number and proportion, specifically number and proportion instantiated in the luni-solar period relationships. For example, there is a fundamental period relationship, the Metonic cycle,[29] well known in ancient astronomy, whereby

19 years = 254 sidereal months = 235 synodic months

---

[25] On Archimedes' orrery see also Cicero, *Tusculan Disputations* 1.63; Ovid, *Fasti* 6.263–83; Lactantius, *Divine Institutes* 2.5.18; Claudian, *Carmina minora* 51 (68). All these sources are conveniently set out in translation in Price 1975: 56–7.

[26] The Egyptian 'wandering' year is displayed on a slip ring so that it can be recalibrated against the tropic year which is approximately one-quarter of a day longer.

[27] The Antikythera Mechanism had gears for outputs other than the year, the sidereal month, the synodic month, and the lunar year, but we do not know what those outputs were.

[28] The inferior planets (Mercury, Venus) would be kept in lockstep with the Sun. No attempt would be made to capture and display the retrograde motion of the five planets proper. I suspect that all seven planets must have been kept in a single plane, i.e. the plane of the ecliptic. To exhibit latitudinal change (not to mention the draconitic month and the precession of the lunar nodes) would surely have been beyond the technology of the times, in practice if not in theory. With the Sun and Moon in the same plane, the orrery would imply an eclipse twice a month. The intent must have been to demonstrate when an eclipse was possible (Sun and Moon in conjunction or opposition), not when an eclipse would actually occur.

[29] Named after Meton, an Athenian astronomer of the 5th cent. BCE.

The Antikythera Mechanism was geared in such a way that nineteen complete revolutions of the Sun and 254 complete revolutions of the Moon on the dial on the front would coincide precisely with 235 complete (synodic) revolutions of the Moon on the lunar dial on the back. Its gear train thus instantiates the numbers in the formula given above, which a Platonist might tell you is the intelligible reality behind the relative motions of the visible Sun and the visible Moon. An orrery must of course also instantiate this ratio so that its model Sun and Moon can replicate the relative motions of their originals. But the addition of the little model luminaries is for the purist something of a distraction, a concession to appearances which, even if they can be replicated precisely, are not really worth replicating since in the strictest sense they are unintelligible.

The orrery, one must suppose, suppressed universal daily motion. The whole point of an orrery is to demonstrate planetary motions and their relationships. If the entire contrivance is spinning in the opposite direction and at a speed more than twenty-seven times faster than the Moon, the fastest of the planets, the phenomena of planetary motion will be lost to the viewer. In any case, Cicero's descriptions make it abundantly clear that the orreries were specifically designed to demonstrate only planetary motion, and that this was their sole 'output'. Where universal motion comes into play is as the 'input'. One turn of the crank produces one day's worth of planetary motion. The gearing should be such that twenty-seven-and-one-third turns bring the model Moon back to her starting point and $365\frac{1}{4}$ turns bring the model Sun back to his. This is how Cicero (*De natura deorum* 2.88) describes the orrery of Posidonius: '. . . in which every single turn produces the same result for the [sc. model] Sun, Moon, and five planets that is produced in the [sc. actual] heavens every single 24-hour day (*cuius singulae conversiones idem efficiunt in sole et in luna et in quinque stellis errantibus quod efficitur in caelo singulis diebus et noctibus*).'[30]

The intent of the orrery's design as a model universe is stated most succinctly by Cicero in his *Tusculan Disputations* (1.63, of Archimedes' exemplar): 'Archimedes achieved the same as that god of Plato's who built the universe so that one single "turn" would govern motions which are utterly dissimilar in speed (*Archimedes . . . effecit idem quod ille qui in Timaeo mundum aedificavit Platonis deus, ut tarditate et celeritate dissimillimos motus una regeret conversio*).' Archimedes, in other words, replicated the Circle of the Different and demonstrated mechanically that even its apparent 'difference' is the product of a single impetus. No wonder Archimedes' orrery became a trope for the divine inventiveness of the human mind, as also for the cosmos as a divinely ordered whole instantiating reason and number.

The orrery's suppression of universal motion is not for us a trivial point. We have noted already that for those on the periphery universal motion does not

---

[30] The orrery was not designed to replicate 'day' and 'night'. The phrase signifies only a unit of time, what in Greek would be called the *nychthēmeron*.

register, because everything there maintains the same spatial relation to everything else. Only by looking inwards at the insignificant pinpoint earth can you become aware of motion and of change. And why ever, to echo 'Scipio's dream', would you want to do that, once you have achieved the heavens? The orrery and the 'Dream' both represent (in our technical sense) the changelessness of the sphere of the fixed stars as vantage point. They are precedents for the Mithraists' benches as representations of the same changeless location. I do not claim that they were consciously claimed as precedents by the Mithraists. Rather we should think of them as prior representations in the stream of representations of the cosmos in which we find, a century or so downstream, the mithraeum as 'image of the universe'.

A more commonplace 'image of the universe' for representing time as 'told' by the motions of the celestial bodies is the sundial. This device, of which many exemplars survive from antiquity, of course tells only solar time, of which there are two measures, the day and the year. A properly calibrated sundial will tell you both the time of day and the time of year.

Figure 4 is a diagram of a horizontal planar sundial.[31] The straight lines (up and down on the page) represent the hours either side of noon. The noon line is of course the local meridian and is so labelled—*mesēnbria*. It runs due north

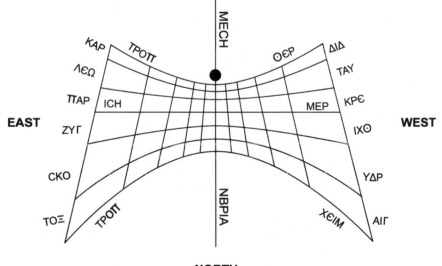

Fig. 4. A horizontal planar sundial from Pompeii (Gibbs 1976: no. 4007)

[31] Redrawn after Gibbs 1976, no. 4007, p. 331.

through the gnomon, the upright pointer which casts the shadow. The Sun, rising in the east, casts a shadow westward. As the Sun moves round to the south and then to the west, the tip of the shadow travels eastward, crossing the hour lines in succession and so 'telling the time'.

Just as the westward progress of the shadow tip tells the time of day, so the northward and southward progress up and down the hour lines tells the time of year. Each day the shadow tip passes eastward along a slightly different day curve. From the summer solstice in July, represented by the southern (upper) margin of the dial and labelled *trop(ikos) ther(inos)*, to the winter solstice in December, represented by the northern (lower) margin and labelled *trop(ikos) cheim(erinos)*, the shadow tip progresses daily northward; from the winter solstice back to the summer solstice, it progresses southward. The day curves drawn in this exemplar are thus boundary markers: when the shadow tip crosses them (or reverses direction at the solstices), the Sun is moving from one sign of the zodiac to the next. The names of the signs (abbreviated) are displayed in columns to the left and right.[32] Finally we should note that one of the day curves is not a curve at all. Uniquely the equinoctial line, labelled *isēmer(inos)*, where the sun crosses from Pisces into Aries and from Virgo into Libra, is straight.

The sundial is a special map for the representation of the Sun's daily and annual progress as motion across a grid of hour lines for the day and day lines for the year. It converts Time into Space, or rather into Change of Place. Manifestly, then, the sundial is a 'cosmic model'. One inscription, from a lost dial (Paris and Delatte 1913: 145–54),[33] calls it precisely that—*eikona kosmou*, the very term transmitted by Porphyry to characterize the mithraeum. The inscription of another lost dial (ibid. 155–6), evidently in the form of a hollow marble hemisphere, the dial form which most closely resembles the celestial sphere as we view it from earth,[34] calls the instrument a 'stony cave' (*lainon antron*). It seems that Mithraists and Neoplatonists were not alone in representing the universe as a 'cave'.

Here too the communicative function of the sundial should be mentioned. The inscription on a recently published sundial (Marengo 1998) records in an elegiac couplet how 'Thaleia, priestess of the divine Hera set me up, a *messenger* of the solar hours to creatures of a day (*hēliakōn hōrōn angelon hēmeriois*)'. The speaking tombstone was of course a long-established convention. But the sundial speaks with authority of a different order altogether. It is a messenger from the

---

[32] No significance should be attached to the placement of the summer and autumn names on the right and the winter and spring signs on the left. Interchanging them would make no difference. The great *horologium/solarium Augusti* in the Campus Martius marked the year by signs of the zodiac up and down the meridian (Buchner 1982: ills. at 70, 107, 110–11). The scale was large enough to distinguish individual days by short cross-bars about 28 cm apart in the short excavated stretch.

[33] The two epigrams discussed by Paris and Delatte were copied in antiquity and transmitted in manuscript.

[34] A fine example of this type, in which a shaft of sunlight falling through a pierced aperture replaces a gnomon's shadow (i.e. a positive rather than negative solar proxy), may be seen in Gagnaire 1999.

gods, specifically the Sun, to mortals,[35] and its news is not some evanescent human biography but the very measure of Time, the 'Sun-given hours'. We shall hear more of and about this 'star-talk' in the next chapter.

In a previous study (Beck 1994a) I compared the horizontal planar sundial and the mithraeum as 'cosmic models' in some detail, emphasizing that both structures are instruments for communication between heaven and earth: the sundial for 'telling time', the mithraeum for symbolic soul-travel to and fro. Here I wish only to draw out the implications of a single striking similarity.

In both structures the longitudinal axis is an equinoctial line. On the sundial, the Sun's surrogate, the shadow point, walks this line on two days in the year, the spring equinox and the autumn equinox. On those two days it is truly 'at the equinoxes'. And since the equinoxes are the points at which the ecliptic and the equator intersect, it is also truly 'on the equator'. In the mithraeum, as we have seen, this equinoctial/equatorial line is represented by the aisle, overseen at the cult-niche end by the tauroctonous Mithras in his 'proper seat' 'on the equator' 'at the equinoxes'.

In the system of planetary identities encoded in the grade hierarchy the surrogate of the Sun is the Heliodromus, the Sun-Runner. Now the Heliodromus in procession is the subject of the scene represented on Side B of the Mainz ritual vessel (Horn 1994). In my study of the scene (Beck 2000: 154–67) I interpreted this 'Procession of the Sun-Runner' as a mimesis of the solar journey intended to validate the mithraeum as an authentic 'image of the universe' and thus as a proper and functional venue for the mystery of soul-travel. Here I shall be more specific and suggest that the Procession of the Sun-Runner might be an equinoctial ritual in which on the two appropriate days of the year the Sun's Mithraic surrogate 'walked the walk' which his other surrogate, the shadow point, walked in the world outside. In both venues to 'walk the walk' is to 'talk the talk'—star-talk. Or put another way, in the ancient cosmos and thus also in its authentic replications Motion is Logos.

11. THE MITHRAEUM AS SYMBOLIC INSTRUMENT FOR 'INDUCTING THE INITIATES INTO A MYSTERY OF THE DESCENT OF SOULS AND THEIR EXIT BACK OUT AGAIN'—WITH SOME MODERN COMPARISONS

'Might be' is not 'is' and 'might have been' is not 'was'. In default of new and direct evidence we cannot prove that the Procession of the Sun-Runner was performed in mithraea twice annually on the days of the equinoxes. We can only

---

[35] In the context of an instrument designed to tell the *hours*, 'creatures of a *day*' is a neat periphrasis.

establish a likelihood, a probability, based on the intent of astronomical discourse and practice on the one hand and astronomical/astrological symbolism on the other.

In speaking of ritual we pass from the design and ideology of the mithraeum to action and experience, from *how and why* the mithraeum is an 'image of the universe' to *how it functions* as an instrument for 'inducting the initiates into a mystery of the descent of souls and their exit back out again'.

In exploring the ancient mysteries one is dealing both with something *done* and with something *experienced*. May we assume then that the descent and return of souls was actually instantiated in a ritual and experienced psychically as a soul journey? Perhaps there was indeed such a ritual with its corresponding experience, but it is only a presupposition, not a certainty, that there was necessarily some special action and some special experience dedicated to each and every major aspect of the mysteries.

It is, then, entirely possible that there never was a Mithraic ritual specific to the soul journey. If the mithraeum/cave was duly consecrated, 'made sacred' by being properly made a model of the universe, then merely by being in the mithraeum and by apprehending it as the universe the initiate would effectively enjoy the freedom of the heavens. The heavy lifting of space travel is achieved *cognitively*. In fact we have already covered most of the 'how' of the mystery in describing what it is that the Mithraist comes to know when he apprehends his mithraeum as an authentic microcosm. At this stage we need scarcely add that the 'knowing' is not acquired doctrinally and catechetically, or at least not primarily so.

Heuristically and hermeneutically, the problem of the mithraeum is much like the problem of the tauroctony. Just as there is no Big Secret encoded in the tauroctony, no all-explaining esoteric identity of Mithras the bull-slayer, so in the mithraeum there is no necessity for a lost ritual to be postulated, deduced from currently available evidence, or anticipated in the recovery of new evidence like the scenes depicted on the Mainz ritual vessel.

There are nevertheless intimations of a relevant ritual or fragment of ritual in a passage from Proclus which I have discussed recently (Beck 2004*a*). In the passage (reproduced below) Proclus is criticizing the second-century CE Neopythagorean Numenius of Apamea for his explication of Plato's cosmology in the 'Myth of Er' at the close of the *Republic*. Now Numenius was Porphyry's source for the cosmology of the *De antro*, and that cosmology, as I have demonstrated earlier in this chapter, was Mithraic.

Numenius says that this place [i.e. the site of posthumous judgement] is the centre of the entire cosmos, and likewise of the earth, because it is at once in the middle of heaven and in the middle of the earth. . . . By 'heaven' he means the sphere of the fixed stars, and he says there are two chasms in this, Capricorn and Cancer, the latter a path down into genesis, the former a path of ascent, and the rivers under the earth he calls the planets . . . and introduces a further enormous fantasy (*teratologian*) with leapings (*pēdēseis*) of souls from the tropics to the equinoxes and returns from these back to the tropics, leapings that are all his own and that he transfers to these matters, stitching the Platonic utterances together with astrological concerns and these with the mysteries (*syrraptōn ta Platōnika rhēmata tois genethlialogikois kai tauta tois telestikois*). He invokes the poem of Homer [i.e. *Od.* 13.109–12] as a witness to these two chasms... (*In remp.* 2.128.26–129.13 Kroll).[36]

Proclus here accuses Numenius of contaminating Platonic discourse with improper discourse of two other types, first astrological (specifically genethlialogical) discourse, and secondly mystery-cult discourse. The accusation is factually correct on both counts. First, astrological as well as astronomical categories, for example the system of planetary houses, play a large part in Porphyry's argument and are there (*De antro* 21) explicitly attributed to Numenius. Secondly, Porphyry's essay is full of allusions to Mithraism and its mysteries, and there is no reason to suppose that this discourse did not also reach Porphyry via Numenius. In fact the simplest and most plausible hypothesis is that both discourses were transmitted in tandem from the Mithraists to Numenius to Porphyry.

What then are we to make of the 'fantasy' of 'leapings of souls from the tropics to the equinoxes and returns from these back to the tropics'? Clearly it is ritual action replicating in the mithraeum the descent and return of souls. Whether the initiates actually 'leapt' is questionable. Characterizing the initiates' movements as celestial hopscotch may be no more than pejorative spin from the disapproving Proclus.

The ritual binds the microcosm to the macrocosm as follows:

To 'leap'
from the mithraeum's 'northern' side-bench
to its 'southern' side-bench
across its 'equatorial' aisle
is to replicate
the soul's journey
from its entry into the world at the northern tropic,
Cautopates presiding,
to its exit from the southern tropic,
Cautes presiding,
through a life under the tutelage of Mithras
on the equator at the equinoxes.

Before we turn from action to experience we shall adduce two comparison rituals. The first is the most familiar of all rituals in the Christian tradition, at least in those parts of the tradition which emphasize symbolic action, whether sacramental or memorial: the Christian eucharist or mass. While still current, in

---

[36] Trans. Lamberton 1986: 66 f., with minor changes and a correction (*isēmerina* = 'equinoxes', not 'solstices'). The last sentence quoted shows that Proclus is indeed drawing on the same passage of Numenius as Porphyry, i.e. an allegorization of Homer's cave of the nymphs in *Odyssey* 13.

origin the rite goes back to antiquity, where it was contemporaneous with the rituals of Mithraism. It is a product, ultimately, of the same culture.

Now the mass is a vast carrier of meaning. In one of its perhaps minor intentions, it is a journey to heaven, a ritual mode of gaining access to another, wider world while still planted firmly in this. *Introibo ad altare dei*, the start of the Old Roman Rite, is more than just voiced stage directions, the priest's matter-of-fact statement that he is about to move up the physical aisle to the physical altar. It is the commencement of a transfer, accomplished in the charged language and the charged action, from earth to heaven. Yet, because this is a ritual journey, the point of departure is never really left—it is not supposed to be—and the destination is only approximated. Heaven, for a time and after a fashion, is realized on earth; earth transported to heaven. As illustration I quote from a description of the mass which concludes a book on ritual by scholars of the biogenetic structuralist school to which I alluded in Chapter 1 (sect. 5). The author of this study is a Jesuit priest (Murphy 1979: 323–4).

The priest incenses the altar... by circling around it in an orbiting motion.... [T]he circling... brings the worship into synchrony with the circling of the planets around the sun, the stars around the galactic center, and even with the heavenly worship conceived of as adoration around the divine throne.... [R]otational motion points to the altar as the central axis of all rotation, the eternal still point.

Note, incidentally, the updating of the cosmology: the physical heavens are re-represented in terms compatible with their representation in modern astronomy.

Our second comparator is as obscure as the first is familiar. In the 1990s two small 'cults', in the modern derogatory sense of the word, achieved considerable notoriety by the suicide and murder of some of their members. These cults were the Solar Temple and Heaven's Gate. They are of interest to us because their intent was the same as the Mithraists', to get their initiates to heaven. But instead of attempting the journey symbolically and ritually, both cults sent their members on their way in real time and in real life—or rather, in real death.[37] But before paranoia drove them to suicide and murder the initiates of the Solar Temple were strong practitioners of ritual. Given their name, it will come as no surprise that they timed their ceremonies to the seasonal cycles of Sun and Moon. I quote from a sociological study of the cult (Hall and Schuyler 1997: 294).[38]

---

[37] For a summary of the incidents of suicide/murder see Beck 1998*b*: 343.

[38] Sociological comparison is as interesting as ritual comparison. Hall and Schuyler emphasize the 'respectable' insider status of the initiates of the Solar Temple as 'hardly a sect of the dispossessed. It appealed mostly to the affluent bourgeoisie and people of the new middle classes. Among the dead in the so-called Transit [i.e. to the heavens by suicide or 'assisted suicide'] were a mayor of a Quebec town, a journalist, an official in the Quebec Ministry of Finance, and a French nuclear engineer' (1997: 287). Particularly worrying to the authorities was the infiltration, as it would be perceived, of Hydro Québec, an iconic institution in Québecois self-definition. The story of how the cult became marginalized and self-marginalized is extraordinarily interesting (ibid. 296–303, Hall and Schuyler's second 'thesis', headed 'the struggle over cultural legitimacy'). Since this was a fate which Mithraism

Once a month, members . . . came from all over Quebec for a meeting on the night of the full moon. Gatherings also marked the transits of the earth around the sun. Jean-François Mayer [a Swiss historian of religion] recalls attending a similar celebration—a bonfire held in the French Savoie countryside to mark the 1987 summer solstice. 'The only ceremonial part was the fire, and people came from several sides, each with a torch, and put it in. And there were also some instructions: we had always to turn around the fire only clockwise.' During the event, Mayer remarked to a Temple representative, 'Oh, this is ritual'. 'Well, no', the man replied. 'Real ritual, it's something much more'.

What now of the subjective experience of the Mithraic mystery? Immediately one must throw in a set of cautions.

First, as said in the preceding section, the nub of the experience may be simply the initiate's apprehension of his 'cave' as an authentic microcosm. There is no need for an experience of space travel, of getting to heaven, when you are already there in your appropriate place on your side-bench.

Secondly, in the twenty-first century let us at last recognize that the tyranny of psychic dualism, the dichotomy between reason and passion, established by Plato and the Greeks and confirmed into modernity by Descartes, is dead. Late twentieth-century cognitive and neuro-science have buried it.[39] Its wraith however continues to haunt the study of the mental life of the ancients, where we are still far too respectful of their psychic taxonomies. It was all very well for Aristotle (Fr. 15) to insist that finally in the mysteries one does not learn (*mathein*) something, one experiences (*pathein*) something. For us however the distinction is or should be of little consequence. As I said at the start of this section, in the Mithraic mystery of the descent and return of the soul 'the heavy lifting of space travel is achieved *cognitively*'. The *feelings* which the Mithraic cosmonaut experiences as he undergoes induction into this mystery are part and parcel of *getting to know* his cave as universe.

Thirdly, although the experience of the initiate may have been in some sense 'extraordinary',[40] we need not suppose that it was necessarily exotic and intense. I used to imagine that it was indeed of a different order of experience altogether, akin to the shaman's soul-travel, and cognate to those celestial ascents found in the ancient Gnostic and magical sources.[41] The problem with this supposition, its naivety apart, is that it would mean that the Mithraic Mysteries somehow managed to make a routine out of what elsewhere seems to have been a solitary

manifestly avoided (until the empire's definitive swing to Christianity), comparison here is a study of contrast: how a group which is 'in the world' but not ultimately 'of the world' maintains or fails to maintain worldly approval, particularly the approval of the political, social, and cultural authorities and arbiters.

[39] As good a telling of psychic dualism's demise as any, at least for the lay person, is the neurologist Antonio Damasio's pair of studies, *Descartes' Error* (1994) and *Looking for Spinoza* (2003). See also, from a philosopher's perspective, R. de Sousa's, *The Rationality of Emotion* (1991).

[40] Walter Burkert's characterization (1987: title of ch. 4).

[41] On the soul's celestial ascent and the scholarship thereon, see Beck 1988: 73–85, 93–100, index s. 'soul, celestial journey'.

and individual experience. Apart from the implausibility of this entailment, it is not documented by any evidence—unless one believes (as almost no one does) that the so-called 'Mithras Liturgy'[42] is an authentic Mithraic experience rather than a magical adventure with gleanings from the Mithraic mysteries. Certainly one is prepared to credit the Eleusinian Mysteries with realizing an initiatory experience which was replicable year after year, effective on a mass of participants, and of great, even life-transforming, intensity for the individual. But in the first place there is a range of explicit testimony to the intensity and singularity of the Eleusinian experience. Secondly, in contrast to the ongoing life of a Mithraic community, the whole Eleusinian experience was concentrated into that one initiation, albeit a climax prepared for over several days. If you did not attain to that experience, you had accomplished nothing. Put somewhat cynically, your investment was too great *not* to experience the experience—or at least to suppose that you had.

12. TO 'EXPERIENCE', TO 'SURMISE', AND TO 'REPRESENT': DIO'S *TWELFTH (OLYMPIC) ORATION*

In *Ancient Mystery Cults* Walter Burkert begins his discussion of the experience of initiation (1987: ch. IV, 89–114)[43] with a passage (ch. 33) from Dio Chrysostom's *Oration* 12, the *Olympicus*:

If one would bring a man, Greek or barbarian, for initiation into a mystic recess,[44] overwhelming by its beauty and size, so that he would behold many mystic views and hear many sounds of the kind, with darkness and light appearing in sudden changes and other innumerable things happening, and even, as they do in the so-called enthronement ceremony (*thronismoi*)[45]—they have the initiands sit down, and they dance around them[46]—if all this were happening, would it be possible that such a man should experience (*pathein*) just nothing in his soul, that he should not come to surmise (*hyponoēsai*) that there is some wiser insight and plan in all that is going on, even if he came from utmost barbary? (Trans. Burkert 1987: 89–90)

---

[42] Dieterich 1923; Betz 2003.

[43] In my opinion, Burkert's exploration of the ancient evidence on the initiates' experience is unsurpassed.

[44] 'Recess': *mychon*, by emendation from the manuscripts' *mython*.

[45] In the Mithraic mysteries we have no evidence for the enthronement of initiands. In the ritual of the Archery of the Father (Scene A on the Mainz vessel) the initiating Father is seated on a chair from where he menaces the initiand with drawn bow and arrow (Horn 1994; Beck 2000: 149–54). Mithras himself, as we have seen, has 'his proper seat at the equinoxes', replicated as the cult-niche in the microcosm of the mithraeum. Finally, an inscription in the 'Pareti dipinte' mithraeum at Ostia records the dedication of a 'throne to the Sun' (V266, *thronum Soli*).

[46] Cf. the description of the Solar Temple ritual quoted above: 'we had always to turn around the fire only clockwise'. The cosmic dance, orchestrated by the Sun, is of course an ancient commonplace.

As Burkert goes on to say (ibid. 90), 'the intended reference is the cosmos, the dance of stars and sun around the earth and other marvels of nature that surpass the artful contrivances of mystery ceremonies'.[47] But my point here is not to reinforce what we have already established, that a mystery hall is a mini-cosmos, but rather to track, as does Dio, the modalities of the initiand's perception or apprehension of the mystery hall as mini-cosmos. A *pathos* of the soul is accompanied by a *surmise* that there is a wise underlying purpose to both the happenings in and the design of the mystery hall. The further inference is then made that just as there is human intent in the plan of the mystery hall and what happens there, so there has to be divine intent in the macrocosm which the mystery hall replicates.

Ultimately, Dio's argument is a variant on the argument from design for a world governed by Providence. What interests us, however, is not the conclusion of the argument but what Dio has to say about the making of representations which are essential components of the initiate's experience. In point of fact the principal topic of the entire *Olympicus* is precisely *representation*. What did the sculptor Phidias intend in his representation of Zeus in the great cult statue at Olympia? How does Phidias' representation of Zeus differ from Homer's in the epics? What mental representations do we, the beholders of the statue, make in conformity with this template which Phidias has left us? What representations *ought* we to make as rational and moral beings? Though in antique guise, Dio asks much the same questions as the cognitivists we met in Chapter 6 now ask— and from much the same premise: religion is a matter of constructing mental and public representations.

How do those who are 'into' religion (or who 'do religion', to use another colloquialism) go about constructing representations? Again Dio has some interesting answers, which he presents in terms of the 'sources' of religion.[48] These are of two types, the second of which comprises the makers of public representations: the poets, the law-givers (who establish the institutions of religion), the visual artists, and the philosophers (39–48). Since Dio is speaking about Phidias' statue of Zeus at Olympia, his focus is naturally on the creators in the third category, the visual artists, whom he also calls the 'craftsmen' (*dēmiourgoi*), no doubt deliberately invoking connotations of Plato's cosmic 'demiurge' in the *Timaeus*.

Dio's other 'source' of religion is human cognition (27–37). Cognition, Dio holds, is innate and autonomous in the sense that we do not need to be taught how to use it in order to form mental representations and so to apprehend our

---

[47] Burkert continues: 'the comparison of the cosmos with a mystery hall goes back to the Stoic philosopher Cleanthes' (*Stoicorum Veterum Fragmenta* 1, no. 538). Interestingly, in the macrocosmic mystery the Sun is the 'torchbearer' (*daidouchos*), though the reference there is of course to the Eleusinian Torchbearer, not the Mithraic pair.

[48] The literal *pēgai* ('springs') is used at ch. 47. See the 'analysis' of the oration in D. A. Russell's edition (1992: 16–19).

environment correctly. Dio does not of course use the language of cognition and mental representation. In the discourse of his times he speaks of *doxa* and *epinoia*, 'opinion' and 'thought' (27), and in the passage quoted above (33) of 'surmise' (as a verb, *hyponoēsai*). But the intent is the same, and Dio's main point is unaffected: that at least some of our capacity for opinions, thoughts, and surmises is innate, not culturally acquired. On this Dio is emphatic and insistent: 'opinion and thought common to the entire human race, both Greeks and barbarians, essential and innate (*anankaia kai emphytos*), naturally occurring in every rational creature, without mortal teacher or mystagogue, never deceptive...'

Dio is deploying a version of the familiar Stoic argument from universal human consensus for the existence and purposeful benevolence of the gods and especially of 'the Leader of All' (27), Zeus as Providence. Now the existence or otherwise of those particular objects of cognition is not at issue here. What matters is rather the process of cognition and the cognizing human mind as Dio construes them. One object of cognition does however concern us closely: it is— or was—an object in the actual human environment, namely the mystery hall, together with what transpires there.

The witness to the mystery, says Dio, reacts both emotionally and intellectually. His/her intellectual reaction is a 'surmise' (*hyponoēsai*). As usual in antiquity, Dio translates this 'surmise' into propositional form, an opinion or thought, which happens to be true in Dio's view, 'that there is some wiser insight and plan in all that is going on'. From a contemporary cognitivist perspective, we might rather say that the witness to the mysteries makes for himself/herself certain mental representations of the place and the events, representations in which we would be unwise to attempt to disentangle an emotional from an intellectual component. These representations are neither proto-propositions on the one hand nor interior videos on the other. They are the product of innate mental capacities, as Dio affirms, but they are thoroughly conditioned culturally. Yes, the visitor 'from utmost barbary' would include 'purpose' in his/her representation, but that would be because he/she would recognize an instrument or tool, a means-to-an-end thing, a category for which our species has a dedicated intelligence.[49] But the barbarian's representation would otherwise bear little

---

[49] On the development of technical intelligence in the human mind, Mithen 1996; on the mental template for 'tool', Boyer 2001: 59–61. Boyer further postulates an 'inference system' dedicated not to the 'domain of man-made objects' but to the more specific task of ' "finding out how to handle tool-like objects" ' (ibid. 93–135, esp. 102). Dio's barbarian, in a Boyeresque scenario, recognizes the mystery hall as an artefact, which flags it for the inference system which processes questions of purpose and intent. All this cognition is of course well below the threshold of consciousness, and the capacity for it, along with other inference systems, is innate. But *pace* Dio, the barbarian gets no further: he can infer a designer, but not the designer's actual intent, and certainly not the intent's superiority ('that there is some *wiser* insight and plan in all that is going on'). Only someone trained in the culture, i.e. a Greek, can apprehend 'what it's for', and the Greek's apprehension, though not realized in propositional form, would be above the threshold of consciousness.

resemblance to the Greek's, for the cosmos replicated in the mystery hall is not the actual cosmos but the cosmos as culturally constructed by the Greeks. A Greek can apprehend it, a barbarian cannot. With good reason the Eleusinian mysteries were restricted to Greek-speakers. Speaking the language is a good index of an ability to apprehend correctly a culture's artefacts and structured activities, to form appropriate representations, in other words.

Dio's use of *hyponoēsai* ('surmise') recalls the use of the same word (in noun form, *hyponoia*) by his contemporary Plutarch, in a passage from *On Isis and Osiris* (27) which we have looked at twice already.[50] Plutarch there relates how the goddess Isis herself founded her mysteries by 'mixing into the holiest rituals images, thoughts, and imitations of her former experiences' (*tais hagiōtatais anamixasa teletais eikonas kai hyponoias kai mimēmata tōn tote pathēmatōn*). As I suggested, one might think of the central term *hyponoiai* (literally 'under-thoughts') as the realization of the mysteries in the mode of cognition, just as their visual realization is the icon (*eikonas*) and their performative realization the ritual (*mimēmata*). The latter two are public representations, the former private representations of the thinking and experiencing mind.

13. RELIGIOUS EXPERIENCE AS MODELLED BY BIOGENETIC STRUCTURALISM AND 'NEUROTHEOLOGY'

'The thinking and experiencing mind.' I warned above against separating thought from emotion, so we shall not move on from *hyponoia* to *pathos* as if they were separable components of the mystery experience. Is there anything more to say of that experience as an integrated whole? On the subjective experience of initiation Walter Burkert (1987: 89–114) has probably interpreted the extant ancient testimonies to the fullest extent possible. I at least have nothing to add on that score.

However, in the last four decades a new subdiscipline composed of neuroscientists, psychologists, religionists, and philosophers has started to address questions of religious experience not just in terms of states of mind and emotion but also in terms of the concomitant neural events taking place in the brain and nervous system of the person undergoing the religious experience. Their models of religious experience are germane to our present study because, while cultures and religions come and go, the human brain which ultimately sustains all cultures and all religions by its ceaseless making of mental representations is still today what it was two thousand year ago.

The scholars and scientists who have proposed these models gave their subdiscipline singularly unhelpful names: first 'biogenetic structuralism' and then

[50] Ch. 1, sect. 1; Ch. 4, sect. 10.

'neurotheology'. The former was merely opaque, but the latter is more seriously suspect because it seems to imply neural access to the supernatural. Indeed, it is not unfair to say that the neurotheologians do seriously entertain concepts of a transcendental reality accessed by and thus independent of the brain/mind representing it in various ways in various religious experiences. Ontologically, altogether too much is postulated for the transcendent, whether it is called God or the Sacred or Absolute Unitary Being (the favoured term in d'Aquili and Newberg (1999),[51] the book which I shall take as the basic source for neurotheology's models and methods).

From our perspective in the secular academy, are biogenetic structuralism and neurotheology (BS/N) hopelessly compromised by their traffic with the transcendental? I think not. Their correlations of neural and other physiological events with states of mind, feelings, and emotion are empirically verifiable, and their consequent models of the workings of the brain and the mind in religious experience can be assessed like other scientific models. Transcendentalism dwells on the margins of the theory, not at its centre.

To reassure the sceptic about the utility and legitimacy of the basic BS/N method, I shall quote from a critique by a self-acknowledged sceptic who is both an evolutionary biologist and a philosopher (Pigliucci 2002: 269–70):

The book [Newberg and d'Aquili 2001] opens with its most informative chapter: the story of an experiment carried out by the authors on a Buddhist immersed in Tibetan meditation (as well as of a similar experiment on praying [Christian] nuns). The practitioner of course thinks that this sort of experience gets him in touch with his inner self, 'the truest part of who he is' and at the same time he is 'inextricably connected to all of creation'. What the single photon emission computed tomography camera to which he is connected shows is quite different. The scan images display an unusual level of activity in the area of the brain called the posterior superior parietal lobe. The known primary function of this area is to orient the individual in space, essentially a neurological device to keep track of what's up or down, judge distances and relative positions, and in general allow us to move around. When injuries occur in this area the subject cannot properly move in its environment, with the brain apparently baffled at all these necessary calculations of distance, angles, depth and so on. The posterior superior parietal lobe accomplishes its task by first drawing a sharp distinction between the individual and everything else, literally separating the physical self from the rest of the universe. This, in turn, is made possible by a continuous flow of information from each of the body's senses—mediated, of course, by the corresponding areas of the brain.

Under normal conditions, not surprisingly, the posterior superior parietal lobe shows a high level of activity: after all, we constantly need to know where we are and what we are doing. However, and here comes the kicker, during meditation (and—according to the authors—many other similar states, including prayer and drug-induced 'mystical' experiences . . .) that whole section of the brain is essentially non-functional. Newberg and D'Aquili suggest that the brain interprets the low level of sensorial input as a failure to

---

[51] With the unfortunate title *The Mystical Mind*: again, a red rag to the secular academy!

find the borderline between self and the rest of the universe, which nicely explains the feeling of 'being one with the cosmos' that these subjects experience.

Newberg and D'Aquili go on... to correctly conclude that mystical experiences are 'real' in the sense of having a neurological counterpart. However, they somehow distinguish this sort of reality from the one induced by epilepsy, schizophrenia, delusions and so on. Why? Aren't all these phenomena real in the same sense? In fact, given that we experience the world through what amounts to a complex virtual reality simulation created by our nervous system, how could any psychological state not be real in the sense of having a neural correlate?

Instead of following their research to what seems to me its logical consequence—that mystical experiences are no different from delusions and drug-induced states because they alter the functioning of the posterior superior parietal lobe—the authors take a surprising turn. 'Gene [d'Aquili] and I [i.e. Newberg]... believe that we saw evidence of a neurological process that has evolved to allow humans to transcend material existence and acknowledge and connect with a deeper, more spiritual part of ourselves perceived of as an absolute, universal reality that connects us to all that is'.

In other words, the authors think that what clearly looks like a malfunctioning of the brain due to an unusual condition of sensorial deprivation, evolved as an adaptation to get in touch with a higher level of reality.

Before staking out some middle ground, let me first dispose of the objection that, whatever the experience of the trained meditator or the shaman, their altered states of consciousness are irrelevant because our concern is with the experience of the religious rank and file, ordinary Mithraists in ordinary mithraea. Now one of the most impressive features of BS/N is its modelling of a *continuum* of religious experience of differing intensity from meditation as described above to the somewhat unfocused participation in routine ceremonial ritual of the ordinary member of a congregation.

On this continuum, the intensity of, and the attention paid to, the experience is by no means the sole distinction. Actually the model postulates two parallel continua, each of which involves the autonomous nervous system (ANS) differently. Meditation activates the ANS primarily on its parasympathetic (trophotropic) side, ritual (especially fast-paced ritual) primarily on its sympathetic (ergotropic) side.[52] As a further complication, more intense and focused engagement in either meditation or ritual activates, according to the model, the less involved side of the ANS, finally causing both parts to 'discharge' together.

In the brain itself different areas and different neuronal circuits are involved in different religious experiences. One must of course avoid thinking in terms of an old phrenologist's chart. There is no area of the brain which 'does' meditation, and none which 'does' ritual either, and there is certainly no super-area dedicated to 'religion'. The human brain—indeed the animal brain—is a superb multi-tasking apparatus, evolved over the millennia to cope with and to survive in a

---

[52] I use here the biogenetic structuralist terminology as in Lex 1979: 130–47. D'Aquili and Newberg (1999: 23–7) speak of 'hyperquiescent' and 'hyperarousal' states.

complex and dangerous environment. No species of higher animal could ever have afforded the luxury of dedicated neuronal circuitry, let alone circuitry dedicated to meditating on transcendental realities.

In the BS/N model there are however different parts of the brain which take the lead, as it were, not in different religious experiences but at the stage prior to any experience or activity at all, the organization and integration of sensory input for processing by the brain/mind as a whole. The model postulates four 'tertiary association areas' (d'Aquili and Newberg 1999: 32–7):[53] (1) 'the visual association area... located in the inferior temporal lobe'; (2) 'the orienta- tion association area... in the posterior superior parietal lobe'; (3) 'the attention association area... in the most forward aspect of the brain, the prefrontal cortex'; and (4) 'the verbal-conceptual association area... at the junction of the temporal, parietal, and occipital lobes but technically... in the inferior parietal lobe'. The posterior superior parietal lobe we have met already in the case of the meditators (above). An important and distinctive role is played by each of the brain's two hemispheres, the left and the right, in all brain/mind processes (ibid. 28–31; Lex 1979: 124–30). Finally, the limbic system (mainly the amygdala, the hippocam- pus, and the hypothalamus) plays the lead in feeling and emotion, the affective coloration of all experience (d'Aquili and Newberg 1999: 37–41).

On the platform of the brain so structured BS/N, like all contemporary theories of neurocognition, builds a model of the structure of our thoughts, sensations, and emotions, all the subjective phenomena of the human mind. The model postulates seven 'primary functional components of the mind' which it calls 'cognitive operators' (ibid. 50–7). 'Cognitive operators are essentially analo- gous to the operators used in mathematics', for example the signs '+' and '×' which tell us to relate numbers by addition and multiplication respectively. The seven primary cognitive operators are (1) the holistic operator, (2) the reduc- tionist operator, (3) the causal operator, (4) the abstractive operator, (5) the binary operator, (6) the quantitative operator, (7) the emotional value operator.

These seven primary cognitive operators 'allow the mind to think, feel, experience, order, and interpret the universe' (ibid. 51). They create 'cognitive structures':

the result of the functioning of the cognitive operators is 'cognitive structures', which simply refer to the subjective manifestations of ways in which reality is organized by the operators. In other words, depending on which operator is functioning, the world is perceived in terms of synthetic unity, abstract causal relationships, relationships of binary opposition and so on. In ordinary, day-to-day-cognitive functioning, all these operators function together, each relating its function to that of the others in order to construct meaning from experience and create a coherent view of the world. (Ibid. 80)

[53] 'Tertiary' because much of the integration of sensory input has already been performed at primary and secondary levels: e.g. 'the primary visual reception area does not receive an image so much as it receives various patterns of lines, shapes, and colors' (d'Aquili and Newberg 1999: 31).

But what, the sceptic will rightly ask, is this 'universe' which is 'interpreted', this 'reality' which is 'organized', this 'world' of which a 'coherent view' is created? In answer, one must point to the philosophical foundation of BS/N on phenomenology.[54] So 'reality', 'the universe', 'the world' is whatever you choose finally to put at the end of your 'intending', your outreach into the world through sensation and thought. You may postulate brute matter or energy, transcendental being, God, or nothing more than an anti-solipsism marker, a mere something to hold us together in a common universe. Your choice. Yes, the neurotheologians do at times treat 'Absolute Unitary Being' as something onto-logically real over and above its subjective attainment as an experience in meditation. That is their privilege, for they write as often as not for a general readership, not just the secular academy. All that need concern us here is the simple question: do their deistic or theistic beliefs invalidate their approach? No, they do not, for they are an optional appendage not a necessary postulate.

Our model of how the brain and mind function does not rely on there being an external mystical object or being . . . If deafferentation[55] of the orientation association area yields a sense of no space and no time, it matters little if the deafferentation causes the state of no space and no time or allows us to enter this state that already exists 'out there'. (Ibid. 49)

BS/N thus distinguishes very precisely between reality and our *constructions* of reality. Unlike the former, the latter are directly accessible and communicable.

We need take our survey of BS/N no further before judging its utility to our project. Pigliucci's criticisms (above) are certainly just. But they are not fatal. And his own reductionism is equally dangerous. Certainly, one must allow that there would be no neurologically discernible difference between, for example, the workings of the brain circuitry of a mystic experiencing union with the One and a person whose posterior superior parietal lobe had been 'deafferentiated' by trauma or by drugs. Certainly, too, we must set aside all questions of ultimate realities accessed by the meditating mystic or the religious practitioner engaged in ritual. All such experiences are brain/mind events—natural events, if somewhat out of the ordinary. Nevertheless, reducing the experiences of the insane, the drugged, the mystic, and the ritual performer to essentially the 'same' neuronal event, while proper in physiology, is far from proper in a social-scientific inquiry such as ours where group behaviour in a particular culture is the issue. Our concern is with the minds of Mithraists, and how in a collective endeavour they 'got to know' their mithraeum as image of the universe and venue for imagined soul-travel. For this BS/N's approach and methods, once pruned of transcenden-talism, are legitimate and useful.[56]

---

[54] Explicitly acknowledged by e.g. d'Aquili and Newberg (1999: 177–93).

[55] i.e. the temporary or permanent cutting off of an area of the brain: see d'Aquili and Newberg 1999: 41–2.

[56] My acceptance of the methods of BS/N is limited to those early heuristic stages which concern the workings of the human brain/mind outlined above. Its evolutionary account of the development of religion I find unpersuasive, and the actual 'theology' in 'neurotheology' is not part of my mandate.

14. THE 'COGNIZED ENVIRONMENT': THE MITHRAEUM AS MATERIAL REPRESENTATION OF THE INITIATE'S COGNIZED UNIVERSE

In the BS/N model our constructions of reality and the world constitute what is called our 'cognized environment'. Brute reality itself, that which lies beyond our senses and our thinking, is our 'operational environment'.[57] You cannot access your operational environment directly, only through the structures of your cognized environment. But your operational environment can and will affect you—drastically if your cognized environment diverges from it too far.[58] That is why humans and other species of higher animals not only construct their cognized environments but also modify them.

Animals modify their cognized environments phylogenetically over the aeons of evolutionary time. Humans have acquired the ability to represent to themselves environments replete with cognitive structures which enable them to do much more than simply navigate their operational environment, survive, flourish, and reproduce themselves. These additional cognitive structures we build ontogenetically and socially, individual by individual and group by group.[59]

I suggest that the mithraeum is a special case of a cognized environment. This is the mithraeum as apprehended, a cognitive structure of the mind. The actual built mithraeum is a material, hence 'public', representation of this mental representation.

What I am *not* saying is that the physical mithraeum is the operational environment. To say so would be to confuse the 'operational environment' in the technical BS/N sense with the immediate physical environment one moves around in, senses, and sometimes thinks about, an environment in the everyday sense.

It is important to make this distinction explicit. The mithraeum was certainly an environment in the banal sense: you could move around in it; you could sense it and 'the things inside' by sight, touch, hearing, and smell. In that sense one might say that it was the environment you 'operated' in. But this, as we have seen, does not make it the 'operational environment' or even a part of the 'operational environment' in the technical BS/N sense.

[57] On the cognized and operational environments see d'Aquili *et al.* 1979: 12–14; Laughlin 1989: 16–17; 1997: 472–3.

[58] No one can entertain a cognized environment which permits him/her to step blithely off a precipice, unless of course he/she belongs to a winged species. Although we will never be able to confirm it, a flawed cognized environment would appear to be the error of the Solar Temple and Heaven's Gate cultists (above, sect. 11).

[59] Cf. the intriguing theory of Nobel laureate Gerald Edelman and Giulio Tononi (2000) that at the *ontogenetic* level the human brain—and the brains of higher animals too—functions as an environment for 'neuronal group selection'; i.e. that the brain/mind evolves by *natural* selection within the lifespan of each and every individual.

Furthermore, this mithraeum which you move around in and which you apprehend by sight, touch, hearing, and smell is not your cognized environment either. Your cognized environment is the construction which your mind and your senses working together put upon this particular bit of the mundane environment.

But of course you are not just someone who has stumbled fortuitously into this particular chunk of three-dimensional space. You are an initiate of Mithras, so it is with the mind of an initiate that you apprehend this space, and you apprehend it not just as a room but as a 'mithraeum'. This mithraeum of the mind is your cognized environment. The actual mithraeum, as I have said, is a material, hence 'public', representation in brick and stone (or natural rock) of this cognized environment. Functionally it ensures that my cognized environment as a Mithraist in a mithraeum matches yours, and vice versa.

Think of a cognized environment as a set of working templates of reality, of 'the way things are'. As humans we have several templates which we can call up and put in place in addition to the template for physical reality which our minds must develop for mere ontogenetic and phylogenetic survival. We all develop, for example, the template of a cognized social environment to relate appropriately to our conspecifics. For the most part the templates of our cognized physical and social environments function automatically and unconsciously. We do not need to think about *not* stepping off a precipice into thin air. These templates can of course be called to consciousness, and those others which are perhaps unique to members of our species we not only construct in the full glare of consciousness but also communicate publicly, conspecific to conspecific. They are the products of education and training, formal and informal, and they are essential parts of our socio-cultural apparatus.

Why do we say that the mithraeum as apprehended by the initiate is a *special* case of a cognized environment? Because (1) it claims to represent more accurately than any secular or profane representation ever could the real universe and the uniquely true operational environment of all ensouled beings everywhere and everywhen, in time and in eternity; and (2) it substantiates that claim by immersing the initiate physically in an isomorphic 'image of the universe' whose 'contents by their proportionate arrangement furnished symbols of the universe's elements and climates' (Porphyry, *De antro* 6).

Mapping the cognized environment of a Mithraist has been our primary task in this chapter, though of course we have not until now entertained the mithraeum's blueprint in these terms. What now remains is briefly to apply the BS/N approach to the Mithraist's apprehension of his mithraeum—qua cognized environment, qua symbolic universe. We shall limit ourselves to this apprehended ritual *context*, leaving aside the apprehension of actual rituals, since we know rather less about them than about the mithraeum. In any case, I suspect that in the Mithraic mysteries *place* is prior to praxis (supposing *per impossibile* that one can meaningfully disentangle the two).

Let us return to our metaphor of the cognized environment as a set of templates, and let us think of the apprehended mithraeum as a special template which the initiate constructs as he is drawn into the life *of* the mithraeum as community *inside* the mithraeum as physical environment. Remember, though, that the cognized mithraeum as special template is only a metaphor, so please do not reify it.

The power of the apprehended mithraeum within the mind of the apprehending initiate, both intellectually and emotionally, is a function of (1) the radical simplification and mathematical structuring of the special template, (2) the subordination of non-cosmological templates to the special template, and (3) the universality of the special template (subjectively the sense that there is no larger reality to be apprehended).

(1). When within the mithraeum, the initiate's cognized environment is reduced to a few simple primary constituents and their relationships in space and time: the fixed stars, the Sun and Moon and their periods, the other planets, their circular orbits, the pinpoint central earth, Mithras, Cautes and Cautopates, the souls of initiates descending and returning.

(2). It is these cosmological features of the initiate's cognized environment which are brought to consciousness, focused on, and privileged as the relevant 'reality'. However, you do not and you cannot switch off or nullify all other aspects of your cognized environment.[60] For example, if you are seated on the mithraeum's 'northern' bench you know that you are 'above' or 'higher' than your colleagues on the 'southern' bench. But you also know and cannot help knowing that as a matter of physical fact the two benches here on earth rise to the same height above the floor of the aisle. But which of the two 'facts' is part of your cognized environment qua Mithraist in a mithraeum, and which accordingly is the 'truer' and more 'real'? Obviously the former.

(3). Your sense of your cognized environment as the totality of all that is or was or will be is greatly heightened by what we termed 'the Marino experience' (above, sect. 2, para. 6.1), the feeling that as you enter the confined space of the mithraeum you are entering something which is in reality *bigger* than its environment (in the everyday sense). That of course is a stark impossibility. Yet it is precisely what the mithraeum as 'image of the universe' asserts: the inside is larger than the outside—or has no outside at all; the contained contains the container. This paradox and the cognitive dissonance it arouses are fundamental to the mystery of cosmic soul travel. Yes, your mithraeum is still a furnished room in which workaday cognition still functions. But it is simultaneously the universe in which initiate's cognition rules; the inside really is bigger than the outside and the contained does indeed contain the container.

---

[60] This is possible only in extreme meditative states (d'Aquili and Newberg 1999: 109–20), but they were not on the regular Mithraic agenda, as far as we know.

Here we may drop the 'template' metaphor—it has served its turn—and think of the apprehended mithraeum purely in BS/N terms as a 'cognitive structure'. You will recall (from the preceding section of this chapter) that cognitive structures are built by the mind's 'cognitive operators'. The structures are 'the subjective manifestations of ways in which reality is organized by the operators' (d'Aquili and Newberg 1999: 80). As mental phenomena they are not themselves located in specific parts of the physical brain—to suppose so would be onto-logically erroneous—but the operators which build and activate them are cor-related with specific parts of the brain, principally with the 'tertiary association areas', which we reviewed together with the operators in the preceding section. Again, the correlation is not exclusive or one-on-one. The brain has no sealed and autonomous compartments, any more than does the mind.

Now it seems to me that a good starting point for exploring the mental structure which is the cognized mithraeum would be the long quotation from Pigliucci's article (2002: 269–70) in the preceding section, since it indicates explicitly where the neurotheologians and their critics are on common ground as well as where their paths diverge. What is under discussion there is activity—an unusually low level of activity—in the posterior superior parietal lobe. This part of the brain is the 'orientation association area' (OAA) in BS/N terminology.

The known primary function of this area is to orient the individual in space, essentially a neurological device to keep track of what's up or down, judge distances and relative positions, and in general allow us to move around. When injuries occur in this area the subject cannot properly move in its environment, with the brain apparently baffled at all these necessary calculations of distance, angles, depth and so on. The posterior superior parietal lobe accomplishes its task by first drawing a sharp distinction between the individual and everything else, literally separating the physical self from the rest of the universe. This, in turn, is made possible by a continuous flow of information from each of the body's senses—mediated, of course, by the corresponding areas of the brain. (Pigliucci 2002: 269)

The function of the OAA in orienting the individual spatially is not in dispute. Note that in answering the question 'where am I?' the OAA also answers part of the question 'who/what am I?' by separating 'me' from 'not me'. It defines identity by distinguishing between the self and the rest of the universe. In humans these cognitive questions can be entertained consciously and reflectively.

In meditation the OAA shows an unusually low level of activity. It appears to be somewhat isolated, 'deafferentated' in BS/N terms, from the rest of the brain. Hence the mystic's sense of the breaking down of the boundaries between self and non-self and of the unity of all being.

It is here that the neurotheologians and the sceptics begin to part company. The sceptics do not deny the 'reality' of the mystic's subjective experience (how could they?); they point instead to the same feeling of radical disorientation experienced by individuals with lesions in the posterior superior parietal lobe and

ask why the mystic's experience should not be explained—and explained away—
as an analogous mental epiphenomenon. Why promote a subjective sense of no
self and no other into an objective Absolute Unitary Being (capitalization *sic*)?
Fortunately our business can all be done before the fork in the road. We are
concerned with the cognitive structures of Mithraists, not with their structures'
independent ontological reality.

The intent of the Mithraic mysteries, it seems clear to me, was not to abolish
but to *redefine* the mind's normal and necessary distinction between 'me' and 'not
me', between the self and the self's environment. Literally this was a process of
reorientation, and it was not reorientation in a trivial sense, as one might tell
someone 'you're here on the map, not there', or 'you're facing east, not west'.
Rather, it was what one might call 'deep reorientation', in which 'here' and 'there'
are radically redefined and a new map substituted for or superimposed on the old.
More important, it was not inculcated by instruction, or not primarily so. No
doubt initiates here and there were taught the relevant cosmology in propositional form. But actually to experience 'the descent and return of souls', rather
than just to know about it as something germane to you before your birth and
after your death, required a more profound reconfiguration of your cognized
environment. Such *re-cognition* could only be acquired by activity within the
mithraeum (moving around, occupying space) and by sense perception of
'the things inside in proportionate arrangement'. Only so could you *recognize*
the mithraeum for what it was intended to be and so accomplish there what you
had to accomplish. In principle, learning cosmic soul-travel in a mini-universe is
no different from learning to drive in a car; for it is in a car and by driving a car,
not in a classroom or from a book, that you learn to drive competently and
successfully. Similarly, you get to know your mithraeum as universe by road-
testing it as universe. Epistemically, we return to the old distinction between
'knowing that' and 'knowing how to', between propositional knowledge and
practical knowledge. Conditioned as we are to ancient hierarchies of the intellect,
we tend to think of the former as the 'higher' form of knowledge. But we may
surely agree that the latter is the 'deeper', for it engages more brain areas and brain
circuitry, not to mention the senses and the autonomic nervous system. Socrates
was intuitively right in valuing the craftsman's understanding of his trade.

To be more precise, we might compare learning how to navigate the universe
in the mithraeum to learning how to drive not on the road but in a simulator.
The mithraeum is indeed the universe, but it is of course a virtual universe. And
the advantage of a simulator, whether a simulated road and car or a simulated
universe, is that you pay no immediate penalty for your mistakes. But sooner or
later you must transfer your newly minted cognized environment from the
simulator to the road, to the context where steering wheel, clutch, gear shift,
accelerator, and brake issue in an actually existing, actually moving car. No more
virtual ritual reality, which means no more make-believe operational environment, no more risk-free crashes. Of your subsequent driving record in your

material car on the material road we can say much, and what we say is all verifiable, in principle if not practice. Of your record as an initiate of Mithras who has graduated from your esoteric simulator at death we can say nothing whatsoever, at least not in the secular academy. But in truth, your postgraduate career, if indeed you have one, concerns us not at all. Rather it is your cognitive processes, your mind/brain states while still among us in your cosmonaut's flight simulator, that claim our attention. These, thanks largely to advances in cognitive science, are now increasingly accessible to us.

Clearly the mental structure of the cognized mithraeum subsists and is activated (for want of better words) in the 'orientation association area' of the brain, but it is activated there not in isolation—the OAA is not 'deafferentated' as in the mystic's contemplation—but in response to sensory input from sight, touch, hearing, smell, taste, all of which is, as it were, pre-programmed. There are two aspects to this pre-programming of sensory stimuli. One is in the 'public' objective world. Everything that the initiate sees, touches, hears, smells, and tastes in the mithraeum, all 'the things inside', are designed 'by proportionate arrangement' to establish the equation 'mithraeum = universe'. The second aspect of the pre-programming is in the private subjective world of the initiate's mind. The structure of the cognized mithraeum does not have to be built anew from sensation and interpretation of sensation each time the initiate enters. It is there 'in mind' and needs only to be reactivated.

Obviously too the 'visual association area' (VAA, 'located in the inferior temporal lobe') is also engaged; or to retain the language used above, one can say that the mental structure of the cognized mithraeum subsists and is activated in the VAA:

The neurons in the [tertiary] visual association area receive highly processed input from the secondary visual areas (in the occipital lobes) from both hemispheres. These neurons scan the entire visual field ... so as to alert the person to objects of interest or motivational importance through the interconnections with the limbic system and the autonomic nervous system. (d'Aquili and Newberg 1999: 32–3)

One need only add that to the Mithraist in his mithraeum 'the entire visual field' and everything in it are pre-fraught with significance: what you see is the universe.

Also engaged is the tertiary 'attention association area' (AAA, 'situated in ... the prefrontal cortex'):

No other area of the entire cerebral cortex is as intimately and richly interconnected with the limbic system as is the attention association area ... Likewise, this area is profusely interconnected with all the secondary and tertiary sensory association cortices. Only the attention association area receives fibers from all sensory modalities (vision, hearing, touch, taste, and smell) as well as from the tertiary association areas ... The attention association area is involved in forming conceptual thoughts by means of its rich inter-connections with the verbal-conceptual association area and can also help in forming complicated visual images... Thus, this area has become involved in many types of behaviors and activity, but goal-oriented behavior or even purposive organization of thought always derives from input from the attention association area. (Ibid. 34–5)

Note here how emotion and value are aroused by the entrainment of the limbic system with which the AAA is 'intimately and richly interconnected'. You will not only recognize your mithraeum as universe but also feel intensely and of course positively and warmly about it. The structure of your cognized mithraeum, in other words, has built-in value.

The intent of the mithraeum, we know, was not merely to replicate the universe in a physical model but to enable 'goal-oriented' action, namely the enactment of the descent and return of souls in a mystery. Clearly this intent, which is an integral part of the initiate's mental structure of the mithraeum, is formed and activated in the AAA.

'The attention association area is involved in forming conceptual thoughts by means of its rich interconnections with the verbal-conceptual association area', the fourth of the tertiary association areas explored by d'Aquili and Newberg, sited 'at the junction of the temporal, parietal, and occipital lobes but techni-cally... in the inferior parietal lobe'.

The verbal-conceptual association area may be the area of the greatest integration of sensory input in the brain. In a sense, it is an association area of association areas, and it maintains rich interconnections with the vision, hearing, and touch association areas... The verbal-conceptual association area is also responsible for the generation of abstract concepts and relating them to words. It accomplishes this task through rich interconnec-tions with the language center, which is primarily located in the left hemisphere and incorporates much of the temporal lobe and parts of the frontal and parietal lobes. The verbal-conceptual association area is also involved in conceptual comparisons, the order-ing of opposites, the naming of objects and categories of objects, and higher-order grammatical and logical operations. (Ibid. 37)

The verbal-conceptual association area's (V-CAA) principal contribution to the cognitive structure of the mithraeum is the logic which binds together and articulates the whole, in fact precisely what we are calling 'star-talk'.

All four of the tertiary association areas of the brain described by d'Aquili and Newberg participate in the creation and activation of the cognized mithraeum. One must not think of this sort of mental structure as some sort of bounded entity residing solely in a defined location of the brain or in a some dedicated bunch of neurons. Of its nature the structure is both composite and diffuse. In a sense it is both nowhere and everywhere. In my layman's opinion, what is unusual about the cognized mithraeum is neither some peculiar quality of the structure itself nor the modalities by which it is created in and by the association areas of an initiate's brain, but rather the restriction of the stream of input through his senses to data pre-programmed in his actual physical environment to carry the sign-ificance 'mithraeum = universe'.

In BS/N theory, just as the brain has its association areas, so the mind has its 'cognitive operators' which are its 'primary functional components'. In the preceding section of this chapter I listed and very briefly described these operators. The function of the operators is to build and articulate the cognitive structures which 'allow the mind to think, feel, experience, order, and interpret the universe'. BS/N theory postulates seven of these cognitive operators, three of which seem to me especially germane to the formation of the cognized mithraeum: the holistic operator, the binary operator, and the emotional value operator.

I must admit to a certain unease about the concept of the cognitive operator. The operators, as psychological rather than neurological constructs, are not as accessible empirically as are the association areas discussed above. However, cognition has to be analysed in one way or another, and the BS/N functional differentiation by operators seems to me as reasonable as any. Perhaps the operators should be considered heuristic devices rather than actual 'components' of the mind. However, it is certainly proper to relate them, though non-exclusively, to certain areas of the brain. Thus the holistic operator correlates with the orientation association area, since it is primarily in the OAA that the brain/mind learns to discriminate between 'me' and 'not-me' and so to define the self over against the rest of the universe. Likewise, the emotional value operator correlates with the limbic system, not of course in isolation but in conjunction with higher (that is, less primitive) cortical areas, since our feelings are thoughts too, not just raw affect or emotion. Lastly the binary operator correlates not with a particular area or areas of the brain but with the brain's binary structure as two interconnected hemispheres (left and right) each of which both complements and duplicates the functions of the other.

The binary operator articulates the rich array of oppositions which are such a prominent feature of the Mithraic mysteries, both internalized as cognitive structure and externalized in words communicated, actions performed, and 'things inside the cave' visually apprehended. I have discussed binary opposition in some detail in Chapter 5, section 8. Binary opposition is so fundamental to the mysteries that I have postulated 'Harmony of Tension in Opposition' as one of their two axioms or ultimate sacred postulates.

One must remember finally that realizing the mysteries in the mithraeum is not an act of solitary contemplation. In the mithraeum we re-cognize our conspecifics present as fellow souls, fellow voyagers in the macrocosm there represented. Our kinship is actualized in communal ritual, not just by being together in the mithraeum but by performing structured, repetitive actions which, as d'Aquili and Newberg put it (1999: 89), 'synchronize affective, per-ceptual-cognitive, and motor processes within the central nervous system of individual participants and ... *among* the various individual participants' (em-phasis added).

15. THE COGNIZED UNIVERSE AND CELESTIAL NAVIGATION: THE CASE OF THE INDIGO BUNTING

Humans of course are not the only species of animal to construct a cognized environment, though we are perhaps the only one to bring it to full consciousness. We not only construct a cognized environment—any animal endowed with locomotion must do this or die—but also think about it and talk to our conspecifics about it. In other words, our cognized environment is more than just the necessary mental proxy for our operational environment.

Together with our human ability to think about and talk to each other about our cognized environment comes the ability to construct alternative environments, one of which, the 'mithraeum = universe', we have been analysing in the present chapter. Other animals presumably do not have this luxury (though who finally knows?). Their cognized environment is their sole template of reality, and for each species natural selection has optimized that template for survival in its operating environment.

In many instances it is possible to infer some particular feature of the cognized environment of a species from the behaviour of the phenotype. As an analogy to the cognized environment constructed by our Mithraic cosmonauts let us take a look at the cognized environment of an animal which must travel vast terrestrial distances from one location to another and back again at regular intervals, a migratory bird—specifically the Indigo Bunting.

The Indigo Bunting (*Passerina cyanea*) was the subject of an elegant experiment to determine empirically how it navigates, what features of its environment it selects and constructs mentally as indicators of 'proper direction'. For long-distance travellers there are no better or more reliable indicators than the celestial bodies, for they are the same at your destination as at your point of departure and they are equally accessible there as here. So it is with buntings. They navigate by the stars. Specifically, the experiment, which was conducted in a planetarium, proved that they navigate by reference to the north celestial pole recognized as the point around which the circumpolar stars revolve (Emlen 1967; Berthold 2001: 153–4).[61]

Now the revolution of the circumpolar stars is nothing but a manifestation of universal daily motion, and universal daily motion is nothing other than the Revolution (or circle or period) of the Same which Plato in the *Timaeus* construes both as the highest visible manifestation of Unity and Reason and as existing, in a more or less deformed copy, in the heads of humans and animals.[62] So by a nice coincidence, which he would surely have savoured, the Indigo Bunting appears to have done in a literal and scientifically verifiable way precisely what Plato urges us

---

[61] See also the Smithsonian's website <http://natzoo.si.edu/Animals/Birdfacts/navigation.htm>.
[62] See esp. *Timaeus* 47b5–c5, 90c6–d7, to which passages we shall return in the next chapter on 'star-talk'.

humans to do. It has cultivated internally the Revolution of the Same. By this it navigates, by this it finds its way.

The venue of the bunting experiment was a planetarium, because in a planetarium the motions of the celestial bodies can be replicated. In this respect a planetarium is a model or image of the universe. The bunting of course cannot discriminate between the model and 'the real thing', which is a comment not on its powers of discernment or of representation but simply on its inability to conceptualize. Nevertheless, a comparison between the bunting's planetarium and the initiate's mithraeum is surely apposite. Each structure is an artificial public representation of the mental representations of the macro-environment of each of the two groups, buntings and Mithraists. In their respective model universes each group constructs its cognized environment and learns to navigate successfully. The difference is that our buntings learn to navigate in a *proxy* model universe, and if they are released they will perform exactly as do their conspecifics in the world outside; in contrast, our Mithraists learn to navigate in an *alternative* universe which, to be sure, shares the same features and structure as our visible cosmos but which, esoterically, one enters and leaves not from and to some workaday earthly venue but by descent of the soul from the heavens at birth and its departure thither at death.

16. CONCLUSION

'What was it like?' Asked of the initiate's subjective experience the question is finally unanswerable, unless of course we construe it in the most literal way as a request for an analogy. The problem is not so much the inability to enter other minds as the 'ineffability' of the experience. It is literally indescribable. This is not because it is or pretends to be something particularly grand or 'sacred'. It is simply that language cannot do the job. 'Unspeakable words which *cannot* be spoken' (*arrhēta rhēmata ha ouk exon anthrōpōi lalēsai*), said the Christian Paul of Tarsus of his own ascent as far as the 'third heaven' (2 Corinthians 12: 2–4), not 'words which are unspeakable because they *may not* be spoken'. Language is linear, sequential, left-brain, and so cannot narrate a quintessentially right-brain experience (visuo-spatial, simultaneous or non-temporal, holistic). It is not that the left hemisphere plays no part in the experience and the formation of representations during it, or that the right hemisphere is entirely incapable of language: glossolalia, significantly, is right-brain. Rather, the experience simply cannot be captured in normal descriptive narrative.[63] Metaphor is the best that regular language can do.

---

[63] On the relevant functions of the two hemispheres of the brain, see Lex 1979: 124–30, Springer and Deutsch 1985: 235–9; on 'ineffability', Watts 2002: 185–6; on glossolalia Lex 1979: 128; on Paul's experience, Shantz 2001.

I have already stated my hypothesis that the Mithraist's experience of 'getting to heaven' was not an 'extraordinary' experience in the sense in which Burkert (1987: 89–114) quite rightly characterizes mystery-cult initiations of the Eleusinian type. Undoubtedly the Mithraic initiations which we see on the side-benches of the Capua Mithraeum (Vermaseren 1971) and on Side A of the Mainz ritual vessel (the 'Archery of the Father'—Beck 2000: 149–54) were of that type, and no doubt the external drama of their enactment was matched by the internal emotional turmoil and cognitive *aporia* of the initiand. In Harvey Whitehouse's bipolar theory of modes of religiosity (Whitehouse 2000; Whitehouse and Martin 2004; Beck 2004*b*) such experiences and the rituals which engender them are manifestations of 'imagistic', as opposed to 'doctrinal', religion. Their representations are held principally in 'episodic' or 'flashbulb', as opposed to 'semantic', memory. But knowing your mithraeum as the universe and experiencing 'the descent and departure of souls' seems to me an experience of a different sort: not the extraordinary subjective pay-off of a single extraordinary ritual, but a habit of mind—admittedly a very strange habit of mind—acquired by repetitive 'assimilation to the holy symbols' in numerous acts of worship and communal festivity played out in the mithraeum, not that different perhaps from the experience of the regular lay participant in the Christian eucharist.[64]

The expression 'assimilating themselves to the holy symbols' (*syndiatithesthai tois hierois symbolois*) is Proclus' phrase from a description of the experience of initiation (*In remp.* 2.108.17–30). Burkert uses that description to good effect in the penultimate paragraph of *Ancient Mystery Cults* (1987: 113–14), and in that context the assimilation of the self to the symbols is both sudden and intensely fraught. But it need not be that way. A Mithraist assimilates himself to the holy symbols by habituation, by re-cognition, by constant renewal in ritual of the initiate's compact: to accept that his mithraeum is the universe and that movement there, whether actual or imagined, is cosmic soul-travel.

We need not suppose that fervent belief and strict attention to every phase of the ritual (whatever it was) were necessary conditions of the Mithraic experience any more than they are of the Christian's experience in the eucharist. Minds wander, and in the ritual context the acceptance of a set of conventions ('let this be so') is what matters, not belief ('this really, really is so'), however strongly held.[65]

The sense of access to some ampler space afforded by ritual is temporary, provisional, and intermittent. This is not intended as a religious statement about humanity's limitations in approaching the divine. Rather, it is meant as a factual, verifiable statement about the experiencing of ritual. Neurocognitively, the altered state of the participant in ritual is indeed intermittent and inchoate.

---

[64] I offer the example as the only one about which I can speak experientially.
[65] Eloquently argued by Roy Rappaport (1999: 107–38).

Exaltation, whether of thought or emotion, is transitory. Getting to heaven is done by fits and starts, and it is achieved by the 'acceptance that what is being acted out is already so'.[66] For the initiate, the path to heaven is already there: the ritual just makes it 'visible and actual'. And that is a matter of commitment to the symbols and what they symbolize rather than the quality or intensity of inner experience.

[66] Murphy 1979: 320–1. Murphy writes about the mass from the perspective both of a priest and of a biogenetic structuralist. His perspective is thus *ex officio* different from a layperson's perspective. Moreover, his template for experience is prescriptive (how the participants ought to represent access to heaven to themselves) rather than descriptive (how they do in fact represent it).

8

Star-Talk: The Symbols of the Mithraic Mysteries as Language Signs

1. INTRODUCTION: 'STAR-TALK'

In our 'template for a re-description of the mysteries' (Ch. 1, sect. 3) I proposed that 'the mysteries' common *symbolic idiom* across axioms, motifs, domains, structures, and modes is the language of astronomy/astrology or *star-talk*' (Proposition F). In Chapter 7 we saw, in the context of the mithraeum, that star-talk is the logic which articulates the symbols and symbol complexes of the mysteries. It is now time to look at star-talk more systematically, for just as the form and function of the mithraeum was literally inaccessible to us without considerable prior discussion both of symbolism (Chapter 5) and of cognition and representation (Chapter 6), so it will be impossible properly to consider the mysteries' other ubiquitous symbolic structure, the tauroctony, without first exploring star-talk.

First, what star-talk is not: it is not just ancient astronomy and astrology under a catchy and shorter name. Secondly, what it is, or rather how it should be construed: it is a language, a language 'talked' by the monuments because that is the logic by which they are articulated, and for the same reason a language silently talked by the representation-forming minds of the apprehending initiate. It is also of course the language spoken (in the usual sense of the word) by astronomers and astrologers. It has, however, other presumed speakers, and therein lies its peculiarity. In the culture of antiquity the celestial bodies were gods, and philosophy endowed them with reason of a very high order. We should never forget that for the ancients the stars spoke—or the gods spoke through them. The fact that we no longer consider them either rational or communicative is of far less importance than the fact that the ancients did.

With the postulate that star-talk is the internal logic of the mysteries' symbol system in place, we should revisit our 'banner text' (Ch. 1, sect. 1) from Origen's *Contra Celsum* (1.12). The 'mysteries' (*teletai*) of the Persians, says Origen, 'are cultivated rationally (*logikōs*) by the erudite but realized symbolically by common, rather superficial persons'. My intent all along (and especially in Chapter 4 on 'doctrine') has been to break down that invidious distinction between the wise and the vulgar, between those who can 'get it' by reason and those who can only 'get it' if it—whatever it is—is mediated to them through symbols. We have established that the mysteries are apprehended in their symbols by the wise as well as the vulgar—since the mysteries are symbolic constructs, how else could they be accessed? We shall now see how the mysteries are also apprehended 'logically' (*logikōs*) by the vulgar as well as the wise. The logic is star-talk, which the initiate learns, at least as listener, in the apprehension of a symbol system imbued with that logic.

2. MITHRAIC ICONOGRAPHY AS 'UN LANGAGE À DÉCHIFFRER' (R. TURCAN)

Before we can study star-talk as the 'language' of Mithraic symbols and repre-sentations, I must first meet a formidable theoretical objection. Are we making a serious category mistake in proposing that symbols can function as language signs to convey definite meanings?

In studies of Mithraic iconography (and not uncommonly in classical studies in general) there is an assumption, usually implicit, that symbols do indeed 'mean' and that 'reading' symbols is legitimate hermeneutics, in principle no more problematic than reading a text. In practice of course it is far from straightforward, and there is all too often wide disagreement on the meanings 'read'. But disagreement is usually seen as an index of better and worse readings (my reading is better than your reading) rather than of invalid hermeneutics (we're both going about it in the wrong way).

We have in fact visited this problem in a different guise as the 'problem of referents' addressed in Chapter 3; for to ask what a complex of symbols 'means' is much the same as asking to what it 'refers'. There we looked at the three principal answers of twentieth-century scholarship (referents in the surrounding culture, Iranian referents, and celestial referents), and we concluded that none was entirely satisfactory and that this line of interpretation has reached something of a dead end. But we did not look at the underlying semantic and semiotic question: do symbols mean, do they function as language signs?

As an exemplar of the best in that line of interpretation of Mithraic iconog-raphy we looked at Robert Turcan's article 'Feu et sang: à propos d'un relief mithriaque'.[1] Turcan is explicit about iconographic symbols as constituting a language:

C'est un langage à déchiffrer, et l'on ne peut guère hasarder de déchiffrement qu'en se fondant sur la sémantique courante des motifs ou des attributs, en fonction de certaines idées communes au monde gréco-romain. (1986: 221)

---

[1] See above, Ch. 4, sect. 2; Ch. 3, sect. 2.

[It is a language to be deciphered, and one can only try deciphering it by relying on the then current semantics of the motifs or attributes, in terms of certain ideas common to the Graeco-Roman world.]

Les images sont un langage dont les éléments sont faits pour être compris en fonction d'un vocabulaire commun au sculpteur et au spectateur de son oeuvre, en l'occurrence au responsable et aux fidèles de la communauté mithriaque. (ibid. 220)

[The images are a language whose elements are made to be understood by means of a vocabulary common to the sculptor and viewer of his work, in context to the person responsible and to the faithful.]

Turcan is commendably aware of the implications of treating iconography as a language, in particular the importance of identifying and characterizing not only the discourse (first excerpt) but also the language users, those who speak it and hear it (second excerpt). However, he does not discuss the validity of this entire hermeneutic approach, for he regards the assimilation of iconography to language as quite unproblematic.

3. CAN SYMBOLS FUNCTION AS LANGUAGE SIGNS? THE QUESTION AS POSED IN CULTURAL ANTHROPOLOGY

To justify the claim that star-talk is the language of the Mithraic mysteries we must look further afield—to cultural anthropology. As one might anticipate, in anthropology the question (can symbols function as language signs?) is posed not just for those visual symbols which constitute an iconography but for entire symbol systems, manifested in deed and word and artefact, which constitute cultures and religions. This broader perspective is welcome here, precisely because our postulated star-talk is multi-media: it is 'spoken' in the symbolic action of ritual quite as much as in the viewed symbolic structures of the monuments. We have to accommodate Mithraists pouring honey on each other's hands and, less strikingly but of no less significance, feasting together on the opposed benches of their mithraeum.

As one might also expect, our question has been posed mainly in the context of, or in reaction against, the symbolist interpretations of cultures, notably those of Mary Douglas, Clifford Geertz, Edmund Leach, and Victor Turner. These anthropologists (significantly, among the least utilized by classicists) have treated symbol systems as language-like, but they have not tested the analogy with the same rigour as the four scholars to be mentioned next.

Frits Staal, Dan Sperber, E. Thomas Lawson, and Robert McCauley (the last two collaboratively) have addressed explicitly the question of the language status of rituals and their constituent symbols and symbolic acts. The titles of their relevant works are illuminating, so we cite them here: Staal 1975: 'The meaninglessness of ritual'; Sperber 1975: *Rethinking Symbolism*; and Lawson and McCauley 1990: *Rethinking Religion: Connecting Cognition and Culture.*

In summarizing their positions, I shall not attempt to adjudicate between them.[2] Justice could not possibly be done in the space available to works of considerable subtlety and sophistication. Besides, my aim in this chapter is not to reach a definitive position so much as to test the hypothesis, encapsulated in Turcan's claim that Mithraic iconography is 'un langage à déchiffrer', that symbols and symbolic actions are language signs.

Staal's position is the most straightforward and radical. For Staal, ritual is indeed language-like—perhaps it is even the Ur-language of our species—because it has rules which are closely analogous to those of syntax.[3] It has, however, no semantics, since its signs, the performative acts, are without external meaning: they refer only to themselves. Clearly, the price to be paid for sending the Mithraic symbol system down that linguistic road would be high indeed!

Staal took as his paradigm case, observed in the field, Vedic ritual and in particular the Agnicayana, a 3,000-year-old fire ritual. Sperber, at the same time, was working with the Dorze, a people of southern Ethiopia, and his study, which confronts the symbols-as-language question more directly than Staal's, covers not only ritual acts but also the full range of a culture's symbolism manifested in artefact and word as well as in deed.

Sperber's position is almost the reverse of Staal's. On the one hand, he denies that symbol systems are languages precisely on the grounds that they fail to meet certain defining criteria, both formal and functional, for natural languages (1975: 90). In particular, he demonstrates that language conveys 'meaning' in ways that symbol systems do not and cannot (ibid. 8–12). Language can do this not only because the references of its signs are stable and agreed (compare the fluidity and polysemy of symbols) but also, and more fundamentally, because its signs can be combined in relationships of 'entailment, paraphrase, contradiction, etc.' which its users understand intuitively how to handle. Symbol systems have no such 'semantic properties';[4] ergo, they are not languages.

On the other hand, although in a strict linguistic sense Sperber finds symbolism 'meaningless', he considers it far from vacuous. To the contrary, for Sperber symbol systems are fundamental cognitive systems by which human societies get to know, to construct mentally, and to represent themselves and the world.

---

[2] For a lengthier survey covering a wider selection of the scholarship (though omitting Sperber), see Bell 1997: 61–72, esp. 68–72. Lawson and McCauley (1990) build on, rather than in opposition to, Staal 1975 and Sperber 1975. For that reason their running critique of the two earlier works is constructive and illuminating.

[3] See Lawson and McCauley 1990: 56–9.

[4] See Lawson and McCauley 1990: 40, whence the phrases in quotation marks are taken.

Lawson and McCauley, in the most detailed of the three studies, agree with Staal, against Sperber, that rituals are languages, or rather that they are generated like utterances according to definable linguistic principles; they disagree with both Staal and Sperber in that they allow 'meaning' in ritual and in other systems of symbols; and they agree with Sperber that symbol systems are cognitive systems, ways to communicate within a culture its particular understanding and ordering of the world.

4. CROSSING SPERBER'S BAR: THE CASE FOR MITHRAIC ASTRAL SYMBOLS AS LANGUAGE SIGNS

I shall concentrate here on Dan Sperber's case against symbols as language signs, principally because it is the most formidable and the most comprehensive. (Staal, and Lawson and McCauley, both allow at least rituals to function as languages.)[5] If I cannot somehow clear Sperber's bar, I cannot establish star-talk as the language of the Mithraic mysteries. At the very least I must be able to make a special case that astral symbolism as deployed in the mysteries meets Sperber's criteria for languages. This I intend to do, while at the same time agreeing with Sperber that symbols *usually* do not function as language signs.

What then are Sperber's criteria for language signs which symbols fail to meet, and why do I claim an exception for astral symbolism in the Mithraic mysteries? Equally important, since Sperber maintains that symbols cannot 'mean', what is it that symbols do which language signs do not do, and can I claim that astral symbols in the mysteries also continue to perform that function as well as their postulated star-talk function as language signs?

'Symbols', says Sperber (1975: 85), 'are not signs. They are not paired with their interpretations in a code structure. Their interpretations are not meanings.' 'Pairing' of sign and meaning 'in a code structure' is the key criterion: languages meet it, symbol systems do not. The language 'code' with its pairings is of course hugely complex. It tells us, for example, not just how to use and comprehend the signs 'cat' and 'dog' in the construction and recognition of empirically true (and false) propositions about the animals signified, but also how to make sense out of a pseudo-propositional exaggeration such as 'it's raining cats and dogs' or the well-known command in the primary school reader 'see Spot run!' And it guides us more or less effortlessly to the generation of contextually appropriate new utterances: 'See Spot chase Ginger up a tree! Spot has treed Ginger!'

---

[5] Lawson and McCauley present a full 'grammar' of ritual in ch. 5: 'Outline of a theory of religious ritual systems' (1990: 84–136). What is outlined is a 'universal grammar' of the 'internalized' language ('I-language') underlying the 'externalized' languages ('E-languages') of the ritual practices of particular religions and cultures. For our purposes, it is unnecessary to pursue language down to this deep Chomskyan level.

Nothing of this sort is enabled by a symbol system. Let us take as an example the densest and most central complex of symbols in the Mithraic mysteries, the symbols in the tauroctony. (For the sake of the experiment we must forgo all astral interpretations except the absolutely unavoidable, for example that the image of Sol refers to the Sun). One looks in vain for the systematic deployment of these symbols ('dog', 'snake', 'scorpion', 'raven', etc.) as signs in other utterances, whether in the Mithraic mysteries or elsewhere; and one looks equally in vain for the shared and accessible code which regulates the use of the symbol system and enables new speech acts in the language.[6]

Only by metaphoric licence do symbols mean. This is the metaphor which allows us to attribute meaning to anything and everything 'from the meaning of life to the meaning of the colour of leaves in autumn' (Sperber 1975: 83). However, 'the attribution of sense is an essential aspect of symbolic development in *our* culture. Semiologism is one of the bases of *our* ideology' (ibid. 83–4, Sperber's emphasis). The Dorze, the people of southern Ethiopia studied by Sperber, 'know nothing of it'. For them, 'the question "What does that mean?" (*awa yusi?*) can only be asked about a word, a sentence, a text or a directly paraphrasable behaviour, such as a nod' (ibid. 83).

However, one should not read too much into Sperber's assertion of the meaninglessness of symbols. He has merely disembarrassed symbolism of a language metaphor which he felt did more harm than good, thereby freeing it to be construed for what it is—here too I agree with him—a *cognitive system*. Sperber's particular target, or rather the subject of his rescue operation, is Lévi-Straussian structuralism:

when we strip the work of Lévi-Strauss of the semiological burden with which he has chosen to encumber it, we will then realize that he was the first to propose the funda-mentals of an analysis of symbolism which was finally freed from the absurd idea that symbols mean. The argument may be summarized in this way: if symbols had a meaning, it would be obvious enough. All these learned terms—signifier and signified, paradigm and syntagm, code, mytheme [—] will not for long hide the following paradox: that if Lévi-Strauss thought of myths as a semiological system, the myths thought themselves in him and without his knowledge, as a cognitive system. (1975: 84)

---

[6] It is true that certain elements of the tauroctony are also deployed in other compositions. For example, in the Trier rock-birth (V985) the dog, the snake, and the raven are witnesses of the birth of the god just as they are witnesses of the bull-killing. Or consider another example, taken from outside the mysteries: in a mosaic from the Antioch area the four subsidiary animals of the tauroctony are found (together with a centipede, a panther, a trident, a sword, and an ithyphallic dwarf) surrounding the evil eye, presumably to ward it off (Levi 1947: 33–4, pl. IVc). The point is not that symbols cannot be redeployed and recombined—obviously they can—but that there are no rules which are intuitively brought into play by a 'speaker' and which can be explicitly displayed by a 'grammarian', for getting from one 'utterance' to another. If there are principles involved, they are those of 'listing'; and listing, though a complex business semantically (for listing within Mithraism, see Gordon 1998), is grammatically primitive. It functions solely by parataxis: one symbol, another symbol, another symbol . . .

'Evocation' is Sperber's key term for the work done by symbols. While language signs *mean*, symbols *evoke*. And to say that symbols evoke is really just another way of speaking of the apprehension of symbols by the cognizing agent when the object of cognition is made the grammatical subject. The initiate apprehends whatever it is that the symbol evokes. An ancient exegete probably would have used the verb *ainittesthai*, to 'intimate' or 'speak in riddles (*ainigmata*) about'.

Traditionally hermeneutics has been largely a matter of explicating what symbols 'evoke' or 'intimate'. A fine early modern example, very germane to our study, is the explication appended to the drawing of the Ottaviano Zeno tauroctony (V335)[7] by the sixteenth-century collector Pighius. There, in the key to the symbols, we learn that the composition is an allegory of agriculture and its necessary virtues. For instance, our four animals participate as follows:

(I) Corvus qui diligentiam significat (The raven which signifies diligence)
(O) Canis quo amor et fides [significantur] (The dog by which love and loyalty are signified)
(P) Serpens quo providentia [significatur] (The snake by which providence is signified)
(S) Scorpio qui generationem [significat] (The scorpion which signifies generation)

It is easy to laugh at such an interpretation. But while we can be fairly sure that the founders of the mysteries did not compose the tauroctony with these exact equations to hand, who is to say that no practising Mithraist ever construed his icon with thoughts of farming, its seasons, and its moral values consciously in mind? To the contrary, it is entirely probable that explications along these lines were both given and received.

Moreover, provided that one does not insist on a single exclusive set of one-for-one meanings, exploring what symbols *evoke*, individually or in combinations, is entirely legitimate.[8] It is likely, for example, that the tauroctony's metamorphosis of the bull's tail into an ear of wheat evokes, and was intended to evoke, agriculture. These and similar evocations were explored by Luther Martin (1994) in a study aimed not at deciphering some fixed meaning injected into the icon by its originators but at tracking and relating the cluster of ideas about sacrifice to which we may suppose the representation of the bull-killing gives expression.

The method is unobjectionable, and in fact almost all modern scholars employ it to some extent, for it merely harnesses known features of the culture of classical antiquity, where self-evidently relevant, to the interpretation of the icon.[9] But it

---

[7] Vermaseren 1978: 7–9, pls. XI, XII.
[8] Richard Gordon's 'Reality, evocation and boundary in the Mysteries of Mithras' (1980*b*) is explicitly Sperberian in method and intent (note 'evocation' in the title).
[9] See above, Ch. 3, sect. 2: 'Referents in the surrounding culture?'

does not treat the interpreted symbols as the signs of a language, except by metaphor ('the language of allegory', etc.), for it does not postulate signs paired with their meanings in a publicly accessible code operative wherever the signs are deployed.

Unlike symbols, language signs *are* 'paired with their interpretations in a code structure' (Sperber 1975: 85). The language code has a set grammar and a set semantics transparent to all users and accessible to anyone who wants to learn the language. There are no arcana, though the grammar and semantics generally operate below the level of conscious manipulation. (If you have to think about them while speaking, you have not yet acquired full competence to the standard of a native speaker.) Finally the language code offers the limitless potential for generating new utterances within the set grammar. Languages, in other words, are recursive.

I must now make the case that Mithraic astral symbols meet Sperberian criteria for language signs. Let us take as our first example the four attendant animals at the bull-killing, whose allegorical 'significances' were explicated by Pighius (above): the raven, the dog, the serpent, and the scorpion. The astral interpretations of the tauroctony which we reviewed in Chapter 7 (sect. 4) read these symbols as signs for the constellations Corvus, Canis Minor, Hydra, and Scorpius.

Now the question, it is important to understand, is not whether the sculpted and painted images of the animals in the tauroctony are or are not symbols of the respective constellations. That question I now regard as settled: lingering sceptics are invited to read my article 'Astral symbolism in the tauroctony: a statistical demonstration of the extreme improbability of unintended coincidence in the selection of elements in the composition' (Beck 2004c: 251–65 = ch. 12). The animal images do indeed symbolize, signify, denote, refer to—whatever term you wish—the constellations; the tauroctony was composed with that intent in mind by the person(s) who commissioned and designed it; and the initiates so apprehended it. The tauroctony is, among other things, a star-chart. Insofar as the astral interpreters were mistaken, it was not their reading of the tauroctony as star-chart which was at fault but the implausible identities for the tauroctonous Mithras which they then claimed the star-chart warranted (ibid. 235–49).

The mere fact that there is a Raven constellation, a Dog constellation (actually two: Canis Major and Canis Minor), a Snake constellation (actually three: Hydra, Draco, Serpens), and a Scorpion constellation (Scorpius) does not in itself imply that some quasi-language is operative in the tauroctony. That hypothesis only becomes plausible when one observes (1) that *all* the standard elements in the composition of the tauroctony have their celestial referents (above, Ch. 5, sect. 4); (2) that the constellations represented were not picked at random from the sphere of the fixed stars but were chosen because they were contiguous in an astronomically definable and meaningful area of the heavens (Beck 2004c: 262–4); (3) that astral symbolism, as we have already seen, is not confined to the tauroctony but pervades the Mithraic mysteries in their entirety, including the other two great constructs of the mysteries, the grade hierarchy under the seven tutelary planets (Beck 1988: 1–11) and the mithraeum as 'cosmic image' (see the preceding chapter). The language of star-talk, if language it is, is the idiom of the mysteries, not just of the icons. We should note too that it is a performative language: it is spoken, for example, in the enactment of the Procession of the Sun-Runner now known to us from the Mainz ritual vessel (Beck 2000: 157–63).

The second of the three considerations above requires elaboration. If it were the case that the selected constellations came from anywhere and everywhere in the heavens, then one might reasonably conclude that they were present as astral symbols for no other purpose than to give a certain 'cosmic' flavour to the scene and/or that other, non-astral reasons drove the selection.[10] But the selected constellations do in fact all fall within the same defined area of the heavens, and that area is astronomically meaningful as a section of the celestial sphere. In other words, the selected constellations are not just contiguous; they also form a block about which one can say something astronomically interesting beyond simply describing its extent and location: it consists of a band of zodiacal constellations extending in a semicircle (neither more nor less) from Taurus eastward to Scorpius together with the southern paranatellonta of the central part of that semicircle. (Paranatellonta are the constellations on either side of the zodiac which 'rise alongside' zodiacal constellations.)

The intent of that selection does not immediately concern us. What does concern us is that there is an astronomical logic at work, just as there is an astronomical logic at work in the plan and ritual use of the mithraeum. This logic is our 'star-talk'.

Now language signs do not normally convey meaning in isolation from each other or by mere accumulation (except in lists). They function in relation to each other. And so it is with star-talk signs. Again, let us take our examples directly from the tauroctony. The bull signifies Taurus and the scorpion Scorpius. In representing the bull and the scorpion the tauroctony is not just saying 'Taurus!' and 'Scorpius!' as independent exclamations. The uttering of those two 'words'

---

[10] The most obvious non-astral reason would be that the raven, the snake, the dog, and the scorpion are there in the composition because in the bull-killing venture Mithras was accompanied by a raven, a snake, a dog, and a scorpion. In the sense that the icon constructs the story, this is true, but only tautologously. One has to ask if there was a *prior* story which required representation of the animals in their own right and not as constellation symbols. Perhaps so; but if there was, the strange, surreal quality of the scene suggests an *allegorical* narrative. In a study of the subject, the emperor Julian rightly states that 'incongruity' (*to apemphainon*) is the hallmark of allegory (*Or.* 7. 217 C, 222 C–D). The cluttered, over-attended scene of the bull-killing is nothing if not 'incongruous'.

However, if the attendant animals (not to mention Sol, Luna, and the torchbearers) are elements in an allegory, surely it has to be a *celestial* allegory; for only in the heavens and with celestial identities can that motley crew of witnesses be rendered congruous. But to treat the animals as symbols in a celestial allegory only returns us to the question: 'an allegory of what?' Rather than once again searching fruitlessly for allegorical meaning in the astral symbols of the tauroctony, we would do better to return to our exploration of astral symbols as language signs throughout the mysteries.

together necessarily brings into play the relationship between the two things signified, the two constellations/signs of the zodiac named. That relationship is one of 'opposition' in the sense of 'opposite each other' on the celestial sphere and on the ecliptic/zodiac.

The opposition of Taurus and Scorpius is not a contingent matter, something which could be otherwise, like for example the opposition of two planets at a particular moment in time. Although it originated in the fact that the group of stars likened to a bull is on the other side of the heavens from the group of stars likened to a scorpion, with the introduction of the 360° zodiac of twelve equal signs the opposition of Taurus and Scorpius develops into a definitional truth: Taurus is the second 30° sector of the ecliptic/zodiac (longitude 30°–60°), Scorpius the eighth (210°–240°). Consequently, nothing except a change in the underlying astronomical convention can ever disconfirm the relationship 'Taurus is in opposition to Scorpius'. It is part of the grammar of star-talk.

Now Taurus lies at the east end of the band of constellations represented in the tauroctony and Scorpius at the west end. From the opposition of these two signs, it follows that the tauroctony represents one half of the zodiac, neither more nor less; and from the signs/constellations actually represented it follows that the semicircle from Taurus eastward to Scorpius is represented, not the semicircle from Scorpius eastward to Taurus. In terms of the design of the tauroctony, all these choices could have been different. That is not the point. What matters is that once the decision has been taken to deploy certain star-talk signs rather than others, what the signs mean and say in collaboration with each other at the literal level is fixed and unalterable. It cannot be otherwise. It is also non-esoteric (not one thing to the wise and another to the vulgar) and accessible to all competent speakers, readers, and hearers.

Prima facie at least we have a case that astral symbols can, and in the Mithraic mysteries do, function as language signs. They meet Sperber's criterion of being 'paired with their interpretations in a code structure' (1975: 85). The 'code structure', star-talk's grammar, is the strict geometry—or rather uranometry—of basic Hellenistic astronomy. Star-talk is thus extremely rich in necessary relationships—opposition is a good example—which serve as the grammatical warp and weft, as it were, to sustain the intricate knotted patterns of its utterances. Clearly, too, star-talk meets the criterion of public accessibility. It is not an idiolect, a private language of the Mithraic mysteries alone. Finally, it is recursive. One can generate new star-talk utterances indefinitely, as a glance at the output of horoscopal astrology will show.

One question which I asked above remains to be answered. If astral symbols function as language signs, do they forfeit their powers of evocation in the same context? They do not: nothing prevents a Pighius (above) from hearing the evocations of 'diligence', 'love and loyalty', 'providence', and 'generation' from the raven, the dog, the snake, and the scorpion respectively; and nothing prevents a Martin (1994) from hearing evocations of the triumphant virtues of the Roman soldier-farmer in the tauroctony's collective symbolism. Certainly, I find the latter's interpretation much more persuasive than the former's. But since symbols do not carry a set complement of designer-approved evocations, neither interpretation can be endorsed as uniquely right and neither interpretation can be dismissed as objectively wrong. What is certain, however, is that the evocative powers of the symbols are in no way compromised or diminished by their other function as star-talk language signs. Evocation and star-talk meaning often reinforce one another. For example, the scorpion in the tauroctony *evokes* 'generation' in that it fastens on the genitals of the dying bull, and in star-talk the same figure *means* the sign/constellation of Scorpius. The link between evocation and meaning is reinforced by the assignment of Scorpius to the genitals in the astrological system by which each of the twelve signs of the zodiac was assigned to a part of the human body. Those relationships between sign and body part are of course star-talk phrases. They are among the necessary truths of the language.

While evocations are finally subjective matters ('hey, it works for me' is irrefutable), star-talk meanings and the relationships between its signs are not. Taurus and Scorpius are opposed signs. If you read or hear 'quadrature', you are simply mistaken: you are misreading or mishearing.

This does not mean that the tauroctony or any other symbolic structure in the Mithraic mysteries can be interpreted in an objective, straightforward, and definitive way simply because it speaks in star-talk. Star-talk, it cannot be emphasized too strongly, is not the key to the encrypted secrets of the tauroctony. It simply lets us read, by correctly apprehending the signs in context, the language in which the tauroctony is written. Star-talk, like natural languages, is 'medium, not message'.

I shall not be presenting anything like a comprehensive grammar of star-talk. In any case, how the language works is best seen in context; so the proper place for more on star-talk grammar will be our penultimate chapter on the tauroctony. However, a few general points about the language still need to be made before we turn to the important topic of how the ancients themselves construed this celestial language.

First, as is usual with languages, star-talk admits both homonyms and synonyms. This is the linguistic equivalent of the polysemy of symbols, a matter we have already raised. The sign 'snake', for example, can signify in star-talk any one of three different serpentine constellations: Hydra, Draco, and Serpens.[11] That it signifies Hydra in the tauroctony is clear by context: Hydra fits into the band of constellations signified by the animals; the other two celestial snakes do not. By

---

[11] The three serpentine constellations are not the only star-talk meanings of 'snake'. From its setting alongside half the zodiac on the ceiling of the Ponza mithraeum, with its head next to Leo and the tip of its tail next to Aquarius, it is evident that it there signifies the nodes of the lunar orbit, personified and subsequently attested as *caput* and *cauda draconis* (Beck 1976a, 1978).

the same token, the sign 'dog' in relation to all the other constellation signs in the contiguous group signifies Canis Minor, but in other relationships signifies Canis Major and its lucida, Sirius the Dog Star.

Secondly, star-talk as spoken, for example, in and by the Mithraic tauroctony differs from natural languages in that it is not constrained by linearity. In the natural languages the signs are deployed in a sequence: a temporal sequence in the spoken language, a spatial sequence in the written language. Moreover, the flow of signs is unidirectional in both the giving and the receiving: one cannot hear in reverse, and while one can read in reverse it literally makes no sense. Star-talk, however, is non-linear and it is unconstrained by sequence and direction. In the tauroctony, for example, one can read and apprehend the meaning of the constellation signs 'at a glance' synoptically. One may also read from right to left or from left to right; either way is meaningful: if you read from left to right you will be tracking the daily motion of all celestial bodies westward; if you read from right to left you will be tracking the peculiar motions of the Sun, the Moon, and the planets eastward. Lastly, since the tauroctony's star-talk utterances are made simultaneously, not sequentially in real time, the same sign can carry double or multiple meanings simultaneously. Thus the dog can signify Canis Minor and Canis Major simultaneously without contradiction; likewise the bull can signify Taurus and the Moon simultaneously without contradiction. Texts in star-talk, one might say, are many-stranded, hence denser and more convoluted than texts in natural languages, although the actual lexicon of star-talk, the inventory of its signs, is much more meagre than the lexicons of the natural languages.

5. STAR-TALK: ANCIENT VIEWS CONCERNING ITS SPEAKERS, DISCOURSES, SEMIOTICS, AND SEMANTICS

> Consider what a demonstration of God's power the celestial signs (*ta ourania sēmata*) furnish, for they are all stamped (*entetypōmenōn*) from the beginning to the end of time on the heavens, the worthy book of God.
>
> (Origen, *Philocalia* 23.20, Junod 1976: 200).

> The gospel ... written on the tablets of heaven and read by all those considered worthy of the knowledge of all things (*to euangelion ... to en tais plaxi tou ouranou graphomenon kai hypo pantōn tōn ēxiōmenōn tēs tōn holōn gnōseōs anaginōskomenon*).
>
> (Origen, *Commentary on John* 1.68, p. 94 Blanc)

I have chosen these epigraphs from Origen for a number of reasons. First, they are intended to forestall the objection that I am inventing a special language of astral symbolism, manifested solely in the Mithraic mysteries, in order to 'solve' a hermeneutic problem peculiar to those mysteries alone. To the contrary, I shall demonstrate that treating the celestial bodies as the signs in a language was not uncommon in antiquity; hence, that 'star-talk' in Mithraic symbolism is but a particular case of a much more widespread convention which the ancients themselves explicitly recognized as a language. Whether there 'really' is such a language is beside the point. As the ancients well appreciated, languages do not exist apart from their speakers. Conversely, if you can identify sign-users and the signs by which they appear to communicate, you are obviously justified in postulating a language.

The epigraphs also let us dispel any residual misunderstanding that by 'star-talk' we mean astronomical and astrological discourse under a catchy (and economical) new term. Astronomical and astrological discourse, as preserved for us in the ancient texts, may well be second-order star-talk, but the primary language is conveyed in and by the celestial bodies themselves and their motions. In star-talk, the visible heavens are the medium of communication, the 'book', and the contents of heaven are the 'signs imprinted' on it. This is no metaphor: Origen clearly intends that everything is to be taken literally.

Why, though, do we go first to a Christian source to illuminate star-talk in a pagan religion? The answer is that in the Christian sources the language of the stars is a topic addressed far more explicitly and in detail than in the pagan sources.[12] In particular, there is an intense concern with the speakers/writers and audience/readers of star-talk, in other words with its language community; likewise with the moral and spiritual status of the language itself and its speakers: God-talk or devil-talk? Among pagans, such concerns are usually absent or at least not as urgent. They had no motive, then, to develop an explicit semiology of star-talk. They could and did take the stars as signifiers for granted.

Another reason for looking first at Christian views on star-talk is the Christians' concern—and paganism's relative lack of concern—with text itself as the vehicle of ultimate meaning and value. It was natural for Christianity, as it developed and interpreted its own scriptural canon, to evaluate other sign systems in terms of text and the language in which text is communicated.

There are two passages of scripture which absolutely compel the Christian exegete to treat the stars as signs and thus to entertain at least a rudimentary semiology in order to explicate them. The first passage is Genesis 1: 14–19, the creation of the Sun, Moon, and stars on the fourth day. God's stated purpose for the celestial bodies is unambiguous: 'God said, "Let there be lights in the vault of heaven to separate day from night, *and let them serve as signs both for festivals and for seasons and years".*' The purpose of the celestial bodies is thus to serve as *measures* of time and as indicators of the *proper* times for celebrating festivals. Any

---

[12] On the topic of early Christian attitudes to astrology I wish to acknowledge my debt to Timothy Hegedus, whose doctoral dissertation, published in 2005, I supervised.

thoughtful pagan, incidentally, would endorse this definition of the function of the celestial bodies.

The second passage is from the Christian New Testament, the well-known story of the 'Star of Bethlehem' and the visit of the Magi to the infant Jesus (Matt. 2: 1–12). In performance, if not in name, the Magi (*magoi*) are astrologers, and the story presupposes, in this instance at least, both the validity and the respectability of astrology. The Magi read the sign aright: the Star indicates the 'child who is born to be king of the Jews' (2: 2). How Christian exegetes reconciled the story with their general hostility to astrology and astrologers is another story.[13] But whatever solution one arrives at, constructing a semiology of sorts to cope with it is unavoidable.

Starting, then, with the Christian authors, we shall attempt to reconstruct something of the semiotics of star-talk in the ancient world. We shall look particularly at star-talk's postulated language communities, both explicit and implicit; also at the extraordinarily varied constructions placed on the language's moral status, its intent, its speech acts, and its signs.

6. ORIGEN'S VIEW: 'HEAVENLY WRITINGS' AND THEIR ANGELIC READERS[14]

> Just as in our books certain things are written for our understanding, such as the creation and other mysteries, and other things such as the instructions and commandments of God, so that knowing them we may take action, even so it is possible that the heavenly writings (*ta ourania grammata*) which the angels and divine powers know how to read well contain both things to be perused by the angels and functionaries of God, so that they may delight in their knowledge, and also instructions which they may receive and act upon.
>
> (Origen, *Philocalia* 23.20, Junod 1976: 200–2)

Our second epigraph from Origen leads us further into the question of star-talk's language community. Origen's answer is somewhat unusual, although in

---

[13] One which we do not have to tell here. It is well explored by Hegedus (2000: 174–93, 268–73), who emphasizes Tertullian's solution (*De Idolatria* 9.4), which was 'to make a simple temporal distinction in the history of astrology, to separate "those magi" from "today's astrologers": "In fact that science [astrology] was only permitted until the Gospel, in order that after Christ's birth no one should henceforth interpret a person's nativity from the stars" ' (Hegedus 2000: 269). Hegedus also shows that some respect was accorded even to star-worship as a *praeparatio evangelii* (ibid. 283–5): e.g. Clement, *Stromateis* 6.110.3: 'He [God] gave the Sun, the Moon, and the stars for religious observation (*eis thrēskeian*); God made them for the gentiles (*tois ethnesin*) . . . so that they would not become complete atheists and so be completely corrupted.' Better a living star than a dead idol, at least before the coming of Christ.

[14] See Hegedus 2000: 283–90, and as background Scott 1991.

identifying supernatural users he is typical of Christian thinkers in antiquity. Origen's readers of celestial writings are angels, divine powers (*dynameis theiai*), functionaries (*leitourgoi*) of God. The writer is God himself, the creator and deployer of the signs. From the receiver's perspective, then, the text and the language itself are 'read only'. God has 'burnt' the text into the CD; it is unalterable by other users.

Despite the supernatural speakers, Origen's linguistics have a strangely modern, Chomskyan ring to them. Rather than limiting inquiry to the syntax and semantics of explicit 'sentences' (which he would in any case consider beyond human comprehension), Origen concentrates on the speakers and functions of star-talk. One could say of Origen what the authors of an introductory text on Chomsky's 'revolution in linguistics' say in their first paragraph: 'he was proposing to draw conclusions from the nature of language to the nature of the... language user' (Smith and Wilson 1979: 9).

Note that Origen's star-talk is not a language whose sole or even primary function is to communicate facts by way of true propositions. Just as our scriptures contain not only things that we should *know* about ('such as creation and certain other mysteries') but also things that we should *act* on (i.e. God's commandments), so, Origen claims, the heavenly writings contain both orders for the supernatural powers to execute and (rather charmingly) things to delight them (*hina euphrainōntai ginōskontes*)—God's video show for his angels, as it were. This emphasis on the *performative* function of language is echoed in modern studies of ritual and myth.[15]

Origen accommodates within his model of star-talk the misunderstanding and deliberate misrepresentation of the utterances of the language by fallen angels. This, as we shall see, accounts for the hit-and-miss record of astrology—and for certain other things more sinister. But before we look at Origen's account of celestial misinformation and disinformation, we should turn to the altogether more sombre views of Augustine on the language of the stars.

7. AUGUSTINE'S VIEW: STAR-TALK AS A DEMONIC LANGUAGE CONTRACT[16]

For Origen, at least in the *Philocalia*, star-talk was angelic. For Augustine, as for most Christian theologians in antiquity, it was diabolic. Augustine's target was what we would call 'astrology', the reading of heavenly signs for predictive ends. For Christians, astrology posed an urgent problem. Especially if the celestial signs are viewed as causal, not merely foretelling terrestrial events but actually bringing them about, then man's free will is diminished and the omnipotence of God

[15] e.g. Bell 1997: 68–83.

[16] On this topic and on Augustine's semiology in general, see R. A. Markus's essays (esp. nos. 1, 4, and 5) in *Signs and Meanings: World and Text in Ancient Christianity* (1996).

infringed.[17] The solution was not only to refute the validity of astrology and its techniques but also to demonize it—literally. Star-talk was the talk of devils. If you started talking it, you found yourself keeping some very bad company indeed. Wittingly or unwittingly, you had entered a chat-room which a prudent and pious person would want at all costs to avoid.

In *Christian Doctrine* (*De doctrina Christiana*), when discussing astrology (2.21.32.78–24.37.95), Augustine concentrates less on the signs themselves than on the speakers and the speech acts, and in this respect he mirrors Origen, though his conclusions are diametrically opposite. For Augustine the danger of star-talk is that it traps the astrologer-speaker by a binding contract in a community of language users whose other members are demonic.

This is not just a matter of guilt by association. The contract is built into the language convention itself.[18] Here we touch on that element in the *De doctrina Christiana* which is nowadays most valued, Augustine's theory of signs and of language.[19] Signs are of two sorts, 'natural' (*signa naturalia*) and 'given' (*signa data*). In natural signs there is a causative link between the sign and what is signified. Smoke, in this sense, is a sign of fire. With given signs, in contrast, there is no such link. It is purely by convention that a particular sign signals a particular signified. The convention is an agreement among a group of users to employ a set of signs with fixed meanings understood by all in the group. For humans the principal conventions are those of the various natural (in the modern sense) languages, communicated in speech and writing. Those who use the set of agreed signs constitute the language community. Whether they wish it or not, then, astrologers have enrolled themselves in a demonic community simply by using astral signs according to the conventions of star-talk. The stars have no prior meaning in and of themselves; they acquire meaning because certain individuals, demonic and human, agree to treat them as signs.

[Of language in general:] All these meanings (*significationes*), then, derive their effect on the mind from each individual's agreement with a particular convention (*pro sua cuiusque societatis consensione*). As this agreement varies, so does their effect. People did not agree to use them because they were meaningful; rather, they became meaningful because people agreed to use them (*nec ideo consensuerunt in eas homines quia iam valebant ad significationem, sed ideo valent quia consensuerunt in eas*). [Of the language of astral signs and other modes of divination:] Likewise the signs by which this deadly agreement with demons (*perniciosa daemonum societas*) is achieved have an effect that is in proportion to each individual's attention to them. (*De doctrina Christiana* 2.24.37.94, trans. Green 1995: 101)

Augustine here differentiates implicitly between stars as things and stars as language signs. This distinction comes into sharper focus at a later point in the

---

[17] On early Christian opposition to astrology and the polemical arguments used against it see Hegedus 2000: 10–173.

[18] See Markus 1996: 31, 108–10, 135–8.   [19] See Markus 1996: 1–35, 105–24.

De doctrina Christiana (2.29.46) when he discusses the stars as objects of knowledge and teaching.

Here, knowledge of the physical heavens and their contents is not of much interest to Augustine. He is frank and straightforward with his reason: since secular scientific knowledge is useful only insofar as it enables biblical hermeneutics, and since the Bible makes but scant reference to the heavenly bodies, the discipline of astronomy has little to offer the Christian scholar. Such interest as it has for Augustine is limited to calendrics, the determination of the date of Easter being the sole and obvious example given of the discipline's practical utility.

This calendric bias does, however, lead Augustine to make some perceptive remarks on the peculiar power of astronomy to make accurate and verifiable predictions—not of course the predictions of astrology (that being the semiological abuse of the discipline), but factual and, as we would characterize them, scientific predictions about the future positions of the heavenly bodies themselves. Moreover, what can be projected into the future can be retrojected into the past. We know where the planets were on a given historical date just as securely as we know where they will be at a date in the future. The celestial past thus belongs to the domain of history, the record of fact which, because it is immutably so and not otherwise, bears the seal of God.

8. ORIGEN AGAIN: THE DEMONIC MISCONSTRUCTION OF STAR-TALK

Origen, we saw (above, sect. 6), postulates a language of the stars spoken by God for the delight and instruction of his angels and other superhuman powers. The problem with this language for us as humans is that we may perhaps overhear utterances in star-talk, but we will not understand them properly, precisely because they are not meant for us at all. We are not their intended audience. By definition, then, the semantics of star-talk on this model are irrecoverable. We can identify the language community and we can grasp several other important facts about both the community and the language: first, that we ourselves are necessarily outside that community (our phenotype not equipped to receive star-talk); secondly, that communication within the language community flows in one direction only (from God to his angels); and thirdly, that the language's signs/words are the stars and its utterences the configurations and motions of the stars. But of the utterances spoken in star-talk we comprehend nothing for certain and never will, at least in our present sinful and mortal condition.[20]

---

[20] Origen allows that 'holy souls rid of the present bondage' may indeed read the celestial writing (*Philocalia* 23.20, p. 200 Junod). In *Contra Celsum* 5.13 he predicts that the stars too, as part of material creation, will themselves be freed from the 'futility' (*mataiotēs*, quoting Rom. 8: 20) of the present dispensation.

What does get through to us, in Origen's account, is a certain amount of celestial misinformation and disinformation. Origen's semiology of star-talk is here extraordinarily ingenious in that it elegantly accommodates both defective utterances and lies. The utterances he must account for within his model are the predictions of astrologers and their statements about astral causation. Here is where the demons make their entrance, though the scenario is fundamentally different from Augustine's. Rather than *inventing* star-talk in a corrupt compact with human astrologers, they *mis-remember* the language which they had once known in their prelapsarian state as angels. They are still language users, but incompetent ones. Hence the hit-and-miss quality of astrology, as they and the astrologers struggle to communicate in a semantically and grammatically inadequate pidgin.

More subtly, the demons use star-talk to tell lies, to convey not misinformation but disinformation. The signs of the language in the heavens are of course beyond their reach, but the events on earth which they are thought to signify are not. So a clever demon can, for instance, manipulate the onset of epilepsy to coincide with the phases of the Moon in such a way as to suggest a causal or indicative relation.[21] Thus, implicit in Origen's full account there is not one language of the stars, but two: the heavenly bodies themselves speak—or rather, act as signifiers in—good star-talk, while demons and astrologers speak bad star-talk. The former is veridical but unknowable (to us); the latter is all too plausible and comprehensible, but it is semantically deceptive. Break the code, if you will, but remember that the deciphered meanings are a pack of lies.

9. STARS TALKING THEOLOGY: THE 'HERETICAL' INTERPRETERS OF ARATUS AS REPORTED BY HIPPOLYTUS (*REFUTATIO* 4.46–50)

We turn next to a marginal sect discussed by the heresiologist Hippolytus of Rome. What is fascinating about this group is that not only did its members read the heavens as a text with both literal and figurative meanings, but they also appealed for legitimacy at both the exegetic and interpretive levels to a second, terrestrial text which is both real and extant: the *Phaenomena*, an astronomical poem composed by Aratus of Soli in the third century BCE.

In attacking these 'heretics', Hippolytus has this to say (*Ref.* 4.46.2):

In order that what I am going to say may appear clearer to my readers, I have decided to discuss the thoughts of Aratus on the disposition (*diatheseōs*) of the stars in heaven, how certain people allegorize those thoughts by transferring the celestial likenesses [i.e. the

---

[21] Thus Origen on the healing of the epileptic boy in Matt. 17: 14–21 (*Comm. in Matt.* 13.6). Common terrestrial language underwrites the connection, for epilepsy in Greek is 'lunacy': as the father explains to Jesus (v. 15), his son 'has been made lunatic' (*selēniazetai*).

constellation figures] to what is said in holy scripture (*hōs tines eis ta hypo tōn graphōn eirēmena apeikonizontes auta allēgorousi*) . . . showing a strange marvel, how[22] their own sayings have been 'catasterized' (*xenon thauma endeiknymenoi hōs katēsterismenōn tōn hyp' autōn legomenōn*).

The semiology of the Arateans[23] (as we may call them) resembles Origen's, in that appeal is made to two sacred texts. Origen postulates the Bible on earth for humans and the stars in heaven for angels. The readership differs for each text, the celestial text being illegible and incomprehensible to terrestrial humanity. The Arateans too postulate both an earthly text, the *Phaenomena* of Aratus, and a celestial text, the visible heavens, the actual 'phenomena' which gave Aratus the title for his work. But the readership of these two texts is the same, humans searching for understanding and salvation.

Hippolytus characterizes the Aratean method as 'allegorizing', of which it is certainly a form. However, it is important to distinguish this form of allegory in which the signifiers are real, actual, related entities (in this case recognized groupings of the stars of heaven) from allegories constructed *ad hoc* from fictional stories or make-believe situations. A good example of the latter class of allegory is that imputed to Homer by Porphyry in an essay on which we have frequently drawn in the present study, *On the Cave of the Nymphs in the Odyssey* (*De antro*).[24] The *De antro* is an extended philosophical and theological explication of the cave described by Homer in *Odyssey* 13.102–12, the cave near which the sleeping hero is set on his return to his native land. So 'full of obscurities'[25] is Homer's description that we cannot believe such a cave ever existed or could exist in the actual world. Obviously, then, since it is neither a real cave to be found on Ithaca nor yet a realistic fiction,[26] Homer must intend something different. That something can only be allegory. Homer's description is indeed bizarre from a naturalistic point of view, so one has every sympathy with Porphyry's premise, if not with his solution.

Unlike the invented elements of allegories of that sort, the elements of the Arateans' story, the stars of heaven, are real and their disposition a fact accessible to all who care to gaze up at them on a clear night. 'Don't believe *us*', say the

---

[22] Or, following Marcovich's emendation of *hōs* to *hōsan*, 'as if'.

[23] It is not necessary to suppose that the Arateans actually existed as an identifiable sect. These unnamed and otherwise unattested heretics may be no more than a fictional construct for Hippolytus to locate the teachings of an anonymous Gnostic writer and to furnish notional converts back to orthodoxy. Since we are not concerned with the sect itself but with its implied semiology, a lone author will support my case just as well.

[24] Allegory, and the allegorical interpretation of Homer in particular, was very much a Neoplatonic project. See Robert Lamberton's study, *Homer the Theologian* (1986, esp. 66–76, 119–33, 318–24). The allegorization of Greek (and Latin) texts is paralleled by the allegorization of Hebrew texts, first by Jews, Philo in particular, and subsequently by Christians.

[25] *Asapheiōn* (*De antro* 4).

[26] As Lamberton points out (1986: 125–6), Porphyry somewhat undercuts his own argument in *De antro* 4 by finding a possible candidate for the Ithacan cave in the works of an earlier geographer, Artemidorus of Ephesus.

Arateans (in effect), 'believe the evidence of your own eyes. Read what you see in the book of heaven, and if you really want to understand what you read, listen to our explications, and check them against another accessible text, by an acknowledged astronomical expert, the *Phaenomena* of Aratus.'

An essential postulate of the Arateans' semiology is that the constellation figures of Aratus coincide with, and carry the same literal identities as, the traditional constellation figures of Graeco-Roman culture, both learned and popular. The astral bears, Ursa Major and Ursa Minor, were the same pair of bears for Aratus as for the astronomers and seafarers of classical antiquity—as indeed they remain in today's celestial cartography, with some tidying of boundaries. Whatever else they were, they were agreed signs in one of the most widespread and durable semiotic conventions of our world. Because they were so widely current, the Arateans could depend on their accrued authority, as well as on the authority of Aratus himself, to legitimate the figurative meanings which they read into them.

It is precisely on the status of the stars as signs that Hippolytus attacks and 'refutes' the Arateans. As he cogently argues (*Ref.* 4.50), the stars themselves long pre-existed the constellation figures which humanity descried in them. The constellations, far from being the archetypes of things on earth (as the Arateans contend),[27] are mere arbitrary groupings, constructed by humans so as to make the stars more easily recognizable (*eusēma*).

However, what seems to us an obvious and self-evidently correct rebuttal would not appear so to many of the ancients. Hippolytus is no modern, making a general semiological point about the arbitrariness of non-natural signs. For him there could be no question of the human construction of meaning entirely by language convention. Meaning, ultimately, is external to humanity. Whence does it come, and by what means? To reply with the Arateans that it comes from the stars in constellation figures forming a salvific text is neither more nor less reasonable than to assert, with Augustine (see Markus 1996: 1–35), that it comes through a certain set of historical facts expressed in the narrative of the Old Testament and construed as God's signs. It all depends, finally, on what one privileges as sacred text.

To illustrate the Arateans' reading of the celestial text, I set out the meanings which they ascribed to their celestial signs in two columns (see table). In the first column are displayed the traditional constellation meanings, in the second the esoteric meanings. In Augustine's semiology this would correspond to the distinction between the literal meanings of Old Testament events and facts, which are the subject of exegesis, and their figurative meanings, the subject of typological interpretation.

It is the Arateans' parallel sacred text, the *Phaenomena*, that enlightens us about the figurative meanings of the signs which at the literal level in the celestial text

---

[27] *Ref.* 4.49: the terms quoted are *eikones, paradeigmata, ideai.*

Traditional meaning (literal)	Esoteric meaning (figurative)
Draco	the diabolic Serpent
Hercules	Adam
Lyra	the harmonious instrument of God's law
Corona Borealis	the crown that rewards those who follow God's law
Serpens	a lesser serpent, offspring of Draco
Ophiuchus	God's Logos that restrains the serpents and comforts man
Ursa Major	the creation (*ktisis*) of Adam; the road and wisdom of the Greeks
Ursa Minor	the creation of Christ; the road and wisdom of the elect
Canis Major	the Logos (alternative sign)
Cepheus	Adam (alternative sign)
Cassiopeia	Eve
Andromeda	the soul (*sic* sing.) of Adam and Eve
Perseus	the Logos (alternative sign); the cosmic axle
Cetus	a diabolic monster (as the serpents)
Cygnus	the divine spirit

signify the constellations. For example, why the Bears, Ursa Major and Ursa Minor, should signify the routes to wisdom for the 'Greeks' and for the elect respectively is entirely opaque until we read Aratus' comparison of the two constellations at *Phaenomena* 37–44. Aratus speaks of the Bears as aids to navigation. Ursa Major, which is used by Greek sailors, is the larger and more obvious. Ursa Minor is used by the Phoenicians; it is smaller, and since it wheels closer to the pole it is the more reliable and accurate guide. These contrasted descriptions intimate to the heresiarch how he might develop and nuance his basic contrast between the two orders of creation, 'that according to Adam' and 'that according to Christ'. The constellations now come to represent not merely the creations themselves, but their opposed systems of 'doctrine and wisdom' (*Ref.* 4.48), by which one navigates life's journey. The Greater Bear is the route and wisdom of the Greeks, of Man's creation, not God's. Being the larger, it is the route of the many. Its error is manifest in an alternative name, used by Aratus in this navigational context: Helice, the Coil. Those who follow it 'go round in circles'. It leads nowhere. The Lesser Bear is the route of the wiser Phoenicians. It is the route of God's creation, not Man's. Being smaller, it is the road of the few, the 'narrow road', with all the soteriological connotations of that term. It is more accurately aligned, it leads 'straight' to its destination, and it is altogether preferable. For does not Aratus say authoritatively that it is 'better for sailors' (line 42) and that 'by it the Sidonians navigate most directly' (line 44)? It too has another name, figuratively relevant in context: Cynosura, the Dog's Tail. The Dog is the Logos, shepherding the elect along the proper path and keeping at bay the beasts which would destroy them. All is clear, if only we 'read' the heavens, Aratus in hand.

The celestial navigation of the Arateans recalls the celestial navigation of the Indigo Bunting discussed in the preceding chapter. Buntings navigate, in the literal sense of planning and implementing a journey in the actual world, by means of a cognitive template of the revolution of circumpolar stars. Arateans plan and implement a metaphorical journey, a journey of salvation. They validate their respective journeys by appeal to the same visible objects in the common environment construed as signs, the wheeling stars of the night sky. A bunting which has successfully educated itself extracts two simple yet vital messages from the signs: 'go towards the centre of revolution' in the spring, 'go away from the centre of revolution' in the fall. The proof of lessons well learnt is successful migration.[28]

As humans, the Arateans enjoyed all the resources of metaphor, communication, and external memory denied the buntings. Using the same objects as signs, they constructed a soteriological journey by superimposing on the celestial text of the constellations two hypertexts:[29] first, the exegetical text of Aratus, the *Phaenomena*, then the interpretive text of their prophet, Hippolytus' unnamed heresiarch.[30] As in Augustinian biblical semiology two centuries later, at the lower level the exegetical text explicates the signs, at the higher level the interpretive text displays their salvific sense and meaning.

Before we leave the Arateans' reading of the constellations, we should note a significant deficiency in the discourse—its monotony. As interpreted by the Arateans, the constellations transmit a single message; they tell the same old story over and over and over again, night after night as the heavens turn. Granted, the message and the story are supremely important, nothing less than the salvation of humanity. The problem, though, is not that the conversation of the stars is boring. From the ancient, Platonic perspective the unvarying revolution of the sphere of the fixed stars is supremely interesting because it is the only visible manifestation of the god who is the cosmos.[31] Rather, the problem is that Aratean star-talk appears to lack what we have already identified as a necessary feature of language. That feature is *recursivity*, the power of natural languages to generate out of a limited number of signs an unlimited number of utterances.

Fortunately, one can immediately identify a set of signs, absent from the celestial text of the Arateans, which enables star-talk to function recursively.

---

[28] Buntings raised in a starless planetarium, the bunting equivalent of a surd universe, 'migrate', i.e. start hopping, in any and every direction. Buntings raised in a planetarium with a shifted north celestial pole, the equivalent of a deceptive and malevolent universe, 'migrate' towards the new pole, thus demonstrating that 'revolution around a centre' is the operative sign, not particular star patterns. It has to be this way, since the pole, i.e. 'true north', describes a wide circle through the northern constellations in a period of *c*.25,000 years, which is quite rapid on an evolutionary time scale, and more often than not there is no 'pole star' at all. Over mere hundreds of bunting generations, the circumpolar constellations by themselves cease to be reliable indicators.

[29] Or, if you will, metatexts or paratexts.

[30] Whether this was an actual book or a body of oral teaching is immaterial.

[31] As Plato himself puts it in the *Timaeus* (34b, trans. Lee): 'So he [the creator] established a single spherical universe in circular motion, alone but because of its excellence needing no company other than itself, and satisfied to be its own acquaintance and friend. His creation, then, for all these reasons, was a blessed god (*eudaimona theon*).'

These signs are seven in number; they are of course the planets. It is the motions of the planets at varying speeds, bringing them into ever-changing positions and relationships both to each other and to the constellations/signs of the zodiac, that enables the generation of new sentences in star-talk virtually without limit. Rightly, Origen (*Philocalia* 23.20, p. 200 Junod) identifies the *revolution* of the celestial bodies (*tēs tōn ouraniōn periphoras*) as the factor which makes them language signs (*hōsperei grammata kai charactēras... anagignōskein ta sēmeia tou theou*).

10. MAKE-BELIEVE STAR-TALK: ZENO OF VERONA'S BAPTISMAL INTERPRETATION OF THE ZODIAC

At Easter, some year during the 360s, Bishop Zeno of Verona preached a sermon (*Tractatus* 1.38, ed. Löfstedt) to the newly baptized in which he Christianized the zodiac by endowing its twelve signs with new salvific meanings.[32] Zeno says that he will indulge his flock's astrological 'curiosity' (otherwise now strictly forbidden) by revealing to them the 'sacred horoscope' of their baptism (1.2): *sicut parvulis morem geram sacrique horoscopi pandam tota brevitate secreta.*

Edifying and rhetorically accomplished though Zeno's sermon may be, it is not star-talk in the way that the discourse which the Arateans read in the heavens most certainly was. The difference is partly a matter of sincerity: that while the Arateans believed that the constellations really did transmit a message, which they could decipher with the aid of the text of Aratus, Zeno's zodiacal message is patently a contrivance, a conceit in which he makes no ontological or semiological investment. The Arateans had wholeheartedly entered into the semiotic convention of stars as signs, but Zeno plays with it allegorically to extract some timely salvific lessons for his newly baptized audience.

What, though, warrants my confidence in Zeno's lack of commitment to his allegorical props? There is an objective reason as well as one's subjective sense of Zeno's rhetorical intent. As a simple matter of fact, Zeno's discourse does not deliver what it purports to deliver—a horoscope. Horoscopes have their rules, both of form and of content; which is to say that, constructed and read as utterances in star-talk, they follow certain quite strict rules of grammar and of semantics. Zeno's 'horoscope' conforms neither grammatically nor semantically to the template. Consequently, read as star-talk, it is utter nonsense—which of course does not mean that it is not both effective and comprehensible as a Christological and soteriological allegory based on the astrological meanings and associations of the twelve signs of the zodiac.

---

[32] See Hübner 1975; Hegedus 2000: 303–20.

Superficially, Zeno's 'horoscope' does look like one, especially to a casual modern reader used to seeing horoscopes which go through the twelve signs of the zodiac daily in the newspapers. Traversing the signs, in the same standard order from Aries round to Pisces, is exactly what Zeno does. He has this, for example, to say about the fifth sign, Leo (2.4): 'Our Leo [i.e. the Christian Leo = Christ], as Genesis bears witness [49: 9],[33] is the "lion cub", whose holy sacraments we celebrate, who "reclined in sleep" for this purpose, that he might overcome death, and for this purpose awoke, that he might confer on us the gift of immortality, his own blessed resurrection.'

What is wrong with this? Nothing, if Zeno were playing the Aratean game. He has discovered, via Genesis 49: 9, a typological meaning for Leo. But Zeno is not playing that language game, at least overtly. He is making, or pretends to be making, a horoscopic statement. As such it is defective to the point of incomprehensibility. A properly formed horoscopic statement must convey the following information (at a minimum) in the following grammatical form:

$$(1)\text{ celestial event E signifies outcome O}$$

or, expressed in terms of the fulfilment of a condition:

$$(2)\text{ if E, then O.}$$

'O' is typically some terrestrial event, but it need not be. Other types of outcomes are, for example, character traits in the subject of a natal horoscope or eventualities that the subject should guard against. In Zeno's context, we would expect some outcome in the spiritual lives of the newly baptized. 'O', we might say is conferral of the gift of immortality through the resurrection of Christ, the Lion Cub. So far, so good.

The problem lies in the protasis. In a well-formed, 'grammatical' horoscope the celestial event 'E' must consist of at least one pair of terms in a contingent relationship, for example, 'Sun in Leo'. Thus, minimally:

$$(3)\text{ E} = \text{A} + \text{B}$$

where 'A' and 'B' are celestial entities (bodies or geometrical constructs, e.g. the Sun and the 30° sector of the zodiac known as Leo), and '+' stands for the contingent relationship (e.g. 'Sun *in* Leo').

From (2) and (3), it follows that a horoscopic statement must, at a minimum, exhibit the form:

$$(4)\text{ if A} + \text{B, then 0.}$$

Zeno's pretended horoscopic statements are defective, and thus unintelligible as such, precisely because they lack the necessary pair of terms in a contingent relationship.

---

[33] In the Genesis context the lion cub is Judah.

(5) *If A (= Leo), then O (= immortality)

is not a well-formed statement in horoscopal star-talk, either grammatically or semantically. A reader competent in star-talk is left with the unanswered question, 'Leo and what?'

But does not a newspaper horoscope exhibit the same form? Superficially, yes; however, all such horoscopes in fact carry a silent but understood second element in the protasis. What the horoscope actually says is:

(6) If you were born when the Sun was in Leo, the prognosis for your day is thus and thus.

Clearly, the formal requirements of (4) are met.

Our digression into horoscopes has shown that a linguistic approach to the significance of the heavens in antiquity, strange though it must initially seem, is both more rigorous and more illuminating than a symbolic or allegorical approach alone. It is a characteristic of natural language that agreement can be reached as to when and why an utterance is ill-formed or nonsensical. Zeno's baptismal sermon with its make-believe 'horoscope' provides a good test case. Star-talk is a language, or can profitably be treated as such, because one can locate a penumbra of defective and nonsensical statements surrounding it.

11. 'ROLLING UP THE SCROLL': MAXIMUS CONFESSOR AND THE END OF HISTORY

For our final Christian source we turn to late antiquity (seventh century) and to a fragment of Maximus Confessor published in the *Catalogus codicum astrologorum Graecorum* (vol. 7: 100–1).[34] To understand it, one must appreciate that it is an exegesis of Isaiah 34: 4, 'all the host of heaven shall crumble into nothing, the heavens shall be rolled up like a scroll, and the starry host fade away' (*NEB* trans.):

The stars in heaven are what letters are in a book. Through both, men gain knowledge of the things that are. Through letters they gain the recovery (*hypomnēsin*) of words, through the stars the diagnosis of seasons and signs in the graphic mode (*tēn tōn kairōn kai sēmeiōn kata tēn graphikēn diagnōsin*). Just as after the book is finally read it is rolled up (*heilissetai*) by its owner, so when the life of humanity is completed the stars of heaven will fall since they serve no further purpose (*hōs achrēsta pesountai*). Heaven will be 'rolled up'; it will not be 'shortened like a sail' (*sustellomenos*) or 'made to disappear' (*aphanizomenos*). It will be useless (*achrēstos*), for there will be no one there to look at it in order to diagnose the things that are (*pros tēn tōn ontōn diagnōsin*).

---

[34] The passage is discussed by F. Messerschmidt (1931: 68–9) as a suitable conclusion to a survey ('Himmelsbuch und Sternschrift') which starts with Euripides (fr. 506 Nauck) a millennium earlier.

For Maximus, reality (*ta onta*, 'the things that are') is accessible to us humans in two texts: (1) ordinary earthly books in which letters lead us to the *hypomnesis* ('recall', in the sense of Plato's *Phaedrus*) of words, and so to the things which words signify; and (2) the book of heaven in which the stars, 'in graphic mode', lead us to the 'diagnosis' (discernment) of 'seasons and signs'. What happens to these two interrelated texts at the end of human history and the Day of Judgement, which are Maximus' ultimate concern in this fragment? The reality of the present dispensation ('the things which are'), to which both texts are keyed, is finished and done with, so the texts serve no further purpose. There is no need any more to consult the celestial text, to puzzle over problems of time and season (when will such-and-such happen?) or of signification (what does such-and-such a configuration mean?); and besides, there is no one left in the here and now to read the text.

Scripture furnishes (of course) the logical and straightforward answer. What happens to a text in scroll form when its owner is finished with it? He rolls it up and puts it away. Ergo, as Isaiah said, 'heaven will be rolled up'. Why would one expect otherwise?—Though nowadays one might rather say, 'click on the icon of the document <startext> and drag to trash'.[35]

12. PAGAN VIEWS (ASTRONOMERS, ASTROLOGERS, PHILOSOPHERS); STARS AS BOTH SPEAKERS AND SIGNS

In their approach to the visible heavens and their phenomena most people in antiquity, Christians for the most part excepted, shared two fundamental assumptions: (1) the location of meaning in the heavens and the stars, independent of any terrestrial reader or speaker of star-talk; and (2) the divinity and rationality of the celestial bodies themselves. These two assumptions have a peculiar consequence semiotically: (3) the stars are both the signs and the speakers of star-talk. Star-talk is the natural language of the denizens of heavens just as Greek and Latin and Hebrew are (some of) the natural languages of humans. The difference is that, unlike Greek and Latin and Hebrew, star-talk is a language in which the signs, qua speakers, talk to and convey meaning to themselves, regardless of any human audience. When humans overhear it and try to speak or write it, it is necessarily second-order star-talk, a replication and elaboration of the primary celestial discourse.

---

[35] Readers disturbed by this Beckettesque End Game might like to know the sequel in Maximus' scenario. Light will return, because 'the righteous will shine like stars'. It will be an intellectual light. Consequently, the damned will be confined in double darkness, for physical light is no more and they have lost irrevocably and eternally the intellectual light.

13. THE DIVINITY AND RATIONALITY OF CELESTIAL
BODIES: PTOLEMY AND PLATO

We shall start with the second assumption above, that the stars, and in particular the Sun, the Moon, and the other five planets, are divine and rational beings—gods, in other words, or at the very least the gods' celestial surrogates and place-markers. Of the two assumptions this second one is the more obvious and the easier to document. It is evident both in the ancients' astronomical terminology and in their religious practices. The names of the planets reveal it: in Greek, the planet Jupiter carries the god's name in the form 'the [sc. star] of Zeus'—*ho tou Dios (astēr)*, when it it is not called simply 'Zeus'.[36] In religion, moreover, any solar cult necessarily presupposes the divinity of at least one of the visible celestial bodies, the Sun. Even within Christianity, we find Origen lauding the stars as beacons of 'true intellectual' (*noēton kai alēthinon*) light as well as physical light (*Contra Celsum* 5.10):[37]

They are living (*zōia*), rational (*logika*), morally serious (*spoudaia*) beings, and they were made to shine with the light of knowledge by Wisdom, which is 'an effulgence of eternal light' [Wisdom of Solomon 7: 26]. Their visible light is the work of the creator of all things, their intellectual light probably comes from their own free agency (*autexousion*).

A Mithraist could not have said it more handsomely. Clearly, such beings would have something interesting and edifying to say—for those with the wits to listen to their talk.

Little point would be served by multiplying examples of how the ancients treated the stars as both divine and rational. For our purposes, two leading but very different authors will suffice: Plato in the *Timaeus* and Ptolemy in the introduction to the *Almagest*. A huge time span and a huge advance in scientific knowledge (in the fullest modern sense) separate the two. Nevertheless, Ptolemy's *Almagest*, the acme of ancient mathematical astronomy, exhibits the same con-viction about the divinity and intentionality of the heavenly bodies as does Plato's *Timaeus*, which had established antiquity's most widely accepted cosmological paradigm half-a-millennium earlier.

Ptolemy was also the author of an astrological handbook, the *Tetrabiblos*, the introduction to which is equally germane. In it he argues (*Tetr.* 1.1) that the stars in their configurations and courses are both signs and causes of things on earth. Predictions based on these celestial signs are necessarily subject to error, since the outcomes belong to the contingent, physical, sublunary world. Exempt from that

[36] On planetary nomenclature see Cumont 1935; Gundel and Gundel 1950: 2025–33. Histor-ically, the change is from the fuller to the abbreviated form, reflecting (according to Cumont 1935: 35) not just a 'linguistic change' but also a 'modification in the religious conception of the planets', i.e. a closer identification of the god with the visible celestial body.

[37] See Hegedus 2000: 283–5; Scott 1991: 113–49.

uncertainty are predictions about the motions of the celestial bodies themselves and the configurations in relation to each other and the earth which those motions produce. These motions and configurations are the subject matter of the primary branch of astronomy (or as we would call it, of astronomy as opposed to astrology).[38] This discipline, in that it is engaged solely with the translunary universe, is self-sufficient (*autotelēs*) and secure (*bebaios*). By 'self-sufficient' Ptolemy means that astronomy proper is a closed system; it depends on nothing and makes reference to nothing beyond the writ of the immutable laws to which the heavens conform. Indeed, astronomy is but the exploration of the necessary outcomes of those laws.

The postulate on which the 'self-sufficiency' and 'security' of those celestial laws depend is the principle of uniform circular motion.[39] Since nothing in our terrestrial world appears to move naturally and under its own impetus in a perfect circle, and to move in that figure perpetually and at a uniform speed, it must be supposed that the celestial bodies which do exhibit motion of that kind are themselves of an entirely different nature and substance. Hence the 'aether' or 'fifth essence' of standard Aristotelian physics. Hence too, historically, antiquity's great divorce of heaven from earth.

The sole scientific bridge across that chasm was astronomy. This is the point which Ptolemy makes in the introduction to the *Almagest* (1.1). Astronomy is a mathematical discipline intermediate between physics and—*theology*. Its objects of study, like those of physics, are material and observable; but unlike those of physics they are not liable to change and decay. On the other tack, astronomy's objects are divine beings, like those of theology; but, unique among the orders of divine beings, they are regularly observable. Since astronomy studies the orderly behaviour of divine beings, it is not only an intellectual pursuit but also a moral and aesthetic pursuit, arguably the best there is:

With regard to virtuous conduct in practical actions and character, this science, above all things, could make men see clearly; from the constancy, order, symmetry and calm which are associated with the divine, it makes its followers lovers of this divine beauty, accustoming them and reforming their natures, as it were, to a similar spiritual state. (*Alm.* 1.1, trans. Toomer)

Some five centuries before Ptolemy, Plato related, through the persona of the cosmologist Timaeus (after whom the dialogue is named), a narrative of creation.

---

[38] Interestingly, Ptolemy's differentiation between astronomy and astrology is less extreme than Augustine's. For Ptolemy it is simply a matter of distinguishing between the sure and certain predictions of astronomy and the less certain, but still frequently correct, predictions of astrology. For Augustine, as we have seen (above, sect. 7), the chasm is vast and unbridgeable: on the one hand, a legitimate science of the motions and positions of the celestial bodies as natural objects; on the other hand, an error-fraught conversation with demons in which the celestial bodies serve as signs in a conventional language. Stripped of its religious garb, Augustine's distinction is actually closer to that drawn by modern science.

[39] See e.g. *Alm.* 1.3.

Plato's primary concern was not to give a Genesis-like catalogue of the contents of creation, though he does, like the author(s) of Genesis, pay close attention to its temporal (or meta-temporal) sequence. Rather, his concern was to explain how everything in creation, including the material universe itself, was created to plan so as to instantiate orderliness, goodness, and rationality, each thing at its appropriate level. With good reason, then, he considers the universe first, what it is, in and of itself, not as the mere sum of its parts. Here is how he characterizes it—and we should bear in mind that the visible proof, the empirical base for his characterization, is the rotation of the prime celestial sphere carrying with it as it turns all celestial bodies:

And so the most likely account must say that this world (*kosmon*) came to be in very truth, through god's providence, a living being with soul and intelligence (*zōon empsychon ennoun te*). (*Timaeus* 30b6–9, trans. Lee)

For of the seven physical motions he [the creator] allotted to it [the kosmos] the one which most properly belongs to intelligence and reason (*noun kai phronēsin*), and made it move with a uniform and circular motion on the same spot. (ibid. 34a1–4)

This was the plan of the eternal god when he gave to the god about to come into existence a smooth and unbroken surface, equidistant in every direction from the centre, and made it a physical body whole and complete...And he put soul (*psychēn*) in the centre and diffused it through the whole and enclosed the body in it. So he established a single spherical universe in circular motion, alone but because of its excellence needing no company other than itself, and satisfied to be its own acquaintance and friend. His creation, then, for all these reasons, was a blessed god (*eudaimona theon*) (ibid. 34a8–b9).

In these passages Plato sets for most of classical antiquity, its scientists included, the benchmark for divinity and rationality. Uniform circular motion is the primary 'outward and visible sign' of those qualities. It is not just a *symbol* of divinity and rationality, in the sense that Plato might have used it metaphorically as a stand-in for qualities that cannot be apprehended visually. Rather, it is the *instantiation* of divinity and rationality in the visible world, in the sense that it *is* divinity and rationality, or as much of it as we can perceive directly with our eyes. Semiologically, it is both an *index* and an *icon*: an index because it indicates divinity and rationality by virtue of an actual relationship (as smoke to fire) rather than a conventional relationship (the word 'fire' to actual fire); an icon—and this is the difficult part for us moderns—because that is what divinity and rationality actually look like (as in signage a drawing of an elevator looks like an elevator and a drawing of an escalator like an escalator). Finally, for our present inquiry, we must not forget that it is also a language sign, or rather an *utterance* which bespeaks divinity and rationality, gods to gods, gods to men, and men to men. As the last of our three quotations above illustrates, it is what the self-sufficient universe communicates to itself as 'its own acquaintance and friend'.

Moving on from the universe in and of itself, Plato treats of the stars and planets which exhibit circular motion as indices of their own and the universe's rationality and divinity. Were there no celestial bodies visible in motion, we could have no conception—at least none mediated through the sense of sight—of divinity and rationality. And that, as Plato later explains (46e7–47b2) when dealing with our physical senses, is precisely why we have eyes in our heads—the spherical human head, by no means coincidentally, being yet another likeness of the cosmos.[40]

We must go on to describe the chief benefit of the function of sight, which was the god's reason for giving it to us. For I reckon that the supreme benefit for which sight is responsible is that not a word of all we have said about the universe could have been said if we had not seen stars and sun and heaven. As it is, the sight of day and night, the months and returning years, the equinoxes and solstices, has caused the invention of number, given us the notion of time, and made us inquire into the nature of the universe; thence we have derived philosophy, the greatest gift the gods have ever given or will give to mortals. That is what I call the greatest good our eyes give us.

Here is how Plato describes the ever-visible gods who are the fixed stars (40a2–b6):

The divine form he [the creator] made mostly of fire so that it should be as bright and beautiful to look at as possible; and he made it spherical like the universe and set it to follow the movement of the highest intelligence (*tithēsi te eis tēn tou kratistou phronēsin ekeinōi synhepomenon*), distributing it round the circle of the heaven to be a kind of universal cosmic embroidery. And he gave each divine being two motions, one uniform in the same place, as each always thinks the same thoughts about the same things (*peri tōn autōn aei ta auta heautōi dianooumenōi*), the other forward, as each is subject to the movement of the Same and uniform; but he kept them unaffected by the other five kinds of motion, that each might be as perfect as possible. This is the origin of the fixed stars, which are living beings, divine and eternal and remain always rotating in the same place and the same sense.

The fixed stars are divine and intelligent *because* they are perfect spheres which both rotate about their own centres and revolve around the common universal centre, unendingly and at an unvarying speed;[41] and they perform those rotations and revolutions *because* they are intelligent and divine. Uniform circular motion is thus the necessary and sufficient condition of divinity and rationality for the fixed stars.

---

[40] 'They [the gods acting on the creator's instructions] copied the shape of the universe and fastened the two divine orbits of the soul into a spherical body, *which we now call the head*, the divinest part of us which controls all the rest' (44d3–6). The 'two divine orbits' (*periodous*) are the rotation of the sphere of the fixed stars westward and the revolution of the planets eastward.

[41] There was no observational evidence, accessible to the ancients, for the axial rotation of the fixed stars. Plato postulates it a priori because the stars must instantiate in themselves as well as in their orbits the prime and only visible property of the divine and rational universe.

Although Plato does not here repeat the specifics of their motions, which he had discussed earlier (38–9), the planets too are spheres manifesting circular motion.[42] Accordingly they too are intelligent and divine.[43]

14. THE PLATONIST VIEW OF HOW THE STARS COMMUNICATE AND HOW WE UNDERSTAND THEM; IMPLICATIONS OF THE COSMOLOGY OF THE *TIMAEUS*

For the most part, we can say, the ancients conceived of the celestial bodies as rational and divine beings, who could accordingly communicate both with each other and with us rational humans. This claim about the ancients' conception of the visible heavens is scarcely controversial.

Our next question, then, must be: what, from the ancient pagan perspective—specifically the Platonist perspective—is the nature of that celestial communication and how is it effected? Is it, or can it usefully be treated as, language communication? Did the pagans construe it as such, whether explicitly, as did certain Christian thinkers in antiquity, or implicitly? If so, can we reconstruct something of its semiotics?

Let us start with how communication is effected across rational species, from the celestial gods to humans. The *Timaeus* has a straightforward but, from a modern perspective, exceedingly strange answer. We have already taken note of the role of the human eye in the reception of the visible gods into our souls (see preceding section). But how do we know and appreciate the true import of these images, what they really signify, or even that they are message-bearing signs at all?

The answer lies in the construction and composition of the human soul. We understand the true significance of the celestial bodies and their motions because our souls were made of the same stuff and behave in the same way (*Timaeus* 43a4–6, trans. Lee): 'And into this body, subject to the flow of growth and decay,[44] they [the divine agents of the creator] fastened the orbits of the immortal soul (*tas tēs athanatou psychēs periodous*).' We know that what we see in the heavens are the *periodoi* (journeys around, circuits, orbits) of divine and rational beings because, and only because, the qualitatively identical soul-stuff is performing its circuits inside our physical heads. Furthermore, this soul-stuff spinning

---

[42] But not, at least in appearances, *uniform* circular motion. Hence the great project of Greek astronomy: to 'save' appearances by accounting for them as epiphenomena of a combination of motions which were not only circular but also uniform.

[43] Fortunately, the vexed question of whether axial rotation is to be inferred for the planets as well as for the fixed stars need not here concern us. Whatever answer is returned to that question, my argument concerning uniform circular motion and the rationality and divinity of the celestial bodies is unaffected. For discussions of this passage (40) and its implications, see Taylor 1928: 221–45; Cornford 1937: 117–37; Dicks 1970: 131–7. For a full discussion of the astronomical aspects of the cosmogony and cosmology of the *Timaeus*, see Dicks 1970: 116–37; Gregory 2000.

[44] Literally, 'subject to influx and efflux'.

within our heads empowers us not only to recognize divinity and rationality when we see them in the heavens but also internally to function as rational beings and to live truly reasonable lives. This is the model of rationality which informs the entire narrative of the creation of humanity (41a2–47e2), the reasoning human mind as an embodied instantiation of cosmic *periodoi*, dwelling originally in the stars and destined thither to return.

In due course I shall discuss certain particulars of this Platonic model of rationality. First, however, we must stress that Plato does not offer just a disguised analogy: that our reason functions *somewhat like* the rotation/revolutions of the stars. No, our rational minds function thus because *they consist of* the same rotating/revolving soul-stuff whose operations we can actually see in the revolving stars and hence infer for the rotating universe. In other words, Plato gives us an ontological as well as a functional explanation of rational mind.

The psychology and anthropology of the *Timaeus* is thoroughly conditioned by this communicative relationship between the rotating/revolving celestial bodies and the mind. As a species of land-going animal we are distinguished by our spherical heads set at the summit of our bipedal bodies. Our heads are spherical so as to accommodate the spinning 'periods' of our rational souls; they are atop our bodies so as to elevate us, literally, toward heaven, our souls' true origin and destination (90a2–9):

We should think of the most authoritative part of our soul as a guardian spirit given by god, living at the summit of the body, which can properly be said to lift us from the earth towards our home in heaven; for we are creatures not of earth but of heaven, where the soul was first born, and our divine part attaches us by the head to heaven, like a plant by its roots, and keeps our body upright.

In contrast, other land-going species are lowered groundwards as quadrupeds or worse, the number of their feet being directly proportional to their affinity with earth and to the depth of their stupidity;[45] and their heads are flattened and distorted because 'their orbits (*periphorai*) have been compressed by disuse' (91e6–92a7). These outcomes and life-forms are not ours or the animals' by necessity of membership in particular species. Rather they are the ontogenetic consequences of each individual soul's use or abuse of its rational 'orbits'.

Perhaps the zoology of the *Timaeus* is more playful than serious—in which case modern science has played a curious posthumous trick on Plato. As we saw in the last chapter (sect. 15), there is as a matter of verified fact one species of bird, the Indigo Bunting, which has mentally internalized the revolution of the stars around the pole as a template for migratory navigation. Whether Plato would have enjoyed the joke one cannot say—a Socrates or an Aristophanes would have loved it, as also the match between actual bunting cognition and

---

[45] Worst is no feet at all: 'the stupidest of the land animals, whose whole bodies lay stretched on the earth, the gods turned into reptiles, giving them no feet, because they had no further need of them' (trans. Lee).

Plato's own characterization of birds as reincarnations of harmless but silly souls who have spent too much time in observational instead of theoretical astronomy (91d6–e1)!

Whatever the case with the animals, we should not doubt that Plato's description of the replication of the celestial 'periods' in the 'periods' of the rational human soul is both deeply serious and intended literally. The function of that replication of the macrocosm in the microcosm is a pedagogy of the soul which begins with sight and ends in understanding, and its goal is the restoration of the orderly motions of the universe in the disordered motions of the soul:

The god invented and gave us vision in order that we might observe the circuits of intelligence in the heaven and profit by them for the revolutions of our own thought, which are akin to them, though ours be troubled and they are unperturbed; and that, by learning to know them and acquiring the power to compute them rightly according to nature, we might reproduce (*mimoumenoi*) the perfectly unerring revolutions of the god and reduce to settled order the wandering motions in ourselves. (*Timaeus* 47b5–c5, trans. Cornford)

Now there is but one way of caring for anything, namely to give it the nourishment and motions proper to it. The motions akin to the divine part in us are the thoughts and revolutions of the universe:

these, therefore, every man should follow, and correcting those circuits in the head that were deranged at birth, by learning to know the harmonies and revolutions of the world, he should bring the intelligent part, according to its pristine nature, into the likeness of that which intelligence discerns (*tōi katanooumenōi to katanooun exhomoiōsai*),[46] and thereby win the fulfilment of the best life set by the gods before mankind both for the present time and for the time to come. (90c6–d7, trans. Cornford)

In the narrative of the soul's descent into the mortal bodies of humans and its return to the heavens, the *Timaeus* (together with the *Phaedrus*) furnishes a companion text to Mithraic soteriology and, more important, to the function of the mithraeum, discussed in the preceding chapter (sect. 11), as venue and platform for 'induction into a mystery of the descent and departure of souls' (Porphyry, *De antro* 6). Notice how, in the first of the passages quoted above, intellectual and moral education is a process in which we are said to 'mime' (*mimoumenoi*) the 'perfectly unerring revolutions of the god' so as to 'reduce to settled order the wandering motions in ourselves'. The Greek distinguishes literally between the 'unwandering' (*aplaneis*) and the 'wandering' (*peplanēmenas*) orbits, which of course are respectively the orbits of the 'fixed' stars and the orbits of the planets. Replicating and relating these orbits, as I argued, is both the structural function of the mithraeum and the ritual task of its initiates. It is also the reason why, theologically, 'they assigned to Mithras the equinoxes as his proper seat' (*De antro* 24), for the equinoxes are, spatially, the points at which the

---

[46] More literally, 'to assimilate the thinking agent to the object thought'.

orbit of the 'unwandering' (i.e. the celestial equator) is tied to the orbit of the 'wandering' (i.e. the ecliptic).

15. THE CELESTIAL LOCATION OF MEANING

The *Timaeus*, we may agree, furnishes a celestially oriented epistemology and model of cognition. That it also furnishes a celestial semiotics is less obvious. That it does so, or rather that it carries certain semiological presuppositions about the celestial bodies as signs, will be the burden of the present section. From the *Timaeus* I shall generalize to ancient preconceptions about the visible heavens as a source of meaning and sign-giving. Of the more explicit views of the early Christians on the stars as signs I have already given an account at the beginning of this chapter.

A general condition for something to function as a sign is that it signify something other than itself. The *Timaeus* actually breaks this rule: its universe, as we have seen, communes with itself about itself, and is happy and fulfilled in doing so. It is a uniformly rotating sphere which talks to a uniformly rotating sphere, which is necessarily none other than itself, about being a uniformly rotating sphere.

When we move down the ontological orders of being to the visible gods in the thereby visible heavens, that is to the 'phenomena' of astronomy, we encounter beings who not only make manifest the universe's interior monologue of uniform spherical rotation but also realize it in their own daily revolutions. Moreover, they instantiate, and are brought into being so as to instantiate, various great principles, necessarily other than and independent of themselves: divinity, rationality, the binary opposition of the Same and the Different, Time.[47]

Here, then, we have a beginning of a semiotics and a semantics set in the visible heavens. The celestial bodies *signify* something other than themselves; they *mean* something other than themselves.

So far, so good. But *how* do celestial bodies 'signify' and 'mean'? What transforms a set of entities into language signs which can express and communicate meaningful utterances? In the case of the stars and planets it is their *motions*, their 'journeyings-around' (*periphorai, periodoi*), which furnish the *syntax* by which the stars and planets both 'signify' and 'mean' as *noun signs* in the utterances of a language. Or we might say, more simply, that the language in which the stars and planets serve as signs *is* their *periphorai/periodoi*. Centuries later, but of course still within the Platonic tradition, Plotinus was to liken celestial motion explicitly to utterance or, rather, writing in a language whose characters (*grammata*) are the celestial bodies (*Ennead* 2.3.7): 'Let us suppose that [the stars] are like characters constantly being written in the heavens or as

---

[47] We should add, from the earlier chapters of the *Timaeus* (35–6), proportion and existence.

characters set in motion once they have been written (*estō toinun hōsper grammata en ouranōi graphomena aei ē gegrammena kai kinoumena*).'

The stars instantiate language in the heavens not simply by being 'written' there as characters once and for all, but either by being *constantly* (*aei*) written there or by being *set in motion* (*kinoumena*) when written. To semi-modernize the simile, we might think in the first instance of moveable type reset to compose new messages and in the second the many individual still frames of a 'motion picture' or 'movie'. What makes the celestial movie or, to return to 'star-talk', the ongoing discourse of the signs of heaven possible is the change imported into the heavens by the various motions of the planets, or in Platonist terms by the orbit(s) of the Different.[48]

In the context of the *Timaeus*, it follows that signification on serious matters such as the nature of Divinity, Reason, Time, and the binary opposition of the Same and the Different takes place in the visible heavens. That is where utterances are made and where meaning originates. We humans read these speech acts with eyes given to us for that purpose and we understand them by virtue of the affinity of the microcosmic orbits of our souls to the macrocosmic orbits of the heavens.

The serious Platonist is not so arrogant as to suppose that star-talk is directed primarily, still less solely, at us humans. That is the vain and vulgar anthropocentric error of the hack astrologer, brilliantly exposed by Plotinus in *Ennead* 2.3.1–6. No, like all species, the divine stars live for themselves and for the All or Whole, not merely to signify, still less to cause, the destinies of humans (2.3.3, trans. Armstrong): 'For each [planetary god] has its own life to itself, and each one's good is in its own act, and has nothing to do with us. The action on us of living beings that have no part with us is always something incidental, not their dominant activity. If, as with birds, their acting as signs is incidental, their work is not directed at us at all.'[49]

---

[48] As we have seen in the case of Hippolytus' Aratean 'heretics' (above, sect. 9), the primary message of the 'fixed' stars alone is necessarily limited, precisely because those stars never change in relation to each other. They are like a single still photograph. They may of course say many different things *figuratively*, but at the *literal* level, the fixed stars cannot say tomorrow anything other than what they are saying today and what they said yesterday.

[49] Interestingly, in *Enn.* 4.4.6–8 Plotinus is at pains to show that the motions of the planets do not and cannot mean the same to us as they do to the planets themselves. To us human observers planetary motion registers as a change of position, for example from one sign of the zodiac to another. But to the planets themselves there can be no change, for change would imply some former state or condition, which would mean a memory of, and hence a separation from, that glorious Now which the planetary gods, unlike us, have never lost. If we relate this argument to 2.3.7. on planetary *grammata*, we would have to say that planet writing is read by us more grossly embodied human souls as movement from one position to another (e.g. from Cancer to Leo), but it is actually not composed and written in that idiom by the planet, because the planetary gods do not experience and reflect on their motions in terms of change of position and so cannot knowingly communicate them as such.

Plotinus was not entirely opposed to astrology in the sense of denying all celestial signification down into our sublunary and contingent world. He objected of course to anything that imputed morally negative traits to the planetary gods, still more to the implication that they could change from benevolence to malevolence and vice versa depending on their 'aspects' to each other and their positions in the heavens relative to the human subject of a horoscope (2.3.1–6). Nevertheless, he allowed that cosmic sympathy, the inter-connectedness of all parts of the universe, might warrant drawing conclusions from celestial signs—if one had the wits to figure out the links from signifier to signified (2.3.7). But in general he preferred to leave the stars to their own proper business and to the business of the Whole. In another use of the simile of writing, he emphasizes the metaphysically upward and universal intent of the discourse of the stars, while acknowledging their other 'service' in communicating downward and predictively to the human 'reader' (3.1.6, trans. Armstrong):

We must rather say that the movement of the stars is for the preservation of the universe (*hōs pheretai men tauta epi sōtēriāi tōn holōn*), but that they perform in addition another service; this is that those who know how to read this sort of writing can, by looking at them as if they were letters, read the future from their patterns, discovering what is signified by the systematic use of analogy—for instance, if one said that when a bird flies high it signifies some high heroic deeds.

As we have already seen (above, sect. 6), Origen reaches very similar conclu-sions about the discourse of the heavens: star-talk is not intended for us mortals, at least not in the time of our mortality. The similarity is of course genealogical, for both Origen and Plotinus were working within the same Platonic tradition. Nevertheless, in the *Timaeus*, and thus in any subsequent Platonist or Platonizing cosomology, the visible heavens are also the *fons et origo* of meaning for rational humanity. The stars, in this mode of signification, are both speakers and signs. If we are wise, we will listen to and assimilate what they tell us, attuning the circuits of our souls to their grand originals, the orbits of the celestial bodies.

16. CONCLUSION

In this chapter we have gone a certain distance into our exploration of star-talk as the language of the heavens and of humans replicating this celestial language in various discourses of their own. We have seen that the ancients themselves sometimes treated the celestial motions explicitly as a language and the ever-changing but predictable *schemata* which those motions produce as utterances or, more usually, writings (*grammata*) in a text. We have seen something of the strange (to us) array of language communities—human, divine, demonic—which speak and listen to these celestial utterances or write and read them as text. We have noted that, unlike the natural languages, the signs of star-talk can themselves function as autonomous speakers (and audience) of the language. Most importantly, we have seen that star-talk can be heard as a language of *figurative* discourse. Those who hear it in this mode necessarily presuppose that the stars, or the powers speaking through the stars, not only declare their past, present, and future *schemata*, but also *intend further meanings thereby*, whether that further meaning is a terrestrial 'outcome' (*apotelesma*) as in astrology or a theological truth as in the constellation interpretations of the Arateans.

In the next chapter I shall apply our insights into 'star-talk' to the principal icon of the Mithraic mysteries, the tauroctony. Since we have crossed what I called 'Sperber's bar' and have satisfied ourselves that astral symbols, if only in the context of the Mithraic mysteries, can and do function as language signs, we may now with some confidence set about *reading* the tauroctony, parsing its sentences, and explicating its meanings.

9

The Mithraic Mysteries as Symbol System: III. The Tauroctony

1. INTRODUCTION: THE EXEGESIS AND INTERPRETATION OF STAR-TALK DISCOURSE

If you are expecting a new interpretation of the tauroctony in this chapter you will, I fear, be disappointed. In fact the interpretation will be essentially the same as that which I put forward more than a decade ago in my essay 'In the place of the Lion: Mithras in the tauroctony' (1994). What is different is the way I now reach my interpretation. I no longer approach the *explananda* as encoded doctrine but instead as symbols apprehended on a structured site and as signs deployed in star-talk discourse.

This revised approach necessarily involves two stages: first, so that we can read the tauroctony at the literal level, an exegesis of what the astral signs actually say; second, the interpretation proper, an exploration of what star-talk in the tauroctony is, or may be, talking about non-literally, in other words its cosmological, theological, soteriological, eschatological intent. For example, at the literal level we shall see that the astral signs speak of a visible celestial hemisphere with Taurus setting in the west, Leo culminating to the south, and Scorpius rising in the east. *Why* they speak of this hemisphere rather than of one defined by, say, the tropic signs (Aries setting, Cancer culminating, and Libra rising) is another matter. To pose the 'why' is to ask an interpretive question, in effect to ask what this star-talk utterance might mean over and above the literal statement 'Taurus is setting, Leo is culminating, Scorpius is rising'.

This two-stage procedure is appropriate to our subject matter. As a method it is grounded in antiquity's differentiation between literal meaning and figurative meaning. Attention had to be paid to both, each at its proper level. For Porphyry, to use a familiar example, it was by no means a trivial question whether or not the cave described by Homer at *Odyssey* 13.102–12 was an actual feature of Ithacan topography or a mere figment of Homer's invention for allegorical purposes (*De antro* 2–4). The factuality, or otherwise, of literal meanings mattered.

This two-stage method culminated in Augustine's exegesis and interpretation of the Old Testament in *De doctrina Christiana* and elsewhere (Markus 1996: 1–35; Rist 1994: 23–40). Following Markus, we may summarize Augustine's semiology as follows:

God makes things and causes events. These things/events are facts. But they are also God's words, and thus signs. He inspires authors to arrange these things/events/signs so as to constitute a text/narrative. This text is the (Christian) Old Testament. The text/narrative is true, literally. It is also meaningful, figuratively/typologically. The human exegete explicates the text at the literal level. He requires knowledge of language (Hebrew, Greek, Latin), and knowledge of things, both natural and human (i.e. of human institutions). The interpreter (who may of course be one and the same as the exegete) searches anagogically for the figurative meaning. On the principle of polysemy there may be several valid figurative meanings. There are two privileged meanings, that intended by the divine author (God) and that intended by the human (e.g. Moses). These two meanings should of course coincide. The intent of the interpreter is paramount. Only an intent founded on charity and thus aligned with the intent of the divine and human authors will successfully discern figurative meaning. Charity is a necessary condition of successful hermeneutics; it is not a sufficient condition.

Augustine constructs a semiology which privileges past events and their narrative as the deeds and words of God, thus sanctifying the record of history:

But, coming to the next point, we are not to reckon among human institutions those things which men have handed down to us, not as arrangements of their own, but as the result of investigation into the occurrences of the past, and into the arrangements of God's providence. (*De doctrina Christiana* 2.27.41)

And even when in the course of an historical narrative former institutions of men are described, the history itself is not to be reckoned among human institutions; because things that are past and gone and cannot be undone are to be reckoned as belonging to the course of time, of which God is the author and governor. (ibid. 2.28.44)

The historical facts which concern Augustine most closely are those which form the chain of events recorded, under divine guidance, in the books of the Hebrew scriptures, the Christian Old Testament. These facts are the privileged signs which, following their literal exegesis, the Christian scholar interprets figuratively.

Nevertheless, the scriptures are not just allegories. Their facts are facts, not quasi-facts, mere fictions designed with anagogic intent as props for the figurative interpretation. The literal inerrancy of scripture is a fundamental given, as is its factuality. The tree of the knowledge of good and evil and the tree of life are just as real and as solid as the wood of Christ's Cross.[1]

To what in the star-talk 'text' of the tauroctony do the persons, things, and events in the Old Testament—the signs, that is, of Augustinian exegesis—correspond? Obviously, to the celestial bodies and their relationships signified by the astral signs deployed in the tauroctony's composition.

Notice that we have bypassed a first level of reference. In the scene of the tauroctony the sculpted or painted raven, for example, refers to the raven which was present when Mithras slew the bull. True—but irrelevant to our inquiry. We are concerned with the raven as a star-talk sign for Corvus, not as the bird who witnessed or participated in the event of the bull-killing.

In treating the image of the raven as a star-talk sign we do not of course deny its function as a sign in the representation of the bull-killing event. That is a given, indeed a tautology within the conventions of narrative art: the referent of the image of the raven in the tauroctony is the raven which participated in the bull-killing event in the myth of Mithras. Exegesis of what one might call the narrative signs in the tauroctony and other scenes is merely the retelling of the story of Mithras as it was presented to his initiates on the monuments of his Mysteries. This story has been retold in every comprehensive study of the cult since Franz Cumont's in 1899. To retell it here would merely return us to the start of the fruitless interpretive project of narrative and doctrinal explication from which we extracted ourselves in the first four chapters. Consequently, since the images as narrative signs do not concern us here, I shall make very little reference to the other events in the myth cycle represented in the side-scenes or in self-contained compositions such as the banquet or the rock-birth.

Exegesis of star-talk signs is seldom if ever a matter of explicating a single sign: after all, there is not much one can say about a one-word utterance. Rather, exegesis is a matter of explicating star-talk signs in relation to each other. In fact, it is only in relation to each other that the images acquire their star-talk meanings in the first place. By itself the image of the raven says nothing beyond 'look, raven present!' Only by association with the images of the other animals does it declare itself the star-talk sign of the constellation Corvus. In particular, in association with the images of the snake and the cup (the latter in Rhine-area tauroctonics) it tells the catasterismic legend of Corvus (Gordon 1980*b*: 27). It is the task of exegesis to rehearse that legend. The exegete will further explicate the moral of the tale: it is an aetiological story which answers the question, why do ravens go thirsty for a long period over the summer? Note that the elaboration and esoteric

---

[1] The distinction between things as things and things as signs and the importance of not forgetting the former are spelt out more fully and explicitly in Augustine's *Commentary on Genesis*, from which our example of the two trees is taken (8.4.8): *diligentius considerandum est, ne cogat in allegoriam, ut non ista ligna fuerint, sed aliud aliquid nomine ligni significent.* See Markus 1996: 3–8.

application of the moral is not the exegete's business; responsible exegetes confine themselves to consensual meanings, explanations which 'everyone knows' are correct. From our perspective these are the factoids of the 'encyclopaedia', antiquity's store of common knowledge, which we have already looked at in the context of the grade hierarchy (Ch. 5, sect. 5).

Exegesis completed, the interpreter takes over. It is the interpreter's task to suggest why the public catasterismic story of the thirsty raven belongs in the esoteric Mithraic story of the bull-killing and thus in the Mithraic mysteries. In point of fact, the functions of both exegete and interpreter of the Corvus story were fully discharged by Richard Gordon in 'Reality, evocation, and boundary' (1980*b*: 25–32). Here we are concerned with firming up the methodological route to conclusions already reached.

We may summarize the tasks of exegete and interpreter as follows. The exegete helps you hear what the star-talk signs are saying at the literal level, in our present example an aetiological story about thirsty ravens. The interpreter helps you hear what the star-talk signs mean or intend by their literal utterances at the anagogic level, which in the present instance is something about the significance of thirst and aridity over a certain period of the summer.

Retrospectively, one can detect a certain irony in twentieth-century interpret-ations of the tauroctony, in that mainline Mithraic scholarship has tended to dismiss as 'speculation' what are actually the most secure readings of the icon and to trust instead in the more speculative. This story I have already told as 'the problem of referents' in Chapter 3, and there is no need to repeat it here. Suffice it to say that scepticism about the astral interpretations was warranted by the failure of their proponents to differentiate between the two stages of explanation: exegesis and interpretation as we have termed them, following Augustine's model. The astral interpreters (myself included) were both too modest in their exegesis and too sanguine in their interpretations. That the images of the animals in the tauroctony function as astral (star-talk) signs to define a particular area of the heavens is a fact, not a conjecture. It has been demonstrated over and over again by us astral interpreters (qua exegetes), and I do not intend to demonstrate it yet again.[2] In contrast, the esoteric inferences one draws from the tauroctony qua star-chart or, as I would prefer to put it here, the esoteric star-talk utterances one hears or reads in the tauroctony, are necessarily tentative, difficult to substantiate, more or less plausible guesswork. Augustine, who was naturally concerned only with the Christian interpreter, listed the cardinal virtue of Charity as the interpreter's necessary qualification. For the secular academic interpreter of Mithraism's mysteries one would have to substitute knowledge of the culture from which the religion was generated, a sense of what is plausible

---

[2] For a formal, 'statistical demonstration of the extreme improbability of unintended coincidence in the selection of elements in the composition' of the tauroctony, see my essay on that topic in Beck 2004*c*: 251–65 = ch. 12.

and what is implausible in context, a recognition of the provisional nature of all interpretation (soft facts at the best), and above all a comprehension of the language of star-talk.

2. THE EXEGESIS OF STAR-TALK IN THE TAUROCTONY: A. THE CONSTELLATION SIGNS

Since for the past quarter of a century I have devoted much of my research to the astral explication of the Mithraic tauroctony and its symbolic structure, I shall here set out the exegesis in summary form only. For more detailed explanations see Beck 1976*c*; 1977 (= 2004*c*: ch. 8); 1984: 2081–3; 1988: 19–28, 91–100; 1994*b* (= 2004*c*: ch. 13); 2001: 62–71; 2004*c*: chs. 11 ('The rise and fall of the astral identifications of the tauroctonous Mithras') and 12 ('Astral symbolism in the tauroctony').

A1. The tauroctony represents a view or map of the heavens extending from Taurus in the west to Scorpius in the east (see the star-chart in Fig. 1).

A2. Nine elements in the composition of the tauroctony are star-talk signs for constellations (see the drawings of tauroctonies reproduced in Figs. 5 and 6). The lion and the crater are elements particularly in tauroctonies from the Rhine and Danube provinces (see Fig. 6 = V1118); the other elements are ubiquitous.

Fig. 5. Tauroctony (V417), after Cumont 1896: 194, fig. 19

CRATER   LION

Fig. 6. Tauroctony (V1118), after Cumont 1876: 374, fig. 283

(1). Bull means Taurus.

(2). Cautes and Cautopates: (*a*) as twins mean Gemini; (*b*) as the scene's margin-definers: torchbearer on right means Taurus, torchbearer on left means Scorpius.

(3). Dog means Canis Minor; also means Canis Major.

(4). Snake means Hydra.

(5). Lion means Leo.

(6). Crater (large two-handled vessel) means Crater; also, in the Danubian motif of a lion plunging down into a crater, means (vessel of) Aquarius.

(7). Wheat ear(s) at tip of bull's tail means Spica (Alpha Virginis, the ear of wheat in the hand of Virgo); thus, by metonomy (more precisely, *pars pro toto*), also means Virgo.

(8). Raven means Corvus.

(9). Scorpion means Scorpius.

Note the alternative constellation meanings of the torchbearers (2), the dog (3), and the crater (6). I shall discuss this polysemy in more detail later.

A3. All nine constellation signs are 'iconic' signs, in that they resemble in appearance what they signify. They are thus icons, not just symbols or arbitrary signs, of their respective constellations. That the constellation figures are actually human constructions is immaterial. The point to remember is that when humans join in star-talk discourse *two* texts are written and read, the celestial text and its facsimile in the human artefact. The authenticity of the human facsimile depends on the closest possible correlation of its signs to the signs in the celestial text. This is achieved by replication, by making the terrestrial signs icons of the celestial signs. Iconic signs are *hiero*-glyphics.

The apparent exception proves the rule. Certainly the torchbearers, qua Taurus and Scorpius (2*b*), the constellations which define the western and eastern boundaries of the celestial map, do not resemble a bull and a scorpion. However, they sometimes carry, or are otherwise closely associated with, a bull's head (or small ox) and a scorpion as secondary attributes (Hinnells 1976: 43–5; Beck 1977: 3–5; 1988: 19–22). The occurrences are numerous enough to infer a normative identity even when not explicit.

A4. Placement within the composition corresponds for the most part to the relative placement of the signified constellation in the actual heavens. The obvious exceptions are (*a*) the bull, which straddles the entire scene from right to left, and (*b*) the raven, which has been moved upwards/northwards from its proper celestial location relative to the neighbouring constellations.[3] The poly-semous signs, of course, can only be 'correctly' located in respect of *one* of the two constellation meanings. Thus, most obviously, the crater by position relative to the other constellation signs means (or intends or signifies) Crater, not Aquarius. The dog in the same context means Canis Minor, although Canis Major, being not far distant, is also intended, though less precisely. The torchbearers in this context of relative celestial position mean Taurus and Scorpius, for they flank and define the scene of the bull-killing, just as the two constellations flank and define the intended star-field.

Notice how I speak of 'meaning' rather than 'identity'. Questions posed in terms of identity, where a case can be made for two or more alternatives, lead either to paradox ('how can it be both this and that?') or to inappropriate exclusion. In contrast, posing the same question in terms of the meaning of a language sign invites the proper riposte, 'what's the context?' or 'give me the whole sentence'. If you are asking, for example, about the meaning of the crater and you tell me that the context is the Danubian motif of the lion plunging down into the crater immediately below (as e.g. in V1958), I will tell you that the crater means Aquarius and the motif refers to the vertical/north–south axis of the tauroctony/star-chart's 'esoteric quartering' (of which more below). If, however, you tell me that the context is the Rhine motif of the trio of signs—lion (left), crater (centre), snake (right)—below the bull (as Fig. 6 = V1118), I will tell you that the crater means Crater and the trio of signs is part of a larger utterance about the constellations between Taurus and Scorpius intended in and by the composition. The example illustrates well how astral symbols in the tauroctony

---

[3] The bull (= Taurus) fills the scene because it is the object of the action. The raven (= Corvus) has been elevated because it is a bird and the natural place for a bird is aloft. If there is a point here, it is that exegesis is often just a matter of common sense.

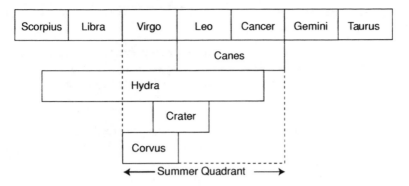

Fig. 7. Southern paranatellonta to the summer quadrant of the zodiac

can and do function as language signs with agreed meanings.[4] The crater in the two contexts is merely an instance of a homonym. It is not at all paradoxical.

A5. Of the nine constellations signified, five (Taurus, Gemini, Leo, Virgo, Scorpius) lie on the band of the zodiac and are thus among those which gave their names to the twelve 'signs' (*zōidia*), in the technical sense of the successive 30° sectors of the ecliptic through which the Sun passes in the course of the year. Accordingly, their star-talk images signify both the zodiacal constellations and the zodiacal signs, depending on context. The four extra-zodiacal constellations signified (Canis Minor, Hydra, Crater, Corvus) all lie to the south of the zodiac and are 'paranatellonta' to, hence surrogates for, certain of the zodiacal constellations signified. Paranatellonta are literally stars or constellations which 'rise alongside' (i.e. together with) specific other stars or constellations. We shall consider their significance in due course. In linguistic terms a surrogate is a synonym, so we may say that in certain contexts the paranatellonta function as synonyms of the zodiacal constellations.[5] The relationship of the paranatellonta represented in the tauroctony to the zodiacal signs is shown in bar form in Figure 7.

3. EXEGESIS (CONTINUED): B. SUN, MOON, MITHRAS, BULL (AGAIN), CAVE

B1. In the upper left corner of the tauroctony we regularly find an image of Sol, the Sun god; in the upper right corner an image of Luna, the Moon goddess. Frequently, these deities are shown with their chariots and teams, Sol in a quadriga drawn by horses, Luna in a biga drawn by oxen. Obviously,

---

[4] See above, Ch. 8, sect. 4, on 'crossing Sperber's bar'.
[5] Rhetorically, the naming of a zodiacal constellation and its paranatellon together could be read/heard as a hendiadys.

(10). Sol means the Sun.

(11). Luna means the Moon.

B2. What, then, of Mithras in the centre of the composition? What does the sign 'Mithras' mean in the tauroctony's star-talk discourse. The answer is literally spelt out. The dedicatory inscription DEO SOLI INVICTO MITHRAE tells us that

(12). Mithras means the Sun.

But is there not already a sign for the Sun, namely Sol in the upper left corner? Of course there is. But remember that our subject here is language, not ontology on the theological plane. The fact that the sign 'Sol' says 'Sun' does not preclude the sign 'Mithras' from saying 'Sun' too. Again, it is simply a matter of synonyms. And the fact that star-talk discourse in the tauroctony is unconstrained by the linearity and temporal sequence of spoken or written language means that the sign 'Sol' and the sign 'Mithras' can say 'Sun' simultaneously. Remember, too, that we are concerned only with 'Mithras' as a star-talk sign. Nothing said in star-talk precludes viewing the tauroctonous Mithras as a distinct character from the Sun god, Sol, with whom he interacts in many other episodes in the mythic narrative.

B3. In the star-talk lexicon used in the tauroctony, the most interesting of the polysemous signs is the bull. The bull, as we have seen, means Taurus, as both sign and constellation. It also means the Moon:

Bull (sign 1) means the Moon.

Why do I confidently claim this other meaning? First, it is warranted by a string of mystery-cult meanings set out by Porphyry in *De antro* 18.

The ancients called the priestesses of Demeter Bees, as initiates of the earth goddess, and the Maiden they called the Honey-sweet and the Moon who presides over genesis the Bee, especially since *the Moon is a bull and the exaltation of the Moon is Taurus*, and souls going into genesis are ox-born,[6] and he who secretly listens to genesis is the cattle-stealing god.

Since the 'cattle-stealing god' (*bouklopos theos*) means Mithras,[7] it is clear that this mystery-talk belongs to his mysteries as much as to Demeter's and the Maiden's.

Secondly, as the same passage also declares, Taurus is the Moon's 'exaltation' (*hypsōma*). This is pure star-talk. The 'exaltations' and 'humiliations' constituted an astrological system whereby each of the planets was allotted a sign of the zodiac in which it was powerful and another, directly opposite, in which it was

---

[6] The allusion here is to the *bougonia*, a process described in Virgil, *Georgic* 4.281–314, by which bees are supposedly generated spontaneously from the putrefying carcass of an ox.

[7] M. J. Edwards (1993) denies this on the grounds that the phrase in the allegedly Eleusinian context can only refer to Hermes. However, Edwards ignores the larger Mithraic context of the entire *De antro*. More serious is the improper posing of mutually exclusive alternatives (it can't mean Mithras because it means Hermes).

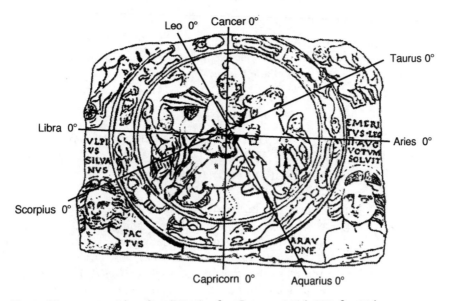

Fig. 8. Tauroctony with zodiac (V810), after Cumont 1896: 389, fig. 304

weak. The sign of the Moon's exaltation was Taurus, the sign of its 'humiliation' (*tapeinōma*) Scorpius. By star-talk metonomy the sign 'bull' in the tauroctony means 'Moon'.

The London tauroctony V810 (see Fig. 8) makes an explicit statement about the different star-talk meanings of the sign 'bull' and their relationships. In the upper right quarter of the composition notice the juxtapositioning of the head of the sacrificial bull with the sign Taurus in the ring zodiac and of the latter with the pair of oxen drawing Luna's chariot.

B4. If Mithras in the tauroctony means the Sun and the bull means the Moon, then the encounter of Mithras and the bull means the conjunction of Sun and Moon, the monthly event we call 'new moon', and the victory of the bull-killing Mithras signifies, whatever its ulterior meaning, the Sun's triumph over the Moon.

Note that the meanings 'new moon' and 'solar victory' are indisputable, once it is agreed that star-talk is the special language of the Mithraic mysteries in general and of the tauroctony in particular. One can argue about the meaning of symbols indefinitely, but the ruling principle for language signs is that words *mean what they say*. This principle holds regardless of any speaker's intent.

B5. We come finally to the sign 'cave'. Here again the sign's meaning is explicit. From Porphyry *De antro* 6 and our discussion of the mithraeum in Chapter 7 (sects. 1 and 2) we know that for the Mithraists:

(13). Cave means universe.

In the context of the tauroctony, the cave at the mouth of which Mithras kills the bull means specifically the entire celestial sphere, one hemisphere of which is signified by the selected constellation signs.

4. EXEGESIS (CONTINUED): C. MAP AND VIEW; BOUNDARIES AND ORIENTATION; TIME AND MOTION. SIMILAR STRUCTURES: THE AUGURAL *TEMPLUM* AND THE ANAPHORIC CLOCK

There are two ways in which we may 'read' the tauroctony as star-talk discourse. One is by reading it as a map or chart, the other by reading it as a view of the heavens. The distinction corresponds, except in one important respect, to that between a geographical map and an actual view of an expanse of terrain. Where the analogy fails is in respect of the terrestrial and celestial views. For while the terrestrial view remains the same as one gazes in the same direction from a fixed vantage point—a car or a cow may come into view or leave, but a hill or a house stays where it is—the celestial view is constantly changing as the celestial bodies (stars and constellations, Sun, Moon, and planets) rise and set in the twenty-four-hour cycle.

C1(*a*). As view, then, the tauroctony represents a window on the heavens which happens to be filled with the particular set of constellations signified. Twelve hours earlier and twelve hours later there was and will be an entirely different set of constellations filling the view.

The view is south-facing. It is defined by the horizon at the bottom and by the zenith at the top; by east to the left and by west to the right. Although in relief sculpture the tauroctony is usually composed in the shape of a rectangle (a trapezium on Danubian stelai), the celestial 'window' should not be so construed. The best approximation one can offer in diagram form is a composite of the two sky-views reproduced in Figures 9 and 10.[8] Figure 9 represents the left/east side of the view: Scorpius is rising; ahead of it are the zodiacal constellations Libra, Virgo, Leo, and Cancer, and the chosen paranatellonta Hydra

---

[8] The views are necessarily latitude-specific and epoch-specific. The latitude is that of Rome. The epoch is 100 CE. The grid is based on the ecliptic, shown here as a dotted line. The co-ordinate lines at right angles to the ecliptic mark the boundaries of the signs of the zodiac. The sign Cancer begins (at the summer solstice = longitude 90°) to the west/right of the constellation Cancer and ends to the east/left at the start of Leo (longitude 120°), some 3° short of the star Regulus. Due to precession, the zodiacal constellations have parted company with the signs of the zodiac named after them. The constellations have all shifted eastwards, so that the constellation Gemini is now, nineteen centuries later, in the sign of Cancer, the constellation Cancer in the sign of Leo, and the constellation Leo in the sign of Virgo.

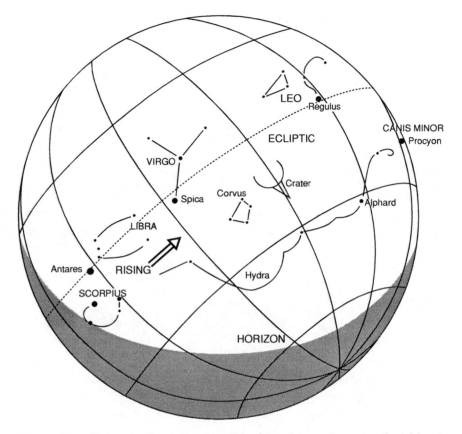

Fig. 9. Constellations in the tauroctony rising from the east (concave celestial hemisphere)

(tail), Corvus, Crater, Hydra (head), Canis Minor. Figure 10 represents the right/west side of the view: Taurus is setting; following it are the zodiacal constellations Gemini, Cancer, Leo, Virgo; of the paranatellonta, Canis Major is setting, to be followed by Canis Minor, Hydra (head), Crater, and Corvus. Figure 11 represents a more formalized version of the same view in its totality, with the zodiac forming a circular frame.

One must bear in mind that this particular celestial view with Taurus setting and Scorpius rising can only be seen at night during a limited time of the year. While the Sun is travelling through the selected signs of the zodiac from Taurus in the spring to Scorpius in the autumn, the scene is invisible—which is not to say that it isn't there, could one but discern it through the Sun's glare. A Mithraist wishing to view the actual scene with mortal eyes would have picked a night in January or February when Cancer or Leo would have culminated at around midnight. For a view earlier than midnight one would pick a night in a

Fig. 10. Constellations in the tauroctony setting in the west (concave celestial hemisphere)

subsequent month, for a view later than midnight a night in an earlier month (i.e. a month late in the preceding year).

The torchbearers construed as Gemini carry a subsidiary meaning in the context of the tauroctony read as view. The celestial Twins are of course the Dioscuri, Castor and Pollux, who contract to share the latter's immortality, spending alternate days in heaven and the underworld. Consequently, they come to symbolize the two hemispheres defined by the horizon, the visible hemisphere above and the invisible hemisphere below. This meaning was public knowledge, so we may assume that it was explicit as well as implicit in the sign of the mysteries' twin torchbearers.[9] Thus,

---

[9] This meaning is rightly emphasized by Ulansey (1989: 112–16).

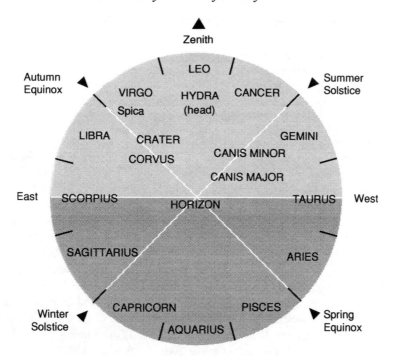

Fig. 11. The circle of the zodiac and the tauroctony constellations

(sign 2) Cautes means the visible hemisphere; Cautopates means the invisible hemisphere.

C1(*b*). As a map or star-chart the tauroctony represents a band of zodiacal constellations together with their southern paranatellonta extending from Taurus on the right of the map eastward to Scorpius on the left. In effect the map shows half of the zodiac, a half of a circular band which has been cut and extended as an elongated rectangle. As in a terrestrial map, north is at the top, south at the bottom. A star-chart, then as now, inverts east and west. The east side of the tauroctony is on the left, the west side on the right. Figure 1 is a star-chart of a more conventional sort covering the same celestial field as the tauroctony. The east–west line is the ecliptic, which is the median line of the band of the zodiac and the apparent path of the Sun in his annual journey. The stars are plotted on the chart in a rectilinear grid according to their coordinates in Ptolemy's catalogue (*Alm.* 7.5–8.1).

C2(*a*). To read star-talk in the tauroctony from left/east to right/west is to read in the direction of universal daily motion. Universal motion is the apparent motion of all celestial bodies around the heavens in a twenty-four-hour period. Looking at the tauroctony as view rather than chart we see the celestial bodies rising on the left, culminating in the centre, and setting on the right. Universal daily motion is 'uttered' principally in (i) the direction of the tauroctonous Mithras towards the right/west with his cloak streaming out behind him as if in the rush of forward impetus, and (ii) the direction of the chariots and teams of Sol and Luna (when shown) which is almost always to the right, meaning that the Sun is mounting the heavens in the east while the Moon is descending in the west.

C2(*b*). To read star-talk in the tauroctony from right/west to left/east is to read in the direction of planetary motion, particularly in the direction of the annual motion of the Sun around the ecliptic and of the monthly motion of the Moon weaving from north to south and back again along the same medial path. (The other five planets also move to and sometimes fro along the same path, but the tauroctony does not speak of them.)[10] The tauroctony does not speak as 'loudly' about this direction of solar and lunar motion as it does about the luminaries' participation in universal motion. We can 'hear' it, though, on certain monuments, for example the London tauroctony (V810) shown in Figure 8, where the Bull in the ring zodiac rushes in the opposite direction from the oxen drawing Luna's chariot (see above, sect. 3, B3) and the Lion likewise in the opposite direction to Sol and his team of horses. The star-talk relationship implicit in the latter parataxis (Leo next to the solar team, as Taurus next to the lunar) is that Leo is the astrological 'house' of the Sun, just as Taurus is the Moon's 'exaltation'.

Leo's leftward/eastward direction in the zodiac of V810 is unusual. Normally, in ring zodiacs which are properly oriented, in that the sequence of signs is counterclockwise and thus corresponds to the sequence of the actual star groups as one reads them in the heavens, Leo is represented facing or moving westward or to the right. He confronts Cancer, not Virgo. That indeed is his direction in the great majority of zodiacs.[11] So unless the designer of V810 has simply 'misspoken' in reversing Leo, we must assume that he intended to make some statement thereby. The intent is obvious. He is drawing attention to the Sun's annual motion in parataxis with the statement about the Sun's daily motion inherent in the eastward direction of the ascending solar quadriga. In the companion lunar statements in the upper right corner of the composition no reversal of Taurus was needed, since leftward/eastward is the sign's proper direction.[12] The abnormality in the direction of Leo is a good example of a detail in the composition which opens a window on the designer's probable intent. But even if Leo's reversal was mere coincidence, the star-talk utterance is made. Words mean what they say. The statement is there on the monument for all to read regardless of what the designer meant or did not mean.

---

[10] Though see Beck 1988: 21–2.
[11] See the catalogue in Gundel 1992. I have not made a precise count.
[12] On the literary allusions to Taurus rising backwards see Hübner 1982: 102, para. 2.133.1.

C3. Since time is defined by celestial motion, direction in the tauroctony signifies the temporal relationships 'before' and 'after', earlier' and 'later'.

(*a*) Daily time (universal motion): the flow of time is from left/east (means 'earlier') to right/west (means 'later').

(*b*) Annual time (solar motion) and monthly time (lunar motion): the flow of time is from right/west (means 'earlier') to left/east (means 'later').

Once again our star-talk approach resolves a seeming contradiction. Left/east cannot *be* both earlier and later, but it can *mean* either 'earlier' or 'later' depending on the temporal context (daily time or annual/monthly time). Moreover, given the icon's freedom from linearity, both meanings can be conveyed simultaneously.

Just as we found structures similar to the mithraeum qua 'image of the universe' in the surrounding culture (above, Ch. 7, sects. 9–10), so we should take note of two structures similar to the icon of the tauroctony, one to the tauroctony as view, the other to the tauroctony as celestial map. The first I have discussed in previous studies (Beck 1977: 9–11; 1994*a*). It is the Roman augural *templum*, which is literally a field of view defined for the observation of bird flight and bird cries ('auspicy' and 'augury') by a watcher facing south. The *templum*, Varro reports (*De lingua Latina* 7.6–8), is so quartered that the left 'part' is to the east, the right to the west, the front to the south, and the rear to the north. The Roman augur or magistrate literally 'con-templates' (*contemplare/-ari*) his *templum* for significant avian behaviour. Just so, one might say, the competent Mithraist 'con-templates' the celestial field of view which is his community's tauroctony for relevant meaning.

Our second analogous structure parallels the tauroctony as celestial map. It is the anaphoric clock (Vitruvius 9.8.8–15; Drachman 1954; Noble and Price 1968; Neugebauer 1975: 869–70). The dial of the anaphoric clock is literally a map of the constellations engraved on a bronze plate. Part of one exemplar survives, discovered near Salzburg a century ago (Benndorf *et al.* 1903; Price 1967: 592–3; Neugebauer 1975: 869–70). The principal constellations on the preserved fragment are Pisces, Aries, Taurus, Andromeda, Perseus, and Auriga. The line of the ecliptic was perforated with small holes: every two days a peg representing the Sun was moved counterclockwise from one hole to the next, tracking the Sun's annual progress around the ecliptic. (The fragment was snapped off at this line of perforations, giving it the appearance of part of a toothed gear wheel.) The entire dial rotated clockwise in the period of a twenty-four-hour day. The rotation of the dial was thus synchronized with, and so replicated, the rotation of the celestial sphere. In front of the rotating dial was a stationary wire web of hour lines radiating in appropriate curves. Time was 'told' by observing the passage of the Sun-marker crossing beneath the hour lines as the dial rotated. Like the more commonplace sundial, the anaphoric clock is constructed as an 'image of the universe' to display the daily and annual travels of the Sun. The following analogy holds:

anaphoric clock : tauroctony :: sundial : mithraeum

5. EXEGESIS (CONTINUED): D. FURTHER MEANINGS OF THE TORCHBEARERS: THE LUNAR NODES; CELESTIAL NORTH AND CELESTIAL SOUTH; HEAVENWARD AND EARTHWARD. MEANINGS OF THE 'TYPICAL' AND 'UNTYPICAL' LOCATIONS (CAUTES LEFT AND CAUTOPATES RIGHT VERSUS CAUTOPATES LEFT AND CAUTES RIGHT)

The principal players in the tauroctony are Mithras and the bull. As agent-signs in the discourse they mean 'Sun' and 'Moon', and those too are the meanings of Sol and Luna in the upper corners of the composition. The tauroctony is thus star-talking about the interaction of Sun and Moon—an essential point grasped by Rutgers (1970—see above, Ch. 7, sect. 4).

D1. Now the Sun and Moon travel essentially the same celestial route in the same direction. The Sun's route, as we have noted many times, is the ecliptic, the median line of the zodiac, while the Moon's is oblique to the ecliptic by approximately 5 degrees. The points at which the lunar orbit and the solar orbit intersect are known as the 'nodes' (Greek *syndesmoi*). The point at which the Moon crosses the ecliptic from south to north is the 'ascending' node (Greek *anabibazōn*), and the point at which she crosses back again from north to south is the 'descending' node (Greek *katabibazōn*) (see Fig. 12).

Anabibazein and *katabibazein* are causative forms of compounds of the verb *bainein* (to 'go'). Hence *anabibazōn* means 'causing to go up' or 'he who causes to

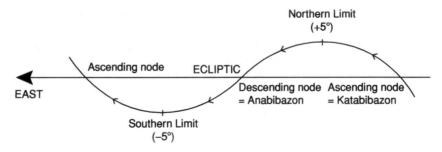

Fig. 12. The Moon's orbit in relation to the ecliptic

go up', and *katabibazōn* means 'causing to go down' or 'he who causes to go down'—more succinctly, 'upper' and 'downer' respectively. So it requires no great feat of the imagination to infer that with their raised and lowered torches the twin torchbearers in the tauroctony mean the lunar nodes. Specifically,

> Cautes means Anabibazon, the ascending node, and Cautopates means Katabibazon, the descending node.

I have discussed this pair of meanings and their interpretation in some detail in Beck 1976*a*: 9–13 (= 2004*c*: 159–63); 1978: 88–106, 135–6 (= 2004*c*: 171–90, 219–20); 1987*b*; 2001: 69–71; 2004*c*: 128, 327–8.

D2. The Moon's crossing of the ecliptic from south to north is represented as an ascent and her passage back again from north to south as a descent. This is but one instance of the semantic conflation of 'north' with 'up' and 'south' with 'down', a conflation as routine in Greek astronomy as in common parlance today. In star-talk we may properly call it a dead metaphor.

It follows that a pair of star-talk agent-signs one of whom carries his torch upright and the other inverted signify north and south, northerly and southerly, northward and southward. Specifically,

> Cautes means north/northern/northward, and Cautopates means south/southern/southward.

D3. There is however an ambiguity in the language of Greek astronomy—hence in star-talk as spoken by mortals—concerning the meaning of 'up' and 'down'. Up and down, above and below, ascent and descent refer not only to north and south, northern and southern, northward and southward, but also to the location of the spheres of the universe relative to the central earth and to motion 'upward' or 'downward' through them.[13] One 'ascends' from the globe of earth to the sphere of the Moon; thence in the standard order of Hellenistic astronomy through the spheres of Mercury, Venus, the Sun, Mars, Jupiter, Saturn, and finally to the sphere of the fixed stars.[14] One 'descends' in the opposite direction, from the sphere of the fixed stars downward through the spheres of the planets. Accordingly,

> Cautes means ascent from earth through the spheres of the planets to the sphere of the fixed stars and Cautopates means descent in the opposite direction.

These meanings take on immense importance in the context of the mystery of 'the soul's descent and departure back out again' (Porphyry, *De antro* 6) which we have seen to be so central to the business of Mithraists in their mithraea.

---

[13] Technically, the term 'depth' (*bathos*) and, less frequently, 'height' (*hypsos, altitudo*) are used for a planet's distance from earth. See Neugebauer 1975: 802 (particularly on Pliny's usage).

[14] On planetary orders (note the plural) in Mithraism see Beck 1988.

D4. We are now in a position to explain, in the sense of rendering a star-talk exegesis of, the one major set of alternatives in the tauroctony's composition: the placement of the torchbearers either with Cautes on the left in the east and Cautopates on the right in the west or vice versa with Cautopates on the left in the east and Cautes on the right in the west. The regional distribution of these alternatives was plotted by John Hinnells (1976), who found that the former type predominated in Rome and Italy in general and the latter in the Rhine and Danube provinces. Tauroctonies of the latter type are the more numerous overall, so Hinnells labelled them 'typical' and tauroctonies of the other type 'untypical', though without any implication that the typical tauroctonies were normative.

The untypical type is easier to explain. Cautes on the left signifies celestial bodies, the Sun in particular, rising in the east; his colleague Cautopates on the right signifies the Sun and all other celestial bodies setting in the west. The tauroctony is here read as celestial 'view' (above, C1(*a*)).

In the typical type Cautopates on the left means Scorpius qua southern sign through which the Sun descends in the 'fall' of the year; Cautes on the right means Taurus qua northern sign through which the Sun ascends in the spring of the year. The tauroctony is here read as celestial 'map' (above, C1(*b*)), although one can also read it as 'view', in which case it is saying that Scorpius is rising in the east while Taurus is setting in the west.

It is a curious fact that the lucidae of the two constellations Aldebaran (Alpha Tauri) and Antares (Alpha Scorpionis) are conspicuous red stars separated by roughly 180° of longitude, in other words half the ecliptic. From this fact was generated the factoid that the stars are exactly opposite each other on the celestial sphere, so that when one of them rises the other sets.[15] This factoid warrants the further pair of meanings for the torchbearers:

> Cautes means Aldebaran (Alpha Tauri) and Cautopates means Antares (Alpha Scorpionis).

This is a good example of a somewhat recherché star-talk meaning which an exegete could quite properly draw from the tauroctony but which it is possible that no actual Mithraic exegete did in fact draw. Mithraic doctrine, as we determined back in Chapter 4, is present on the monuments as a latent potentiality as well as an intended actuality.

---

[15] For the details see Beck 1977: 6–8. The author who preserves this factoid is Cleomedes (1.8.46–51 Todd), a teacher of elementary astronomy, *c*.200 CE. Cleomedes transmits other highly germane pieces of star-talk which I shall present in the following chapter.

6. EXEGESIS (CONTINUED): E. BEING IN THE NORTH/ ABOVE OR IN THE SOUTH/BELOW VERSUS GOING NORTHWARD/UP OR SOUTHWARD/DOWN. THE SOLSTICES, THE EQUINOXES, AND YET FURTHER MEANINGS OF THE TORCHBEARERS

As we have seen, the ecliptic, which is the Sun's orbit, is divided into two semicircles, one in which the Sun is 'above' (to the north of) the celestial equator and the other in which the Sun is 'below' (to the south of) the celestial equator. The Sun enters the 'upper' semicircle on/at the spring equinox (temporally in March, spatially at the start of the sign of Aries) and leaves it on/at the autumn equinox (temporally in September, spatially at the start of the sign of Libra). The Sun then enters the 'lower' semicircle and traverses the winter signs until it once again crosses the equator on/at the spring equinox.

One may also divide the ecliptic into two semicircles at the solstices. In the semicircle from the winter solstice (temporally in December, spatially at the start of Capricorn) the Sun 'ascends' northward as far as the summer solstice (temporally in June, spatially at the start of Cancer). In the semicircle from the summer solstice back to the winter solstice the Sun 'descends' southward.

The dividing lines between these two pairs of semicircles are at right angles to each other. Accordingly, the circle of the ecliptic/zodiac may be further divided into four quadrants (see Fig. 13):

(1). In the spring quadrant from Aries through Taurus to Gemini the Sun is in the north and ascending.

(2). In the summer quadrant from Cancer through Leo to Virgo the Sun is still in the north but is now descending.

(3). In the autumn quadrant from Libra through Scorpius to Sagittarius the Sun continues to descend but is now in the south.

(4). In the winter quadrant from Capricorn through Aquarius to Pisces the Sun is still in the south but is once again ascending.

These four statements convey important definitional truths. They furnish the star-talk terms and grammatical relationships on which one can articulate facts about the seasonal cycle which governs the ebb and flow of life on earth. Note especially the meanings which are drawn from the winter solstice as nadir, the southern extreme of the solar orbit, the point at which the debilitated Sun begins to wax again. Small wonder then that the date, the nominal solstice on 25 December, becomes the Sun's birthday, the 'Natalis Invicti', as the Calendar of Filocalus famously notes—to which phrase in Greek (*hēliou geneth-lion*) the less well-known Calendar of Antiochus appends 'light increases' (*auxei*

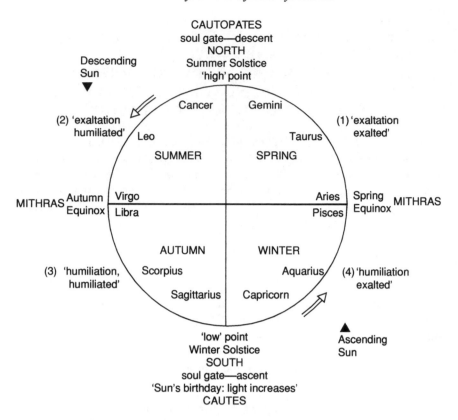

Fig. 13. A Mithraic version of a star-talk story of the solar year

phōs).[16] According to Macrobius (*Sat.* 1.18.10), not only was the Sun's birthday celebrated at the winter solstice but he was also displayed as a baby on that day: 'These differences in age [in the representations of various gods] relate to the Sun, who is made to appear very small (*parvulus*) at the winter solstice. In this form the Egyptians bring him forth from the shrine on the set date to appear like a tiny infant (*veluti parvus et infans*) on the shortest day of the year.'

In many cultures, perhaps universally, 'up' correlates with success, victory, and 'high' status and 'down' with failure, defeat, and 'low' status. Since star-talk equates 'north' with 'up' and 'south' with 'down', it follows that 'north' in certain star-talk contexts means 'success/victory/high status' and 'south' means 'failure/defeat/low status'.

The standard seasonal quartering of the ecliptic/zodiac formalizes and expresses in star-talk the important distinction between success and succeeding, between failure and failing. At the pinnacle of success one can start to fail, and at

---

[16] Calendar of Filocalus, Salzman 1990: 149–53; Calendar of Antiochus, Boll 1910: 16, 40–4.

the nadir of failure one can start to succeed. At the winter solstice the weakened Sun can sink no further to the south; he begins again the climb back northward to overpowering heat and brilliance.

The astrologer Antiochus of Athens captured well the significance of the four quadrants in respect of power and status by applying the terminology of 'exaltation' and 'humiliation'.[17] We have already encountered the terms as indicating a pair of opposite signs of the zodiac, one of which is a planet's 'exaltation', the other its 'humiliation' (above, sect. 3, para. B3). In the present context, they are applied to the solar quadrants (*CCAG* 7.128):

(1) The Sun ascends in the north from Aries to the start of Cancer; accordingly his exaltation is said to be exalted (*hypsos hypsoutai*).[18]

(2) From Cancer to the start of Libra he descends in the north; so his exaltation is said to be humiliated (*hypsos tapeinoutai*), since from the zenith he begins to be abased.

(3) From Libra to Capricorn he descends in the south; so his humiliation is said to be humiliated (*tapeinon tapeinoutai*).

(4) From Capricorn to Aries he ascends in the south; so his humiliation is said to be exalted (*tapeinon hypsoutai*), since from the nadir he begins to be exalted.

It is impossible to overestimate the metaphorical freight carried by the star-talk utterances of the solar journey. In addition to the ebb and flow of the seasonal, natural cycle, the Sun's stages and progressions (high or low, upward or downward?) speak—or can be made to speak—of success and failure both as states and as tendencies in all activities human and divine.

We may accordingly assign the following additional star-talk meanings to the torchbearers in (and beyond) the tauroctony:

E1. Cautes means the northern/higher semicircle of the ecliptic and the spring and summer signs of the zodiac. Cautopates means the southern/lower semicircle and the autumn and winter signs.

E2. Cautes means the semicircle of the ecliptic in which the Sun ascends northward; hence the winter and spring signs. Cautopates means the semicircle of the ecliptic in which the Sun descends southward; hence the summer and autumn signs.

E3. Cautes means the summer solstice where/when the Sun is at his northern extreme and zenith. Cautopates means the winter solstice where/when the Sun is at his southern extreme and nadir.

---

[17] It is probable that Antiochus first applied the terminology to a lunar quartering which we shall meet in a later section. Throughout this chapter I avoid the customary translation 'depression' for Greek *tapeinōma* = Latin *depressio*. 'Depression' today both carries irrelevant psychological connotations and fails to convey the proper implications of low status.

[18] Helios may be the grammatical subject of *hypsoutai* and *hypsos* an internal accusative: 'he is exalted in respect of his exaltation'. The meaning remains unchanged. The same goes for the other three sentences.

E4. Cautes means the spring equinox where the Sun is at the midpoint of his ascent northward. Cautopates means the autumn equinox where/when the Sun is at the midpoint of his descent southward.

E5. Cautes means ascent northward from the winter solstice. Cautopates means descent southward from the summer solstice.

One of these meanings (E5) we have encountered already: Cautes as ascent from the winter solstice, Cautopates as descent from the summer solstice. It is the prime meaning of the torchbearers in the mithraeum where, as we saw in Chapter 7, it is a crucial definition in the construction of the mithraeum's own meaning as 'universe'. Meaning E5, as we also saw, is one of the few pieces of Mithraic star-talk preserved in a literary source, Porphyry *De antro nympharum* 24: Mithras 'at his proper seat . . . on the equator . . . at the equinoxes' has Cautopates on his right at the summer solstice and Cautes on his left at the winter solstice.

These meanings are naturally crucial to Mithraic anthropology and soteriology. It is not just the Sun who begins to descend from the summer solstice and to ascend from the winter solstice. The human soul too begins its descent into genesis through the gate of the summer solstice in Cancer and completes its ascent 'back out again' into apogenesis through the gate of the winter solstice in Capricorn. In talk about the Sun's seasonal descent and ascent the torchbearers carry their E5 meaning: descent from celestial north southward and ascent from celestial south northward; in talk about the descent and ascent of souls they carry their D3 meaning: descent inwards and downwards to earth, ascent outwards and upwards to heaven. This a good example of a shift in meaning accompanying a shift from one domain to another. In my descriptive template (Ch. 1, sects. 1 and 3) I postulated four 'domains' in which 'the initiate apprehends the "axioms" and "themes"' of the mysteries. The second of these domains is 'the cosmos', the fourth 'the destiny of human (especially initiates') souls'. In star-talk in the fourth domain the torchbearers will probably carry their D3 meaning, while in the second domain only a narrower context ('what particular aspect of the cosmos?') will indicate their meaning.

7. EXEGESIS (CONTINUED): F. TWO PARADOXES: (1) COLD NORTH AND HOT SOUTH VERSUS HOT NORTH AND COLD SOUTH; (2) DESCENDING FROM HEAVEN AND GROWING UP ON EARTH VERSUS DYING DOWN ON EARTH AND ASCENDING TO HEAVEN. TERRESTRIAL MEANINGS OF THE TORCHBEARERS

The solstices are archetypal 'turning points' (*tropai*). At the summer solstice the Sun is 'up' at the northern limit of his orbit where he turns back 'down' south; at the winter solstice he is 'down' at the southern limit and turns back 'upward' towards the north. In the Mithraic mysteries then either torchbearer can mean either solstice: it simply depends on the sentence uttered.

There is however a more fundamental paradox concerning 'north' and 'south' which affects the meanings of the torchbearers. Fortunately, this paradox is posed explicitly in our prime literary source for Mithraic star-talk, Porphyry's *De antro nympharum* (21–9). In the Mithraic mysteries Cautopates is located at the gate of descent at the summer solstice in the north and Cautes at the gate of ascent at the winter solstice in the south, locations warranted, as we saw in the preceding section, by the star-talk truism that from a zenith one can only descend and from a nadir one can only rise. But although that truism is latent in Porphyry's explanation, the actual logic pursued is quite different. Cautopates presides over descent into mortality from the north because the north with its invigorating cold is appropriate to souls entering mortal genesis, while his colleague Cautes presides over ascent via apogenesis into immortality from the south because the heat of the south 'dissolves' or 'releases' (*dialuei*).[19]

But wait a moment: how can the summer solstice where/when the Sun reaches his zenith be 'cold' and how can the winter solstice where/when the Sun reaches his nadir be 'hot'? The answer is that we have shifted domains. In the heavens north is indeed 'hot' and south 'cold'; but on earth north is just as surely 'cold' and south 'hot'. Star-talk here asserts a paradox, but it does not flatly contradict itself.

The paradox here explicated is especially manifest in the design and seating of the mithraeum (see above, Figs. 2 and 3). The initiates on the bench to the right of Mithras are 'hot' because they occupy the signs of the zodiac where the Sun resides in spring and summer; they are 'cold' because the very same signs are northerly. Conversely their colleagues opposite on the bench to Mithras' left are 'cold' because they occupy the signs of the autumnal and winter Sun, but they are 'hot' because those signs are southerly.

The distinction between heavenly and earthly meanings resolves, or rather clarifies, a second paradox.[20] One of Cautopates' meanings in the celestial domain and his primary meaning in the anthropological/soteriological domain is descent into mortal genesis; and the corresponding meaning of Cautes is apogenesis and ascent into immortality. However, these meanings have been largely overlooked by Mithraic scholars in the main stream,[21] who have usually interpreted the torchbearers first as symbols of the rising and setting Sun or of the Sun in spring and the Sun in autumn and secondly as symbols of the seasonal waxing and waning of vegetation. Terrestrially, on this interpretation,

---

[19] The argument is made in terms of the different effects of the north and south winds.
[20] On the two paradoxes addressed in this section see Beck 1994*a*: 114, n. 31.
[21] But see Campbell 1968: 29–43.

Cautes signifies seed-time, growth, and the season of spring, while Cautopates signifies harvest, and the dying down of vegetation in autumn ('fall' in North American usage).

This terrestrial sense, in which Cautes is genetic and Cautopates apogenetic, appears to contradict the celestial sense in which it is Cautopates who means (descent into) genesis and Cautes who means (ascent into) apogenesis. The contradiction is more apparent than real, and it can be resolved by pointing to the now familiar distinction between *proceeding into* a state and *being in* a state. But the paradox so generated must be allowed to stand as an element—a very important element—in the Mithraists' construction of reality, *their* world as they comprehended it. It is of course a version of the dualist *sōma/sēma* model: 'the body is a tomb'; life is death and death is life.

Here the exegete must quickly put on his interpreter's hat and warn that the paradox as articulated in the mysteries is not anti-materialistic. The world in which we grow and flourish is a good place. You will scan the monuments in vain for signs of hatred of the flesh or the natural order. Robert Turcan (1982) was surely right in characterizing Mithraic 'salvation' as '*bio*-cosmic' (my emphasis) and the mysteries as robustly life-affirming; right too in pointing to Mazdaism as the likely source of this attitude.

To conclude, this is a good example of the limits of literal star-talk exegesis. Star-talk, at least in this context, does not tell you whether celestial descent and terrestrial growth are good things or bad things or merely indifferent. That sort of question requires other, more traditional skills in comparing and interpreting religious representations. For my own money, I would hazard that the Mithraic line was 'genesis good, apogenesis better', but I cannot demonstrate it in the way I can demonstrate the mysteries' star-talk propositions.

8. EXEGESIS (CONTINUED): G. WHERE AND WHEN? 'MITHRAS THE BULL-KILLER' MEANS 'SUN-IN-LEO'

(1) Since the tauroctony represents a view or map of the heavens extending from Taurus in the west to Scorpius in the east (above, sect. 2, A1),

(2) and since the torchbearers on either side of the scene signify Taurus and Scorpius (above, sect. 2, A2.2, A3),

(3) and since Mithras in the centre of the scene means the Sun (above, sect. 3, B2),

(4) and since Leo as sign and constellation is midway between Taurus and Scorpius,

(5) it follows that the tauroctonous Mithras means Sun-in-Leo. In temporal terms, this means the Sun during the last third of July and the first two thirds of August.

Notice that we have *deduced* the meaning of the tauroctonous Mithras by star-talk logic from the four premises. We did not reach the conclusion *inductively* by adducing evidence from within and outside the mysteries to establish that the initiates did in fact ascribe that identity to Mithras as bull-killer.

The weaknesses of the inductive approach are all too evident. There is almost no internal evidence (other than the dedications which tell us that Mithras is a god, that he is the Sun, and that he is invincible) for the ascription of further esoteric identities to the tauroctonous Mithras by the initiates. Consequently, we can only assemble data to show that since Leo is the Sun's own 'house' and a fiery sign associated with sovereignty, and since the Sun when in Leo is at the acme of his seasonal power, Sun-in-Leo would have been a highly appropriate identity for the Mithraists to have ascribed to their god.[22] Certainly such data from the ancient 'encyclopaedia' is germane and one may readily agree that the ascription of the postulated identity was highly probable. But between 'highly probable' and 'actually did' there will always be a gap—a gap which 'must therefore have ascribed' does not span.

In asserting Sun-in-Leo as the star-talk meaning of the sign 'Mithras' in the context of the tauroctony we are on altogether more secure ground. Once we agree that the question is one of language and semantics, the deduced meaning Sun-in-Leo stands or falls on the logic and accuracy of the four premises which lead to it. If you are going to tell me that Mithras does not mean Sun-in-Leo, you must tell me what is wrong with my reading of the text of the tauroctony or with my understanding of the grammar of its language.

Sun-in-Leo is the meaning of Mithras in the tauroctony read as 'map' (above, sect. 4, C1 (*b*)). In the tauroctony read as 'view' (C1 (*a*)), Mithras means the culminating midday Sun at the zenith of his daily journey from his rising in the east/left to his setting in the west/right.

When the Sun blazes at the zenith no other celestial body is visible. Likewise, for the month when the Sun is in Leo, the stars of Leo and nearby constellations are invisible, since whenever they are above the horizon so is the Sun. There is thus an implicit irony in the tauroctony: you cannot read it with corporeal eyes, only with the mind's eye.

There is however, one creature who can gaze at Sun-in-Leo (or anywhere else) and still 'see'—the eagle; and from Porphyry (*De abstinentia* 4.16) we know that in esoteric parlance the Fathers of Mithraic communities were called 'eagles'. Richard Gordon in his exploration of the animal lore of the ancient 'encyclopaedia' explains why the sobriquet was so appropriate (1980*b*: 66–7). The ability to look at the Sun without blinking is the test for legitimacy by which eagles recognize and acknowledge their true offspring (Aelian, *De natura animalium* 2.26). On this criterion, we may now add, the Eagle-Father is he who can bear to gaze on the cult icon and read it with undazzled eyes.

[22] This necessary task I have already performed (Beck 1994*b*: 44–7).

9. FROM EXEGESIS TO INTERPRETATION. AN ESOTERIC QUARTERING OF THE HEAVENS

The boundary between exegesis and interpretation is quite fluid. The end of the preceding section is a good example of how the former flows seamlessly into the latter. We brought together a basic meaning—actually, *the* basic meaning—in the star-talk discourse of the tauroctony (Mithras means Sun), an esoteric sobriquet (Mithraic Fathers were called 'Eagles'), and a factoid about actual eagles looking at the Sun. From these three items we inferred something— admittedly a rather small something—about the ethos and world view of the Mithraic mysteries, namely the moral and intellectual qualifications for viewing the tauroctony.

Notice first that the object of our interpretation here was not the tauroctony itself but the Mithraic mysteries as a whole; secondly, that the interpretation, unlike the prior exegesis, is not completely secure. We simply do not know whether all those connections were in fact widely made, or indeed whether they were ever made explicitly. Nevertheless, what we can say with some confidence is that they were there for the making.

From this point in the chapter we shall be blending exegesis with interpret- ation, and the proportion of the latter to the former will gradually increase. There is no need to track the shift with any precision. In the end, exegesis and interpretation are but two stages in a single enterprise. Notionally it is important to distinguish them, but in any given instance it is not crucial to say at what point the one yields to the other.

I want to continue by posing the question, why in the tauroctony do the mysteries adopt an unusual quartering of the heavens? In place of the usual quartering by the solstitial and equinoctial signs (or points), the tauroctony declares a celestial quartering by the signs which *follow* the four tropic signs: Taurus, Leo, Scorpius, and Aquarius. In astrology these are called the 'solid' (*sterea, solida*) signs because they 'confirm' the terrestrial conditions introduced by the four tropic signs (Bouché-Leclercq 1899: 152). This quartering is explicitly stated by (1) the torchbearers on the east/left and west/right margins of the tauroctony with their 'Scorpius' and 'Taurus' meanings (above, sect. 2, A2.2(*b*)); (2) the tauroctonous Mithras in the upper centre meaning 'Sun-in-Leo' (above, sect. 8); (3) the Danubian motif of the lion plunging down into the crater signifying Leo–Aquarius as the tauroctony's vertical axis (above, sect. 2, A2.6 and A4), at right angles to the horizontal Taurus–Scorpius axis.

'Why?' asks an interpretive question. 'Why' questions often arise in the context of something unusual. Had the composition of the tauroctony followed the standard quartering by tropic (i.e. equinoctial and solstitial) signs, the question would not arise at all.

Our first answer is commonsensical—and none the worse for that. Mithras slew a bull, not a ram, and he did so with a scorpion present and active, not a pair of scales; a lion, moreover, is a much more impressive symbol of solar power than a crab. True enough, and probably sufficient; certainly, a salutary reminder that quartering the zodiac was not the primary concern of the designer(s).

So is the question improper? Should we just say that the appearance of an unusual celestial quartering is a mere epiphenomenon of the subject matter. After all, when zodiacs are explicit parts of the composition, as in the London tauroctony V810 (Fig. 8), the standard quartering, not the esoteric quartering, is usually observed.

This would be an overreaction. Epiphenomenon it may be in terms of implicit priorities, but the esoteric quartering is a fact of the composition, a star-talk statement actually made, particularly and emphatically by the torchbearers defining the east–west, left–right, horizontal axis of the tauroctony as star-chart. Consider also the scorpion. Is its presence really determined by a prior narrative of the bull-killing which included all the accessory animals, or is it rather determined by star-talk logic which requires it as the complement to Taurus the Bull in statements about opposition and the tauroctony's east–west, left–right, horizontal axis? Surely the latter. In the priorities of the composition the bull precedes Taurus but Scorpius precedes the scorpion. If, then, the esoteric quartering does not drive the composition, it is certainly more than a meaningless epiphenomenon.

In his interpretation of the tauroctony (1989—see above, Ch. 7, sect. 4) David Ulansey was surely right to focus on the privileging of Taurus and Scorpius in the composition. His mistake was to draw the implausible inference that Taurus and Scorpius were selected by the designers because they were the constellations in which the equinoctial points had resided two millennia before. This hypothesis about the design and composition implies that the designers knew the then very recherché fact that the equinoxes do indeed slowly shift position, the so-called precession of the equinoxes. Very few serious scholars either of the Mithraic mysteries or of the history of astronomy have accepted Ulansey's theory. My own view (Beck 2004c: 243–4) is that, wrong though the theory is, this much can be said for it: had you explained precession to a Mithraic Father and pointed out that the torchbearers, the scorpion, and the bull could be related to the equinoxes of an earlier era, he would have gratefully added it to his portfolio of explications. Simply as a matter of star-talk syntax, the archaic equinoxes were and are potentially present as meanings in the composition of the tauroctony. What makes it extremely improbable that precession was ever elicited as a meaning, let alone deliberately encoded in the tauroctony as a 'plumbed-in' meaning, is the need to postulate Mithraists or Ur-Mithraists with the requisite knowledge. Nothing in the reception-history of the astronomical theory of precession suggests that such people ever existed. Since one can account for Mithraism's esoteric quartering without invoking them, they serve no useful function and are best dismissed.

To ascertain the significance of the esoteric quartering in context we must first explore its occurrence in star-talk outside the Mithraic mysteries. Were there precedents for the esoteric quartering in the public domain? Or, to avoid the implication of temporal priority, do we find parallels to our 'esoteric' quartering of the zodiac in secular astrology?

There are in fact two parallels, and both are highly germane. The first is the system of planetary 'houses' (Bouché-Leclercq 1899: 182–92). In Graeco-Roman astrology the signs of the zodiac are distributed among the planets as their 'houses' (*oikoi*), as places where by definition they are most 'at home' and hence most powerful and influential. The problem of dividing twelve signs among seven planets was solved by assigning one house to each of the two luminaries and two each to the remaining five planets. Leo was assigned to the Sun and Cancer to the Moon. In the order of the signs (counterclockwise) from Leo and against the order of the signs (clockwise) from Cancer, the other signs are then distributed pair by pair to the other planets in the order of the planets' distance from the earth (see table). Thus Mercury, the nearest of the planets proper, acquires Virgo and Gemini, and so on in opposite directions around the two semicircles of the zodiac to Capricorn and Aquarius, the final pair, which fall to Saturn, the most distant of the planets.

Planet	Diurnal/Solar House	Nocturnal/Lunar House
Sun	Leo	
Moon		Cancer
Mercury	Virgo	Gemini
Venus	Libra	Taurus
Mars	Scorpius	Aries
Jupiter	Sagittarius	Pisces
Saturn	Capricorn	Aquarius

Vertically, then, the system of houses divides the zodiac at the cusp of Cancer and Leo at the 'top' and the cusp of Capricorn and Aquarius at the 'bottom'. This vertical division is of course the same as that of our esoteric quartering.

May we then say that the system of planetary houses was 'structured into' the composition of the tauroctony? Yes, as a truism, in that the tauroctony, structured as it is, cannot help talking 'houses' in its star-talk utterances. Probably, but not certainly, in the sense that the original designer(s) had the system of houses in mind when they composed the icon. What the tauroctony actually says is 'Sun in Leo, his house', and there are indications, to be noted below, that the icon was in fact read that way.

Does the tauroctony also say 'Moon in Cancer, her house'? We have seen that a particular tauroctony (V810: above, sect. 4, C2(*b*); and see Fig. 8) alludes to

Taurus as the Moon's exaltation 'in the same breath', one might say, as it alludes to Leo as the Sun's house[23] But the composition in general, as we have also seen (above, sect. 3, B4), speaks of an *encounter* of the Sun, the meaning in context of the sign 'Mithras the bull-killer', and the Moon, the meaning in context of the sign 'bull killed by Mithras'. So, yes, the tauroctony does indeed say that the Moon is in Cancer, her house, or more precisely at the end of Cancer where she encounters the Sun at the beginning of Leo, his house.[24]

Paradoxically, of all the extant framing zodiacs on Mithraic monuments it is the zodiac surrounding a birth scene, not a tauroctony, which speaks most clearly of planetary houses. A monument from Housesteads on Hadrian's Wall (V860) shows the young Mithras emerging from the lower half of a split eggshell (rather than the customary rock), sword and torch in hand. A zodiac arches around and above him in the shape of a horseshoe, the open side at the bottom. The signs begin on the lower left side with Aquarius and run clockwise around to Capricorn on the lower right.[25] With six signs on either side, the zodiac culminates at the cusp of Cancer and Leo. Those two signs are separated from the ten below by the sword and torch respectively. The following table is a schematization of the two halves of the zodiac (the planets 'at home' in each are shown in parentheses).

Left	Right
Cancer (Moon)	Leo (Sun)
sword	*torch*
Gemini (Mercury)	Virgo (Mercury)
Taurus (Venus)	Libra (Venus)
Aries (Mars)	Scorpius (Mars)
Pisces (Jupiter)	Sagittarius (Jupiter)
Aquarius (Saturn)	Capricorn (Saturn)

That the disposition of the signs announces the system of planetary houses is obvious. Note that in this structure a 'horizontal' division effecting an actual quartering into four equal quadrants would be irrelevant. Consequently it is absent from the composition because it would not say anything meaningful. The

[23] Another tauroctony (V75 Sidon) so places its zodiac that Taurus is shown leaping towards the bust of Luna, and Aries, the sign of the Sun's exaltation, towards the bust of Sol. To achieve this effect while preserving the zodiac's proper counterclockwise order the busts of the luminaries are reversed: Sol is on the right, Luna on the left. In this tauroctony the representation of the scorpion does double duty as both sign of the zodiac and animal at the bull's genitals.

[24] Modern Leo 0° = ancient Cancer 30°.

[25] Aquarius, most unusually, is represented like Capricorn as a fish-tailed creature. The assimilation, as well as balancing the composition at the two ends of the zodiac, suggests what the two signs have in common: they are the two houses of the same planet, Saturn.

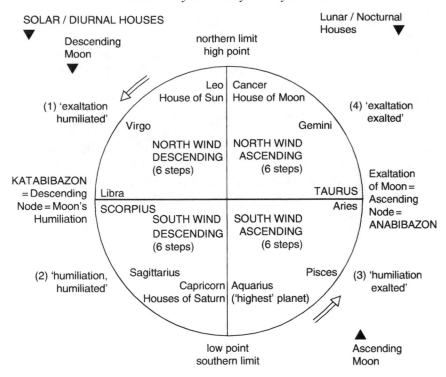

Fig. 14. A star-talk story of an ideal draconitic month

meaningful horizontal divide (sword and torch) separates the houses of the two luminaries from the houses of the remaining five planets.[26]

The second parallel to our esoteric quartering in exoteric astrology is what we may call the lunar quartering (Fig. 14). The lunar quartering effects for the Moon what the standard quartering by tropic points effects for the Sun: it divides the zodiac into four equal quadrants in which the Moon is (1) north of the ecliptic and moving northward, (2) still north of the ecliptic but moving southward, (3) south of the ecliptic and still moving southward, and (4) still in the south but now moving northward. All the meanings which we saw attached to the standard or solar quartering remain, in particular those of 'exaltation' and 'humiliation'; likewise the meanings of the torchbearers which we examined in section 6 (E1–5). What has changed is the definition of the quadrants: the cardinal points have shifted 30 degrees (one hour on a clock dial) counterclockwise.

Here anyone at all knowledgeable in astronomy may properly object that the lunar quartering is astronomically nonsensical. Indeed it is, for while the solar

---

[26] On the zodiac of V860 and the planetary houses see also Beck 1988: 35–9.

quartering is based on astronomical fact—the Sun really is to the north of ('above') the equator from the start of Aries to the end Virgo—the lunar quartering is a fiction. The Sun does indeed always cross the celestial equator from south to north at the start of Aries, but the equivalent proposition for the Moon is false: the Moon does *not* always cross the ecliptic from south to north at the start of Taurus. If she does so one month, the following month she will cross the ecliptic at a point slightly to the west in Aries, and so on for the next 18.6 years until she returns once more to the vicinity of her original crossing point. In other words, the lunar nodes themselves circle the ecliptic in a period of approximately 18.6 years. The lunar quartering is thus an arbitrary construct which freezes the Moon's orbit in a fixed track with respect to latitude. There was, presumably, some astrologically cogent reason for fixing the ascending node at the start of Taurus, the northern limit at the start of Leo, the descending node at the start of Scorpius, and the southern extreme at the start of Aquarius; but what it was we do not yet know. My sense is that it is part of the definition of an *ideal* lunar orbit and an *ideal* month within a certain tradition of star-talk to which the Mithraic mysteries belonged.

The lunar quartering brings with it a peculiar idiom. The four quadrants of the solar quartering, as we have seen, are seasonal: spring, summer, autumn, winter. In the lunar quartering, one speaks of 'winds' (*anemoi*) north or south and of 'ascending' or 'descending' sectors, and it was customary to begin the quartering not at the midpoint of ascent (the equivalent of the spring equinox) but at the northern extreme (the equivalent of the summer solstice).[27] To complicate matters further, the quadrants are measured not in 30° signs ($3 \times 30° = 90°$) but in 'steps' (*bathmoi*) of 15°. Each quadrant thus consists of six steps ($6 \times 15° = 90°$). The system is described by the second-century CE astrologer Vettius Valens in a chapter entitled 'How to find the steps and winds of the Moon' (*Anthologies* 1.18). Antiochus of Athens, who we saw applied the language of exaltation and humiliation to the solar quartering (above, sect. 6), also mentions it (*CCAG* 7.128.14–16). One may tell the story of a lunar cycle accordingly (Fig. 14):

1. Leo to Libra: North Wind descending: six steps down from zenith; exaltation humiliated.

2. Scorpius to Capricorn: South Wind descending: six more steps down to nadir: humiliation humiliated.

3. Aquarius to Aries: South Wind ascending: six steps up from nadir: humiliation exalted.

4. Taurus to Cancer: North Wind ascending: six more steps up to zenith: exaltation exalted.

---

[27] This order is almost certainly related to the ancient astronomical practice of measuring ('for reasons unknown', Neugebauer 1975: 80) the 'argument of latitude' from the Moon's northern extreme, not from the ascending node as in modern practice.

The great historian of ancient astronomy, Otto Neugebauer, properly points out that in astrology the wind of the Moon or other planet 'simply means the direction of the motion in latitude and not an atmospheric phenomenon; probably "vector" would better represent the actual meaning' (1975: 670–1). As someone seeking to free ancient mathematical astronomy from the clutter of irrelevant metaphor, he is of course right. But one person's trash is another's gold, and as a historian and semiotician of star-talk in the Mithraic mysteries I value the 'winds' as a precious lexical nugget. For example, it helps me read and better comprehend the meaning of the two wind gods in the London tauroctony V810 (Fig. 8); likewise the inclusion of the winds Boreas and Notos in Porphyry's extended treatment of the solstitial soul-gates in the mysteries (see above, sect. 7). In star-talk in a religious context very few signs 'simply' mean or mean only by metaphor.

The lunar nodes, it will be remembered, are star-talk meanings of the Mithraic torchbearers (above, sect. 5, D1). Cautes means Anabibazon, the ascending node, and Cautopates means Katabibazon, the descending node. But we have already established that as the limiting signs and constellations to the right/west and left/east of the tauroctony as star-field Cautes means Taurus and Cautopates Scorpius (sect. 2, A2.2(*b*)). It follows, then, syllogistically that:

Cautes means Anabibazon in Taurus; Cautopates means Katabibazon in Scorpius.

We can read much the same sort of star-talk exegesis in a comment by a later writer appended to Vettius Valens' chapter (1.18) on the 'steps' and 'winds' of the Moon cited above:[28] 'For Taurus is the exaltation (*hypsōma*) of the Moon and, as it were (*hoion*), Anabibazon; and Scorpius as it were Katabibazon; and Leo as it were the northern limit (*peras*) of Anabibazon; and Aquarius as it were the southern limit of Katabibazon.' No direct influence from or on our piece of Mithraic exegesis need be postulated. Both pieces merely belong to the same stream of star-talk chatter, the same 'epidemic' (in Dan Sperber's sense)[29] of astral representations. Both have to do, I suggest, with the definition of an ideal lunar orbit.

10. THE IMPLICATIONS OF SUN-IN-LEO AND THE ESOTERIC QUARTERING. CONJUNCTIONS AND ECLIPSES; VICTORIES AND DEFEATS

An extraordinarily valuable but neglected snippet of Mithraic exegesis is preserved in the late antique scholiast to Statius' *Thebaid*, Lactantius Placidus. In the Statius passage (*Thebaid* 1.719–20) Apollo is invoked under various names ending with Mithras: '...or as Mithras beneath the rocks of a Persian cave

---

[28] See David Pingree's edition (1986: 397, App. VII).
[29] Sperber 1996; and see above, Ch. 1, sect. 2.

twisting the horns loath to follow.' The allusion to the tauroctony, to the event if not to the icon, is patent.[30] The scholiast has this to say (Cumont 1896: 47–8):

The sense is as follows: the Persians worship the Sun in caves, and here the Sun is called by his proper name Mithras, who, because he suffers eclipse, is accordingly worshipped inside a cave. He is the very Sun with a lion's face (*leonis vultu*), in Persian dress, and with both hands pressing on the ox's horns. This reading relates to the Moon who, 'loath to follow' her brother, gets in his way and obscures his light. The author has laid bare part of the mysteries. The Sun, as if leading the Moon, his inferior, 'twists' the bull. The author has placed the word 'horns' wonderfully well so as to bring out the meaning 'Moon' more clearly, not the animal by which she is represented as conveyed. However, because this is not the place to discuss the secrets of those gods along the lines of esoteric philosophy, let us say a little about the images and metaphors [hendiadys for *figuris*] to which it is entrusted. The ineffable Sun, because he treads upon and bridles the principal sign of the zodiac, that is Leo, for that reason he too is represented with this [i.e. a leonine] visage (*Sol ineffabilis, quia principale signum inculcat et frenat, leonem scilicet, idcirco et ipse hoc vultu fingitur*); or else because this god excels among the others in the violence of his divinity and the onslaught of his power, as the lion among other wild beasts; or else because the lion is a fierce and swift [hendiadys for *rapidum*] animal. The Moon, because close by she overpowers and leads a bull, is accordingly represented as a cow.

Lactantius Placidus asserts that in the mysteries of Mithras, the name under which the Persians worship the Sun, the god is represented with a lion's face. This of course is patently false: the tauroctonous Mithras is entirely and always anthropomorphic. The scholiast, it seems, had never set eyes on a tauroctony. But just as clearly there is nothing in the text of Statius from which, in the usual scholiast's way, he could have inferred Mithras' leonine visage. What, then, is the origin of his error? The answer is obvious and simple: he or his source has mistaken exegesis for description. He thought that because the tauroctonous Mithras means Sun-in-Leo he must somehow have been represented as a lion.

Notice that the scholiast has also got hold of some of the star-talk logic behind the meaning 'Sun-in-Leo': that Leo is the astrological house of the Sun. More-over, he senses that Leo is somehow 'the primary sign' (*principale signum*). However, even the import of this simple proposition he does not really under-stand. Absurdly, he thinks it has to with the Sun 'trampling and bridling' (*inculcat et frenat*) Leo in the way that Mithras overpowers the bull. But as we have seen, there are only two star-talk constructs in which Leo rules as the 'primary sign'. One is the system of houses, in which Leo, as the Sun's house stands at the head of the 'diurnal' houses; the other is the lunar quartering, the first quadrant of which begins with Leo.

From the same star-talk exegesis of the tauroctony the scholiast received the lunar meaning of the bull. A single word in the text reveals that he either received

---

[30] As is often pointed out, Statius' Mithras grasps the bull by the horns, not by the nostrils as in the standard composition of the icon.

it in garbled form or else himself misconstrued the more precise lunar meaning of the bull: the Moon in Cancer, her house. The word is *propius* in the sentence, 'the Moon, because *close* by she overpowers and leads a bull, is accordingly represented as a cow'.

The scholiast's argument is as follows: both luminaries overpower and master an animal; the Sun overpowers a lion and is accordingly represented with a lion's visage, the Moon overpowers a bull and is accordingly represented as a cow. If the lion overpowered by the Sun is Leo, 'the leading sign', who then is the bull overpowered by the Moon? Taurus the Bull, obviously.[31]

Lactantius Placidus seems to be unaware or unconcerned that his argument has parted company from the actual scene of the tauroctony in which what Mithras overpowers is not a lion but a bull and the bull is not in a position to overpower anything, being itself overpowered by Mithras. However, lack of correspondence with the scene represented by Statius and the tauroctony is not the scholiast's only problem. He speaks of the Moon overpowering Taurus 'close by' (*propius*) the Sun overpowering Leo. But Taurus is not near Leo. It is three signs away in quadrature. A further, formal difficulty is that it is *not* the case, strictly speaking, that

Taurus : Moon :: Leo : Sun,

for while Leo is the Sun's house Taurus is not the Moon's house but rather the Moon's exaltation.

Beneath the surface Lactantius Placidus' argument is sheer nonsense. But nonsense, as every textual critic knows, often reveals more than does sense, especially when it preserves enough to indicate an original sense. The original exegesis which our scholiast has garbled is

Cancer : Moon :: Leo : Sun

where 'is to' means 'is the house of'. The word *propius* confirms it, for Cancer is indeed the sign 'near by' to the immediate west of Leo. Not finding a crab either in Statius or in his source's description of the tauroctony, the scholiast substituted Taurus. His talk of overpowering is simply a conflation of the scene of mastery in the tauroctony and the power relationship inherent in the system of houses: a planet has heightened power in his or her own house.

Behind the scholium is a piece of esoteric exegesis of the tauroctony actually made, solid evidence that some learned Mithraist really did explicate the tauroctony in terms of the encounter of the Sun and Moon on the cusp of their respective houses, Leo and Cancer. As an immediate caution I add that the anonymous exegete did not *interpret* the encounter of Sun and Moon as the

---

[31] In fact the question hardly arises except in translation, where one must choose to render the single Latin word *taurum* with or without an article; if with, then definite or indefinite; capitalized or not; or finally and unambiguously, untranslated as Taurus.

message of the tauroctony. Rather, he explicated the star-talk meanings which 'Mithras' and 'the bull' necessarily have as language signs in the medium carrying the message. One can appreciate the scholiast's puzzlement, for like modern scholars he looks for message where there is medium, and finding nothing much to his satisfaction—can this really just be about eclipses?—he not unreasonably supposes some grander philosophical mystery of which the author has 'laid bare a part' with 'images and metaphors' (*figuris*).[32]

If the Sun and the Moon encounter each other on the cusp of their houses, or anywhere else on the ecliptic for that matter, what happens? Usually nothing, or more precisely nothing observable. The Moon, at the same longitude as the Sun but somewhat to the north or south, is invisible. So one may say that the Moon is overcome by the Sun whose invincibility is thereby confirmed. This solar victory is routine: it occurs once a (synodic) month and marks the month's beginning ('new moon'). But every so often the Sun and the Moon arrive together not only at the same degree of longitude but at the same degree of latitude (by definition latitude 0° since the Sun never departs from the ecliptic). Since the Moon is the nearer of the two bodies, she passes in front of the Sun and so causes a solar eclipse. Thus at the very moment of his customary triumph the Sun is cata-strophically defeated. Certainly this defeat is quite rare and seen by few, for unlike lunar eclipses which are seen from any point on earth where the eclipsed Moon is above the horizon, total solar eclipses are seen only along a fairly narrow 'shadow path'. Nevertheless their occurrence is a universally known fact which no assertion of the Sun's invincibility, however vociferous, can gainsay. A serious solar cult—'serious' in the sense of cognizant of the science of its culture—simply has to take eclipses seriously. It is no more possible for such a cult to ignore solar eclipses than it would be for a religion to assert the benevolence and omnipotence of God and ignore the problem of evil. Bad stuff happens, to modify a saying, and it happens now and again to the Sun.

Fortunately, we now have on record a monument which shows that some Mithraists at least took the problem of eclipses very seriously indeed. The zodiac on the ceiling of the Ponza Mithraeum, published by M. J. Vermaseren (1974), shows within the circle of signs a huge semicircular snake with its head in Leo and its tail in Aquarius.[33] In my detailed study of the Ponza zodiac (Beck 1976a, 1978 = 2004c: chs. 9 and 10) I argued that the snake is an early representation (actually the first in the West) of a cosmic dragon which causes eclipses and which eventually gave its name, in the form *caput* and *cauda draconis* (the 'head and tail of the dragon'), to the lunar nodes Anabibazon and Katabibazon. During my researches I was alerted to two outside facts: first that the shadow path of a solar eclipse passed across or very close to the island of Ponza on 14 August 212 CE;

---

[32] *Figura* can mean 'a form of speech departing from the straightforward and obvious' (*OLD*, sense 11). What I see as a means of *expressing* something the scholiast sees as a means of *disguising* it. Interestingly, with this sense of *figura* we both see it as a strategy of language.

[33] Also, closer to the centre, a large bear and a small bear, obviously Ursa Major and Ursa Minor.

secondly that the fact that the eclipse took place in Leo,[34] the Sun's own house, was noted by those who witnessed or heard about it in North Africa. Tertullian reports (*Ad Scapulam* 3.3) that it was not thought possible that 'positioned in its own exaltation and house' (*positus in suo hypsomate et domicilio*)[35] the Sun could suffer 'the extinction of its light' as the consequence of 'an ordinary eclipse' (*ex ordinario deliquio*). The zodiac of the Ponza Mithraeum, read in its historical context, shows that from an initiate's perspective a solar eclipse in Leo was memorable, so memorable that it merited a unique type of monument to record it. How the local Mithraists interpreted this solar defeat we have no idea. All we can say is that they did not evade what star-talk told them was inevitable in the course of time but dealt with it explicitly.[36]

Actually, there is something we can say about the Mithraic strategy for coping with a solar eclipse in Leo. If an eclipse in Leo is the worst defeat the Sun can suffer, what are the circumstances in which this outcome is impossible? The answer is simple: since eclipses by definition occur at the lunar nodes, an eclipse of the Sun in Leo can only occur when one or other of the nodes is in Leo. Remove the nodes from Leo and its opposite sign, Aquarius, and an eclipse in Leo becomes an impossibility. If you wish to locate the nodes as far as you can from Leo and Aquarius, the pair of opposed signs to pick is the pair in quadrature, Taurus and Scorpius. But we have already established (sect. 9, above) that the Mithraic torchbearers mean *inter alia* the lunar nodes in this pair of signs, Anabibazon in Taurus and Katabibazon in Scorpius. Do we conclude that they were assigned these meanings for the very purpose of representing an ideal lunar month in which Leo, the Sun's house, is necessarily eclipse-free? No, we do not so conclude, for that would be to confuse *result* with *intent*. Certainly, a star-talk *entailment* of the tauroctony's design is 'no solar eclipse in Leo this month'.[37] That is irrefutable, for that is what the tauroctony actually says, and in star-talk, as in other languages, words in syntactically proper arrangements must be presumed to mean what they say. However, it is a very different matter to claim designer's intent or even designer's awareness. For awareness one can easily make a case. Intent is more problematic, for it means disentangling the designer's priorities in structuring the tauroctony along the

---

[34] At the ascending node: consequently in the Ponza zodiac it is the snake's head which is juxtaposed with the sign of Leo.

[35] Strictly speaking, Tertullian is right about the domicile, wrong about the exaltation. The Sun's exaltation is Aries.

[36] Although Mithras is apparently undefeated in the biographical episodes represented in the side-scenes, his career, as Giulia Sfameni Gasparro has pointed out (1979*a*: 324, 345), is not without 'vicissitudes': 'tuttavia è protagonista di una vicenda complessa che conosce rischio, fatica, contrasti.' For Sol Mithras surely the most terrible of vicissitudes is to undergo eclipse in his own house.

[37] Or for at least three years before or after, approximately the length of time it takes the nodes to regress across two intervening signs (e.g. for the descending node to regress from the start of Scorpius to the end of Leo while the ascending node regresses from the start of Taurus to the end of Aquarius).

lines of the esoteric quartering, and that presents the same difficulties as finding the 'real motives' behind any complicated human enterprise.

11. THE ORIGINS OF THE ESOTERIC QUARTERING AND THE DEFINITION OF AN IDEAL MONTH

There is actually good monumental evidence that the esoteric quartering and the ideal lunar month which it defines descended to the Mithraic mysteries from an earlier form of Mithras-worship. That earlier form was the Mithras-worship of the Graeco-Iranian kingdom of Commagene in the first century BCE. I have argued elsewhere that the antecedents of the mysteries lie there and that one of the agents of transmission in the following century was the astrologer-politician Ti. Claudius Balbillus (Beck 1998*a*; 2001: 62–71; 2004*c*: 323–9), a kinsman by marriage of the ruling dynast of Commagene.

It is worth noticing how our exegesis has moved from the entirely synchronic to the partially diachronic. We are talking now of origins and events—in a word, of history. This shift to diachronic history is inevitable when treating of an enterprise committed to relating earth to heaven in star-talk discourse. For we are in the unusual position of dealing with two stories simultaneously, one of which is recoverable in its entirety. I mean of course the celestial story, in the very literal sense that we can reconstruct the positions of the celestial bodies relative to each other as viewed from any location on earth at any time on any date.[38] We can reconstruct what the ancients saw (weather permitting), what they could not have seen (celestial events not observable at the relevant longitudes and latitudes because they occurred either in daylight or below the horizon), and, much more importantly, what any minimally competent astronomer or astrologer would have known from tables and calculations regardless of visibility. Not all of the events in this celestial history would have been germane to the mysteries, and we cannot tell a priori which were and which were not: 'may have been' is reasonable methodologically, 'must have been' is not. But when we have evidence clearly relating the celestial story to the terrestrial story of the Mithraic Mysteries—the Ponza zodiac is obviously the best example—we can bring an unusual degree of clarity to the actual history of the Mysteries here on earth.

The next piece of evidence we have to consider is the great Lion monument of Nemrud Dagh (V31) together with the statues of the enthroned gods and the reliefs of the gods in 'right-handshake' (*dexiōsis*) with King Antiochus I of Commagene.[39] The Lion monument is generally and rightly considered to be

---

[38] There are inexpensive astronomical software programs which can display precisely these views on a computer screen. For example, I generated Figs. 9, 10, and 15 from the 'Voyager II Dynamic Sky Simulator' program.

[39] I have discussed the Lion monument and its intent in Beck 1999 (= 2004*c*: ch. 14): 12–14; 2001 [2003]: 62–4.

a horoscope of sorts. In form it is a bas-relief on which a huge lion, moving to the right with his vast maned head confronting the viewer, fills most of the field. His body and the surrounds are covered with stars, one of which on his chest is cradled in a crescent moon. The three large stars above his back are labelled from left to right *Pyroeis Hērakleous, Stilbōn Apollōnos,* and *Phaëthōn Dios* ('the fiery [star] of Heracles, the glittering [star] of Apollo, the radiant [star] of Zeus'), which identifies them respectively as the planets Mars, Mercury, and Jupiter.[40] The monument's explicit star-talk about the planets makes it certain that the star-studded Lion is the constellation of Leo, and the moon-cradled star on his chest Regulus, the lucida of Leo.

Before I start my exegesis of the Lion monument, I want to make it clear that I am *not* unveiling the origin of an esoteric doctrine later adopted by the founders of Mithraism and passed down more of less unchanged from generation to generation among the 'wise and learned' in the mysteries. What I shall be explicating is an early representation in a certain star-talk tradition which issued in the Mithraic mysteries—and elsewhere.[41] What holds these representations to the same template is not transmitted doctrine, but the logic of star-talk, an exoteric system independent of the mysteries and so resistant to the imposition of aberrant meanings. No inventive Mithraic Father could propose, for example, a house for the Sun other than Leo, and only the most ignorant would fail to draw the inference: Sun in Leo means Sun at home.

Now to our Lion. It is generally agreed, again rightly, that he commemorates an astronomical event: the simultaneous presence of the Moon and the three named planets in Leo. On the assumption that their absence from the monument means that the other three planets (Sun, Saturn, Venus) were *not* then in Leo, a definitive date can be found within the relevant time span when those presences and those absences actually obtained. And so it was: 7 July 62 BCE. The solution was proposed by O. Neugebauer and H. B. Van Hoesen in their magisterial *Greek Horoscopes* (1959: 14–16). The date was definitively explicated by Heinrich Dörrie (1964: 201–7) as the foundation horoscope of the great mountain-top *hierothesion* and of the establishment of the royal cult there. The gods in dexiosis with the king are the identified planetary powers greeting him in the person of the star Regulus, Cor Leonis, 'the royal star on the heart of the Lion' (Pliny, *NH* 18.235, 271).

So far, so good. What follows, however, is a cautionary tale on the limits of positivism in the history of astronomy and astrology. The problem is the supposed absence of the Sun. Now 'as everyone knows', if Mercury is present the Sun is also present—if not in the same sign, then in one or other of the signs next door.[42] Far from saying 'Sun absent', what our Lion actually says, as a glance

---

[40] On alternative planetary names see Cumont 1935.

[41] 'Elsewheres' I hope to pursue in another study.

[42] In angular distance Mercury is never more than 28°, i.e. less than one 30° sign, away from the Sun.

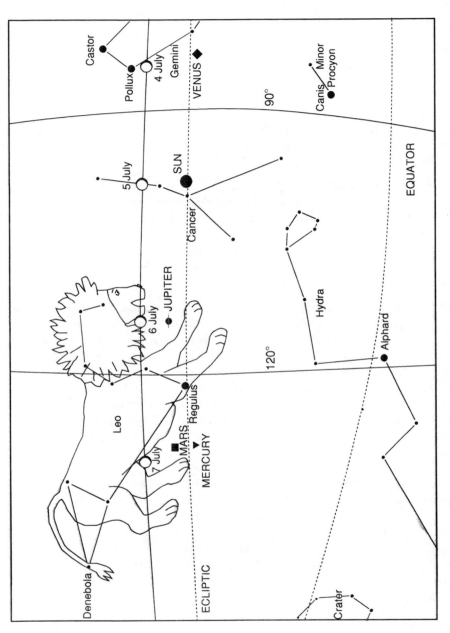

Fig. 15. Planetary positions at new moon (conjunction) on 5 July 62 BCE, 2:40 p.m. (Commagene LMT). The positions of the Moon one day earlier and two days later are also shown.

at Figure 15 will show, is 'Sun *soon* present' or on Dörrie's interpretation 'the Sun will be the next to greet our king'.

The Lion monument was never meant to be read as a self-contained document whose intent was to state an exclusive horoscopal date: 7 July 62 BCE and no other day. Rather, it is a sophisticated and polysemous star-talk text whose full range of meanings only emerge when read together with the dexiosis reliefs, the colossal statues, and the foundation inscription (V32).[43] The inscription is the obvious starting point, for it spells out precisely who are the gods represented enthroned and in dexiosis with the king. They are ('as you see') 'Zeus Oromasdes', 'Apollo Mithras Helios Hermes', 'Artagnes Heracles Ares', and 'my fatherland all-nurturing Kommagene' (lines 54–7). In terms of celestial signification,

(1) 'Zeus Oromasdes' and 'Phaëthon Dios' mean the planet Jupiter;

(2) 'Artagnes Heracles Ares' and 'Pyroeis Herakleous' mean the planet Mars;

(3) 'Apollo Mithras [Helios] Hermes' and 'Stilbon Apollonos' mean the planet Mercury;

(4) 'Apollo Mithras Helios [Hermes]' and the Lion mean the Sun;

(5) 'my motherland all-nurturing Kommagene' and the lunar crescent mean the Moon.

The last of these five meanings is established by process of elimination: if three of the four gods represented enthroned and in dexiosis intend the three named planets on the Lion monument, what planet does the personification of Commagene intend and what is her sign on the Lion monument? Obviously, the Moon and the lunar crescent.

The foundation text and the dexiosis reliefs make it abundantly clear that five, not four, planetary gods were involved in the astral foundation event, despite the fact that only four anthropomorphic gods are named and represented both enthroned and greeting the king. This is so because one of the anthropomorphic gods is, and is a sign for, two planets. 'Apollo Mithras Helios Hermes' is, and is a sign for, both the Sun and the planet Mercury. Consider the number of elements in his name, four. Like his two male colleagues he has an Iranian name and an Iranian persona, Mithras (corresponding to Oromasdes and Artagnes). Like them he carries the customary Greek planetary name and with it the planetary persona, Hermes = Mercury (corresponding to Zeus = Jupiter and Ares = Mars). Like Artagnes he carries an alternative planetary name, Apollo = planet Mercury (corresponding to Heracles = planet Mars).[44] But the fourth name and persona

---

[43] For bibliographic references to the monuments and inscription see Beck 1999: 32, n. 12.

[44] On the alternative system of divine names see Cumont 1935: 13–16. The planet Jupiter is 'Zeus' in both systems. 'Apollo' in the Commagenian context is actually ambiguous, since 'Apollo Epēkoös' is the name of an entirely Hellenic Sun god with halo and rays on a dexiosis relief which pre-dates the foundation on Nemrud Dagh (the Sofraz Köy stele, Wagner 1975: 54–9; see also Beck 1998*a*: 124, n.49).

of this deity has no counterpart among the titles of his colleagues. Yet the name refers to another planet, in fact to the greatest of the planets, Helios = the Sun. So do we pretend that 'Helios' does not mean 'the Sun' because the Sun was not in Leo on 7 July 62 BCE? That would be truly a counsel of despair, especially when we recall the impressive solar halo surrounding the deity's head in the dexiosis relief. Do we then assert that although this deity means two planets, Mercury and the Sun, the solar identity is suppressed in the Lion monument because the Sun on 7 July 62 BCE, though close, was not yet 'in Leo'? The supposition is just as absurd, for it implies that, before or after the event, the king and his advisers selected as an auspicious day for the foundation a date on which Mithras was present as Mercury, but not as the Sun! It was as if they welcomed the messenger of the Sun king but slammed the door in the Sun king's face!

The only solution is to follow the star-talk logic of the monumental complex as a whole and to 'read' the Sun into the Lion monument. And as soon as we admit the necessity, we 'see' the Sun there. The Sun is the Lion. Or rather, in star-talk terms, we may say that

the Lion means not only Leo but also the Sun;

or, if you are still uncomfortable with polysemy,

the Lion means Leo occupied and glorified by the presence of the Sun his master.

In context could that superb radiate mane really signify anything else?

The Lion monument, then, tells of the encounter of five, not four, planets in Leo. Here are the dates of the successive conjunctions with Regulus, the royal star who, following Dörrie,[45] we understand as the king's celestial surrogate.

Mars	25 June
Mercury	1 July
Moon	6 July
Sun	28 July
(Moon	3 August)
(Venus	6 August)
Jupiter	6 August

Notice that between the Regulus conjunctions of Mars and Jupiter there occurred not only the Moon's conjunction of 6 July and the Sun's conjunction but also a second conjunction of the Moon (in the next lunation) and a conjunction of Venus. The latter was suppressed on the Nemrud Dagh monuments but arguably commemorated elsewhere. Texts from Arsameia on the Nymphaios and Arsameia

---

[45] I have corrected Dörrie's dates (1964: 205) where necessary and have added those for the conjunctions of the Sun and Venus with Regulus and for the Moon's second conjunction; see Beck 1999: 14.

on the Euphrates substitute Hera Teleia for Commagene,[46] and Hera was the name for the planet Venus in the alternative nomenclature that called the planet Mercury Apollo and the planet Mars Heracles.

One must not give too free a rein to the imagination and envisage these celestial events as observations made by actual astrologers from the summit of Nemrud Dagh. In the first place, the Sun is far too close for any of the conjunctions except the first, that of Mars, to be observable with any certainty, even if the weather permitted. Secondly, the prosaic fact is that at least in the Greek tradition celestial events of this sort, even when observable in principle, were calculated, not literally watched for. It was enough that the events were real and knowable, and that they could be imagined 'in the mind's eye' and endowed with whatever significance the astrologer chose within the constraints of exegetical and interpretive star-talk.

The Lion monument, in the context of Antiochus' *hierothesion* on the summit of Nemrud Dagh, announces an assembly of planetary gods, the Sun included, in Leo. As a document in the history of astrology it is relatively early. In fact it is the earliest of all the horoscopes in Neugebauer and Van Hoesen's collection. One consequence of this, as Neugebauer and Van Hoesen were of course aware (1959: 15), is that we cannot assume that the system of signs measured from the vernal equinox at Aries 0° was yet definitively in place. 'In the Lion' could refer to somewhat different tracts of the ecliptic, including the tract occupied by Leo the constellation and its immediate surrounds. In our Figure 15 the curved vertical line on the right represents longitude 90° and the curved vertical line on the left longitude 120°, respectively the beginnings of the signs Cancer and Leo in the classic astronomical system (vernal equinox at Aries 0°). Various other systems would move those two lines to the right.[47] In the same way, if we define 'Leo' as constellation rather than sign, his western boundary must move a good half sign to the right, since his head as shown is entirely in Cancer the sign!

I do not think that a definite answer can or should be returned to the question, on which system did Commagenian astrologers of the first century BCE measure celestial longitude? Neugebauer and Van Hoesen chose the system of the much earlier Greek astronomer Eudoxus of Cnidus (fourth century BCE), which in our figure would move the longitudinal lines a full 15° (half a sign) to the right. This meets the desiderata of having the three named planets and the Moon 'in Leo' on 7 July (two days after the date of our Figure 15).[48] It also has the happy result of

---

[46] Waldmann 1973: 89 (Text A, line 251) and 130 (Text G, line 183). While the introduction of Hera as the planet Venus is accurate star-talk (the planet really was present then), I am not suggesting that this was necessarily in the drafters' minds when they added her to the text at those two sites.

[47] Including the two Babylonian systems, 'A' and 'B', which set the vernal equinox at Aries 10° and 8° respectively. System B remained in vogue in Greek astrology long after the standard system (equinox at Aries 0°) had prevailed in astronomy.

[48] For a chart of the situation on 7 July see Beck 1999: 25, fig. 4. Note there how the fast-moving Moon is now to the east of Mars and Mercury by the Lion's left hind leg.

returning to 'Leo' all the stars of his head and forelegs, which for me is a much more important consideration.

There is a second reason for keeping in mind the Lion monument's early date as a document in the history of astrology. Previously I spoke of Leo as the Sun's house without chronological qualification. But what can be taken for granted in the star-talk of a monument of the second century CE or later, such as the Housesteads birth scene (V860, discussed above, sect. 9), cannot be assumed for a monument a good two centuries older. Did the Commagenian astrologers even know of the system of houses? Was it even current then? There is no Greek or Latin source to confirm its existence at that early date, and unlike the system of planetary exaltations and humiliations there is no evidence for it in Babylonian astronomy.[49] Fortunately, my argument here does not depend on the knowledge or availability of the full system of planetary houses at this early date, only on the awareness of a special relationship between the Sun and Leo. Indeed, I would like to reverse the argument: far from being evidence for the existence of the system of houses at that date, I suggest that the celestial events of 62 BCE and their interpretation in Commagene mark a significant stage in the *development* of the system of houses within the tradition of star-talk in those astrological circles.

A glance at Figure 15 will reveal why I have chosen 5 July 62 BCE as the particular date to illustrate what was then happening in the heavens. The horoscopal configuration of 7 July, though real enough (the heavens do not lie, neither do historians of astronomy), is an irrelevance, for it corresponds, *pace* Neugebauer and Van Hoesen, to no horoscope actually cast by men on earth. In other words, there was nothing in the terrestrial history to match what certainly occurred in the celestial. What could perhaps be said in favour of 7 July is that on that evening it might have been possible, weather permitting, actually to view the brighter elements of the configuration on the western horizon after sunset but before Leo itself had set.[50] I might also have chosen the moment of the Moon's conjunction with Regulus on 6 July, since that is what the Lion monument actually 'says' by showing Regulus cradled in the crescent. Instead, I have chosen the moment of another conjunction of the Moon, her conjunction with the Sun on 5 July.

All this may seem like a monstrous digression. But remember the reason why the celestial and terrestrial stories of 62 BCE, a century-and-a-half before the appearance of the Mysteries of Mithras in the Roman empire, were of concern to us. Our topic was the worst thing that could happen to a Sun god—a Sun god, that is, constructed by the star-talk of Graeco-Roman antiquity. The 'worst thing'

---

[49] The earliest horoscope in Neugebauer and Van Hoesen's collection which refers to the system of houses has a natal date of 81 CE but was almost certainly cast later in the native's life (1959: 21–8). Of the theoretical astrologers the earliest to describe and use the system was Dorotheus of Sidon (1.1.8, 2.28–33), who wrote in the period *c.*25–75 CE (Pingree 1976: p. x). For exaltations in Babylonian astronomy see Rochberg-Halton 1988.

[50] See the sky-chart in Beck 1999: 25, fig. 4, which includes the local horizon and the positions of the stars and planets relative to it at 8:00 p.m. local mean time.

was a solar eclipse in Leo, the seat of his power, an event which when it actually happened—more importantly, was *seen* to have happened—on 14 August 212 was commemorated by the Mithraists on the island of Ponza.

In our contingent world this 'worst thing' is inevitable: the structures and motions of the cosmos make it so. But star-talk furnishes two consolations. First, formidable though it seems, it is just an appearance: the god's light is hidden, not extinguished; secondly, there are long periods of time when it cannot happen, times when the lunar nodes are not in Leo and Aquarius and you know for certain that the invisible Moon will pass well to the north or south of the Sun. Such an occasion was the 'new moon' of 5 July 62 BCE. As you can see, the Moon passed to the north of the Sun; at latitude 4° 40′ she was almost at her northern extreme, the point she in fact reached on the following day at the Lion's muzzle in Figure 15.

Now the fact that the Lion monument speaks about a conjunction of Sun and Moon when the Moon was close to her northern limit does not imply that it was part of the designer's intention to celebrate or memorialize that 'no-eclipse' situation. The logic of star-talk compels a star-talk monument to mean what it says, but one cannot therefore impute everything it says to the conscious intent of those who commissioned or designed it. In this instance, however, there is some powerful external evidence to suggest that memorializing avoidance of the 'worst thing' and defining an ideal month which would have that effect was indeed a matter of actual intent, not just an unconsidered star-talk entailment.

Two pieces of evidence belong to the celestial history of star-talk; they are actual celestial events, things said by the stars themselves. A third piece of evidence belongs to the terrestrial history of star-talk, a report of certain views concerning lunar eclipses attributed to the followers of the Stoic philosopher and polymath Posidonius of Apamea, active in the first half of the first century BCE. To address these pieces of evidence we must start with the correlative of 'no eclipse in Leo'. If no eclipse can occur in Leo because that is where the northern extreme of the lunar orbit currently resides, it follows that eclipses *can* occur in Taurus and Scorpius because that is where the lunar nodes currently reside. This is not to say that eclipses *will* occur in Taurus and Scorpius, merely that one of several necessary conditions for their occurrence there is met.

An eclipse may of course be solar or lunar. So far we have concentrated on solar eclipses, necessarily construed in a solar religion as a setback, albeit temporary and apparent rather than real, for the Sun god. Lunar eclipses, in which the Sun projects the earth's shadow on to the Moon's disk and so deprives her of her borrowed light when at the full, are solar victories and lunar defeats. The Sun thus achieves at 'full moon' what he routinely achieves at 'new moon'. Though infrequent in absolute terms (a very small proportion of full moons are eclipsed), lunar eclipses occur more often than solar eclipses and are witnessed by more people.[51]

---

[51] As noted above, a total solar eclipse is witnessed only by those in the shadow path, while a lunar eclipse is witnessed from anywhere on the earth's surface where the eclipsed Moon is above the horizon.

Although, as we have seen, the primary star-talk meaning of Mithras killing the bull is the monthly conjunction of Sun and Moon when the light of the former overwhelms the latter, lunar eclipses qua solar victories are also intended. In this utterance of the tauroctony, the torchbearers will mean the nodes, the points at which the lunar and solar orbits intersect. For an eclipse to occur the Sun and the Moon must arrive at the nodes simultaneously, at the same node for a solar eclipse and one at each node for a lunar eclipse. But, as we saw above (sect. 9), the torchbearer Cautes means specifically 'Anabibazon in Taurus' and his colleague Cautopates means 'Katabibazon in Scorpius'. It follows then that when speaking of lunar eclipses what the tauroctony specifically says is 'lunar eclipse at the ascending node in Taurus' and/or 'lunar eclipse at the descending node in Scorpius'. These are solar victories and desirable, just as the antitype, the solar eclipse in Leo, is the 'worst thing' and highly undesirable.

I am now going to suggest that a tradition concerning lunar eclipses in Taurus and Scorpius descended to the Mithraic mysteries from Commagenian star-talk of the first century BCE, and that this tradition originated in exegesis and interpretation of the celestial events of 62 BCE *and the preceding year*. This is the point at which to introduce the two pieces of evidence from the celestial story, the actual celestial events. Because of the way in which I have been telling the celestial and terrestrial star-talk stories it will now come as no surprise that these two celestial events of 63 BCE were total lunar eclipses, both visible from Commagene (weather permitting), the first on 3 May at the descending node in Scorpius, the second on 27 October at the ascending node in Taurus. The particulars are given in the table.

Date	3 May 63 BCE	27 October 63 BCE
Lunation no.[52]	−24263	−24257
Saros cycle	59	64
Node	descending	ascending
Time of mid eclipse[53]	3:30 a.m.	6:00 p.m.
Altitude of Moon above horizon	16° SW	9° E
Longitude of Moon	218° 30'	32° 15'
Constellation	Scorpius	Taurus

Viewed from Commagene, the second eclipse would have been particularly striking. The Moon was already totally eclipsed when she rose. Normally the full Moon can be seen rising opposite the setting Sun. On this day she would have been invisible until advancing twilight disclosed a view of her deep within the umbra. In longitude she was about 1° west of the Pleiades, one of the most conspicuous celestial markers. Nightfall would quickly reveal two of the planets ahead of her to the west, Saturn 5° degrees away and Mars 11°.

---

[52] Meuss and Mucke 1979: 105.   [53] Local mean time, Commagene.

That there is no extant record of the observation of these eclipses need not trouble us unduly. The first centuries BCE and CE are the silent years in the records of ancient astronomical observation. In the run of ninety-four observations in the *Almagest* there is a gap between 127 BCE and 92 CE (nos. 50 and 51 in Pedersen 1974: 415). More important is our third piece of evidence which implies that human star-talk, at least in one tradition, did indeed take cognizance of the eclipses of 63 BCE.

A curious and vexed passage in Diogenes Laertius' *Lives of the Philosophers* (7.146, p. 531.5–7 ed. Marcovich), in discussing Stoic astronomy and eclipse theory in particular, attributes to 'those around Posidonius' the opinion that the Moon reaches the latitude of the ecliptic (i.e. crosses it) 'in the Claws [i.e. Libra] and the Scorpion and the Ram and the Bull', that is, at the Libra–Scorpius and Aries–Taurus cusps or, as we would put it, at Scorpius 0° and Taurus 0°. The attribution to the circle of Posidonius yields a date in the first half of the first century BCE.

The passage has troubled historians of astronomy (Neugebauer 1975: 671), for it seems to imply that the Posidonians denied what was by that time widely known, that the lunar nodes are not fixed at any one pair of points but travel around the ecliptic in a period of some eighteen and two-thirds years, as we have seen. However, regardless of the Posidonians' intended meaning and whether or not their views have been correctly reported, it seems to me more than likely that the empirical and observational basis for this piece of star-talk were the actual lunar eclipses of 63 BCE when the nodes were in fact in Taurus and Scorpius.

The configurations and conjunctions of July and August 62 BCE were construed, I suggest, by the star-talk experts of Commagene as the culmination of the celestial events of the preceding year. From these events they constructed a narrative of solar triumph and lunar subordination. The story told of an ideal month in which the Sun would be invulnerable and the Moon's subordination regularly and dramatically demonstrated. The ideal month was quartered in such a way as to set both the point of conjunction which initiates the lunation and the northern limit of the Moon's orbit at the start of Leo, the descending node at the start of Scorpius, the southern limit of the lunar orbit at the start of Aquarius, and the ascending node at the start of Taurus—all as in Figure 14.[54] An approximation to this ideal occurred in July 62 BCE. Or rather, the lunation beginning on 5 July 62 BCE furnished the parameters for formulating an ideal month, as did the lunations of the preceding year in which the Moon had suffered total eclipses. But the ideal lunar month was precisely that—a fiction. No actual month exhibited precisely those features, and even if one had, the next most certainly would not. The point of conjunction would have moved a full sign or so to the east and the

---

[54] There is a nice paradox in this ideal month. The Moon passes to the north of the Sun at conjunction. In 'altitude' she is thus 'above' the Sun.

nodes and northern and southern limits a small but significant distance to the west.[55] Not for nothing did the Moon get her reputation for variability.

Here then is the origin of our esoteric quartering, not an invention of the Mithraic Mysteries but an inheritance from a prior form of Mithras-worship in Anatolia on the cultural marches of Greece and Iran. This highly artificial royal cult—a 'top-down' religion if there ever was one—created composite Greek and Iranian deities by star-talk logic, and it used that logic to assert that Mithras is the Sun and the Sun is Mithras. The sign of one is the sign of the other.

From the royal cult of Commagene both Mithras-worship and star-talk as the proper idiom of Mithras-worship were transmitted to the Roman Mysteries. By now we know enough to resist the fantasy of an esoteric doctrine passed down from adept to adept. What flows down the generations are discrete representations, mental representations transmitted by way of public representations; and as Dan Sperber has taught us (1996: 31), output never precisely matches input: 'The most obvious lesson of recent cognitive work is that recall is not storage in reverse, and comprehension is not expression in reverse. Memory and communication transform information.' What disciplined the descent of representations in Mithras-worship from mid-first-century BCE Commagene to late first-century CE Rome (or wherever in the empire you choose to locate the emergence of the Mysteries) was the logic of star-talk—which is to say, the systems of Hellenistic astronomy and astrology. By listening closely to their star-talk utterances we can tell that the Mithraic tauroctony is a true descendant of the Lion of Nemrud Dagh.

'Listening closely' means paying attention to representations in cognate streams of star-talk. The flow of representations which leads from Commagene to Rome is by no means self-contained. Indeed its representations are comprehensible only in relation to other streams of star-talk which flow into and out of it. For example, the representation of an ideal month, as we have seen, shows up in the circle of Posidonius, but that is no reason for assimilating the Posidonians to the Commagenians.

The broader star-talk tradition we see at work in Commagene, in the circle of Posidonius, and later in the Mysteries of Mithras is peculiarly opaque to the modern investigator. That is because it cannot be readily placed in either of the two categories into which historians of science and culture have corralled ancient star-talk. It is manifestly neither 'astronomy', defined as scientific inquiry, nor 'astrology', at least in the predominant form of astral prediction or horoscopy. So a fresh point of view and new methods are necessary to address it.

The testimony of Diogenes Laertius on the Posidonians' placement of the lunar nodes is a case in point. The great historian of ancient astronomy Otto Neugebauer (1975: 671) was puzzled by the Posidonians' apparent ignorance of the regression of the nodes and was at pains to offer an explanation to exculpate

---

[55] At the same time the Moon's points of apogee and perigee, about which the ideal month is silent, would have shifted somewhat to the east.

them. My alternative explanation, that the testimony has to do with the creation of an *ideal* month, would simply not have occurred to him. Positivist historians of astronomy—and Neugebauer was a most aggressive positivist—do not willingly treat of constructs such as an ideal month, especially when, as here, the construct would mark a retreat from knowledge already gained. Why would anyone who already knew about the regression of the lunar nodes want to tie them back in place again?

To an inquirer dealing primarily with the culture and religion of ancient star-talkers, the question is not rhetorical and the answer is quite straightforward. In a religious context—and what pre-modern context was not profoundly religious?—people concern themselves not only with what *is* but also with what *should be*. So they construct ideal models, in Clifford Geertz's famous formulation (1973: 93–5), not models *of* but models *for*. To the Commagenians, as later to the Mithraists, it mattered not merely how the Moon does in fact behave but how the Moon *ought* to behave in an ideal cosmos. Hence the representation of the ideal month with its distinctive quartering and the echo of that representation in the star-talk of the Posidonians.

That an idealist in the Greek intellectual tradition might have constructed such a lunar model is entirely plausible, given the premier postulate of Greek astronomy, that principles of uniformity *must* underlie the apparent irregularities of observed celestial phenomena. To postulate a radically simplified model of what ought to be, but in the present dispensation is not, would be just an extension of that idealizing tendency in Greek astronomy.

Idealizing cosmological speculation of this sort would fit well into the other intellectual tradition current at that time in that part of the ancient world, the Iranian, a religious culture that we know, from explicit sources, contributed one-half to the syncretistic Commagenian pantheon. In an important article Philip Kreyenbroek (1994) drew attention to the tension in cosmogonic thinking between what was to become the main stream of Zoroastrianism and other ancient Iranian—indeed, Indo-Iranian—traditions. In both, creation was a two-stage process, the second stage being the endowment of a static cosmos with motion, growth, and change. In both, the second stage is good and necessary. However, in the Zoroastrian tradition it is necessitated by the evil Ahriman's destruction of the first, more perfect creation, while in the alternative tradition it is an unqualified amelioration in that it vivifies a mere inert potential. Kreyenbroek suggests that Roman Mithraism may have descended from a western Iranian branch of that alternative tradition which worshipped Mithra as the cosmic vivifier in the second stage of creation, an important part of which was the setting in motion of the luminaries and hence the alternation of day and night, light and darkness.

Regardless of the question of Mithra's agency, Kreyenbroek's study shows that the comparison of the actual cosmos with an ideal archetype (is the former the fulfilment of the latter or a temporary expedient, and will the present dispensation return to a purer, less complex form?) could well have engaged thoughtful Iranian Anatolians in the late Hellenistic age. Fixing the lunar nodes at Taurus 0° and Scorpius 0°, contrary to the then known facts, does not necessarily indicate astronomical ignorance. From the ancient Iranian perspective as from the Greek, it is equally explicable as part of a model of lunar motion in an ideal cosmology.

Of course to show that something 'would have fitted well' into such-and-such a context only raises the something's probability; it cannot establish the something's existence. I have argued here for the existence and Commagenian origin of a lunar quartering which furnished the structural archetype and much of the star-talk meaning of the tauroctony, on the basis of (1) the actual celestial events of 63 and 62 BCE, (2) the monumental complex of King Antiochus on Nemrud Dagh 'thickly' described, and (3) the curious testimony of Diogenes Laertius on the placement of the lunar nodes at the beginnings of Taurus and Scorpius 'by those around Posidonius'. My hypothesis makes sense of Diogenes' testimony and so solves a minor problem of star-talk history. My hypothesis also offers a solution to another couple of minor historical problems, the origins of (1) the practice in Greek astronomy of measuring the Moon's 'argument of latitude' from the northern limit rather than one or other of the nodes (Neugebauer 1975: 80), and (2) the astrological calculation of the Moon's 'steps' (ascending and descending) and 'winds' (north and south) from the same point arbitrarily fixed at Leo 0° (above, sect. 9). There is further evidence to indicate the existence of a geometrical and kinematic model of lunar motion which correlates with, and so confirms, the postulated ideal month. That evidence I shall address in the following chapter. It is indispensable, but less astronomically oriented readers have probably been subjected to as much star-talk data as they can reasonably be expected to bear, and may prefer to proceed directly to the Conclusions.[56]

---

[56] However, let me close this chapter with mention of a tiny scrap of an astronomical papyrus of uncertain date from Roman Egypt, *P. Oxy.* 4141 (Jones 1999: I.101, II.25), which appears to confirm at least the existence there of our lunar quartering, though for what ends it is impossible to tell. In this papyrus, mention is made of the first degree of each of three signs which can be safely restored as Taurus, Leo, and Scorpius in that order, and presumably of the first degree of Aquarius either before or after the other three signs. The verb *bainei* ('goes') is repeated each time, and the editor (Alexander Jones) has supplied the appropriate prefix *ana-* or *kata-* to yield 'goes up' in connection with Taurus 1° and 'goes down' in connection with Leo 1° and again with Scorpius 1°. Following each occurrence of the verb he supplements the line with *t/a boreia* ('the north') for Taurus 1° and Leo 1° and *t/a notia* ('the south') for Scorpius 1°. The heavily restored text thus yields the same latitudinal trajectory as our esoteric quartering, but the name of the planet which thus 'ascends' and 'descends' is unfortunately lost. Since the fragment appears to imply fixed nodes, Jones (ibid. I.101) opts for one of the superior planets, settling on Mars, 'with its ascending node located at approximately Taurus 5° about A.D. 100'. I think it much more likely that the fragment relates in some way to the scheme of the lunar nodes reported for 'those around Posidonius' by Diogenes Laertius and thus to our 'ideal' or 'esoteric lunar quartering'. Another possibility is that the scheme as we find it both in the papyrus fragment and in Diogenes Laertius may have to do not with ideally fixed lunar nodes but with a postulated position of the lunar nodes at creation, in other words not with where the nodes ideally 'ought to be' but where they were actually thought to have been when the cosmos was first endowed with motion (and perhaps to where they will return at the end of time).

10

Excursus: the esoteric quartering, a lost helicoidal model of lunar motion, and the origin of the 'winds' and 'steps' of the Moon. The identity of 'Antiochus the Athenian'

The apparent fixing of the lunar nodes at Taurus 0° and Scorpius 0° by 'those around Posidonius' is not the only peculiarity in Diogenes Laertius' summary of Stoic astronomy in Book 7 of his *Lives of the Philosophers*. At 7.144 (p. 529.14–17, ed. Marcovich) he reports the view 'that the Sun makes his route (*poreian*) through the zodiacal circle oblique (*loxēn*) and similarly the Moon makes hers helicoidal (*helikoeidē*)'. The obliquity of the ecliptic, the Sun's route, is of course utterly commonplace, and perhaps 'helicoidal' is intended merely as a synonym for 'oblique'. In that case the view attributed to the Stoics would be no more than their recognition of the banal fact that the Moon's orbit is oblique to the ecliptic as the ecliptic is oblique to the celestial equator. But if so, why introduce the new term at all? And is not 'helicoidal' a strange choice of synonym for 'oblique'? A helix and an oblique line seem at first glance entirely different figures.

What else might a 'helicoidal route' mean? Obviously the first thing to do is to see how other geometrical and astronomical sources use the term 'helix/helicoidal'. Let us look first at Theon of Smyrna (first half of second century CE), because he does in fact use the term in the sense of an oblique orbit dipping north and south of the ecliptic. In the second half of ch. 43 of Book 3 of his work on 'mathematical matters useful for reading Plato' (330.1–15, ed. J. Dupuis), he describes a helix as just such a line undulating to infinity on a plane surface. Figure 12 in our present study shows the lunar orbit in this form. However, in the first half of chapter 43 (328.15–28) Theon defines another form of helix to describe different celestial appearances. This helix is inscribed on a solid surface, not a plane surface. The surface is a cylinder. You will generate this sort of helix if you hold your pen against a cylinder which is simultaneously rotating and moving one way or the other longitudinally.[1] This figure is nowadays the primary meaning of the word 'helix', especially since the discovery of the famous 'double helix' of DNA. In Theon's context it is applied to the product of the two motions which all seven planets exhibit, universal daily motion to the west and planetary motion to the east. It is in fact what we see, and it is best envisaged in the case of the Sun. Each day we can watch the Sun (apparently) circling the earth, but each day from the winter solstice to the summer solstice the Sun's arc is a little higher in the sky, a little more to the north; and each day from the summer solstice back again to the winter solstice the arc is a little lower, a little more to the south. One of the preconditions for mathematical astronomy is to break apart the planetary and universal components of this apparent helicoidal motion.[2]

This other application of the helix is clearly not what the Stoic sources reported by Diogenes Laertius had in mind. It may however be germane to Mithraic representation. In star-talk the snake spiralling round the 'snake-encircled figure' surely means the Sun's apparent helix and the two measures of time which the helix combines: the day (going once around) and the year (a cycle of ascending and descending). This complex meaning is very much to the fore in the Danubian side-scene in which a reclining snake-encircled figure hails Mithras mounting the solar chariot behind Sol.[3] Travelling round and round in a rising and falling spiral is the solar 'way to go': it is what the Sun actually does—or appears to do.

There is, though, yet a third sense in which Theon speaks of planetary helixes, and it is in this sense, I shall argue, that the Posidonians called the Moon's path helicoidal. Theon sets out his model in chapters 31, 33, and 41, in the last of which he attributes it to Eudemus, a pupil of Aristotle and thus more than four centuries prior to himself. Theon and Eudemus before him were countering the model of multiple concentric spheres, first advanced by Eudoxus and subsequently refined by Callippus and Aristotle. Retrospectively, we know that the problems intrinsic to the Eudoxan model were eventually solved by Hipparchus and Ptolemy with the radically different model of epicycles and eccentrics. But two centuries or so separate Hipparchus from Eudoxus and almost another two separate Ptolemy from Hipparchus. In the long years between these great figures, and especially in the astronomically ill-attested years between Hipparchus and Ptolemy, there was plenty of scope for alternative models and plenty of scope for

[1] T. L. Heath (1956: 158–65) has an interesting discussion of the place of the helix in the taxonomy of lines in Greek geometry. The cylindrical helix is one of only three 'homoeomeric' types of line. The other two are the straight line and the circle. A homoeomeric line is one in which any segment is congruent with any other segment.

[2] The combination of solar motions is explicitly called a 'helix' in (Pseudo-) Timaeus of Locri, *On the Nature of the Universe and the Soul* (29), and in the *Ars Eudoxi* (27). Unfortunately the date of both works is uncertain. The former has a *terminus ante* at the end of the first century CE and the latter, in its final form, a *terminus ante* of 165 BCE.

[3] The scene is in the lower right corner of the composition. Good examples are V1935, 1958, 1972.

them to disappear with few traces into the silence of the historical record. In Theon's model of helicoidal planetary motion, I suggest, we can trace the outlines of just such a losing competitor to the epicycle-and-eccentric model of Hipparchus and Ptolemy.[4] Why would I want to pursue an astronomical dead end in this book about the Mithraic mysteries? Fair question. The answer is that the model is part and parcel of a complex stream of star-talk, a tradition of representations, which includes the Mithraic mysteries and the earlier form of Mithras-worship in Commagene. Comprehending the mysteries means comprehending that larger tradition of representations, that larger stream of star-talk.

In this third sense Theon uses the term 'helix/helicoidal' to refer not to actual planetary paths but to epiphenomena, mere appearances, generated by the actual rotation, for each planet, of only two dedicated spheres (in addition of course to rotation of the sphere of the universe which makes everything in the heavens revolve once every day). The first of each planet's pair of spheres is 'hollow' (*koilē*) in the sense that it has a skin or shell of a certain thickness. The center of this sphere is the center of the universe. The sphere rotates eastward in the planet's sidereal period (e.g. twenty-seven and a third days for the Moon, about twenty-nine and a half years for Saturn). Between the outer and inner surfaces of this sphere and carried round by its rotation is a second sphere which is 'solid' (*sterea*) and which carries the planet itself on its circumference.[5] This solid sphere too rotates, and it is these rotations which cause the epiphenomena of figures which can properly be called 'helicoidal' to be traced in the heavens.

In the three diagrams of Figure 16 let us see how the helix is composed. The first two diagrams show cross-sections of the two spheres. (1) Figure 16*a* shows a vertical cross-section. The two large arcs represent the outer and inner surfaces of the hollow sphere; the small circle between the two arcs represents the solid sphere. Our point of view is a spot in the middle of the hollow sphere's shell equidistant to its inner and outer surfaces. The solid sphere is moving towards us impelled by the rotation of the hollow sphere. The solid sphere carrying the planet rotates as shown by the arrows, carrying the planet on its surface from the northern extreme to perigee, then to the southern extreme, then to apogee, and back again to the northern extreme. (2) The second diagram, Figure 16*b*, shows a horizontal cross-section of the two spheres. It is a view from 'above', in the sense of from the north. From this perspective the planet on the surface of the solid sphere would appear to be moving to and from between apogee and perigee.

---

[4] The model appears to have escaped the notice of historians of mathematical astronomy, partly because it is conveyed in sources who for the most part did not themselves fully understand it; partly because, at least after Hipparchus, it was manifestly a loser; but mainly, I think, because its traces in the sources, with one exception, carry no quantitative data of the sort which would attract the historians' attention.

[5] Theon raises the possibility that a single hollow sphere serves for the Sun and the inferior planets Mercury and Venus. Between the inner and outer surfaces of this common hollow shell nest the three concentric solid spheres of (from smallest to largest) the Sun, Mercury, and Venus. This is essentially the model of limited heliocentrism proposed by Heraclides of Pontus.

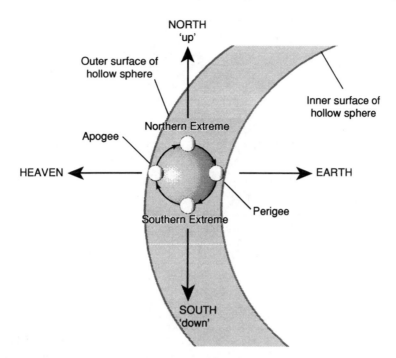

Fig. 16a. The 'helicoidal' model of lunar motion, 1. Vertical cross-section of 'hollow' and 'solid' spheres, showing Moon's motion in *platos* (latitude) and *bathos* (depth).

(3) The third diagram, Figure 16c, shows a cross-section of the solid sphere alone as seen from our actual viewpoint on earth. As the solid sphere moves east (to the left) along the ecliptic, which is its axis of rotation, it carries the planet up to a northern extreme and down to a southern extreme which will be reached at points on the celestial sphere along the 'tropic' lines shown. Putting these three two-dimensional diagrams together into a single three-dimensional (mental) model, we envisage (i) a torus (doughnut) formed by the revolution of the solid sphere as it is carried round within the 'skin' of the rotating hollow sphere; (ii) a helix traced on the surface of this torus by the planet revolving on the circumference of the rotating solid sphere. The number of turns of the helix per rotation of the hollow sphere (<1, 1, >1) depends on the speed of rotation of the solid sphere relative to the speed of rotation of the hollow sphere.

The good news, for an astronomer in the early Hellenistic period, is that the model for the first time introduces the concept of motion in 'depth' (*bathos*). The previous model, that of Eudoxus, Callippus, and Aristotle, kept the planets at unvarying distances from the earth, their motions governed by the rotations of an increasingly complex system of nested concentric spheres. The bad news is that while the helicoidal model imports motion in 'depth' (*bathos*) into planetary

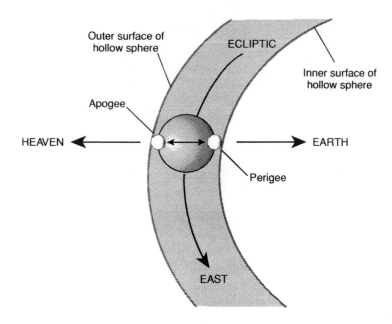

Fig. 16*b*. The 'helicoidal' model of lunar motion, 2. Horizontal cross-section of 'hollow' and solid spheres, seen from 'above' (i.e. north), showing Moon's motion in *mēkos* (longitude) and *bathos* (depth)

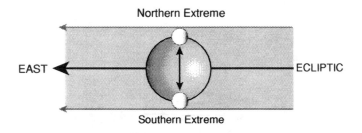

Fig. 16*c*. The 'helicoidal' model of lunar motion, 3. Vertical cross-section of 'solid' sphere as seen from earth, showing Moon's motion in *mēkos* (longitude) and *platos* (latitude)

theory, it does not by itself address the problem of 'anomaly', the observed fact that all the planets travel eastward at non-uniform speeds and five of them interrupt eastward motion with periods of westward or 'retrograde' motion. We know the classic solution to anomaly in the models of Hipparchus and Ptolemy. Apparent differences in speed are accommodated by postulating either eccentric orbits[6] or epicycles.[7] The epicycle/eccentric theory solves the problem of anomalies in speed by constructing figures which put the planets at varying depths in space, in the process saving Greek astronomy's first principle of uniform circular motion. The helicoidal model cannot have been intended to solve anomaly. Rather it was put forward, if one may infer so from Theon several centuries later, on a priori philosophical grounds in order to maintain a minimum number of uniformly rotating spheres after the pattern of Eudoxus but without his insistence that all the spheres be concentric.

The helicoidal model lingered on, ill-understood, through Hellenistic times and beyond. What kept it in play was its appeal to philosophical cosmologists, not to mathematical astronomers. It is no coincidence that the title of Theon's work (in Dupuis's French translation, 1892) is *Exposition des connaissances mathématiques utiles pour la lecture de Platon*, or that another author who speaks of helixes and helicoidal orbits is the Stoic Cleomedes (1.2.60, 61 Todd, 99–100 Goulet, 42 Bowen and Todd);[8] nor, for that matter, is it a coincidence that Cleomedes' prime source is Posidonius (Bowen and Todd 2004: 5–11), a philosophical cosmologist if there ever was one (Goulet 1980: 10–11). It was among 'those around Posidonius', as we have seen (ch. 9, sect. 11), that the 'ideal month' with the nodes fixed in Taurus and Scorpius was developed.

Posidonius furnishes a sure *terminus post* for Cleomedes. He may have lived and written at any time in the first or second centuries CE but not much later, for as Bowen and Todd argue (2004: 2–4) pedagogical Stoic lectures of his type and style were out of vogue by the third century.[9] We cannot say whether he lived before or somewhat after or contemporaneously with Theon. Nothing suggests that he influenced or was influenced by Theon in regards to the idea of helicoidal planetary motion. As is usual in this sort of inquiry, filiation is not the issue. Rather, we attempt first to identify a certain cluster or family of representations and then to see in what sources these representations show up as they drift down the course of time.

For that reason it is of the greatest interest to us that having spoken about helicoidal planetary orbits Cleomedes immediately characterizes the four quadrants of a single turn of the spiral in precisely the same terms as Antiochus of Athens (Ch. 9, sects. 6 and 9): exaltation humiliated, humiliation humiliated, humiliation exalted, exaltation exalted. In this context it is clear that by 'exaltation' (*hypsos*) Cleomedes intends 'north' and by 'humiliation' (*tapeinōma*)

---

[6] The planet at apogee appears to move more slowly than at perigee.

[7] The planet, revolving on the circumference of an epicycle the centre of which revolves on the circumference of a deferent circle whose centre is the earth, will appear to be moving eastward at varying speeds or even backwards if its westward speed on the epicycle is greater than the eastward speed of the centre of the epicycle on the deferent.

[8] Because of the complexities of numeration in Cleomedes, I follow the citation to Todd's edition (1990) with page numbers in the translations of Goulet (1980) and Bowen and Todd (2004).

[9] Goulet (1980: 6–8) and Bowen and Todd (2004: 4, 89, n. 16) are properly sceptical of Neugebauer's fourth-century date (1975: 960).

'south'. Later, however, he applies the same pair of terms to apogee and perigee or rather to the far and near semicircles of a planet's eccentric orbit. He is unaware of this contradiction, which suggests that he did not properly understand how the two motions in 'height', latitudinal motion north and south of the ecliptic, and motion in 'depth' (*bathos*) away from and towards the earth, were integrated in the helicoidal model.

As late as Proclus in the fifth century CE we find, specifically in his *Commentary on Plato's Timaeus* (*In Timaeum*), the indiscriminate conflation of the various directions of planetary motion under the term 'helix'. Proclus has to use the term because Plato did (*Timaeus* 39a6), but the way in which he actually employs it in his explication of what the master must have meant (*In Timaeum* 3.78.29–80.22 Diehl) betrays a poorly understood memory, similar to Theon's and Cleomedes', of the post-Platonic and post-Eudoxan helicoidal model. We can see this best at 3.79.7–11, where Proclus relates the helix to two pairs of opposite motions:

(1*a*) motion 'to the east' = planetary motion in longitude (*mēkos*)

(1*b*) motion 'to the west' = universal daily motion

(2*a*) motion 'in depth' (*kata bathos*) = 'nearer to the earth' (*prosgeioteros*) and 'further from the earth' (*apogeioteros*)

(2*b*) motion 'in latitude' (*kata platos*) = 'more to the north' (*boreioteros*) and 'more to the south' (*noteiōteros*)

In our helicoidal model it is the rotation of the solid sphere (as in Fig. 16*a*) that causes the planet to move simultaneously in depth and in latitude. Had Proclus fully understood the model, he would have realized that because it introduces motion in depth it is no more capable of retaining strict Platonic or Eudoxan concentricity than the epicycles and eccentric circles of mainline astronomy which he rejected.[10]

A single change to Proclus' description would return it to coherence, logic, and a rough reconciliation with facts and appearances. I do not propose emendation, of course, for my point is precisely that Proclus and probably his sources before him did not fully understand what they were talking about. Proclus' mistake was to leave universal daily motion (1*b*) in his account of the helix. What generates the helix by turning the circle formed by the rotation of the solid sphere (2*a* + 2*b*) into a spiral is planetary motion in longitude alone (1*a*). For the Sun and the Moon eastward motion is all that need be accounted for. For the other five planets westward, retrograde motion must also be accommodated, but this does not require a separate principle of westward motion.

It is time to bite the bullet of anomaly. As we saw above, the helicoidal model in itself cannot solve anomaly, the fact, that is, that the planets do not move eastward (in longitude, *mēkos*) at uniform speeds. The Sun and the Moon move now faster, now slower, and the other five planets even slow to a stop

---

[10] On Proclus' rejection of epicycles and eccentrics see Pedersen and Hannah 2002: 74–5.

and reverse direction westward (termed 'retrograde' motion). The only way in which the helicoidal model can account for varying speeds and retrograde motion is by conceding non-uniformity and reversibility to the revolutions of the hollow spheres which carry the solid spheres around the heavens. In other words, to persevere with the helicoidal model one must say in effect: 'What problem of anomaly? The varying speeds and reversals which you see are real.' In a recent article S. Pedersen and R. Hannah (2002) have suggested that Proclus argued precisely that (although of course not in terms of the 'helicoidal model' first postulated here). *In Timaeum* 3.56.31–57 demonstrates that their contention is correct:

Plato at least in the *Republic* [10.616d–e], when he makes the weights [i.e. the composite whorl of the 'Spindle of Necessity'] homocentric and in these the seven circles, and mentions only these, but not the epicycles, seems to attribute irregularity (*anōmalian*) to the stars themselves, this same irregularity also having orderliness (*to tetagmenon*) (for it is restored to itself in ordered periods of time), as to beings intermediate between those moved entirely regularly (*homalōs*) and those moved entirely irregularly (*anōmalōs*); for they have been assigned a movement regularly irregular or irregularly regular. (trans. Pedersen and Hannah 2002: 74)

Interestingly, what is needed to restore regularity to irregularity is another dimension altogether—time: 'for it is restored to itself in ordered periods of time' (*apokathistatai gar pros heautēn dia tetagmenōn chronōn*). Whether for that reason or not, Proclus closes the section on the helix with mention of a 'helicoidal' time god (3.80.12–17): 'Surely the Theurgist,[11] when he hymned "Time the Helicoidal" as at the same time young and old, was not unconcerned with this very fact, that the measures of all sorts of temporal periods become visible to us through the motion of the planets in a helix.' One cannot help but think of Mithraism's snake-encircled time god and the reclining snake-encircled figure, mentioned above, who hails Mithras as he joins Sol in the ascending sun-chariot. Again, I throw in the necessary caution. The mysteries did not self-consciously encode a particular model of helicoidal motion. Think rather of the flow of representations down the linked channels of a common star-talk culture.

However he construed the figure itself, Proclus is clear about the place of the planetary helix in the grand cosmological hierarchy.

The helix is proper to the planets as beings which are spatially intermediate between the fixed stars and things below the Moon. The fixed stars move only in a circle and things below the Moon only in a straight line (3.79.12–18).

The figure of the helix is not a meaningless epiphenomenon (*symptōma kenon*). Rather, it is the intermediary [lit. 'fills the middle'] between bodies which move in straight lines and

---

[11] Proclus refers here to one or other of the Julians to whom the Chaldaean Oracles, a late second-century CE collection, were attributed. This fragment was omitted from des Places' edition (1971).

bodies which move in circles; for as was said, the circle belongs to the realm of the fixed stars, the straight line to the realm of genesis, and the helix to the realm of the planets (3.80.5–9).

Dangerous though it is to draw parallels between a fifth-century philosopher and mysteries moribund or dead at the time when he wrote, we can appeal to Proclus' intense conservatism in claiming that these are echoes not of the Mithraic mysteries themselves but of a stream of cosmological thinking which in the mysteries issued in representations of a Sun god worshipped as the great inter-mediary between heaven and earth.

In the extant sources there is, to my knowledge, only one authority who came anywhere near to understanding the helicoidal model, the by-now familiar Antiochus of Athens. He it is who preserves a single priceless nugget of quanti-tative data.

Antiochus, like Theon and Cleomedes, uses the language of helicoidal orbits (*CCAG* 8.3.112.30–6 = 7.127.27–33):[12]

Carried round in a helix (*helikoeidōs*) in the depth (*en tōi bathei*) of the signs, the planets make four figures (*schēmata*): (1) the first when descending from the highest point of orbit (*apo tēs anōtatou apsidos katabainontes*) they are said to be humiliated with respect to their exaltation (*hypsēlon tapeinousthai*); (2) the second when [sc. descending] from there to their lowest [sc. point of orbit] they are said to be humiliated with respect to their humiliation (*tapeinon tapeinousthai*); (3) the third when ascending from the lowest humiliation to the middle (*ek tou katōtatou tapeinou epi to meson anabainontes*) they are said to be exalted with respect to their humiliation (*tapeinon hypsousthai*); the fourth when [sc. ascending] from the middle to the highest [sc. point of orbit] they are said to be exalted with respect to their exaltation (*hypsēlon hypsousthai*).

Antiochus' rather murky description at least makes it clear that he is speaking of a figure formed in three dimensions, and that 'height' and the 'up/down' opposites refer to location and motion *both* on the vertical north–south axis *and* on the horizontal apogee–perigee axis (see Fig. 16*a*).

In the particular case of the Moon, for whom I think the helicoidal model was primarily developed, Antiochus takes anomaly into account (*CCAG* 8.3.112.36–113.2 = 7.127.33–5). This he does in the only way possible, by factoring in different speeds of eastward (longitudinal) motion depending on the sector of the helix occupied by the Moon. On the 'up helix' (*tēn anō helika*) she travels 11° a day, on the 'down helix' (*tēn katō helika*) 14°. That can only mean that when the Moon is on what we would call the 'outer' sector of her orbit and the Greeks the 'higher' or 'deeper' she moves more slowly *eastward* than when she is on the 'inner' (to us) or 'lower' (to the Greeks) sector. In terms of rotating spheres, as the Moon's solid sphere rotates *at a constant speed* it is carried eastward

---

[12] The two citations represent versions of the same passage in two different manuscripts. I have translated, as literally as possible, from the first cited.

by the rotation of the hollow sphere *at varying speeds*. Strictly speaking, it is immaterial whether the hollow sphere rotates clockwise or counterclockwise, but imaginatively it makes more sense for the sphere to rotate clockwise (from the point of view in Fig. 16a) so that the 'upper' or 'deeper' sector of the helix coincides with the 'ascending' or northward sector.

Just how sure was Antiochus' grasp of the helicoidal model and the theory of two rotating spheres which underlies it? That is impossible to tell, because much may have been distorted in subsequent transmission,[13] but it hardly matters. For the Moon at least he transmits enough data for us to reconstruct the model and the crucial modification which makes it work. The variation in the speed of the Moon eastward is of great significance, for it wears its Babylonian origins on its sleeve. For the Greeks it was axiomatic that all anomaly be resolved into uniform circular motion; hence their increasingly elaborate geometrical models. For the Babylonians, varying speed was an acceptable reality. In fact what Antiochus preserves is precisely analogous to the Babylonian 'step function' for the Sun in the so-called 'System A'.

Generating a helicoidal orbit from the rotation of two spheres is of course as Greek as formulating a step function is Babylonian. There is however one other datum relevant to the helicoidal model that comes from Babylon, and this too concerns specifically the orbit of the Moon. In Chapter 9 (sect. 9) we noticed the strange practice, most fully discussed by the astrologer Vettius Valens,[14] of measuring the 'argument of latitude', which is the Moon's distance travelled in orbit, (a) from the northern extreme rather than the ascending node, and (b) in units not of degrees but of 'steps' and 'winds':

(1) first quadrant = north wind descending = six steps down
(2) second quadrant = south wind descending = six steps down
(3) third quadrant = south wind ascending = six steps up
(4) fourth quadrant = north wind ascending = six steps up

In Greek star-talk steps and winds are reducible to degrees of longitude. A step is 15°, a wind is 90°. The system is completely redundant; so presumably it was retained in a limited circle of star-talkers out of an archaizing sense of the appropriate units of measure in the context of the argument of latitude. But redundancies are seldom invented; they are the vestiges of once useful constructs. What was the original construct which the steps and winds served to measure? I suggest that it was a construct which employed the Babylonian parameter for the width of the lunar orbit—12° or 6° north plus 6° south of the solar orbit or ecliptic (Neugebauer 1975: 514–15, 520, 1345 (Fig. 67 to Book 2)). We know that this value was indeed taken over into pre-Hipparchan Greek astronomy (ibid. 626).

---

[13] The passage immediately following (*CCAG* 8.3.113.2–7 = 7.127.35–128.4) appears garbled.

[14] Antiochus also explains the winds and steps, but he applies the system to the solar orbit, not the lunar orbit (*CCAG* 7.128.14–24).

In Babylonian mathematical astronomy lunar latitude was expressed 'in units called "barley corn" (*še*)' (Neugebauer 1975: 514), seventy-two of which make a degree.[15] I suggest that at some stage in the transmission of star-talk from the Babylonian to the Greek world these units underwent a name change, not into degrees but into equivalent units called 'steps' (one step = 1°). On this hypothesis the step would originally have been simply a unit of lunar latitude. From her northern extreme the Moon takes (1) six steps down to the ecliptic ('north wind descending'), then (2) another six steps down to the southern extreme ('south wind descending'), then (3) six steps back up to the ecliptic ('south wind ascending'), and finally (4) another six steps up to the northern extreme (see Fig. 17a).

At some later stage, to continue the story, this measure of lunar latitude was applied to a helicoidal kinematic model, self-evidently a Greek construct, and a Babylonian step-function parameter for anomaly (11° per day on the 'up helix', 14° per day on the 'down helix') was also applied. As a result, what you see in Figure 17a as a vertical bar and scale of latitude becomes a vertical cross-section of the Moon's 'solid' sphere seen edge on. From our vantage point on earth the Moon is carried up and down this cross-section as the solid sphere rotates. At the same time the Moon is also carried eastward (to the left) as the solid sphere is carried in that direction by the rotation of the 'hollow' sphere (see Fig 17b).

The Moon's apparent motion up and down the cross-section is non-uniform. It will appear to move from south to north or from north to south more rapidly when at the ecliptic than when at the extremes. This lack of *uniformity*, which is what one actually sees, is a consequence of the sphere's *uniform* rotation (compare the rise and fall of gondolas on a Ferris wheel seen sideways on). It is a grand

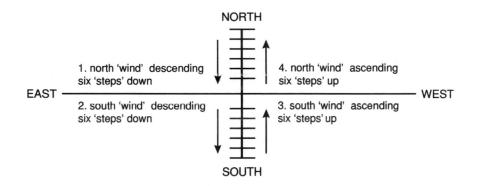

Fig. 17a. The winds and steps of the Moon, 1

[15] J. M. Steele is currently researching an analogous lunar band in the observational records of Babylonian astronomy (lecture, University of Toronto, Jan. 2005). The unit there is the 'cubit' (= 2°). The band measures 6 cubits in breadth from northern to southern extreme.

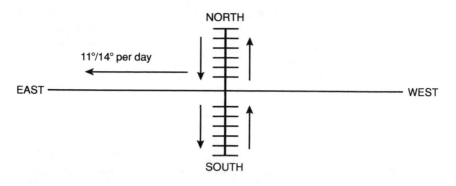

Fig. 17*b*. The winds and steps of the Moon, 2

example of what Proclus (above) was to call anomaly in uniformity and uniformity in anomaly.

When you combine this apparently non-uniform south–north/north–south motion with eastward motion the figure you see will be the familiar sinusoidal curve of the lunar orbit traced on a plane surface, as in Figure 12. It is at this stage of development that the 'step' migrates, as it were, from latitude to longitude. Instead of a 1° unit of latitude, the step becomes the distance in longitude corresponding to a 1° change in latitude. More precisely, it becomes the distance in longitude covered during a 1° change in latitude. That distance will vary: it will be greatest when the Moon is at her northern or southern limits and least when she is at one or other of the nodes.[16] Originally, then, a step was not precisely 15° (one-sixth of a 90° quadrant). It became so, in my scenario, only when its original metrological function and underlying kinematic model were forgotten.

Logically, the next step in the development of a helicoidal model for lunar motion would be to factor in the different lengths of the tropical, draconitic, and anomalistic months. The tropical month is the time taken by the mean Moon to return to the same longitude (27.32 days). In the helicoidal model this return is effected by the rotation of the hollow sphere. The draconitic month is the time taken for the Moon to return to the same latitude (27.21 days). In the helicoidal model this return is effected by the rotation of the solid sphere. The anomalistic month is the time taken for the Moon to return to the same point in the cycle of speed of eastward motion (27.55 days). In the helicoidal model (as refined by Antiochus or his source) this will occur when the rotation of the hollow sphere has completed a cycle of varying speed at 11° per day and 14° per day. Since these three months are of different lengths, the Moon herself, in successive cycles of the helix, will return to different points on the torus formed by the revolution of the solid sphere.

[16] The precise distance will also depend on her eastward speed, i.e. whether 'slow' or 'fast' in the cycle of anomaly.

Whether those three lunar periods were actually factored into the helicoidal model, and if so by whom, we do not know. It may well be that the model remained a work in progress, an elegant geometrical and kinematic construct with some interesting cosmological implications, but abandoned by serious mathematical astronomers in favour of the Hipparchan and Ptolemaic model of epicycles and eccentric circles.

The point of departure for this excursus was the occurrence together in the same source, Diogenes Laertius' brief report of Stoic star-talk (*Lives of the Philosophers* 7.144–6), of references to (1) the Moon's 'helicoidal' orbit, and (2) the fixing of the lunar nodes at Taurus 0° and Scorpius 0°. In section 11 of Chapter 9 I proposed that the latter reference, the fixing of the lunar nodes at those two points by 'those around Posidonius', relates to a larger project, namely the definition of an 'ideal' month in which the Moon will reach her northern extreme in Leo, the house of the Sun. In such a month, should the Sun also be in his house, he cannot suffer eclipse. The impetus for the creation of this ideal month, I argued, were the total eclipses of the Moon in 63 BCE, the first on 3 May when the Moon was at the descending node in Scorpius, the second on 27 October when she was at the ascending node in Taurus. (Both eclipses were visible in Anatolia, weather permitting.) The inauguration of this ideal month, I further argued, was memorialized in the massive complex of statues and reliefs in the *hierothesion* of King Antiochus of Commagene on the summit of Nemrud Dagh. The inauguration occurred in July of 62 BCE, when the actual month coincided quite well with the ideal month. As you may see in Figure 15, conjunction and new moon occurred on 5 July with the two luminaries approaching Leo.[17] The Moon reached her northern extreme the following day, 6 July, just below the Lion's jaws. The planet Jupiter was then immediately to her south. That night she passed Regulus, 'the royal star at the heart of the Lion', and the next day, 7 July, she joined Mercury and Mars below the Lion's belly. On the evening of that day the waxing crescent might have been visible for the first time setting in the west after sunset. All preceding events were invisible, even when above the horizon, because of the proximity of the Sun, as of course was the following conjunction which closed the month late on 3 August with the Sun and Moon below the Lion's belly (and all three well below the horizon). So by 'inauguration' I do not mean a ceremonial star-watching there and then,[18] but a

---

[17] On any definition of the signs and constellations, the Moon and the Sun were still in Cancer, the Moon's house.

[18] By a felicitous coincidence, we do actually have a reference to star-watchers on the Taurus mountains, of which Nemrud Dagh is one of the highest, in Manilius (*Astronomica* 1.402), the astrological poet writing half-a-century or so later. Manilius' star-gazers are precisely the fantasy that the actual memorial complex on Nemrud Dagh would generate. Another nice coincidence: what Manilius' mountaintop observers are watching for is the heliacal rising of Sirius in the second half of July; omens indicated by the position of the Moon ('in what house') at the rising of Sirius are the subject of an excerpt from—our ubiquitous Antiochus of Athens (*CCAG* 4.153–4)!

recognition that the cluster of celestial events, subsequently memorialized at the *hierothesion*, had indeed taken place and an approximation to a Sun-worshipper's ideal month had occurred.

The 'ideal month', I propose, was itself part of the project which we have explored in this chapter, a helicoidal model of planetary and, in particular, lunar motion, initiated, if we are to believe Theon of Smyrna (above), by Eudemus in the late fourth century BCE as a corrective to the over-elaborate model of concentric spheres propounded by Eudoxus, Callippus, and Aristotle. The model, as we have seen, retained pure spherical motion but abandoned concentricity. Its most remarkable innovation was to treat anomaly as an actual variation in speed rather than as an epiphenomenon of uniform motion on an epicycle or eccentric circle. Antiochus of Athens preserves for us a two-speed function for the Moon of obvious Babylonian origin. The helicoidal model was also, as we have seen, the matrix for lunar measurements in 'winds' and 'steps', ultimately also from Babylon.

It has not been my intent here to trace the precise filiation of the helicoidal model or of the ideal month and the esoteric quartering of the Mithraic mysteries, still less to propose these star-talk constructs as arcana of the mysteries transmitted from Commagene and then handed down from learned Mithraic Father to learned Mithraic Father as explicit elements of doctrine. Rather, as I have insisted throughout, they descend in a loosely cohering stream of representations transmitted through both text and visual image. What are still extant are the merest fragments of these star-talk constructs, represented as often as not in sources which did not properly understand them. So the best we can hope for is to isolate the typical markers of the star-talk constructs, such as the characterization of planetary orbits as 'helicoidal', and to see in what sources they show up. Remember too that our stream of representations is but one of several cross-currents which merge and separate. No current is ever entirely distinct or self-contained. I claim no more than that certain Mithraic representations, for example what I have called the 'esoteric' or 'lunar' quartering, belong to a larger tradition of star-talk with identifiable markers, and that they can be better understood by exploring this tradition both upstream and downstream.

There are further explorations to be made, but not here. Instead I shall close with a conjecture concerning one of the names which has cropped up again and again both here and in Chapter 9—the astrologer Antiochus of Athens (Cumont 1934; Gundels 1966: 115–17; Pingree 1977). But another Antiochus has also made an appearance, Antiochus I of Commagene. The name Antiochus recurs in the annals of the dynasty, and we find it held for the last time by a prominent Athenian at the turn of the first and second centuries CE, C. Iulius Antiochus Epiphanes Philopappus, the grandson on his father's side of the last reigning king of Commagene, Antiochus IV, and on his mother's side of the politically powerful astrologer Ti. Claudius Balbillus.[19] I have argued elsewhere that the Mithraic mysteries originated in the circle of the deposed but still highly regarded Commagenian dynasty in exile (Beck 1998a). That is why features of the astrology of Balbillus, their kinsman by marriage, resonate with the star-talk of the Mithraic mysteries (Beck 2001, 2004c: 324–9). What conclusions may we draw from the fact that the astrology of 'Antiochus of Athens' likewise resonates with the star-talk of the Mithraic mysteries and with Commagenian star-talk before? Perhaps that 'Antiochus of Athens' was the 'grandfather-loving' C. Iulius Antiochus Epiphanes Philopappus.

Two final 'coincidences'. First, it is Antiochus of Athens who preserves for us a prediction of 'cosmic apokatastasis' as the simultaneous conjunction of all the planets on the cusp of Cancer and Leo (*CCAG* 1.163.15–23):

Saturn makes the grand (*megistēn*) apokatastasis in 265 years, Jupiter in 427, Mars in 284, the Sun in 1461, Venus in 1151, Mercury in 480, the Moon in 25. The cosmic (*kosmikē*) apokatastasis takes place in 1,753,005 years,[20] and then the conjunction of all the stars [i.e. planets] in the thirtieth degree of Cancer or the first of Leo [i.e. Cancer 30° = Leo 0°] takes place, and Fulfilment (*ekplērōsis*) occurs.

The cusp of Cancer and Leo, as we saw in Chapter 9 (sects. 9–11) and throughout this chapter, was a cardinal point—*the* cardinal point—in the esoteric quartering of the Mithraic mysteries and cognate star-talk traditions, including the Commagenian. It is worth recalling the emphasis placed on apokatastasis in this tradition as that which restores regularity to irregularity.[21]

Our second 'coincidence' comes from Antiochus' calendar (Boll 1910), the same calendar which marks 25 December with 'Birthday of the Sun—light increases' (above, Ch. 9, sect. 6). For 2 August, the Sun being then in Leo, the calendar announces: 'the exultation of the Dog with the leaping-out of the Lion (*gauriama Kynos syn exhalmati Leontos*).' These two striking star-talk phrases refer, in more matter-of-fact terms, to the heliacal rising, or first visibility in the pre-dawn twilight, of Sirius and Leo. Sirius, the Dog-star, is the brightest star in the heavens, and its heliacal or morning rising was eagerly anticipated as one of the most significant markers in the seasonal and astronomical year. In Egypt its appearance traditionally marked the flood season and the beginning of the 'Sothic' year. As we saw (above, n. 18), Antiochus himself transmitted, probably

[19] C. Iulius Antiochus Epiphanes Philopappus = *Prosopographia Imperii Romani*[2] 4.141 Iulius no. 151. Philopappus retained the courtesy title of 'king' (*basileus*). He was *archōn* and *agōnothete* at Athens, suffect consul (109) and an arval brother in Rome. He belonged to the intellectual and cultural circle of Plutarch. His monument, a sort of mini-Nemrud-Dagh adapted to a Graeco-Roman context, still stands on the Hill of the Muses facing the Acropolis at Athens.

[20] One need not emend, but the 'correct' number is 1,753,200, i.e. 1,200 × 1,461 (Neugebauer 1975: 605–6, 618). 'Years' in this context are Egyptian years of 365 days: it takes 1,461 Egyptian years for the Sun to complete 1,460 true years of $365\frac{1}{4}$ days. On this passage see also Beck 1988: 41; 1994b: 288.

[21] See above on Proclus, *In Timaeum* 3.56.31–57; see also Pedersen and Hannah 2002: 74–8.

from Babylonian sources, a list of omens indicated by the position of the Moon at the rising of Sirius, and Manilius has his not altogether imaginary watchers on the Taurus mountains observe the event in order to 'learn the various outcomes for crops' (1.403).

The date on which a star 'rises' depends on the latitude of the observer. Antiochus records three dates for the rising of Sirius: 19 July in Egypt, 25 July for the fourth *klima* (i.e. the latitude of Rhodes), and 29 July for the sixth *klima* (i.e. the latitude of mid-Pontus). Presumably, then, the Dog 'exults' on 2 August because he is newly risen in all *klimata*.

The rising of a constellation takes place over a number of days even at the same site, since it occupies an extended area, not just a single point like a star. For the heliacal rising of Leo Antiochus gives three dates: the first, presumably for the westernmost stars, falls on 1 August, the day before the Lion 'leaps out'; the second, for Regulus 'on the Lion's heart', falls on 11 August; and the third, for the star on the Lion's tail, on 28 August. *Exhalma* is an astrological technical term, first attested in Balbillus (*CCAG* 8.3.104),[22] although Antiochus does not use it in its technical sense (Boll 1910: 28). In this context it appears to be a dramatic star-talk synonym for 'rising' (*anatolē*). The Lion 'leaps out' into visibility once more as the Sun, its master, moves through and beyond it.

In star-talk the rising of Sirius, the Sun's sojourn in Leo, and the sequential risings of Leo's stars are intimately linked. Technically, both Canis Major and Canis Minor (with their respective lucidae, Sirius and Procyon) are paranatellonta of Leo, constellations which 'rise alongside' the Lion as both sign and constellation (see Ch. 9, sect. 2. A5, and Fig. 7). Manilius has this to say of Sirius as the paranatellon of Leo (5.206–11, trans. Goold): 'But when the Lion of Nemea lifts into view his enormous gaping jaws, the brilliant constellation of the Dog appears: it barks forth flame, raves with its fire, and doubles the burning heat of the Sun. When it puts forth its torch to the earth and discharges its rays, the earth foresees its conflagration and tastes its ultimate fate.' This is but the introduction to twenty-eight lines on the rising of Sirius, a topic to which Manilius has already devoted sixteen lines in Book 1 (396–411). Both passages dwell on the violence and destructiveness of the heat which Sirius/Canicula and the Lion—more precisely the Sun in Leo—bring to earth. 'No star reaches the lands more violently (*violentius*) than Sirius' (1.397). It is Sirius of course who brings the 'dog days' and with them the heat prostration and lassitude of late summer.[23] In the passage from Book 5 quoted above Manilius sees in the annual rising of Sirius a foretaste of those Last Days which Antiochus was to define as the

---

[22] i.e. Antiochus' grandfather, on my hypothesis.

[23] Notice how Manilius uses the language of cause and effect. Sirius at its rising not only signals the summer heat; it also causes it. The astronomer Geminus (first cent. CE) effectively challenges this causative view of risings specifically in the case of Sirius (17.26–45).

grand conjunction of all seven planets *in the same part of the heavens*, where Cancer ends and Leo begins.

The celestial Dogs are not the only southern paranatellonta of Cancer and Leo. Hydra's head rises at the same time of year (see Figs. 1, 7, and 15). As Aratus, who also describes the paranatellonta at some length, writes: 'Up rises (*antellei*) the head of Hydra and the bright-eyed Hare [the constellation Lepus] and Procyon and the forepaws of the blazing Dog' (*Phaenomena* 594–5). Now observe how in the tauroctony:

> the dog,
> whose star-talk meaning is the celestial Dogs,
> and the snake,
> whose star-talk meaning is Hydra,
> dart up at the blood flowing from the wound struck by Mithras,
> whose star-talk meaning is Sun-in-Leo.

Our new-won familiarity with the more exotic reaches of star-talk discourse lets us appreciate how Antiochus intends the same celestial event and the same spatio-temporal configuration with his calendar entry:

> 2 August—the exultation of the Dog with the leaping-out of the Lion.

Conclusions: a new basis for interpreting the mysteries

In the first chapter (sect. 3) I set out what I called a 'template' for the re-description of the Mithraic mysteries in the form of six propositions. To these six propositions I now return to see what sense they make at the end of our explorations. Remember that they are in no sense Articles of Religion. You may want to review their status, as I see it, in the first two sections of Chapter 1.

The propositions were advanced in two versions, the first in neutral language (e.g. 'The mysteries give symbolic expression to...'), the second in language reflecting the point of view of the initiate (e.g. 'In the mysteries, the initiate apprehends symbolically...'). Clearly the second version is prior; the first is merely a scholar's construct which feigns objectivity. So I shall recapitulate our six propositions from the initiate's perspective.[1]

A. In the mysteries, the initiate apprehends symbolically two axioms or ultimate sacred postulates:
   (1) DEUS SOL INVICTUS MITHRAS,
   (2) 'Harmony of tension in opposition'.

B. The initiate apprehends these axioms in an indeterminate number of themes or motifs, e.g. the theme of descent and ascent.

C. The initiate apprehends the axioms and themes in one or more of four domains:
   (1) the sacred story, the deeds of Mithras,
   (2) the cosmos,
   (3) the sublunary world,
   (4) the destiny of human (especially initiates') souls.

---

[1] In Beck 2004c (46–9), as an imaginative experiment, I set out a third version in which the six propositions were expressed from the *divine* perspective in the first person, as e.g. in an Isiac aretalogy. What warrants this version is the fact that initiates perceive their mysteries as the gift of the god, not as their own cognitive experiences. In the academy we can deal only with the latter, recognizing that in the mithraeum the former prevailed.

D. The initiate apprehends the symbol complexes conveying the axioms and motifs of the mysteries in their various domains on structured sites. In the mysteries there are three principal and distinctive structures:
(1) the physical structure of the icon of the tauroctony (with its reverse = the banquet scene, plus peripheral scenes),
(2) the physical structure of the mithraeum,
(3) the organizational structure of the seven grades.

E. The initiate apprehends the symbols in one or more of four modes:
(1) ritual action,
(2) the perception of meaningful iconography,
(3) the giving and receiving of words (logia, explications, teaching, esoteric epigraphic formulae),
(4) ethical behaviour consonant with the mysteries (e.g. Mithraic Lions behave in an esoterically appropriate leonine way).

F. The mysteries' common symbolic idiom across axioms, motifs, domains, structures, and modes is the language of astronomy/astrology or star-talk.

On reviewing the six propositions it strikes me that more needs to be said on only one of them, Proposition B on themes or motifs. Chapter 9 was entirely devoted to star-talk as the idiom of the mysteries (F), and Chapter 8 to establishing that a symbol system can in certain circumstances function as a language and that the ancients themselves treated the heavens as text and the stars as intelligent communicators. As regards Proposition D on the initiate's apprehension of symbols in complexes on three principal structured sites, we have explored at some length how this was effected in the tauroctony in Chapter 9 and in the mithraeum in Chapter 8.[2] The 'modes' of apprehending and engaging with symbols (in ritual action, perception of iconography, explications, appropriate ethical behaviour, and so on—Proposition E) do not need systematic treatment either, once the chimaera of a coherent Mithraic doctrine and belief system has been exorcised, as it was in Chapters 2–4. The 'domains' (C) are likewise self-explanatory. In Chapter 9 (end of sect. 6, start of sect. 7) we saw how a change of domain sometimes entails a change of meaning for a star-talk sign. This was important, for it shows how apparent paradox can sometimes be explained—but not explained away!—as an instance of the lexical and semantic flexibility of language.

To say nothing further about Mithraism's two axioms or ultimate sacred postulates (Proposition A) might seem bizarre in a Conclusion. But is it really? If it still needs to be established that the two axioms, (1) DEUS SOL INVICTUS MITHRAS and (2) 'Harmony of tension in opposition', are the golden threads running through and holding together the Mithraic mysteries, then I have failed

---

[2] In the grade hierarchy in Ch. 5, sect. 5.

in my task. One does not prove these things, one shows them by demonstration and iteration.

If anything further needs to be said about the axioms it can be said in the context of some brief remarks about the 'motifs' or 'themes' in and through which the initiate apprehends them (Proposition B). In principle at least there was no limit to the number of themes, unlike the axioms (A), domains (C), structured sites (D), and modes (E). In their explications Mithraic Fathers could and no doubt did develop many themes which have disappeared from the record. Some of these were probably quite idiosyncratic. But all save the most evanescent would have instantiated one or both of the axioms. More successfully or less successfully, each would have said something explicitly or implicitly about the solar invincibility of the god Mithras and the tensed harmony of opposites. If we think of the mysteries as an evolving stream of mental and public representations, we might think of effective instantiation of the axioms as the main factor in the selection of successful representations. Those which effectively instantiated the axioms survived; those which did not did not survive. The principal themes which we can still discern are the 'fit' survivors of a process of selection at work at a level well below the conscious choice of initiates.[3]

In the summary above I cited 'descent and ascent' as an example of a theme, and we saw in Chapter 9 how that theme operated in different domains: in the cosmic domain in the elevation and subordination of the journeying Sun and Moon; in the domain of the sublunary world in the growth and dying down of vegetation; in the domain of human destinies in the descent and return of souls. Our first conclusion must therefore be that themes of consequence both span domains and integrate them. Secondly, nowhere was our theme simple or unparadoxical. Indeed, part of its function appears to have been precisely to generate paradox. Thirdly, complexity and paradox were never pointless; meaning was always present and discernible in star-talk utterances. Fourthly, the theme, while complex in its applications, was reducible to a straightforward polarity: descent versus ascent.

Here we face the problem of circularity. Having proclaimed 'harmony of tension in opposition' the second 'ultimate sacred postulate' of the Mithraic mysteries, themes of opposition are the rabbits I am going to pull out of the top hat. The question then becomes, how authentic is that second postulate? In answer, I can point to the most explicit symbol of opposition in the mysteries, the pair of torchbearers, the 'twins' who are identical in appearance yet also polar opposites in that one carries his torch raised, the other lowered; and I can demonstrate, as I did in Chapter 9, how they function as star-talk signs conveying paired oppositional meanings. I can also argue, as I did in Chapter 5 (sect. 8) that Porphyry, *De antro* 29 is based on a Mithraic list of star-talk oppositions. Yet of

---

[3] I realize my 'themes' are starting to sound suspiciously like Richard Dawkins's 'memes'. I had not intended it that way, but so be it.

course it was I who chose to privilege the torchbearers and Porphyry's *De antro nympharum* in my explications and I who imported the concept of 'star-talk'. In the end, formal circularity just has to be accepted.

The identification of themes is a large part of interpretation—scholarly interpretation, that is, not the esoteric explications of Mithraic Fathers. Identifying themes, however, is not an analytical task. One is not breaking something down into its components. Rather it is a matter of seeing what principles emerge as one explores symbolic structures and star-talk narratives. Baldly listing themes is not an appropriate hermeneutic strategy.

In this study, now at its conclusion, I have begun the task of reinterpreting the Mithraic mysteries on what I hope are sounder heuristic and hermeneutic principles and a sounder theoretical base. Begun, but not completed; for the project of interpretation is open-ended, and I hope not only to go further myself but also that others will venture along this road.

References

ANDRESEN, J. 2001*a*, 2001*b*. 'Introduction: towards a cognitive science of religion', 'Conclusion: religion in the flesh: forging new methodologies for the study of religion'. Chs. 1 and 11 in J. Andresen (ed.), *Religion in Mind: Cognitive Perspectives on Religious Belief, Ritual, and Experience* (Cambridge).

'Arethusa edition' = Seminar Classics 609, State University of New York at Buffalo (ed.). 1969. *Porphyry: The Cave of the Nymphs in the Odyssey* (Buffalo).

ARMSTRONG, H. A. (trans.), 1966–8. *Plotinus: Enneads*, 7 vols. (Cambridge, Mass.).

BARKOW, J. H., COSMIDES, L., and TOOBY, J. 1992. *The Adapted Mind: Evolutionary Psychology and the Generation of Culture* (New York).

BARNES, T. D. (ed.), 1994. *The Sciences in Greco-Roman Society.* Special issue, *Apeiron*, 27: 4 (Edmonton).

BARRETT, J. L. 2004. *Why Would Anyone Believe in God?*, Cognitive Science of Religion Series (Walnut Creek, Calif.).

BAUSANI, A. 1979. 'Note sulla preistoria astronomica del mito di Mithra', in *MM*: 503–13.

BEARD, M., NORTH, J., and PRICE, S. 1998. *Religions of Rome.* Vol. 1: *A History*; Vol. 2: *A Sourcebook* (Cambridge).

BECK, R. L. 1976*a*. 'Interpreting the Ponza zodiac, I', *JMS* 1: 1–19. (= Beck 2004*c*: ch. 9, pp. 151–69).

—— 1976*b*. 'The seat of Mithras at the equinoxes: Porphyry, *De Antro Nympharum* 24', *JMS* 1: 95–8 (= Beck 2004*c*: ch. 7, pp. 129–32).

—— 1976*c*. 'A note on the scorpion in the tauroctony', *JMS* 1: 208–9.

—— 1977. 'Cautes and Cautopates: some astronomical considerations', *JMS* 2: 1–17.

—— 1978. 'Interpreting the Ponza zodiac, II', *JMS* 2: 87–147 (= Beck 2004*c*: ch. 10, pp. 171–231).

—— 1979. 'Sette Sfere, Sette Porte, and the spring equinoxes of A.D. 172 and 173', in *MM*: 515–29.

—— 1982. 'The Mithraic torchbearers and "absence of opposition"', *Classical Views*, 26, NS 1: 126–40.

—— 1984. 'Mithraism since Franz Cumont', *ANRW* 2.17.4: 2002–15.

—— 1987*a*. 'Merkelbach's Mithras' (review article of Merkelbach 1984), *Phoenix*, 41: 296–316.

—— 1987*b*. 'The Anabibazontes in the Manichaean Kephalaia', *Zeitschrift für Papyrologie und Epigraphik*, 69: 193–6.

—— 1988. *Planetary Gods and Planetary Orders in the Mysteries of Mithras*, EPRO 109 (Leiden).

—— 1991. 'Thus spake not Zarathustra'. An Excursus in Boyce and Grenet 1991: 491–565.

—— 1994*a*. 'Cosmic models: some uses of Hellenistic science in Roman religion', in Barnes (ed.): 99–117 (= Beck 2004*c*: ch. 16, pp. 335–53).

BECK, R. L. 1994*b*. 'In the place of the Lion: Mithras in the tauroctony', in *SM* 29–50 (= Beck 2004*c*: ch. 13, pp. 267–91).

—— 1998*a*. 'The Mysteries of Mithras: a new account of their genesis', *JRS* 88: 115–28 (= Beck 2004*c*: ch. 2, pp. 31–44).

—— 1998*b*. '*Qui mortalitatis causa convenerunt*: the meeting of the Virunum Mithraists on June 26, A.D. 184', *Phoenix*, 52: 335–44 (= Beck 2004*c*: ch. 17, pp. 355–64)

—— 1999. 'The astronomical design of Karakush, a royal burial site in ancient Commagene: an hypothesis', *Culture and Cosmos*, 3: 10–34 (= Beck 2004*c*: ch. 14, pp. 297–321).

—— 2000. 'Ritual, myth, doctrine, and initiation in the Mysteries of Mithras: new evidence from a cult vessel', *JRS* 90: 144–79 (= Beck 2004*c*: ch. 4, pp. 55–92).

—— 2001 [2003]. 'New thoughts on the genesis of the Mysteries of Mithras', *Topoi*, 11, no. 1: 59–76.

—— 2004*a*. 'Dancing at the spirit gates: a Mithraic ritual recovered from Proclus (*In Remp.* 2.128.26 ff. Kroll)', in R. B. Egan and M. Joyal (eds.), *Daimonopylai: Essays in Classics and the Classical Tradition Presented to Edmund G. Berry* (Winnipeg): 1–6.

—— 2004*b*. 'Four men, two sticks, and a whip: image and doctrine in a Mithraic ritual', in Whitehouse and Martin (eds.), 2004: 87–103.

—— 2004*c*. *Beck on Mithraism: Collected Works with New Essays*, Ashgate Contemporary Thinkers on Religion: Collected Works. (Aldershot and Burlington, Vt.).

BELL, C. 1997. *Ritual: Perspectives and Dimensions* (New York and Oxford).

BENNDORF, O., WEISS, E., and REHM, A. 1903. 'Zur Salzburger Bronzescheibe mit Sternbildern', *Jahreshefte des österreichischen archäologischen Institutes in Wien*, 6: 32–49.

BERTHOLD, P. 2001. *Bird Migration*, 2nd edn., trans. H.-G. Bauer and V. Westhead (Oxford).

BETZ, H. D. 1968. 'The Mithras inscriptions of Santa Prisca and the New Testament', *Novem Testamentum*, 10: 62–80.

—— (ed. and trans.), 2003. *The Mithras Liturgy: Text, Translation, and Commentary*, Studien und Texte zu Antike und Christentum, 18 (Tübingen).

BIANCHI, U. 1979. 'The religio-historical question of the mysteries of Mithra', *MM*: 4–60.

—— (ed.), 1979. *Mysteria Mithrae*, Atti del Seminario Internazionale su 'La specificità storico-religiosa dei Misteri di Mithra, con particolare riferimento alle fonti documentarie di Roma e Ostia', Roma e Ostia, 28–31 Mar., EPRO 80 (Leiden).

—— and VERMASEREN, M. J. (eds.), 1982. *La soteriologia dei culti orientali nell' Impero Romano*, Atti del Colloquio Internazionale, Roma, 24–28 Sept. 1979, EPRO 92 (Leiden).

BIDEZ, J., and CUMONT, F. 1938. *Les Mages hellénisés: Zoroastre, Ostanès, et Hystaspe d'après la tradition grecque*, 2 vols (Paris).

BIVAR, A. D. H. 1999. *The Personalities of Mithra in Archaeology and Literature*, Biennial Yarshater Lecture Series 1 (New York).

BLAKELY, J. A. 1987. *The Joint Expedition to Caesarea Maritima, Excavation Reports, the Pottery and Dating of Vault 1: Horreum, Mithraeum and Later Uses* (Lewiston, NY).

BOLL, F. 1910. *Griechische Kalender: 1. Das Kalendarium des Antiochos*, Sitzungsberichte der Heidelberger Akademie der Wissenschaften, philos.-hist. Klasse, Jahrgang 1910, 16. Abhandlung (Heidelberg).

BONNET, C. 2000. 'Franz Cumont et les risques du métier d'historien des religions', *Hieros* (Bulletin annuel de la Société belgo-luxembourgeoise d'Histoire des Religions), 5: 12–29.

BOUCHÉ-LECLERCQ, A. 1899. *L'Astrologie grecque* (Paris).

BOWEN, A. C., and TODD, R. B. 2004. *Cleomedes' Lectures on Astronomy: A Translation of* The Heavens *with an Introduction and Commentary* (Berkeley and Los Angeles).

BOYCE, M., and GRENET, F. 1991. *A History of Zoroastrianism*, vol. 3, Handbuch der Orientalistik, 1. Abt., 8. Bd., 1. Abschn., Lfg. 2 (Leiden).

BOYER, P. 2001. *Religion Explained: The Evolutionary Origins of Religious Thought* (New York).

BOYS-STONES, G. R. 2001. *Post-Hellenistic Philosophy: A Study of its Development from the Stoics to Origen* (Oxford).

BRASHEAR, W. 1992. *A Mithraic Catechism from Egypt: P.Berol. 21196*, Tyche Supplementband (Vienna).

BROMLEY, A. G. 1986. 'Notes on the Antikythera Mechanism', *Centaurus*, 29: 5–27.

BUCHNER, E. 1982. *Die Sonnenuhr des Augustus* (Mainz).

BULL, R. J. 1978. 'The mithraeum at Caesarea Maritima', in *EM*: 75–89.

BURKERT, W. 1987. *Ancient Mystery Cults* (Cambridge, Mass., and London).

CAMPBELL, L. R. 1968. *Mithraic Iconography and Ideology*, EPRO 11 (Leiden).

Catalogus Codicum Astrologorum Graecorum (various eds.). 1898–1953. 12 vols. in 20 parts (Brussels).

CHADWICK, H. (trans.), 1953. *Origen: Contra Celsum* (Cambridge).

CLAUSS, M. 1990. *Mithras: Kult und Mysterien* (Munich).

—— 1992. *Cultores Mithrae: Die Anhängerschaft des Mithras-Kultes*, Heidelberger Althistorische Beiträge und Epigraphische Studien, 10 (Stuttgart).

—— 2000. *The Roman Cult of Mithras: The God and his Mysteries*, trans. R. L. Gordon (Edinburgh).

—— 2001. 'Mithras und die Präzession' (review article of Ulansey 1989), *Klio*, 83: 219–25.

COLEMAN, K. M. 1990. 'Fatal charades: Roman executions staged as mythological enactments', *JRS* 80: 44–73.

CORNFORD, F. M. 1937. *Plato's Cosmology: The Timaeus of Plato, Translated with a Running Commentary* (London).

CROSSAN, J. D. 1998. *The Birth of Christianity: Discovering What Happened in the Years Immediately After the Execution of Jesus* (San Francisco).

CUMONT, F. 1896. *Textes et monuments figurés relatifs aux mystères de Mithra*, vol. 2 (Brussels).

—— 1899. *Textes et monuments figurés relatifs aux mystères de Mithra*, vol. 1 (Brussels).

—— 1903/1956. *The Mysteries of Mithra*, trans. T. J. McCormack (London; repr. New York, 1956).

—— 1912/1960. *Astrology and Religion Among the Greeks and Romans* (London; repr. New York, 1960).

—— 1913. *Les Mystères de Mithra*, 3rd edn. (Brussels).

—— 1934. 'Antiochus d'Athènes et Porphyre', *Annuaire de l'Institut de philologie et d'histoire orientale* (Brussels, Université libre), 2: 135–56.

—— 1935. 'Les Noms des planètes et l'astrolatrie chez les Grecs', *L'Antiquité Classique*, 4: 5–43.

CUMONT, F. 1937. *L'Égypte des astrologues* (Brussels).

—— 1946. 'Un bas-relief mithriaque du Louvre', *Revue Archéologique*, 25: 183–95.

D'AQUILI, E. G., and NEWBERG, A. B. 1999. *The Mystical Mind: Probing the Biology of Religious Experience* (Minneapolis).

—— LAUGHLIN, C. D., and McMANUS, J. (eds), 1979. *The Spectrum of Ritual* (New York).

DAMASIO, A. 1994. *Descartes' Error: Emotion, Reason, and the Human Brain* (New York).

—— 2003. *Looking for Spinoza: Joy, Sorrow, and the Feeling Brain* (Orlando, Fla.).

DE BOER, M. B., and EDRIDGE, T. A. (eds.), 1978. *Hommages à Maarten J. Vermaseren*, 3 vols. with continuous pagination, EPRO 68 (Leiden).

DE SOUSA, R. 1991. *The Rationality of Emotion* (Cambridge, Mass.).

DES PLACES, É. (ed.). 1971. *Oracles chaldaïques* (Paris).

—— (ed.). 1973. *Numénius: Fragments* (Paris).

DICKS, D. R. 1970. *Early Greek Astronomy to Aristotle* (London).

DIETERICH, A. 1923/1966. *Eine Mithrasliturgie* (Leipzig and Berlin/Stuttgart).

DÖRRIE, H. 1964. *Der Königskult des Antiochus von Kommagene im Lichte neuer Inschriften-Funde* (Göttingen).

DRACHMAN, A. G. 1954. 'The plane astrolabe and the anaphoric clock', *Centaurus*, 3: 183–9.

DUCHESNE-GUILLEMIN, J. (ed.), 1978. *Études mithriaques*: Actes du 2ᵉ Congrès international, Téhéran. Acta Iranica, Series 1, 4 (Leiden).

DUPUIS, J. (ed. and trans.), 1892/1966. *Théon de Smyrne, philosophe platonicien. Exposition des connaissances mathématiques utiles pour la lecture de Platon* (Paris/Brussels).

EDELMAN, G. M., and TONONI, G. 2000. *A Universe of Consciousness: How Matter Becomes Imagination* (New York).

EDWARDS, M. J. 1993. 'Porphyry and the "cattle-stealing god"', *Hermes*, 121: 122–5.

EMLEN, S. T. 1967. 'Migratory orientation in the Indigo bunting, *Passerina cyanea*', *Auk*, 84: 309–42, 463–89.

GAGNAIRE, P. 1999. 'The Scaphe of Carthage', *Bulletin of the British Sundial Society*, 9, no. 2: 87–90.

GEERTZ, C. 1973. *The Interpretation of Cultures: Selected Essays* (New York).

—— 1983. 'Centers, kings, and charisma: reflections on the symbolics of power', in *Local Knowledge: Further Essays in Interpretive Anthropology* (New York): 121–46 (= ch. 6).

GIBBS, S. L. 1976. *Greek and Roman Sundials* (New Haven).

GLAZIER, S. D. (ed.), 1997. *Anthropology of Religion: A Handbook* (Westport, Conn.).

GOOLD, G. P. (trans.), 1977. *Manilius: Astronomica* (Cambridge, Mass., and London).

GORDON, R. L. 1975. 'Franz Cumont and the doctrines of Mithraism', in *MS*: 215–48.

—— 1976. 'The sacred geography of a *mithraeum*: the example of Sette Sfere', *JMS* 1: 119–65 (= Gordon 1996: ch. 6).

—— 1978. 'The date and significance of *CIMRM* 593 (British Museum Townley Collection)', *JMS* 2: 148–74 (= Gordon 1996: ch. 7).

—— 1979. 'The real and the imaginary: production and religion in the Graeco-Roman world'. *Art History*, 2, no. 1: 5–34 (= Gordon 1996: ch. 1).

—— 1980*a*. 'Panelled complications', *JMS* 3: 200–27 (= Gordon 1996: ch. 9).

—— 1980*b*. 'Reality, evocation and boundary in the Mysteries of Mithras', *JMS* 3: 19–99 (= Gordon 1996: ch. 5).

—— 1988. 'Authority, salvation and mystery in the Mysteries of Mithras', in J. Huskinson, M. Beard, and J. Reynolds (eds.), *Image and Mystery in the Roman World: Three Papers Given in Memory of Jocelyn Toynbee* (Cambridge): 45–80 (= Gordon 1996: ch. 4).

—— 1994*a*. 'Mystery, metaphor and doctrine in the Mysteries of Mithras', in *SM*: 103–24.

—— 1994*b*. 'Who worshipped Mithras?' (review article of Clauss 1992), *Journal of Roman Archaeology*, 7: 459–74.

—— 1996. *Image and Value in the Graeco-Roman World*, Variorum Collected Studies Series CS551 (Aldershot).

—— 1998. 'Viewing Mithraic art: the altar from Burginatium', *Antigüedad: Religiones y Sociedades*, 1: 227–58.

—— 2001. '*Persei sub rupibus antri*: Überlegungen zur Entstehung der Mithrasmysterien', in M. Vomer Gojkovic *et al.* (eds.), *Ptuj in römischen Reich: Mithraskult und seine Zeit*, Akten des internat. Symposium Ptuj, 11–15 Oct. 1999, Ptuj, *Archaeologia Poetoviensis*, 2: 289–301.

—— 2004. 'Small and miniature reproductions of the Mithraic icon: reliefs, pottery, ornaments and gems', in Martens and De Boe (eds.): 259–83.

GOSSEN, G. H. 1979. 'Temporal and spatial equivalents in Chamula ritual symbolism', in W. A. Lessa and E. Z. Vogt (eds.), *Reader in Comparative Religion* (New York): 116–29.

GOULET, R. 1980. *Cléomède, Théorie élémentaire ('De motu circulari corporum caelestium')*. *Texte présenté, traduit et commenté*, Histoire des doctrines de l'antiquité classique, 3 (Paris).

GREEN, R. P. H. (ed. and trans.), 1995. *Augustine: De Doctrina Christiana* (New York).

GREGORY, A. 2000. *Plato's Philosophy of Science* (London).

GRIFFITH, J. G. (trans.), 1970. *Plutarch: De Iside et Osiride* (Cambridge).

GUNDEL, H. G. 1992. *Zodiakos: Tierkreisbilder im Altertum*, Kulturgeschichte der Antiken Welt 54 (Mainz).

GUNDEL, W. and H. G. 1950. 'Planeten', *Real-Encyclopädie d. klassischen Altertumswissenschaft*, 20: 2017–185.

—— —— 1966. *Astrologoumena: Die astrologische Literatur in der Antike und ihre Geschichte*, Sudhoffs Archiv, Beiheft 6 (Wiesbaden).

GUTHRIE, S. E. 1993. *Faces in the Clouds: A New Theory of Religion* (New York).

—— 1997. 'The origin of an illusion', in Glazier 1997: 489–504.

HALL, J. R., and SCHUYLER, P. 1997. 'The mystical apocalypse of the Solar Temple', in T. Robbins and S. J. Palmer (eds.), *Millennium, Messiahs, and Mayhem: Contemporary Apocalyptic Movements* (New York and London): 285–311.

HANNAH, R. 1996. 'The image of Cautes and Cautopates in the Mithraic tauroctony icon', in M. Dillon (ed.), *Religion in the Ancient World* (Amsterdam): 177–92.

HARTNER, W. 1965. 'The earliest history of the constellations in the Near East and the motif of the lion–bull combat', *Journal of Near Eastern Studies*, 24: 1–16.

HAYWOOD, C. T. R. 1996. *The Jewish Temple: A Non-biblical Sourcebook* (London).

HEATH, T. L. (ed. and trans.), 1956 (repr.). *Euclid, Elements*, vol. 1 (New York).

HEGEDUS, T. M. J. 2000. 'Attitudes to astrology in early Christianity: a study based on selected sources', dissertation, University of Toronto.

—— 2005. *Attitudes to Astrology in Early Christianity* (Baltimore).

HINNELLS, J. R. 1975. 'Reflections on the bull-slaying scene', in *MS*: 290–312.

—— (ed.), 1975. *Mithraic Studies*, Proceedings of the First International Congress of Mithraic Studies, 2 vols (continuous pagination) (Manchester).

—— 1976. 'The iconography of Cautes and Cautopates, 1: the data', *JMS* 1: 36–67.

—— (ed.), 1994. *Studies in Mithraism*, papers associated with the Mithraic panel [at] the XVIth Congress of the IAHR, Rome 1990, Storia delle Religioni, 9 (Rome).

—— and GORDON, R. L. 1977–8. 'Some new photographs of well-known Mithraic monuments', *JMS* 2: 198–223.

HOPKINS, K. 1999. *A World Full of Gods: Pagans, Jews and Christians in the Roman Empire* (London).

HORN, H. G. 1994. 'Das Mainzer Mithrasgefäß', *Mainzer Archäologische Zeitschrift*, 1: 21–66.

HÜBNER, W. 1975. 'Das Horoskop der Christen (Zeno 1,38 L.)', *Vigiliae Christianae*, 29: 120–37.

—— 1982. *Die Eigenschaften der Tierkreiszeichen in der Antike*, Sudhoffs Archiv, Zeitschrift für Wissenschaftsgeschichte, 22 (Wiesbaden).

INSLER, S. 1978. 'A new interpretation of the bull-slaying motif', in de Boer and Edridge (eds.): ii. 519–38.

JACOBS, B. 1999. *Der Herkunft und Entstehung der römischen Mithrasmysterien: Überlegungen zur Rolle des Stifters und zu den astronomischen Hintergründen der Kultlegende.* Xenia: Konstanzer Althistorische Vorträge und Forschungen, 43 (Konstanz).

—— 2000. 'Die Religionspolitik des Antiochos I von Kommagene', in Wagner (ed.) 2000: 45–49.

JONES, A. 1994. 'The place of astronomy in Roman Egypt', in Barnes (ed.), 25–51.

—— 1999. *Astronomical Papyri from Oxyrhynens (P. Oxy. 4133–4300a)*. Memoirs of the American Philosophical Society, 233 (Philadelphia).

JOSEPH, R. (ed.), 2002. *NeuroTheology: Brain, Science, Spirituality, Religious Experience* (San Jose, Calif.).

JUNOD, É. (ed. and trans.), 1976. *Origène, Philocalie 21–27: Sur le libre arbitre*, Sources Chrétiennes, 226 (Paris).

KINGSLEY, P. 1990. 'The Greek origin of the sixth-century dating of Zoroaster', *Bulletin of the School of Oriental and African Studies*, 53: 245–65.

—— 1995. 'Meetings with Magi: Iranian themes among the Greeks, from Xanthus of Lydia to Plato's Academy', *Journal of the Royal Asiatic Society*, 5: 173–209.

KREYENBROEK, P. G. 1994. 'Mithra and Ahreman in Iranian Cosmogonies', in *SM*: 173–82.

LAMBERTON, R. (trans.), 1983. *Porphyry: On the Cave of the Nymphs* (Barrytown, NY).

—— 1986. *Homer the Theologian: Neoplatonist Allegorical Reading and the Growth of the Epic Tradition*, Transformation of the classical heritage, 9 (Berkeley).

LAUGHLIN, C. D. 1989. 'Ritual and the symbolic function: a summary of biogenetic structural theory', *Journal of Ritual Studies*, 4: 15–39.

—— 1997. 'The cycle of meaning: some methodological implications of biogenetic structural theory', in Glazier 1997: 471–88 (= ch. 17).

LAWSON, E. T., and McCAULEY, R. N. 1990. *Rethinking Religion: Connecting Cognition and Culture* (Cambridge).

—— —— 2002. *Bringing Ritual to Mind: Psychological Foundations of Cultural Forms* (Cambridge).

LEE, D. (trans.), *Plato: Timaeus and Critias* (Harmondsworth).

LEVI, D. 1947. *Antioch Mosaic Pavements*, 2 vols. (Princeton).

LÉVI-STRAUSS, C. 1955. 'The structural study of myth', *Journal of American Folklore*, 78: 428–44.

LEX, B. W. 1979. 'The neurobiology of ritual trance', in d'Aquili *et al.* (eds.), 1979: 117–51 (= ch. 4).

LLOYD, G. E. R. 1966. *Polarity and Analogy: Two Types of Argumentation in Early Greek Thought* (Cambridge).

L'ORANGE, H. P. 1942. 'Domus Aurea—der Sonnenpalast', *Symbolae Osloenses*, suppl. 11: 68–100.

LYLE, E. B. 1984. 'The circus as cosmos', *Latomus*, 43: 827–41.

McCAULEY, R. N. 2000. 'The naturalness of religion and the unnaturalness of science', in F. Keil and R. Wilson (eds.), *Explanation and Cognition* (Cambridge, Mass.): 61–85.

MACK, B. L. 2001. *The Christian Myth: Origins, Logic, and Legacy* (New York).

MARCOVICH, M. (ed.), 1986. *Hippolytus: Refutatio omnium haeresium*, Patristische Texte und Studien, 25 (Berlin and New York).

—— (ed.). 1999. *Diogenes Laertius: Vitae philosophorum* (Leipzig).

MARENGO, S. M. 1998. 'Orologio solare sferico da Matelica', in G. Paci (ed.), *Epigrafia romana in area adriatica* (Pisa and Rome): 161–75.

MARKUS, R. A. 1996. *Signs and Meaning: World and Text in Ancient Christianity* (Liverpool).

MARTENS, M., and DE BOE, G. (eds.), 2004. *Roman Mithraism: The Evidence of the Small Finds*, Archaeologie in Vlanderen, Monografie 5 (Zellik and Tienen).

MARTIN, L. H. 1994. 'Reflections on the Mithraic tauroctony as cult scene', in *SM*: 217–24.

MERKELBACH, R. 1965. 'Die Kosmogonie der Mithrasmysterien', *Eranos-Jahrbuch*, 34: 218–57.

—— 1984. *Mithras* (Königstein/Ts.).

MESSERSCHMIDT, F. 1931. 'Himmelsbuch und Sternschrift', *Römische Quartalschrift*, 39: 63–9.

MEEUS, J., and MUCKE, H. 1979. *Canon of Lunar Eclipses, −2002 to +2526* (Vienna).

MITHEN, S. 1996. *The Prehistory of the Mind: The Cognitive Origins of Art, Religion and Science* (London and New York).

MOMIGLIANO, A. 1975. *Alien Wisdom: The Limits of Hellenization* (Cambridge).

MURPHY, G. R. 1979. 'A ceremonial ritual: the Mass', in d'Aquili *et al.* (eds.), 1979: 318–41 (= ch. 10).

NEUGEBAUER, O. 1975. *A History of Ancient Mathematical Astronomy*, Studies in the History of Mathematics and Physical Sciences, 1, 3 vols. (with consecutive pagination) (Berlin, Heidelberg, and New York).

—— and VAN HOESEN, H. B. 1959. *Greek Horoscopes*, Memoirs of the American Philosophical Society, 48 (Philadelphia).

NEWBERG, A. B., and d'AQUILI, E. G. 1998. 'The neuropsychology of spiritual experience', in H. G. Koenig (ed.), *Handbook of Religion and Mental Health* (San Diego, Calif.): 75–94.

NEWBERG, A. B., and D'AQUILI, E. G. 2001. *Why God Won't Go Away: Brain Science and the Biology of Belief* (New York).

NILSSON, M. P. 1967/1974. *Geschichte der griechischen Religion*, vol. 2, 2nd/3rd edn., Handbuch der Altertumswissenschaft, 5, 2 (Munich).

NOBLE, J. V., and PRICE, D. J. DE SOLLA. 1968. 'The water clock in the Tower of the Winds', *American Journal of Archaeology*, 72: 345–55.

NOCK, A. D. 1937. 'The genius of Mithraism,' *JRS* 27: 108–14, repr. in Z. Stewart (ed.), *Essays on Religion and the Ancient World* (Oxford, 1972): 452–58.

NORTH, J. D. 1990. 'Astronomical symbolism in the Mithraic religion', *Centaurus*, 33: 115–48.

PARIS, J., and DELATTE, A. 1913. 'Deux nouvelles épigrammes sur des cadrans solaires', *Revue de Philologie Classique*: 145–56.

PEDERSEN, O. 1974. *A Survey of the Almagest*, Acta Historica Scientiarum Naturalium et Medicinalium, 30 (Odense).

—— and HANNAH, R. 2002. 'Celestial dynamics at the crossroads: Proclus' reassessment of Plato in the light of empirical science', *Antichthon*, 36: 65–79.

PIGLIUCCI, M. 2002. 'Neuro-theology: a rather skeptical perspective', in Joseph (ed.), 2002: 269–71.

PINGREE, D. (ed.), 1976. *Dorothei Sidonii carmen astrologicum* (Leipzig).

—— 1977. 'Antiochus and Rhetorius', *Classical Philology*, 72: 203–23.

—— (ed.), 1986. *Vettii Valentis Antiocheni Anthologiarum Libri Novem* (Leipzig).

PRICE, D. J. DE SOLLA. 1967. 'The Tower of the Winds', *National Geographic*, 131 (Apr. 1967): 586–96.

—— 1975. *Gears from the Greeks: The Antikythera Mechanism, a Calendar Computer from ca. 80 B.C.* (New York).

PYYSIÄINEN, I. 2004. *Magic, Miracles, and Religion: A Scientist's Perspective*, Cognitive Science of Religion Series (Walnut Creek, Calif.).

—— and ANTTONEN, V. (eds.). 2002. *Current Approaches in the Cognitive Science of Religion* (London and New York).

RAPPAPORT, R. 1999. *Ritual and Religion in the Making of Humanity* (Cambridge).

REICHARD, G., *Navaho Religion*, 2 vols. (New York, 1950).

ROCHBERG-HALTON, F. 1988. 'Elements of the Babylonian contribution to Hellenistic astrology', *Journal of the American Oriental Society*, 108: 51–62.

RUSSELL, D. A. (ed.), 1992. *Dio Chrysostom: Orations VII, XII and XXXVI* (Cambridge).

RUSSELL, J. R. 1994. 'On the Armeno-Iranian roots of Mithraism', in *SM*: 83–93.

RUTGERS, A. J. 1970. 'Rational interpretation of the ritual of Mithra, and of various other cults', in *Anamnesis: Gedenkboek A. E. Leemans*. Univ. te Gent, Werken uitg. door de Fac. van de Lett. en Wijsbeg. 149: 303–15.

SALZMAN, M. R. 1990. *On Roman Time: The Codex-Calendar of 354 and the Rhythms of Urban Life in Late Antiquity* (Berkeley).

SANDELIN, K.-G. 1988. 'Mithras = Auriga?' *Arctos, Acta Philologica Fennica*, 22: 133–5.

SANDERS, D. H. 1996. *Nemrud Dagi: The Hierothesion of Antiochus I of Commagene*, 2 vols. (Winnona Lake, Ind.).

SAXL, F. 1931. *Mithras: Typengeschichtliche Untersuchungen* (Berlin).

SCOTT, A. 1991. *Origen and the Life of Stars* (Oxford).

SEGAL, R. A. 1989. 'Symbolic anthropology applied to religions of the Greco-Roman world', in *Religion and the Social Sciences*, Brown Studies in Religion 3 (Providence, RI): 147–65.

SFAMENI GASPARRO, G. 1979*a*. 'Il mitraismo nell'ambito della fenomenologia misterica (with an abstract in English)', in *MM*: 299–348.

—— 1979*b*. 'Il mitraismo: una struttura religiosa fra "tradizione" e "invenzione"', in *MM*: 349–84.

—— 1979*c*. 'Riflessioni ulteriori su Mitra dio "mistico"', in *MM*: 399–408.

—— 1985. *Soteriology and Mystic Aspects in the Cult of Cybele and Attis*, EPRO 103 (Leiden).

—— 1994. 'I misteri di Mithra: Religione o culto?', in *SM*: 93–102.

SGUBINI MORETTI, A. M. 1979. 'Nota preliminare su un mitreo scoperto a Vulci', in *MM*: 259–76.

SHANTZ, C. 2001. 'The neural pathway to paradise: a medical-anthropological reading of 2 Corinthians 12: 1–4', paper read at the annual meeting of the Canadian Society for Biblical Studies, Québec, 26 May 2001.

SIMONINI, L. (ed.), 1986. *Porfirio: L'antro delle ninfe* (Milan).

SMITH, J. Z. 1982. 'The devil in Mr. Jones', in *Imagining Religion: From Babylon to Jonestown* (Chicago): 102–20.

—— 1987. *To Take Place: Toward Theory in Ritual* (Chicago).

—— 1990. *Drudgery Divine: On the Comparison of Early Christianities and Religions of Late Antiquity*, Jordan Lectures 1988 (London).

SMITH, N., and WILSON, D. 1979. *Modern Linguistics: The Results of Chomsky's Revolution* (Bloomington, Ind.).

SPEIDEL, M. 1980. *Mithras-Orion: Greek Hero and Roman Army-god*, EPRO 81 (Leiden).

SPERBER, D. 1975. *Rethinking Symbolism*, trans. A. L. Morton (Cambridge).

—— 1996. *Explaining Culture: A Naturalistic Approach* (Oxford).

SPRINGER, S. P., and DEUTSCH, G. 1985. *Left Brain, Right Brain* (New York).

STAAL, F. 1975. 'On the meaninglessness of ritual', *Numen*, 26: 2–22.

STAHL, W. H. (trans.), 1952. *Macrobius, Commentary on the Dream of Scipio* (New York).

STARK, K. B. 1869. 'Die Mithrassteine von Dormagen', *Jahrbücher des Vereins von Altertumsfreunden im Rheinlande*, 46: 1–25.

STIERLIN, H. 1986. *L'Astrologie et le pouvoir* (Paris).

SWERDLOW, N. M. 1991. 'On the cosmical mysteries of Mithras' (review article of Ulansey 1989), *Classical Philology*, 86: 48–63.

TAYLOR, A. E. 1928. *A Commentary on Plato's Timaeus* (Oxford).

THEISSEN, G. 1999. *The Religion of the Earliest Churches: Creating a Symbolic World*, trans. J. Bowden (Minneapolis).

TODD, R. (ed.), 1990. *Cleomedis Caelestia (Meteòra)* (Leipzig).

TOOBY, J., and COSMIDES, L. 1992. 'The psychological foundations of culture', in Barkow, Cosmides, and Tooby (eds.): 19–136.

TOOMER, G. J. (trans.), *Ptolemy's Almagest* (London).

TURCAN, R. 1975. *Mithras Platonicus: Recherches sur l'hellénisation philosophique de Mithra* EPRO 47 (Leiden).

—— 1981. 'Le Sacrifice mithriaque: innovation de sens et de modalités,' *Entretiens Fondation Hardt*, 27: 341–73.

TURCAN, R. 1982. 'Salut mithriaque et sotériologie néoplatonicienne', in U. Bianchi and M. J. Vermaseren (eds.), *La Soteriologia dei culti orientali nell'Impero romano*, EPRO 92 (Leiden): 173–91.

—— 1986. 'Feu et sang: À propos d'un relief mithriaque', *Comptes Rendus de l'Académie des Inscriptions et Belles-Lettres*: 217–31.

—— 1999. 'Hiérarchie sacerdotale et astrologie dans les mystères de Mithra,' in *La Science des cieux: Sages, mages, astrologues, Res Orientales*, 12: 249–61.

—— 2000. *Mithra et le mithriacisme*, 2nd edn., rev. (Paris).

UBEROI, J. P. S. 1978. *Science and Culture* (Delhi).

ULANSEY, D. 1989/1991. *The Origins of the Mithraic Mysteries: Cosmology and Salvation in the Ancient World* (New York).

VERMASEREN, M. J. 1956–60. *Corpus Inscriptionum et Monumentorum Religionis Mithriacae*, 2 vols. (The Hague).

—— 1960. *Mithra, ce dieu mystérieux*, trans. M. Léman and L. Gilbert (Paris and Brussels).

—— 1963. *Mithras, the Secret God*, trans. T. and V. Megaw (London).

—— 1971. *Mithriaca 1: The Mithraeum at Santa Maria Capua Vetere*, EPRO 16.1 (Leiden).

—— 1974. *Mithriaca 2: The Mithraeum at Ponza*, EPRO 16.2 (Leiden).

—— 1978. *Mithriaca 4: Le monument d'Ottaviano Zeno et le culte de Mithra sur le Célius*, EPRO 16.4 (Leiden).

—— 1982. *Mithriaca 3: The Mithraeum at Marino*, EPRO 16.3 (Leiden).

—— and VAN ESSEN, E. E. 1965. *The Excavations in the Mithraeum of the Church of Santa Prisca in Rome* (Leiden).

WAGNER, J. 1975. 'Neue Funde zum Götter- und Königskult unter Antiochos I. von Kommagene', in F. K. Dörner (ed.), *Kommagene, Antike Welt*, Jahrgang 6, Sondernummer: 51–9.

—— 2000. 'Die Könige von Kommagene und ihr Herrscherkult', in Wagner (ed.): 11–25.

—— (ed.), 2000. *Gottkönige am Euphrat: Neue Ausgrabungen und Forschungen in Kommagene. Antike Welt*, Sonderband (Mainz).

WALDMANN, H. 1973. *Die kommagenischen Kultreformen unter König Mithradates I Kallinikos und seinem Sohne Antiochos I*, EPRO 34 (Leiden).

WATTS, F. 2002. 'Interacting cognitive subsystems and religious meanings', in Joseph (ed.), 2000: 183–8.

WEISS, M. 1994. *Die Stiertötungsszene der römischen Mithrasaltäre: Schöpfung, Endzeitakt, Heilstat oder Sternkarte* (Osterburken).

—— 1996. *Als Sonne verkannt* [sic]—*Mithras: Eine neue Deutung des Mithras und der mithraischen Kultbilder aus dem Awesta* (Osterburken).

—— 1998. 'Mithras, der Nachthimmel: Eine Dekodierung der römischen Mithraskultbilder mit Hilfe des Awesta', *Traditio*, 53: 1–36.

—— 2000. 'Kultbilder des Mithras im Licht einer neuen Deutung unter besonderer Berücksichtigung des Reliefs von Mannheim', *Mannheimer Geschichtsblätter*, NF 7: 11–55.

WHITE, L. M. 1989. *Building God's House in the Roman World: Architectural Adaptation Among Pagans, Jews and Christians* (Baltimore and London).

WHITEHOUSE, H. 2000. *Arguments and Icons: Divergent Modes of Religiosity* (Oxford).

—— 2004. *Modes of Religiosity: A Cognitive Theory of Religious Transmission*, Cognitive Science of Religion Series (Walnut Creek, Calif.).

—— and LAIDLAW, J. (eds), 2004. *Ritual and Memory: Toward a Comparative Anthropology of Religion*, Cognitive Science of Religion Series (Walnut Creek, Calif.).

—— and MARTIN, L. H. (eds.), 2004. *Theorizing Religions Past*, Cognitive Science of Religion Series (Walnut Creek, Calif.).

WIDENGREN, G. 1966. 'The Mithraic Mysteries in the Greco-Roman world with special regard to their Iranian background,' in *La Persia e il mondo greco-romano*, Accademia Nazionale dei Lincei, Anno 363, Quaderno 76 (Rome): 433–55.

—— 1980. 'Reflections on the origins of the Mithraic Mysteries', in *Perennitas: Studi in onore di Angelo Brelich* (Rome): 645–68.

WILL, ERNEST. 1955. *Le Relief cultuel gréco-romain: Contribution à l'histoire de l'art de l'Empire romain*, Bibl. des Éc. franç. d'Athènes et de Rome, 183 (Rome and Paris).

WUILLEUMIER, P. 1927. 'Cirque et astrologie', *Mélanges d' archéologie et d'histoire de l'École française de Rome*, 44: 184–209.

ZWIRN, S. R. 1989. 'The intention of biographical narration on Mithraic cult images', *Word & Image*, 5: 2–18.

Index of Mithraic Monuments

Index of Ancient Authors

General Index

Aemilianus Corfinius Olympius 98
'aether' ('fifth essence') 180
Ahriman 238
Aldebaran 208
allegory 85–6, 159, 161 n., 170–5
Anabibazon and Katabibazon, *see* nodes, lunar
anaphoric clock, the 38, 205–6
Andromeda 173
angels 167
anomaly (astronomical) 244–53
Antares 208
Antikythera Mechanism, the 124–5
Antiochus I of Commagene 227, 253
Antiochus IV of Commagene 253
Antiochus of Athens (*see also* Index of Ancient Authors) 209–11, 221, 245, 248–9, 253–6
apogee/perigee, *see* motion, in 'depth' (*bathos*)
apokatastasis (Great Return/Year) 254–6
Apollo 222
Apollo, star of, *see* Mercury
'Apollo Mithras Helios Hermes' 230–1
Aquarius 163 n., 195–7, 216–26, 234–9
Aratus, Gnostic interpreters of 170–5
'Archery of the Father' (ritual) 6 n. 8, 133 n. 45, 151
Archimedes 123–5
'argument of latitude' 239, 249
Aries, *see* equinoxes; opposition(s), Aries (spring equinox) vs. Libra (autumn equinox)
'Artagnes Heracles Ares' 230–1
astronomy, astrology, and astral lore 7–8, 30–9, 49–50, 51, 60, 61, 72, 77–9, 103–16, 128–30, 153, 160–239, 240–56
astronomy, Babylonian 233, 249–50

augural *templum* 205
Augustine (*see also* Index of Ancient Authors)
  on astrology 167–9
  semiotics of 191–2
Aurelius Victor Augentius 98
Auriga 35
'axioms' 5–6, 10, 11, 66, 81–5, 148, 257–9
axis, universal 109–11

Balbillus, *see* Claudius Balbillus, Ti.
banquet scene (Mithraic) 7, 21–2, 23, 27–8, 70, 96, 258
Barberini mithraeum, *see* Index of Mithraic Monuments, V389–90
bathos (t.t. for distance from earth) 207, 243–51
Bausani, A. 36
bears 109, 225 n. 33
bees 198
belief system (faith) 2, 40, 53–6, 62
benches, side-, *see* opposition(s)
Bianchi, U. 51–2
biga (ox-drawn) 197, 199, 204
biogenetic structuralism 13, 131, 136–48, 151–2
blood 28
Boyer, P. 65, 93, 135 n.
bull 31, 37, 107, 161–4, 195–9, 217, 219, 223–5
bull-killing, *see* tauroctony
Burkert, W. 133–4, 136, 151

caduceus 27–8
Campbell, L. A. 28, 49 n. 15, 80 n.
Cancer 200–3, 218–27, 252 n. 17, 254; *see also* opposition(s), Cancer (summer solstice) vs. Capricorn (winter solstice); solstices
Canis Major/Minor 31, 160–4, 173, 195–7, 201–3, 255–6